SOL JUSTITIAE

LAW

Robert B. L. Murphy

The foundations of
modern political thought

VOLUME ONE: THE RENAISSANCE

The foundations of modern political thought

VOLUME ONE: THE RENAISSANCE

QUENTIN SKINNER
PROFESSOR OF POLITICAL SCIENCE
UNIVERSITY OF CAMBRIDGE

CAMBRIDGE UNIVERSITY PRESS

CAMBRIDGE

LONDON   NEW YORK   NEW ROCHELLE
MELBOURNE   SYDNEY

Published by the Press Syndicate of the University of Cambridge
The Pitt Building, Trumpington Street, Cambridge CB2 1RP
32 East 57th Street, New York, NY 10022, USA
296 Beaconsfield Parade, Middle Park, Melbourne 3206, Australia

First published 1978
Reprinted 1979,1980

Printed in the United States of America
Typeset by Western Printing Services Ltd, Avonmouth, England
Printed and bound by Vail-Ballou Press, Inc.,
Binghamton, New York

Library of Congress Cataloguring in Publication Data (Revised)

Skinner, Quentin

The foundations of modern political thought.

Bibliography: v. 1, p.
Includes index.
CONTENTS: vol. 1. The Renaissance. – vol. 2. The
age of Reformation.
1. Political science – History – Collected works.
I. Title.
JA81.S54   320.5′09′03   78–51676
ISBN 0 521 22023 8 (vol. 1) hard covers
ISBN 0 521 29337 5 (vol. 1) paperback

Contents

VOLUME ONE: THE RENAISSANCE

VOLUME TWO: THE AGE OF REFORMATION

Preface

I have three main aims in this book. The first is simply to offer an outline account of the principal texts of late medieval and early modern political thought. I discuss in turn the chief political writings of Dante, Marsiglio of Padua, Machiavelli, Guicciardini, Erasmus and More, Luther, Calvin and their disciples, Vitoria and Suárez, and the French constitutionalist theorists, including Beza, Hotman, Mornay and especially Bodin. No such survey of the transition from medieval to modern political theory has I think been attempted since the publication of Professor Pierre Mesnard's *L'essor de la philosophie politique au XVIe siècle*. Professor Mesnard's study is of course a classic one, and I cannot hope to emulate either his range or the depth of his scholarship. However, it is more than forty years since his book first appeared, and a number of major advances in the subject have been made since that time. Many new editions have been produced, often embodying important scholarly discoveries. And a large secondary literature has grown up, adding a great deal of new information, as well as challenging many received opinions about the leading texts. For these reasons it has seemed worthwhile to try to furnish a more up-to-date survey of the same period, taking account as far as possible of the more significant findings of recent research.

My second aim has been to use the texts of late medieval and early modern political theory in order to illuminate a more general historical theme. I hope to indicate something of the process by which the modern concept of the State came to be formed. To mention this wider ambition is at the same time to explain the chronological boundaries of this book. I begin in the late thirteenth century, and carry the story down to the end of the sixteenth, because it was during this period, I shall seek to show, that the main elements of a recognisably modern concept of the State were gradually acquired.[1] The decisive shift was made from

---

[1] As I seek to make clear in my Conclusion, this is not to say that precisely *our* concept of the State was acquired. The theorists I discuss remained confused about the relationship between the people, the ruler and the State. And of course they lacked the post-Enlightenment conception of the relationship between the nation and the State.

the idea of the ruler 'maintaining his state' – where this simply meant upholding his own position – to the idea that there is a separate legal and constitutional order, that of the State, which the ruler has a duty to maintain. One effect of this transformation was that the power of the State, not that of the ruler, came to be envisaged as the basis of government. And this in turn enabled the State to be conceptualised in distinctively modern terms – as the sole source of law and legitimate force within its own territory, and as the sole appropriate object of its citizens' allegiances.[1]

After considering the historical developments which prompted this conceptual change, I turn briefly in the Conclusion from history to historical semantics – from the concept of the State to the word 'State'. The clearest sign that a society has entered into the self-conscious possession of a new concept is, I take it, that a new vocabulary comes to be generated, in terms of which the concept is then articulated and discussed. So I treat it as a decisive confirmation of my central thesis that, by the end of the sixteenth century, at least in England and France, we find the words 'State' and 'l'État' beginning to be used for the first time in their modern sense.

My third concern is to exemplify a particular way of approaching the study and interpretation of historical texts. I have already discussed this approach in a series of articles published over the past twelve years, and it hardly seems appropriate to rehearse their arguments here.[2] I hope in any case that, if my method has any merits, these will emerge as I try to practise my own precepts in the body of this book. However, it may be worth indicating very briefly what is at issue by comparing my approach with the more traditional method of studying the history of political ideas – the method employed, for example, by Professor Mesnard. He treats the subject essentially as a history of the so-called 'classic texts', producing successive chapters on the chief works of Machiavelli, Erasmus, More, Luther, Calvin and the other major figures. By contrast, I have tried not to concentrate so exclusively on the leading theorists, and have focused instead on the more general social and intellectual matrix out of which their works arose. I begin by discussing what I judge to be the most

---

[1] For this famous definition see Max Weber, *Economy and Society*, ed. Guenther Roth and Claus Wittich, 3 vols (New York, 1968), vol. 1, p. 56.

[2] For any reader who may be interested, I have listed the titles of these essays in the bibliography at the end of this volume. I should like to add that, in arriving at my views about the nature of interpretation, I have been much influenced by a number of writers whose works I have also mentioned in the bibliography. I should especially like to record my debt to the theories of R. G. Collingwood, my admiration for the work done by Alasdair MacIntyre on the philosophy of action as well as on the history of moral concepts, and my more specific obligations to the methodological writings of Martin Hollis, J. G. A. Pocock and especially John Dunn.

relevant characteristics of the societies in and for which they originally wrote. For I take it that political life itself sets the main problems for the political theorist, causing a certain range of issues to appear problematic, and a corresponding range of questions to become the leading subjects of debate. This is not to say, however, that I treat these ideological super-structures as a straightforward outcome of their social base. I regard it as no less essential to consider the intellectual context in which the major texts were conceived – the context of earlier writings and inherited assumptions about political society, and of more ephemeral contemporary contributions to social and political thought. For it is evident that the nature and limits of the normative vocabulary available at any given time will also help to determine the ways in which particular questions come to be singled out and discussed. I have thus tried to write a history centred less on the classic texts and more on the history of ideologies, my aim being to construct a general framework within which the writings of the more prominent theorists can then be situated.

It may well be asked why I adopt this somewhat elaborate approach, and I should like to end these preliminary remarks by sketching an answer. One dissatisfaction I feel with the traditional 'textualist' method is that, although its exponents have generally claimed to be writing the history of political theory, they have rarely supplied us with genuine histories. It has rightly become a commonplace of recent historiography that, if we wish to understand earlier societies, we need to recover their different *mentalités* in as broadly sympathetic a fashion as possible. But it is hard to see how we can hope to arrive at this kind of historical understanding if we continue, as students of political ideas, to focus our main attention on those who discussed the problems of political life at a level of abstraction and intelligence unmatched by any of their contemporaries. If on the other hand we attempt to surround these classic texts with their appropriate ideological context, we may be able to build up a more realistic picture of how political thinking in all its various forms was in fact conducted in earlier periods. One merit I should thus like to claim for the approach I have described is that, if it were practised with success, it might begin to give us a history of political theory with a genuinely historical character.

The adoption of this approach might also help us to illuminate some of the connections between political theory and practice. It is often observed that political historians tend to assign a somewhat marginal role to political ideas and principles in seeking to explain political behaviour. And it is evident that, as long as historians of political theory continue to think of their main task as that of interpreting a canon of classic texts, it will remain difficult to establish any closer links between political theories and political life. But if they were instead to think of themselves essentially as students of ideologies, it might become possible to illustrate one crucial way in which the explanation of political behaviour depends upon the study of political ideas and principles, and cannot meaningfully be conducted without reference to them.

Some sense of the nature of these interactions will I hope emerge in the course of this book. But the point I have in mind can readily be expressed in more general terms if we consider the position of a political actor who is anxious to engage in a particular course of action which he is also anxious, in Weberian phrase, to exhibit as legitimate. Such an agent may be said to have a strong motive for seeking to ensure that his behaviour can plausibly be described in terms of a vocabulary already normative within his society, a vocabulary which is capable of legitimating at the same time as describing what he has done. Now it may appear – and many political historians have assumed – that the nature of the connection this suggests between ideology and political action is a purely instrumental one.[1] The agent has a project he wishes to legitimate; he accordingly professes just those principles which best serve to describe what he is doing in morally acceptable terms; and since the selection of these principles relates to his behaviour in a wholly *ex post facto* way, it hardly seems that the capacity to explain his behaviour need depend in any way on referring to whatever principles he may happen to have professed. It is arguable, however, that this is to misunderstand the role of the normative vocabulary which any society employs for the description and appraisal of its political life. Consider, for example, the position of an agent who wishes to say of an action he has performed that it was honourable. To offer this description is certainly to commend as well as to describe what has been done. And as Machiavelli shows, the range of actions which can plausibly be brought under this heading may turn out – with the exercise of a little ingenuity – to be unexpectedly wide. But the term obviously cannot be applied with propriety to describe *any* Machiavellian course of action, but only those which can be claimed with some show of plausibility to meet the pre-existing criteria for the application of the term. It follows that anyone who is anxious to have his behaviour recognised as that of a man of honour will find himself restricted to the performance of only a certain range of actions. Thus the problem facing an agent who wishes to legitimate what he is doing at the same time as gaining what he wants cannot simply be the instrumental problem of tailoring his normative language in order to fit

[1] For an attempt to document in detail one case in which this has clearly been assumed, see Skinner, 1974a.

his projects. It must in part be the problem of tailoring his projects in order to fit the available normative language.

It will now be evident why I wish to maintain that, if the history of political theory were to be written essentially as a history of ideologies, one outcome might be a clearer understanding of the links between political theory and practice. For it now appears that, in recovering the terms of the normative vocabulary available to any given agent for the description of his political behaviour, we are at the same time indicating one of the constraints upon his behaviour itself. This suggests that, in order to explain why such an agent acts as he does, we are bound to make some reference to this vocabulary, since it evidently figures as one of the determinants of his action. This in turn suggests that, if we were to focus our histories on the study of these vocabularies, we might be able to illustrate the exact ways in which the explanation of political behaviour depends upon the study of political thought.

My main reason, however, for suggesting that we should focus on the study of ideologies is that this would enable us to return to the classic texts themselves with a clearer prospect of understanding them. To study the context of any major work of political philosophy is not merely to gain additional information about its aetiology; it is also to equip ourselves, I shall argue, with a way of gaining a greater insight into its author's meaning than we can ever hope to achieve simply from reading the text itself 'over and over again' as the exponents of the 'textualist' approach have characteristically proposed.[1]

What exactly does this approach enable us to grasp about the classic texts that we cannot grasp simply by reading them? The answer, in general terms, is I think that it enables us to characterise what their authors were *doing* in writing them. We can begin to see not merely what arguments they were presenting, but also what questions they were addressing and trying to answer, and how far they were accepting and endorsing, or questioning and repudiating, or perhaps even polemically ignoring, the prevailing assumptions and conventions of political debate. We cannot expect to attain this level of understanding if we only study the texts themselves. In order to see them as answers to specific questions, we need to know something about the society in which they were written. And in order to recognise the exact direction and force of their arguments, we need to have some appreciation of the general political vocabulary of the age. Yet we clearly need to gain access to this level of understanding if we are to interpret the classic texts convincingly. For to understand what questions a writer is addressing, and what he is doing with the concepts

[1] For this injunction see J. P. Plamenatz, *Man and Society*, 2 vols (London, 1963), vol 1, p. x.

available to him, is equivalently to understand some of his basic intentions
in writing, and is thus to elicit what exactly he may have meant by what
he said – or failed to say. When we attempt in this way to locate a text
within its appropriate context, we are not merely providing historical
'background' for our interpretation; we are already engaged in the act of
interpretation itself.

As a very brief indication of what I have in mind, consider the possible
significance of the fact that John Locke in his *Two Treatises of Government*
makes no appeal to the alleged prescriptive force of the ancient English
constitution. An examination of the prevailing ways of thinking about the
concept of political obligation at the time reveals that this could only have
been seen by his contemporaries as a remarkable lacuna. This discovery
may well lead us to ask what Locke may have been doing at this point in
his argument. We are bound to reply that he was rejecting and ignoring
one of the most widely accepted and prestigious forms of political reasoning available to him. This may in turn lead us to ask whether he may not
have had the intention to convey to his original readers that he saw the
claims of prescription as unworthy of his attention, and thus that he was,
so to speak, stating his attitude to the theory in the form of his silence.
The example is of course over-schematised, but it serves well enough to
hint at the two major claims I have in mind: we can scarcely be said to
have understood Locke's meaning until we have considered his intentions
at this point; but we can scarcely hope to attain this understanding unless
we are prepared to focus not simply on his text, but also on the more
general context within which it was written.

The reader may wonder whether I have any new findings to report as a
result of applying this methodology. I should like to mention two general
points. In volume I I have sought to emphasise the remarkable extent to
which the vocabulary of Renaissance moral and political thought was
derived from Roman stoic sources. A great deal of work has been done –
for example by Garin – on the Platonic origins of Renaissance political
philosophy. And recently a strong emphasis has been placed – notably by
Baron and Pocock – on the contribution of Aristotelian doctrines to the
formation of 'civic' humanism. But I do not think it has been fully
appreciated how pervasively the political theorists of Renaissance Italy,
and of early modern Europe in general, were also influenced by stoic
values and beliefs. Nor do I think it has been fully recognised how far an
understanding of this fact tends, amongst other things, to alter our picture
of Machiavelli's relationship with his predecessors, and in consequence
our sense of his aims and intentions as a political theorist. In volume II I
have tried in a similar way to uncover the sources of the vocabulary

characteristic of Reformation political thought. I have sought in particular to emphasise the almost paradoxical extent to which the Lutherans as well as the radical Calvinists relied on a scheme of concepts derived from the study of Roman law and scholastic moral philosophy. A considerable literature has been devoted in recent years to discussing the formation of 'the Calvinist theory of revolution'. But I argue that, strictly speaking, no such entity exists. While there is no doubt that the revolutionaries of early modern Europe were in general professed Calvinists, it has not I think been sufficiently recognised that the theories they developed were almost entirely couched in the legal and moral language of their Catholic adversaries.

Acknowledgements

My greatest debt is owed to those friends who have read and commented on the whole manuscript of this book, in some cases reading it in several successive drafts. I am deeply grateful to them all: to John Burrow, Stefan Collini, John Dunn, Susan James, John Pocock and John Thompson. They have offered me constant support and advice, as well as providing me with a large number of helpful suggestions, almost all of which I have tried to incorporate into my final draft. I should like to add two special words of thanks. One is to John Burrow, who originally supervised my work in political theory when I was an undergraduate at Gonville and Caius College, Cambridge, and has continued to guide me in the subject (and in much else) ever since. The other is to John Dunn, to whom I owe most of all. I have discussed my work with him at every stage, never ceasing to learn from his insights and the amazing breadth of his reading, and benefiting immeasurably from his unfailing kindness and encouragement as well as from his many detailed criticisms.

I am scarcely less indebted to those who have commented on particular sections of my work. Jimmy Burns has read practically the whole of my script, helping me in particular with the intricacies of late scholastic thought as well as checking my translations with meticulous scholarship. John Elliott has read the chapters on the counter-reformation and prompted me to revise them extensively in the light of his criticisms. Julian Franklin has read the chapters on the Calvinist revolution, putting his massive knowledge of early modern constitutionalism at my disposal in a series of exceptionally helpful letters and conversations. Peter Gay has read the second volume, and has spent a great deal of time and effort in an attempt to make me think and write more clearly. Felix Gilbert has read virtually the whole of the first volume, bringing to bear his unsurpassed understanding of Renaissance political thought, and thereby saving me from many errors of judgment and fact. Martin Hollis has read the second volume, correcting my Latin, making numerous suggestions, and above all helping me to articulate the methodological assumptions on which I have tried to base my work. And in the final months of revision I have received a great deal of help from Donald Kelley, who has not only read the whole of my script and enabled me to avoid a number of mistakes, but has also supplied me with much bibliographical detail as well as valuable general advice.

I have also incurred a number of more general obligations in the course of writing this book, and these too I record with deep gratitude. I owe a great deal to Peter Laslett for his generous help and advice in the early stages of my research. And I owe a very large debt to Jack Plumb for his continual encouragement and many kindnesses. It was he who originally suggested, in his capacity as an adviser to Penguin Books, that I should be commissioned to write a synoptic survey of early modern political thought. It was only after I had worked for some time on the projected book – which was to have covered the whole period from the early sixteenth to the early nineteenth century – that I found the undertaking to be far beyond my powers. I am grateful to Penguin Books for having agreed at that point to release me from the obligation I had formed. My thanks are also due to many past pupils at Cambridge University, with whom I have discussed my work in lectures and seminars. I must especially mention Richard Tuck, originally a pupil and now a colleague at Cambridge. I always learn from our conversations, and I am sure that many of them must have left their mark on this book. I should also like to acknowledge the expert assistance as well as the many kindnesses I have received from Mrs Peggy Clarke and the secretarial staff attached to the School of Social Science at the Institute for Advanced Study, who have typed my manuscript with great skill and speed, and from Clare Scarlett, who has checked quotations, references and bibliographies. Finally, I should like to offer my thanks to the staff of the British Library, the Firestone Library at Princeton, and especially the University Library at Cambridge. Much of my research has been done in the rare-book rooms of these collections, where I have always been received with unfailing patience and courtesy.

I am also much indebted to the various institutions which have supported and encouraged me in my work. Christ's College, Cambridge has given me material help as well as its fellowship. The Faculty of History and the University of Cambridge have shown me exceptional generosity, especially in allowing me three years' leave of absence from my lectureship in 1976, thus giving me the leisure to complete several pieces of work, of which this book is one. Finally, I owe a special debt to the Institute for Advanced Study at Princeton. I first went there as a visitor in 1974, and I am deeply grateful to Clifford Geertz, Albert Hirschman and Carl

Kaysen for having proposed that I be invited to return in 1976 for a three-year stay. During these visits I have not only been able to write virtually the whole of the final draft of these volumes; I have also been privileged to discover that, as a setting for scholarly work, the Institute is beyond praise.

As these volumes go to press, I am very pleased to learn that there is still time to express my thanks to Jeremy Mynott of the Cambridge University Press, who has shown unfailing patience, efficiency and tact.

Notes on the text

(1) *References*. I have tried as far as possible to dispense with the use of footnotes. However, I am of course anxious that the sources of all the quotations and other information I have given should be readily identifiable. The solution I have adopted is as follows. When citing from an original source I mention the author and identify the work immediately before quoting from it. I then give the page-reference in brackets at the end of the quotation. When taking information from a modern work of scholarship, I place the name of the author, the date of the work and the appropriate page-reference in brackets immediately after citing from it. Full details of all the editions I am using can be found in the bibliographies. It must be admitted that the use of these devices places certain constraints on my prose, and doubtless destroys any lingering pretensions to elegance. But the only alternative, in a book containing so many quotations, would be to disfigure the pages with an intolerable clutter of footnotes.

(2) *Editions*. In the case of original sources I generally use what I judge to be the most readily available edition. However, where a modern critical edition has been produced, embodying new scholarly findings, I always use this in preference to other and perhaps more readily accessible versions of the text. When quoting from Shakespeare's plays, my line-references are to the Oxford edition, edited by W. J. Craig and first published in 1905.

(3) *Translations*. I have generally made use of existing translations, except where they seem defective in significant respects. Where I cite from a source originally written in a language other than English, and where no translation exists, all translations are my own. I have also rendered all titles into English. The reader who wishes to recover the original titles of foreign works I have translated will find them included in the bibliographies of primary sources.

(4) *Bibliographies*. The bibliographies at the end of each volume are simply check-lists of primary sources I have actually discussed in the text, and of secondary works I have cited for specific pieces of information. They make no pretence of being full introductions to the very large literature on early–modern political thought. I have also added very brief bibliographies at the end of each group of Chapters. These contain what I take to be the most important works a student might begin by consulting if he or she wished to gain more information about one or other of the major writers discussed.

(5) *Names*. I have followed the conventional (though not very consistent) practice of anglicising the names of rulers and towns, while leaving the names of authors in their original form. Thus I speak of Francis I (not François Ier·) but I speak of Jean (not John) Calvin. A special problem arises with those medieval and Renaissance writers who liked to classicise their names. These I have generally turned back into their vernacular forms. Thus I speak of Marsiglio (not Marsilius) of Padua, and of John Mair (not Major). In some cases, however, the classical versions have become so well-known that to do this would be absurd, and in these cases I have opted for familiarity rather than consistency. For example, I speak of Philipp Melanchthon (not Philipp Schwartzerd) and of Justus Lipsius (not Joost Lips).

(6) *Modernisation*. I have modernised wherever possible. All dates are expressed in the new style, with the year beginning on January 1st. Spelling and punctuation have been modernised in all citations from original sources. Archaic formulations (such as 'doth' for 'does') have been given in their modern equivalents, and all titles have been modernised – so that, for example, I speak of *The Book Named the Governor*, not *The Boke Named the Gouernour*. I have followed these procedures even when citing from modern scholarly editions in which the original spelling and punctuation have been preserved. I recognise that this last decision may be felt to offend against the best scholarly etiquette, but the alternative seems to impose a gratuitous quaintness on the writers with whom I am concerned, with the consequent danger that their arguments may not be taken as seriously as they deserve.

(7) *Terminology*. Where key terms present special problems of translation, the rule I adopt is to follow as closely as possible the translations used at the time. This means, however, that in several important cases the English

terms I employ need to be understood in their early-modern rather than in their current and somewhat different senses. There are three main examples of this:

(i) *Princeps* and *Magistratus*. Following early-modern practice, I normally render these terms respectively as 'prince' and 'magistrate'. In early modern Europe, however, these translations still carried the (much wider) connotations of the original Latin, connotations which have since been lost. The term 'prince' was frequently used to refer to kings and emperors as well as princes. And 'magistrate' was standardly used to describe a much wider class of legal officials than the word currently denotes. In order to preserve consistency, I have generally employed both these terms – even when not translating – in their older and wider sense.

(ii) *Respublica*. Sometimes this term was used simply to mean 'Republic'. Where the context makes it clear that this is the intended meaning, this is naturally the translation I adopt. But sometimes it was used to refer to kingdoms and principalities as well. Some modern scholars in consequence translate it – even in editions of fifteenth- and early sixteenth-century texts – as 'State' But this is misleadingly anachronistic, since no political writer before the middle of the sixteenth century used the word 'State' in anything closely resembling our modern sense. I have accordingly preferred in all such cases to follow the early-modern practice of translating *Respublica* as 'commonwealth'. This may appear slightly mandarin, but it seems the only way to maintain consistency, as well as to signal the crucial fact that, in the period with which I am largely concerned, the term *Respublica* still carried with it a number of normative overtones (mainly suggestive of the common good) which have subsequently withered away in the increasingly individualist atmosphere in which our political arrangements have come to be discussed.

(iii) *Studia humanitatis*. Some modern scholars, translating this Ciceronian concept as 'the humanities' (and its cognates as 'humanism', 'the humanists', etc.) have gone on to use these terms with unfortunate vagueness. As a result, several authorities have recently proposed that, in order to avoid further confusion, the word 'humanism' ought to be excised from any future accounts of early-modern thought. (Professor Hay, for example, has tried to banish the word altogether from his survey of the Italian Renaissance.) (See Hay, 1961, p. 8.) Again, however, it seems to me – and here I simply follow the lead of Professor Kristeller's seminal essays – that the answer lies not in evading the use of the term, but in confining its employment to its original Renaissance meaning, using it simply to refer to the students and protagonists of a particular group of disciplines centred around the study of grammar, rhetoric, history and moral philosophy. Understood in this way, the term is I think valuable as well as perspicuous, and I have accordingly felt able to use it freely, though always, I hope, in this older and more restricted sense.

PART ONE

The origins of the Renaissance

I

The ideal of liberty

As early as the middle of the twelfth century the German historian Otto of Freising recognised that a new and remarkable form of social and political organisation had arisen in Northern Italy. One peculiarity he noted was that Italian society had apparently ceased to be feudal in character. He found that 'practically the entire land is divided among the cities' and that 'scarcely any noble or great man can be found in all the surrounding territory who does not acknowledge the authority of his city' (p. 127). The other development he observed – which struck him as even more subversive – was that the cities had evolved a form of political life entirely at odds with the prevailing assumption that hereditary monarchy constituted the only sound form of government. They had become 'so desirous of liberty' that they had turned themselves into independent Republics, each governed 'by the will of consuls rather than rulers', whom they 'changed almost every year' in order to ensure that their 'lust for power' was controlled and the freedom of the people maintained (p. 127).

The earliest known case of an Italian city electing such a consular form of government occurred at Pisa in 1085 (Waley, 1969, p. 57). Thereafter the system began to spread rapidly in Lombardy as well as Tuscany, with similar regimes appearing at Milan in 1097, at Arezzo in the following year, and at Lucca, Bologna and Siena by 1125 (Waley, 1969, p. 60). During the second half of the century a further important development took place. The rule of consuls came to be superseded by a stabler form of elective government centred on an official known as the *podestà*, so called because he was invested with supreme power or *potestas* over the city. The *podestà* was normally a citizen of another city, a convention designed to ensure that no local ties or loyalties should interfere with his impartial administration of justice. He was elected by popular mandate, and generally ruled with the advice of two main councils, the larger of which might be up to six hundred strong, while the inner or secret council would normally be restricted to some forty leading citizens (Waley 1969, p. 62).

The *podestà* enjoyed comprehensive powers, since he was expected to act as the city's supreme judicial as well as administrative officer, and to serve as its leading spokesman on its various embassies. But the crucial feature of the system was that his status was always that of a salaried official, never that of an independent ruler. His term of office was customarily restricted to six months, and throughout that time he remained responsible to the citizen body which had elected him. He had no authority to initiate political decisions, and at the end of his tenure he was required to submit to a formal scrutiny of his accounts and judgments before he could gain permission to depart from the city which had employed him (Waley 1969, pp. 68–9).

By the end of the twelfth century this form of Republican self-government had come to be adopted almost universally by the leading cities of Northern Italy (Hyde, 1973, p. 101). While this brought them a measure of *de facto* independence, however, they continued to count *de iure* as vassals of the Holy Roman Empire. The legal claims of the German Emperors over Italy extended as far back as the age of Charlemagne, whose Empire had straddled Germany and Northern Italy at the start of the ninth century. These claims had been forcefully revived in the course of the tenth century, when Otto I in particular had decisively linked the *Regnum Italicum* with his German possessions.[1] By the time of Frederick Barbarossa's accession to the Imperial throne in the middle of the twelfth century, the Emperors had come to have two special reasons for wishing to insist once again on the true status of the North Italian *Regnum* as a mere province of the Empire. One was the fact that, as Otto of Freising puts it, the cities had begun to flout the authority of the Emperor and to 'receive in hostile fashion him whom they ought to accept as their own gentle prince'. The other reason, as Otto ingenuously adds, was that if the Emperor could manage to subjugate the whole of Northern Italy, this would make him the master of 'a very garden of delights', since the cities of the Lombard plain had by this time come to 'surpass all other states of the world in riches and in power' (pp. 126, 128). The outcome of adding this hope of instant treasure to the venerable claims of Imperial jurisdiction was that a succession of German Emperors, beginning with

---

[1] The term *Regnum Italicum* thus refers only to that part of Northern Italy which corresponds to the Lombard kingdom of the Dark Ages, which Otto I reincorporated into the German Empire in 962. It is this area alone which the theorists of the Italian City Republics have in mind when they speak, as for example Marsiglio of Padua regularly does in his *Defender of Peace*, of the *Regnum Italicum*. It is thus misleading to translate the term (as for example Alan Gewirth does in his edition of *The Defender of Peace*, p. 4 and *passim*) as 'the Italian State'. Apart from the anachronism involved in using the term 'state', this might be taken to imply that Marsiglio is referring to the whole area of modern Italy, which is never the case.

Frederick Barbarossa's first expedition to Italy in 1154, struggled for almost the next two centuries to impose their rule on the *Regnum Italicum*, while the leading cities of the *Regnum* fought with no less determination to assert their independence.

Frederick Barbarossa's first two expeditions virtually succeeded in winning him control over the whole of Lombardy. He began by attacking the allies of Milan, the greatest and most fiercely independent of the cities, and on his second expedition laid siege to Milan itself, which he captured and razed to the ground in 1162 (Munz, 1969, pp. 74–5). By this time he had already capitalised on his early victories by convening a General Diet at Roncaglia in 1158, where he proclaimed in unequivocal terms his sovereignty over the whole of the *Regnum Italicum* (Balzani, 1926, p. 427). This very success, however, served to unite the normally factious cities against him. Milan took the lead in 1167 in building up a Lombard League to resist his demands, and soon won the adherence of twenty-nine other cities (Waley, 1969, p. 126). When Barbarossa returned in 1174 to reimpose his authority, the combined forces of the League managed to inflict a lucky but absolutely decisive defeat on the Imperial armies at Legnano in 1176 (Munz, 1969, pp. 310–11). After this the Emperor had no option but to compromise with the League, and at the peace of Constance in 1183 he effectively renounced any right to interfere with the internal government of the Lombard cities (Munz, 1969, pp. 361–2).

The next Emperor who attempted to realise the idea of the Holy Roman Empire by trying to resume control of the *Regnum Italicum* was Frederick II, who announced this grand design to the General Diet of Piacenza in 1235, calling in minatory tones on the Italians to 're-enter the unity of the Empire' (Schipa, 1929, p. 152). Again the Emperor was at first successful in imposing his will on the cities. He captured Vicenza in 1236, so bringing about the surrender of Ferrara in the following year, and at the end of 1237 he imposed a crushing defeat on the armies of the revived Lombard League at Cortenuova (Van Cleve, 1972, pp. 398–407). Again, however, the scale of his victories served to reunite his enemies under the leadership of the implacably hostile Milanese (Van Cleve, 1972, pp. 169, 230, 392). They recaptured Ferrara in 1239, seized the Imperial port of Ravenna in the same year, and carried the war all over Tuscany as well as Lombardy throughout the next decade (Schipa, 1929, pp. 155–6). Although they suffered a number of reverses, they eventually succeeded in bringing the dreams of the Imperialists to an ignominious close: in 1248 the Emperor lost his entire treasure at the capture of Vittoria; in 1249 his son was taken prisoner when the forces of the League regained Modena; and at the end of the following year Frederick himself died (Van Cleve, 1972, pp. 510–12; Schipa, 1929, pp. 162–4).

The early fourteenth century saw two further efforts by the German Emperors to make good their claim to be the legal rulers of the *Regnum Italicum*. The first was led by Dante's hero, Henry of Luxemburg, who arrived in Italy in 1310 (Armstrong, 1932, p. 32). Like his predecessors he began victoriously, quelling rebellions in Cremona and Lodi and laying siege to Brescia in 1311 before proceeding to Rome to be crowned by the Pope in 1312 (Bowsky, 1960, pp. 111–12, 114–18, 159). But once again his triumph drove his enemies to unite, this time under the leadership of Florence, the chief defender of Republican liberties since the Milanese had succumbed to the despotism of the Visconti in the previous generation. The Florentines succeeded in raising revolts at Padua, Genoa and Lodi, as well as repelling the Emperor's forces from their own city at the end of 1312 (Armstrong, 1932, p. 38). The outcome was again disastrous for the Imperial cause: after waiting nearly a year for reinforcements before making a further assault on Florence, the Emperor died at the outset of his campaign and his armies immediately dispersed (Bowsky, 1960, pp. 173–4, 204–5). By this time it had become clear that Italy would never submit to Imperial rule, so that the final attempt by Louis of Bavaria in 1327 to insist on his Imperial rights was an abject failure. Perceiving that his meagre funds could never match his grandiose designs, the cities simply bided their time, avoiding any large-scale engagements until the Emperor's unpaid armies duly melted away (Offler, 1956, pp. 38–9).

During this long struggle the cities of Lombardy and Tuscany not only succeeded in repulsing the Emperor on the field of battle, but also managed to build up an armoury of ideological weapons with which they sought to legitimate this continued resistance to their nominal overlord. The essence of their response to the Emperor's demands consisted of the claim that they had a right to preserve their 'liberty' against any external interference. It is true that some doubts have recently been expressed about the extent to which this ideology was self-consciously developed. Holmes has argued, for example, that the cities never succeeded in articulating their concept of 'liberty' in anything more than a 'vague and ambiguous sense' (Holmes, 1973, p. 129). It is arguable, however, that this is to underestimate the early extent of their civic consciousness. It is apparent from a number of official proclamations that the city propagandists usually had two quite clear and distinct ideas in mind when defending their 'liberty' against the Empire: one was the idea of their right to be free from any outside control of their political life – an assertion of their sovereignty; the other was the idea of their corresponding right to govern themselves as they thought fit – a defence of their existing Republican constitutions.

The way in which the term 'liberty' thus came to connote both political independence and republican self-government has been traced in two important studies of fourteenth-century Florentine political thought. Bueno de Mesquita has established from a study of Florentine diplomatic letters at the time of Henry VII's invasion in 1310 that when the Florentines took the lead in opposing the Emperor by proclaiming 'the liberty of Tuscany', their essential concern was with 'throwing off the yoke of servitude to German rule' and reaffirming their right to govern themselves (Bueno de Mesquita, 1965, p. 305). Similarly, Rubinstein has shown that the concepts of *libertas* and *libertà* came to be employed 'almost as technical terms of Florentine politics and diplomacy' in the course of the fourteenth century, and that they were almost invariably used in order to express the same ideas of independence and self-government (Rubinstein, 1952, p. 29). Nor was this distinctive analysis of 'liberty' merely an invention of the *trecento*. We already find the same ideals being invoked as early as 1177, in the course of the first negotiations which ever took place between the Italian Cities, the Emperor and the Pope. These followed the decisive defeat of Barbarossa's armies by the forces of the Lombard League in the previous year. According to the account given in Romoaldo's *Annals*, the speech presented in the course of the resulting discussions by the ambassadors from Ferrara included a stirring apostrophe to 'the honour and liberty of Italy', together with an assurance that the citizens of the *Regnum* would have 'preferred to incur a glorious death with liberty rather than live a miserable life of servitude'. The ambassadors made it clear that in appealing to the ideal of liberty they had two main ideas in mind. By liberty they meant first of all their independence from the Emperor, for they insisted that 'we shall be willing to accept the Emperor's peace' only 'so long as our liberty remains inviolate'. And by liberty they also meant their right to maintain their existing forms of government, for they added that although they had 'no wish to deny the Emperor any ancient jurisdictions', they were bound to insist that 'our liberty, which we have inherited from our forefathers, we can under no circumstances relinquish, except with life itself' (pp. 444–5).

There was undoubtedly a weakness, however, in these affirmations of *libertas* against the Empire: the cities had no means of investing them with any legal force. The source of this difficulty lay in the fact that, ever since the study of Roman law had been revived at the universities of Ravenna and Bologna at the end of the eleventh century, the Roman civil code had come to be used as the basic framework of legal theory and practice throughout the Holy Roman Empire. And ever since the jurists had begun to study and gloss the ancient texts, the cardinal principle of legal interpretation – and the defining characteristic of the so-called school of Glossators – had been that of following with absolute fidelity the words of Justinian's Code, applying the results as literally as possible to prevailing circumstances (Vinogradoff, 1929, pp. 54–8). Now there could be no doubt that the ancient law-books stated in so many words that the *princeps*, whom the jurists agreed in equating with the Holy Roman Emperor, had to be regarded as the *dominus mundi*, the sole ruler of the world. This meant that as long as the literal methods of the Glossators continued to be employed in the interpretation of the Roman law, the cities had no possibility of vindicating any *de iure* independence from the Empire, while the Emperors were assured of the strongest possible legal support in their campaigns to subjugate the cities (Vinogradoff, 1929, pp. 60–2).

This problem was sharply underlined at the outset of the quarrel between the cities and the Empire, when all four of the leading Bolognese Doctors of Law not only agreed to sit on the commission which drew up Frederick Barbarossa's Roncaglian Decrees in 1158, but went on to defend in fulsome terms his legal rights as a sovereign over the Italian cities.[1] They described the Emperor as 'the supreme ruler at all times over all his subjects everywhere', and insisted that even within the Italian cities he retained 'the power of constituting all magistrates for the administration of justice' and 'removing them if they neglect their duties' (pp. 245, 246). The effect of these contentions was of course to deny the cities any authority even to appoint or control their own *podestà*, and so to divest their demands for liberty of any semblance of legality.

It was evident that if the cities were to succeed in putting these claims against the Empire on a proper legal footing, a fundamental change would first of all have to take place in the attitude of their own jurists towards the authority of the ancient law books. Such a change of outlook was never possible for the Glossators, who continued to assume that the Emperor must be equated with the *princeps* of Justinian's Code and endowed with an identical set of legal rights. By the beginning of the fourteenth century, however, in the face of renewed threats from the Empire, the necessary alteration of perspective was finally achieved. The great figure in this

---

[1] See Vinogradoff, 1929, p. 61. The view that the Roncaglian Decrees should themselves be seen as an expression of the Roman Law concept of *merum Imperium* has been discredited, since they were in fact largely concerned with feudal and other local regalian rights. There can be no doubt, however, that the influence of the Bolognese jurists on the commission helped to give the Decrees their strongly absolutist tone. For a discussion of these issues and a bibliography, see Munz, 1969, pp. 167–9. For the decrees themselves, see *sub Diet of Roncaglia : Decrees* in the bibliography of primary sources.

reorientation, the founder of the so-called school of post-Glossators, was Bartolus of Saxoferrato (1314–57), perhaps the most original jurist of the Middle Ages.

Bartolus was a native of the *Regnum Italicum*, a student at Bologna and subsequently a teacher of Roman Law at several different universities in Tuscany as well as Lombardy (Woolf, 1913, pp. 1–2). He clearly set out with the intention of reinterpreting the Roman civil code in such a way as to supply the Lombard and Tuscan communes with a legal and not merely a rhetorical defence of their liberty against the Empire. The result was not only to initiate a revolution in the study of Roman Law (which was later consolidated by his great pupil Baldus) but also to take a large step towards establishing the distinctively modern concept of a plurality of sovereign political authorities, each separate from one another as well as independent of the Empire.

Bartolus's primary contribution was thus a methodological one. He abandoned the cardinal assumption of the Glossators to the effect that, when the law appears to be out of line with the legal facts, the facts must be adjusted to meet a literal interpretation of the law. He instead made it his basic precept that, where the law and the facts collide, it is the law which must be brought into conformity with the facts (Woolf, 1913, p. 5). As he himself puts it in his commentary on the Code, 'it should not be a matter of surprise if I fail to follow the words of the Gloss when they seem to me to be contrary to the truth, or contrary either to reason or to the law' (vol. 8, p. 195).

The effect of this change was to make possible a complete reversal of the Emperor's legal claims against the Italian cities. It is true that Bartolus begins his commentary on the Code by conceding that *de iure* the Emperor is the sole *dominus mundi* (vol. 7, p. 7). He is even prepared to agree with the Glossators that technically the Empire constitutes the sole jurisdictional unit in Europe, with the independent kingdoms or *regna* being no more than Imperial provinces, while the City Republics or *civitates* are equivalent to Roman Imperial cities (vol. 7, p. 7). He then oberves, however, that even though the Emperor may claim *de iure* to be the sole ruler of the world, there are 'many peoples who *de facto* do not obey him'. It is clear that Bartolus is thinking in particular of Italy, for he notes that 'the Imperial laws do not, for example, bind the Florentines, or others who refuse *de facto* to obey the Emperor's decrees' (vol. 7, p. 7). He later underlines the same point in the course of discussing the authority to delegate in his commentary on the Digest. He concedes that *de iure* the Emperor alone wields *merum Imperium*, the highest power to make laws. But he immediately adds that 'in our day all the governors of cities throughout Italy' in fact take it upon themselves to exercise the same law-making powers (vol. 5, p. 69).

Now technically, as Bartolus admits, such behaviour on the part of the Florentines must be irregular and against the law (vol. 9, p. 64). But it seems misleading to infer, as Keen has done, that Bartolus is still essentially concerned to vindicate the universal authority of the Emperor, and is genuinely reluctant to assign any independent powers to the cities (Keen, 1965, p. 115). This is to underestimate the significance of his basic axiom that the law must yield to the facts. As soon as Bartolus combines this contention with the observation that the Italian cities contain 'free peoples who 'are in fact able to make laws and statutes in any way they choose', he proceeds without hesitation to open up an entirely new perspective on the conventional analysis of *merum Imperium*: he insists that the *de facto* situation is one which the law and thus the Emperor must now be prepared to accept (vol. 9, p. 64).

The first point at which Bartolus unequivocally makes this move is in connection with asking whether the Italian cities may be said to have the right to make and execute their own laws. His major discussion of this question occurs in his commentary on the Digest, at the point where he is analysing the status of public judges (vol. 6, p. 411). One of the problems he raises is 'whether a single city is able to make dispensations' in the case of 'infamous conduct' by its legal officers. He first answers in the conventional style of the Glossators that 'it seems it cannot, for a single city cannot make statutes in such matters' (vol. 6, p. 423). He next points out, however, that 'cities which recognise no superior do in fact impose penalties and grant dispensations' in such cases (vol. 6, p. 422). He then argues that the only way to resolve this dilemma is to invoke the basic principle that the law must accommodate itself to the facts. This allows him to conclude that 'in the case of the cities of present-day Italy, and especially those of Tuscany where no superior is recognised, I judge that they constitute in themselves a free people, and hence possess *merum Imperium* in themselves, having as much power over their own populace as the Emperor possesses generally' (vol. 6, p. 423).

The same point is later brought out even more forcefully in Bartolus's commentary on the Code, in the section where he discusses 'whether a long period of time serves to confirm a contract' (vol. 7, p. 159). After offering a general analysis, he moves on as usual to consider the issue in relation to the Italian cities, broadening the question to ask whether the *merum Imperium* which they have in fact been arrogating may be said to have any legal basis to it. The usual answer, he begins by admitting, is that 'if it is the case that the cities are wielding *merum Imperium*', it is essential 'that they should be able to show that they hold this concession from the Emperor' (vol. 7, p. 160). His own answer, however, again depends on applying his key principle that the law must be accommodated to the facts. This leads him to see it as crucial that '*de facto* the cities have been wielding *merum Imperium* for a very long time'. And this prompts him to conclude that 'even if they cannot prove a concession from the Emperor, I submit that, as long as they can prove that they have in fact been exercising *merum Imperium*, then their claim to exercise it is a valid one' (vol. 7, p. 160).

There is clearly a revolutionary political claim implicit in this defence of the Italian cities and their *Imperium*: the claim that they ought to be recognised as fully independent sovereign bodies. This conclusion is finally spelled out by Bartolus in the form of an epigram which may be said to embody the essence of his attack on the Glossators and the other defenders of the Empire. He declares that since the cities are governed by 'free peoples' wielding their own *Imperium*, they may be said in effect to constitute *sibi princeps*, a *princeps* unto themselves. After this it was only a short step to generalise this doctrine from the Italian cities to the kingdoms of northern Europe, and so to arrive at the view that *Rex in regno suo est Imperator* – that every king within his own kingdom is equivalent in authority to the Emperor. This suggestion had already been advanced by Huguccio and other canonists, who were anxious to elevate the rights of secular kingdoms over the Empire as part of their anti-Imperialist campaign on behalf of the Church. But it was left to Bartolus and Baldus – with a number of French jurists under Philip the Fair – to take the revolutionary step of introducing the same doctrine into the civil law, thus making the first decisive move towards articulating the modern legal concept of the State (Riesenberg, 1956, pp. 82–3).

The attainment of this conclusion in turn enabled Bartolus to perform his major ideological service on behalf of the Italian cities: it enabled him to place on a proper legal footing both the claims about their liberty which they had been trying to make good throughout their long struggle against the Empire. First he deployed his concept of *sibi princeps* in order to vindicate the claim that the cities possess liberty in the sense of being free from any lawful interference in the internal running of their political affairs. Bartolus endorses this contention most emphatically in his commentary on the Digest, in the course of analysing one of the key features of sovereignty, the right to delegate jurisdiction to lesser judges (vol. 1, p. 428). When discussing this topic in relation to the cities, he first concedes that no such delegation is possible in 'cities which recognise a superior', since 'they are obliged to refer themselves to the Emperor'. But he then argues that the situation is altogether different 'in the case of cities which refuse to recognise the lordship of the Emperor', since 'they are able to make their own statutes' and to organise their government in any way they choose. The reason is that 'in such a case the city itself constitutes *sibi princeps*, an Emperor unto itself' (vol. 1, p. 430).

Finally, Bartolus uses the same concept to vindicate in legal terms the other claim made by the cities about their liberty: the claim that they must be free to choose their own political arrangements, and in particular to maintain their established style of Republican self-government. Bartolus mounts his main defence of this principle in his commentary on the Digest, in the course of discussing the right of appeal (vol. 6, p. 576). He begins by outlining the conventional hierarchy of appeals from lower to higher judges which is taken to culminate in the supreme figure of the *princeps* or Emperor. He then recognises that there might well be a free city whose procedures cannot be accommodated to these standard rules. Such would be the case of a city – like Florence – which claims complete 'liberty' in the sense that it not only 'recognises no superior', but also 'elects its own governor, and has no other government'. The question in such a case is 'who will then be judge of appeals?' The unequivocal answer Bartolus gives is that 'in such a case the people themselves must act as judge of appeals, or else a special class of citizens appointed by their government'. The reason he again gives is that 'in such a case the people themselves constitute the only superior to be found, and so constitute *sibi princeps*, an Emperor unto themselves' (vol. 6, p. 580).

THE CITY REPUBLICS AND THE PAPACY

Throughout their struggle against the Empire, the major ally of the Italian cities had been the Papacy. The alliance was first forged by Pope Alexander III, after Barbarossa had refused to countenance his elevation to the Papal throne in 1159 (Balzani, 1926, pp. 430–2). When the Lombard cities founded their League in 1167, Alexander supplied them with funds and encouraged them to build a fortified city – which they duly named Alessandria – to block the pathway of the Emperor's advance (Knapke, 1939, p. 76). And when the League rallied against Barbarossa in 1174, it was Alexander who led the attack, and who subsequently initiated the negotiations which culminated in the peace of Constance in 1183 (Knapke, 1939, pp. 77–8). The same alliance was later revived in the face of Frederick II's invasions in the 1230s. Gregory IX concluded an anti-Imperial treaty with Genoa and Venice in 1238, and in the following year excommunicated the Emperor and formally renewed his ties with the Lombard League (Van Cleve, 1972, p. 419; Waley, 1961, pp. 145, 148–9). The same policies were continued by his successor Innocent IV after his election in 1243. He used papal forces to attack the Imperial garrisons in Lombardy, and re-entered negotiations with the Tuscan cities to strengthen his anti-Imperialist crusade (Schipa, 1929, p. 157). (It was at this point that the term 'Guelf' first came into use in Tuscany to denote those who were in alliance with the Pope.) This at first brought about a truce with the Emperor in 1244. But when Frederick showed signs of wishing to modify its terms, Innocent excommunicated him, summoned a Council which proclaimed him deposed, and at the same time led the Lombard Cities in the series of military victories which brought the Imperial intervention to an end in 1250 (Van Cleve, 1972, pp. 484–6; Partner, 1972, p. 256).

There was a danger inherent in this alliance, however, as the cities soon discovered to their cost. This was that the Popes began to aspire to rule the *Regnum Italicum* themselves. This ambition first became obvious in the face of the attempts by Frederick II's illegitimate son Manfred to use his power-base as King of Naples in order to continue his father's Italian policies during the 1260s. Urban IV responded by excommunicating Manfred in 1263 and calling on Charles of Anjou to oppose him as the champion of the Church (Runciman, 1958, pp. 65, 70, 81). Charles arrived in Rome with his armies at the end of 1265, and at the beginning of the following year won a decisive victory at Benevento, a battle at which Manfred was killed and his forces scattered (Runciman, 1958, pp. 88–95). When Frederick's last surviving son Conradin tried to counterattack by invading Italy from Germany in 1267, Charles went on to inflict a fortunate but final defeat on the Imperial armies at Tagliacozzo, an outcome which left the Papacy as the dominant power throughout a wide area of northern as well as central and southern Italy (Runciman, 1958, pp. 105, 108–12).

By this time the Popes had also begun to pursue their temporal ambitious more directly by seeking to manipulate the internal politics of the Northern Italian cities. The first moves were made in Lombardy, where Ezzelino da Romano, the chief ally of the Imperialists, had succeeded by the 1240s in winning control of an unprecedentedly large territory which included Verona, Padua, Ferrara and most of the surrounding countryside (Hyde, 1966a, p. 199). Alexander IV proclaimed a crusade against him in 1255 and appointed Philip, the Archbishop of Ravenna, to lead it. Philip succeeded in liberating Padua in 1256, and after three more years of fighting managed to defeat and capture Ezzelino at Adda in 1259, a victory which greatly enhanced the Papacy's control over the cities of eastern Lombardy (Allen, 1910, pp. 76–87). Next the Popes turned their attention towards Tuscany and central Italy. Clement IV concentrated on Orvieto, perceiving the strategic significance of its central position between Florence and Rome. He actually moved the Curia into residence there in 1266, a policy followed by Gregory X in 1272 and by Martin IV and Nicholas IV at several points later in the century (Waley, 1952, p. 48). Meanwhile the Popes also began to extend their influence over the major cities of Tuscany. Martin IV concluded an alliance with the Guelf League in 1281, assigning the right to collect Papal taxes to Florence, Siena and Volterra as a means of binding them decisively to his cause (Previté-Orton, 1929, p. 202). During the following decade Boniface VIII began to dabble in the internal factions of Florence, hoping to gain control of the city in order to improve his revenues and secure the northern frontier of his existing territories (Boase, 1933, p. 84). When the Florentines sent an embassy in 1300 (on which Dante is said to have served) to protest against these machinations, Boniface responded by excommunicating the entire *Signoria*, summoning Charles of Anjou to seize the city and so promoting the *coup d'état* which overthrew the hostile government of the 'Whites' in 1301 (Armstrong, 1932, pp. 12–14; Boase, 1933, pp. 249–50). Finally, the Popes managed during the same period to impose their authority on the Romagna, traditionally the major pro-Imperial stronghold. When Gregory X successfully promoted Rudolf of Hapsburg's candidacy to the Imperial throne in 1273, one of the conditions he exacted was that the whole area around Bologna as well as the Romagna should be ceded by the Empire and placed under direct Papal rule. The negotiations were completed by 1278, at which point both provinces were formally annexed by Nicholas III (Larner, 1965, pp. 40–2). The outcome was that, by the end of the thirteenth century, the Papacy had succeeded in winning direct temporal control of a large area of central Italy, as well as a considerable measure of influence over most of the major cities of the *Regnum Italicum*.

These policies were matched by the formation of an ideology designed to legitimate the most aggressive of the Papacy's claims to rule *in temporalibus*. The intellectual framework for this development was originally furnished by Gratian in the 1140s, when he reduced the accumulated Papal Decrees to a system and effectively founded the code of canon law (Ullmann, 1972, pp. 179–80). There followed a succession of lawyer-popes who continued to refine and extend the legal basis of the Papacy's claim to exercise its so-called *plenitudo potestatis* or plenitude of temporal as well as spiritual power. The first was Alexander III, a pupil of Gratian's at Bologna, who effectively frustrated Barbarossa's attempts to convert the

Church into a mere patriarchate of the Empire (Pacaut, 1956, pp. 59–60, 179–81). The next was Innocent III, a pupil of the canonist Huguccio, who has come to be regarded as the most important exponent of the canonist theory of Papal supremacy in temporal affairs (Watt, 1965, p. 72; Ullmann, 1972, p. 209). The same doctrines were further extended in the middle of the thirteenth century by Innocent IV, especially in his decree *Ad Apostolice Sedes*, the first systematic exposition by a canonist of the assumption that Christian society is essentially a single unified body with the Pope as its ultimate head (Watt, 1965, p. 72). And finally, Boniface VIII at the end of the century reiterated the same doctrines in a uniquely high-flown style, especially in his notorious Bull of 1302, *Unam Sanctam* (Boase, 1933, p. 317). This begins with the traditional claim that in Christian society 'there are two swords, the spiritual and the temporal one'. But it immediately goes on to insist that 'it is necessary that one sword should be below the other, and thus that the temporal should be subordinate to the spiritual power'. It ends on an even loftier note by making it clear that the ultimate power of the temporal as well as the spiritual sword must be held by the vicar of Christ, since 'the spiritual power possesses the authority to institute earthly power and to stand in judgment over it if it should fail to act properly' (p. 459).

Faced by this growing aggression from the Papacy in its propaganda as well as its policies, a number of Italian cities began to fight back. This happened first in Lombardy, the original centre of communal liberties. The city of Padua began a major dispute with its local churches in 1266 over their refusal to pay taxes, and in 1282 virtually deprived the Paduan clergy of the protection of the law (Hyde, 1966a, p. 239). The same sort of disaffection soon began to spread throughout Tuscany and central Italy. There was an uprising in Orvieto against the presence of the Curia in 1281, and another much more serious insurrection in 1284 (Waley, 1952, pp. 52–8). There were denunciations of Church courts and clerical immunities in Florence in 1285, and an attack on the privileges of the local clergy at Pisa in 1296 (Boase, 1933, pp. 85, 87). The faction of the 'Whites' in Florence strove throughout this period to stave off the interference of the Pope, and after the *coup* of 1301 entered into an alliance with Pistoia in the hope of displacing the pro-Papal *signoria* of the 'Blacks' (Herlihy, 1967, p. 226). Finally, the direct rule of the Papacy in the Romagna came under continual pressure in the closing decades of the century. There were uprisings at Faenza as soon as the Papal *podestà* arrived in 1278, a renewal of unrest at Forli as well as Bologna in 1284, and a further series of revolts affecting the whole of the province throughout the 1290s (Larner, 1965, pp. 44–7).

As well as offering this increasing resistance to the Popes, a number of Lombard and Tuscan cities began to develop a political ideology designed to legitimate their attack on the powers and immunities being claimed by the Church. This happened above all in Florence, the self-appointed guardian of 'Tuscan liberties', and in Padua, the leading exponent of Republican values in Lombardy ever since it had regained its communal government in 1256.

One obvious way of attacking the Church's claims to temporal dominion was to call in the Emperor to redress the balance of the Pope. It was possible, that is, simply to concede the age-old Imperial claim that the *Regnum Italicum* was indeed a part of the Holy Roman Empire, and so to argue that the Papacy could not possibly be the legitimate ruler of Lombardy and Tuscany, since this would involve a usurpation of the Emperor's legal rights. This was a particularly tempting strategy to adopt at the start of the fourteenth century, when the descent of Henry of Luxemburg into Italy in 1310 appeared for a brief moment to be turning the ideal of the Medieval Empire into a reality once again.

One political writer who developed this line of argument was the Florentine historian Dino Compagni (*c.* 1255–1324) in his *Chronicle* of these years. He claimed that a government led by the Emperor would be 'most just', insisted that Henry of Luxemburg's aim in coming to Italy was simply that of 'making peace', and threatened the pro-Papal 'Blacks' in Florence with the prospect that, unless they changed their allegiances, 'the Emperor with his power' would cause them 'to be seized and robbed by sea and land' (pp. 223, 259). But by far the most important Florentine writer of these years to offer his full support to the Emperor as a counter-balance to the Pope was Dante in his treatise on *Monarchy*. This was almost certainly written between 1309 and 1313, at the moment when the hopes of the Imperialists were at their greatest height.[1] Dante's fundamental plea is for a restoration of 'the quietude and tranquillity of peace', since he believes that 'universal peace is the most excellent means of securing our happiness' (pp. 8, 9). When he goes on to consider why there is no peace or tranquillity in the Italy of his own day, he focuses on two principal causes. The first, to which he devotes Book II of his tract, is the denial of the legitimacy of the Empire. The other, the theme of Book III, is said to be the false belief 'that the authority of the Empire depends upon the authority of the Church'. On this issue Dante regards the Popes as the leaders amongst those 'who resist the truth', since they refuse to accept that the Papacy has no genuine temporal power, and so fail to recognise

---

[1] For references to the debate about the dating of Dante's *Monarchy*, see Reeves, 1965, p. 88.

that 'the authority of the Empire in no way depends upon the Church' (pp. 64, 67, 91).

Dante's eventual perspective on these problems in *The Divine Comedy* takes him far beyond the realm of politics, and leads him to stress the ideal of religious regeneration, the need for a change of heart, as the only means of saving the world.[1] Before conceiving his great poem around 1313, however, the answer he suggested was strictly on the political plane. His tract on *Monarchy* asks for total trust to be placed in the figure of the Emperor as the only unifying force capable of overcoming the factions of Italy and bringing peace. The opening Book is accordingly devoted to defending this solution by arguing that the acceptance of a single, universal ruler is essential if the disorders of the *Regnum Italicum* are ever to be resolved. Dante begins by arguing formally, in a somewhat Averroistic style, with an appeal to the special value of unity and the superiority of wholes over parts (pp. 9–14). But he then adds two purely political arguments in favour of the same conclusion. The first is that the overlordship of the Emperor would maximise the rule of justice, since 'a dispute may arise between two princes' which may require the arbitration of 'a third person enjoying wider jurisdiction who by right rules over both of them' (p. 14). His other argument – even more in line with the prevailing ideology of the City Republics – is that the rule of the Emperor would also maximise liberty, 'God's most precious gift to human nature', since 'only under a Monarchy is mankind self-dependent and not dependent on another' (p. 19).

As Gilson has emphasised, this defence of the Empire is based on a remarkably radical set of premises, since it assumes a complete separation between the spheres of philosophy and theology, and thus of nature and grace. Dante explicitly repudiates the orthodox assumption that there is a single 'final goal' for mankind, that of eternal beatitude, and thus that there ought correspondingly to be a single overlordship in Christian society, that of the Church. He insists instead that there must be *duo ultima*, two final goals for man. One is salvation in the life to come, to be attained through membership of the Church. But the other is happiness in our present life, to be attained under the guidance of the Empire – which is thus treated as a power both equal to and independent of the Church (Gilson, 1948, pp. 191–4).

It is commonly claimed that while this vindication of the Empire may have been innovative in the realm of theory, it was hopelessly anachronistic

---

[1] This has prompted D'Entrèves to argue that the tract on *Monarchy* merely represents a middle phase in the development of Dante's thought, eventually rejected and surpassed in his later works. See D'Entrèves, 1952, esp. pp. 62–74. For a defence of the essential unity of Dante's thought, cf. Limentani, 1965, esp. pp. 128–31.

in practice, amounting to little more than 'the vision of an idealist' out of touch with political realities (Ullmann, 1949, p. 33). It is of course true that neither Henry of Luxemburg nor any of his successors ever succeeded in re-establishing their control over the *Regnum Italicum*. But it is arguable that the accusation of anachronism arises in part out of ignoring the context in which Dante was writing, and in particular the nature of the dilemma which his *Monarchy* was evidently intended to resolve (Davis, 1957, pp. 169–70). Dante had been in exile from Florence ever since the *coup* of 1301 engineered by the aristocratic 'Blacks' with the connivance of Boniface VIII. One of his main hopes was thus to find an effective leader under whose banner it might be possible to gather the exiles and displace the city's pro-Papal government. It was evident that any such champion would need to possess a considerable measure of authority in order to serve as an immediate and attractive rallying-point, together with a considerable amount of sheer military strength in order to have any hope of success. Given these problems, it is not at all surprising – and it is only with hindsight that it could possibly seem irrational – that Dante should have chosen, at the moment when Henry VII was actually marching into Italy, to pin all his hopes on the Emperor as a way of saving the *Regnum Italicum* from the continued domination of the hated Pope.

There is no doubt, however, that from the point of view of the Lombard and Tuscan republics, jealous as ever of their liberties, Dante's proposal can hardly have seemed a very tempting solution to their difficulties. While it allowed them to deny the right of the Pope to interfere in their affairs, it did so at the expense of branding them once again as vassals of the Holy Roman Empire. It was obvious that what they needed most of all was a form of political argument capable of vindicating their liberty against the Church without involving them in ceding it to anyone else. Just as Bartolus had sought to defend their independence from the Empire, they were in quest of a parallel form of argument proclaiming their independence from the Pope.

The answer to this problem was first formulated in Padua, the leading Lombard Republic, soon after the failure of the Imperial expedition of 1310–13 had ruled out the sort of solution Dante had proposed. The key contribution was made by Marsiglio of Padua (*c*. 1275–1342) in his famous treatise *The Defender of Peace*, which he completed in 1324 (p. 432). The answer he proposed, which occupies the second and much longer of the two Discourses into which *The Defender of Peace* is divided, unquestionably involved a great imaginative leap. But it was also a direct outcome of the context we have sketched, in the sense that it provided – and was clearly intended to provide – exactly the sort of ideological backing which the City Republics of the *Regnum Italicum* most needed at this juncture in order to defend their traditional liberties against the Pope.

Marsiglio's answer consists in essence of the simple but daring claim that the rulers of the Church have altogether misunderstood the nature of the Church itself in supposing it to be the sort of institution which is capable of exercising any legal, political or other form of 'coercive jurisdiction' (pp. 168, 181). He begins by devoting the first eleven chapters of the second Discourse to attacking the entire priesthood – all the 'priests or bishops and their supporters' – for promoting this misconception in order 'to impose their unjust despotism upon Christian believers' (p. 98). His first move is to reject the Church's claim to immunity from ordinary taxation, a privilege which had already led, as we have seen, to much disaffection in the cities, and which Boniface VIII had vehemently defended in his Bull *Clericis Laicos* of 1296. This had included a demand for exemption for all 'ecclesiastical persons' from all 'halfs', 'tenths' and 'hundredths', together with a threat to excommunicate any secular ruler who attempted to infringe these alleged rights (p. 457). Marsiglio's response is that this constitutes a complete reversal of the teachings of Christ. When Christ was shown the tribute money, he indicated 'by word and example' his belief that we ought to render unto Caesar the things that are Caesar's (p. 119). He thereby made it clear that he 'wanted us to be subject in property to the secular ruler', and that he rejected any idea that it might be 'improper for his successors in the priestly office to pay tribute' (pp. 119, 120). Marsiglio next argues that the same objection applies in the case of the clergy's demands to be exempted from the authority of the civil courts, and to have the right 'to interfere with coercive secular judgments' (pp. 125, 168). This again is said to be contrary to the teaching of Christ and the Apostles. Marsiglio appeals in particular to the thirteenth chapter of St Paul's Epistle to the Romans, a text which was later destined to play a central role in Reformation debates about the proper relationship between the secular authorities and the Church. St Paul's doctrine, Marsiglio stresses, is that everyone must be 'subject to the higher powers', since 'the powers that be are ordained of God', and 'whosoever resisteth the power resisteth the ordinance of God'. The implication of this doctrine is said to be that no member of the Church can possibly lay claim to any special treatment in the Courts, since 'all men alike, without exception' are 'subject in coercive judgment to the secular judges or rulers' (p. 130; cf. p. 140).

These arguments culminate, to speak anachronistically, in a remarkably 'Lutheran' vision of the powers and jurisdictions which Marsiglio thinks it legitimate to claim on behalf of the clergy and the Church. He insists that Christ deliberately excluded 'his apostles and disciples and their successors, the bishops or priests' from the exercise of any 'coercive authority or worldly rule' (p. 114). So he concludes that the Church founded by Christ cannot be regarded as a jurisdictional body at all. It can only be a congregation, a *congregatio fidelium*, a voluntary gathering together of 'the whole body of the faithful who believe in and invoke the name of Christ' (p. 103). This in turn means that the only authority God can possibly have intended any priest to exercise 'with respect to his office' is 'to teach and practice' – an authority which obviously allows him 'no coercive power over anyone' (p. 155). The outcome of Marsiglio's attack on the immunities and jurisdictions of the Church is thus an un-mitigatedly congregationalist theory of the Church – a doctrine unique at this stage in medieval thought (Reeves, 1965, p. 101).

After this general denunciation of the clerical estate, Marsiglio moves on to the major theme of his second Discourse, his attack on the *plenitudo potestatis* claimed by the Popes (p. 313). As Marsiglio himself concedes, it is easy to anticipate the conclusion he is bound to reach, since he has already laid it down that it constitutes a misunderstanding to assign any jurisdictional powers to the Church (pp. 113, 268). He now proceeds to trace out the implications of this belief, seeking in particular to establish that 'when the Roman or any other Bishop ascribes to himself plenitude of power over any ruler, community, or individual person, such a claim is inappropriate and wrong, and goes outside, or rather against, the divine Scriptures and human demonstrations' (p. 273).

Marsiglio begins by isolating five main aspects of the Papal *plenitudo potestatis*: the claim to give 'definitions of meanings' of the Scriptures; to summon General Councils of the Church; to excommunicate or place under interdict any 'ruler, prince or country'; to appoint 'to all the Church offices in the world'; and finally, to make decisions about the defining characteristics of the Catholic faith (pp. 272–3). He then attacks these features of Papal ideology in two ways. He first opposes the concept of Papal monarchy by defending the doctrine of conciliarism – the doctrine that the chief executive power in the Church lies not with the Pope but rather with 'a General Council composed of all Christians', including 'non-priests' (pp. 280, 285). This leads him to repudiate three aspects of the Papacy's thesis about its own plenitude of power. He maintains that the 'determination of doubtful questions' in the scriptures, 'the authority to excommunicate any ruler' and the 'regulations concerning Church ritual' and other features of the faith are all matters over which 'only the General Council, and no bishop or priest or particular group of them' has the authority to legislate (pp. 282, 292–3). This is said to be manifest both from the evidence of the scriptures and from the earliest traditions of the Church, which reveal that it was only 'the later Roman bishops' who began 'to assume a greater authority', and so 'issued and commanded the observance of decrees or ordinances for the universal Church' (p. 271).

The other way in which Marsiglio attacks the supremacy of the Popes is by elevating to an unparalleled height the rights of the secular authorities over the Church. He has already laid it down that no member of the Church is entitled to wield any 'coercive jurisdiction' in virtue of his office (pp. 100, 113). It follows that whatever coercive powers may be necessary for the regulation of Christian life must all by right be exercised exclusively by 'the faithful human legislator' – Marsiglio's term for the highest secular power within each kingdom or City Republic (p. 287). Once he has arrived at this deduction – the climax of his second Discourse – Marsiglio is able to dismantle the rest of the Papacy's contentions about its plenitude of power. He first treats it as a corollary that the right 'to make and approve appointments, and to establish all offices' in the Church – including the office of 'the Roman Pontiff' himself – must be lodged not with 'the Roman Bishop, either alone or with his College of Cardinals', but entirely with 'the authority of the faithful legislator', who alone possesses the power 'to make appointments to the priesthood and other holy orders' (pp. 287–90). He then adds that the right 'to call a General Council' and 'to have it duly assembled, solemnised and consummated' must again belong 'not to any priest or priestly College' but entirely to 'the faithful human legislator' (p. 287). It is this authority alone which is endowed with the power 'to call or command such a council, to appoint and designate suitable persons to it, to order the observation of its decisions and decrees, and to punish transgressors thereof' (p. 292). Since Marsiglio has already concluded, moreover, that all other aspects of the Papal *plenitudo potestatis* belong properly to the General Council of the Church, this elevation of the Legislator to a controlling position over the Council has the final effect of freeing the secular authorities from any vestiges of ecclesiastical influence.

With this transfer of the *plenitudo potestatis* from the Papacy to the 'faithful human legislator', Marsiglio fulfils his main ideological task in the second Discourse of *The Defender of Peace*. He claims to have demonstrated that the figure of the Legislator in each independent kingdom or City Republic is the sole rightful possessor of complete 'coercive jurisdiction' over 'every individual mortal person of whatever status' (pp. 427–8). He claims in consequence to have shown that the attempts of 'the Roman bishops and their accomplices' to secure their hold over Northern Italy can be dismissed as nothing more than a series of 'usurpations and seizures' of jurisdictions which properly belong exclusively to the secular authorities (pp. 95, 98, 101). The vital contribution he is thus able to make to the ideology of the City Republics is to vindicate their total *de iure* independence from the Church, and so to stigmatise the Papacy's efforts to dominate and control their affairs as an 'unjust despotism', a 'vicious outrage' which has 'distressed the *Regnum Italicum* and has kept it and still keeps it from tranquillity and peace' (pp. 95, 98, 344). The corresponding moral of the book – as well as the key to understanding its title – is that anyone who aspires to be a defender of the peace in Northern Italy must above all be a sworn enemy of the alleged jurisdictional powers of the Church.

2

Rhetoric and liberty

THE RISE OF THE DESPOTS

The spreading of what Sismondi called 'this brilliant flame of liberty' throughout the Italian City Republics proved to be a sadly short-lived spectacle (Sismondi, 1826, vol. 3, p. 245). By the end of the thirteenth century most of the cities had become so riven with internal factions that they found themselves forced to abandon their Republican constitutions, to accept the strong rule of a single *signore* and to make the move from a free to a despotic form of government in the name of attaining greater civic peace.

The root cause of this erosion of Republican liberty must be sought in the class divisions which began to develop early in the thirteenth century (Jones, 1965, p. 79). The quickening pace of trade brought into prominence new classes of men, *gente nuova*, who soon grew rich as merchants in the cities and the surrounding *contada* (Jones, 1965, p. 95). Despite their increasing wealth, however, these *popolani* had no voice in the governing Councils of their cities, which continued to remain firmly under the control of the older magnate families (Waley, 1969, pp. 187–97). As these divisions widened, they began to generate an alarming increase in civic violence, with the *popolani* struggling for recognition while the magnates fought to maintain their oligarchic privileges.

The first move in this battle generally came from the disenfranchised *popolani*. Characteristically this took the form of setting up their own Council, or *Popolo*, headed by their own elected leader, the *Capitano del Popolo*. This was intended as a direct challenge to the traditional form of government by *podestà*, since these officials tended to be nominees of the leading magnate families. Such councils were established at Lucca and Florence in 1250, at Siena in 1262 and soon afterwards in most of the leading Lombard as well as Tuscan cities. (Pullan, 1973, pp. 116–18; Waley, 1969, pp. 185–92). Once this breach in the governing monopoly of the nobles was opened up, the next and even more aggressive move which the *popolani* usually made was to force through a series of measures designed to curtail or even prevent the access of nobles to positions of political power. This happened, for instance, at Florence in 1282. The faction of the 'Whites' based on the *popolani* managed to oust the magnate faction of 'Blacks', and in 1293 went on to establish a constitution which systematically excluded the older nobility from the ruling Priorate (Becker, 1960, p. 426). The same pattern was soon repeated elsewhere. One nearby example was that of Siena, where the *Popolo* seized complete control from the *podestà* in 1287, exiled many of the nobility and inaugurated the 'Board of Nine Governors', a merchant oligarchy which continued to rule the city uninterruptedly until 1355 (Bowsky, 1962, pp. 368, 370, 374).

The more the *popolani* fought for recognition, however, the more the older nobility and their allies fought back. This first gave rise to endemic civil violence as soon as the *popolani* began to protest against their exclusion from government. One of the most notorious instances was that of Verona, where the Montecchi – Shakespeare's model for the feuding Montagues in *Romeo and Juliet* – fought for over twenty years on behalf of the *popolani* against fierce opposition from the older nobility, finally managing to seize control of the city in 1226 (Allen, 1910, pp. 45–52). But the most serious internal violence developed once the *popolani* succeeded in establishing their own regimes. The government of the 'Whites' in Florence, for example, was immediately challenged and overthrown by the 'Black' faction of the nobles under the leadership of Corso Donati in 1301. Similarly, the rule of *popolani* in Siena was subjected to a dangerous attack in 1318 and another in 1325, both of them engineered by the Tolomei, a leading noble family ousted in the *coup* of 1287 (Bowsky, 1967, pp. 14, 16).

Given this background of worsening civil strife, it is not surprising that by the end of the thirteenth century a majority of cities in the *Regnum Italicum* had reached the conclusion – more or less voluntarily – that their best hope of survival lay in accepting the strong and unified rule of a single *signore* in place of such chaotic 'liberty' (Hyde, 1973, p. 141; Waley, 1969, p. 237). The first city to experiment successfully with the hereditary government of a single family was Ferrara. There the Etensi managed to make an undisputed transition in 1264 from Azzo d'Este's informal domination of the city to the formal signory of his son Obizzo, who was installed as 'permanent lord' of Ferrara allegedly 'by the consent of all'.[1] The next important city to follow suit was Verona. There the process began with the election of Mastino della Scala as *Capitano del*

---

[1] See Gundersheimer, 1973, pp. 23–5 and Bueno de Mesquita, 1965, p. 315. Waley, 1969, p. 236 cites the formula by which Obizzo was established as 'permanent lord' of the city.

Popolo in 1262. He used this position to maintain a largely personal ascendancy over the city, and thereby succeeded in founding a dynasty. When he was murdered in 1277, his brother Alberto was immediately accepted as Lord of Verona and Captain General for life. And when Alberto died in 1301, his son Bartolomeo – Dante's first patron after his exile from Florence – was able to take over as hereditary *podestà* of the city (Allen, 1910, pp. 94–6, 124, 141–3). After these experiments, the system of government by *signori* began to spread rapidly throughout the *Regnum Italicum*. During the 1270s the Buonaccolsi managed to gain control of Mantua by exploiting the position of *Capitano del Popolo*, and by the end of the next decade there were similar lordships established at Treviso under Gerardo da Cannino, at Pisa under the Count Ugolino, at Parma under Ghiberti da Correggio and at Piacenza under Alberto Scotti (Brinton, 1927, pp. 41–3; Previté-Orton, 1929, p. 203; Armstrong, 1932, pp. 33, 45). Finally, the same period saw the direct rule of the Papacy in the Romagna being widely challenged by the rise of local despots. Guido da Polenta became *podestà* of Ravenna in 1286 and went on to govern the city from that position for nearly a decade (Larner, 1965, pp. 51–2). Similarly, the Malatesta family rose to dominate Rimini in the 1280s, driving out the last of their rivals by 1295 and establishing their hereditary right to rule (Jones, 1974, pp. 31–3, 47). It was thus entirely accurate of Dante to observe in the *Purgatorio*, although his phrasing may have been tendentious, that 'all the cities of Italy' had by that time become 'full of tyrants' (p. 63).

With the coming of the *Signori*, a new style of political theory began to develop, a style of panegyric in which they were praised as the bringers of unity and peace (Bueno de Mesquita, 1965, pp. 321–8). One of the earliest exponents of this *genre* was Ferreto de Ferreti (*c.* 1296–1337), a member of the circle of pre-humanist *literati* at Padua, who composed a long account in Latin verse of *The Rise of the della Scala* soon after they gained control of the city in 1328 (vol. 1, p. xiii; Hyde, 1966a, p. 282). Since the aim of his eulogy was to legitimate their rule, Ferreti made no reference to the liberty of the Paduans so recently celebrated by Marsiglio. He instead devoted much of his second Book to complaining about the 'turbulence' and 'lawlessness' of the city before the coming of the della Scala, while insisting that the main desire of the citizens had always been for peace (vol. 1, pp. 28ff.). Since the government established by Cangrande was undoubtedly more stable than that of the Republic he displaced, this insistence on peace rather than liberty as the fundamental political value had the effect of portraying him as the true liberator of Padua, freeing it from a legacy of chaos and misrule. Ferreti thus felt able to conclude his poem by expressing the unabashed hope that Cangrande's descendants might 'continue to hold their sceptres for long years to come', so maintaining the people in peace and quietness (vol. 1, p. 100).

This shift from government *in libertà* to government *a signoria* was smoothly as well as rapidly accomplished in most cities of the *Regnum Italicum*, doubtless in consequence of war-weariness induced by the background of incessant feuds and faction-fights. But there were several important exceptions to this rule. A few of the cities devoted themselves to resisting the rise of the despots with vigour and in some cases with success, developing in the process a heightened self-consciousness about the special value of political independence and Republican self-government.

The first city to mount a determined defence of its Republican constitution was Milan. When the *popolani* exiled their opponents and appointed Martin della Torre as '*signore* of the people' in 1259, this led to nearly twenty years of fighting between the exiles and the supporters of the *signoria*. It was only when the exiles accepted their own leader, Orto Visconti, as 'perpetual lord of Milan' after his final victory over the forces of the della Torre regime in 1277 that the Milanese republic was finally dissolved (Sismondi, 1826, vol. 3, pp. 260, 435–7). A similar and even more protracted struggle was mounted in Padua soon afterwards. The danger in this case came from the neighbouring city of Verona, where the della Scala had consolidated and begun to expand their power. Alberto della Scala started a war against Padua in 1277, but this was settled by a compromise peace in 1280 (Hyde, 1966a, pp. 227–8). Cangrande della Scala returned to the attack in 1312, but still found himself facing a determined opposition, led by such staunch Republicans as Alberto Mussato, who refused to contemplate surrendering the city into the hands of a tyrant (Hyde, 1966a, pp. 256–7, 266). It was only after fifteen years of fighting, in the course of which Mussato and the rest of his war party were proscribed by their more faint-hearted compatriots, that Cangrande was eventually able to take over the government in 1328 (Hyde, 1966a, pp. 267, 275, 278). But the city which did most of all to check the advance of the despots at this time was of course Florence. As we have seen, the Florentines succeeded in fighting off every external challenge to their independence throughout the thirteenth century. When Manfred attacked them in the 1260s, they allied with Charles of Anjou and quickly repulsed the threat (Schevill, 1936, pp. 139–44). When Arezzo allied with the Imperialists against them later in the century, they responded by winning a major victory at Campaldino in 1289 – a battle at which the young Dante may well have fought (Larner, 1971, p. 208). And when the Emperor descended on Italy in 1310, they not only turned back his attempts to lay siege to their own city, but went on to lead the counter-attack which rapidly brought his expedition to an ignominious end.

These efforts to resist the coming of the *signori* were accompanied in each case by the development of a political ideology designed to vindicate and emphasise the special virtues of Republican civic life. It is arguable that the emergence of this ideology in the late *duecento* and early *trecento* has been too little recognised by the historians of Renaissance thought.[1] Hans Baron in particular has sought to argue that no such defence of Republican liberty was ever produced until the work of the Florentine 'civic humanists' of the early *quattrocento* (Baron, 1966, pp. 49, 58). The same contention has recently been reiterated by a number of other historians of the early Renaissance. Hyde has claimed, for example, that in facing the need to defend their liberty against the despots at the end of the thirteenth century, the City Republics had no ideology to which they could hope to appeal, since their prevailing social and political assumptions were 'aristocratic and chivalric rather than civic' and 'there was no alternative set of ideals to which laymen could turn' except those of an ascetic religious life (Hyde, 1973, p. 171). Holmes has similarly argued that 'the obstacles to the creation of an independent lay ideology' in the late thirteenth and early fourteenth centuries proved to be so great that no such pattern of values was ever successfully articulated in the City Republics until the coming of 'the humanist revolution' in early *quattrocento* Florence (Holmes, 1973, pp. 111, 124, 131).

Although these are orthodox contentions, they give a misleading view of the development of Renaissance political thought. There were in fact two distinct traditions of political analysis available to the protagonists of Republican self-government at the end of the thirteenth century. One had developed out of the study of rhetoric, which had been a major focus of teaching – together with law and medicine – in the Italian universities ever since their foundation in the eleventh century. The other had emerged out of the study of scholastic philosophy, which had first been introduced into Italy from France in the latter part of the thirteenth century. Both these traditions made it possible for the protagonists of Republican 'liberty' to conceptualise and defend the special value of their political experience, and in particular to argue that the disease of faction might be

---

[1] A notable exception is Rubinstein's important essay on the intellectual context of Marsiglio of Padua's political thought. I do not altogether agree with his analysis, which seems to me to treat in too undifferentiated a way two different and often contrasting intellectual traditions of the early *trecento*, one derived from the study of rhetoric, the other based on scholastic arguments. An attempt is made below to separate out these different strands of thought. But Rubinstein's account is a brilliant and learned one, from which I have greatly profited.

susceptible of a cure, and thus that the upholding of liberty might be compatible with the preservation of peace. If we wish to understand the evolution of these central themes of Renaissance political theory, it seems essential to go behind the works of the *quattrocento* humanists and to focus on their origins in these two strands of pre-Renaissance thought.

THE DEVELOPMENT OF THE 'ARS DICTAMINIS'

To understand the process by which the study of rhetoric in the Italian universities eventually gave rise to an influential form of political ideology, we need to begin by considering the practical purposes underlying the teaching of rhetoric itself. The basic aim of rhetorical instruction was to furnish the student with a highly marketable skill: the ability to draft official letters and other such documents with maximum clarity and persuasive force. The underlying concept of letter-writing as a special technique, capable of being embodied in rules and learnt by heart, was first developed at Bologna early in the twelfth century as an offshoot of the University's basic concern with the training of lawyers and judges.[1] The leading master of rhetoric at Bologna during this period was Adalbert of Samaria, who seems to have been the first to describe himself specifically as a *dictator* or instructor in the *Ars Dictaminis* (Murphy, 1974, p. 213). His chief work was a handbook entitled *The Precepts of Letter-Writing*, which he evidently completed between 1111 and 1118 (Haskins, 1929, p. 173). Within a generation of his death, the rules he had laid down became elaborated into a rigid system, the basic principle of which was that all formal letters should be constructed out of, and capable of being resolved into, five distinct parts. The first textbook to insist on this pattern was an anonymous treatise entitled *The Principles of Letter-Writing*, which appears to have been produced at Bologna around 1135.[2] After this the same fivefold classification came to be repeated almost without variation by all the leading rhetoricians throughout the rest of the Middle Ages (Haskins, 1929, pp. 182–7).

[1] For this account see Wieruszowski, 1971b, p. 361. Haskins originally proposed Alberic, a monk of Monte Cassino writing in the 1080s, as the first teacher of the practical art of letter-writing. (See Haskins, 1929, pp. 171–2.) Wieruszowski disputes this suggestion on the grounds that Alberic's approach still concentrated on the use of classical models rather than on formulating rules capable of being taught independently of such authorities. See Wieruszowski, 1971b, p. 361.

[2] This is Haskins's dating (Haskins, 1929, p. 181), which has been adopted by Murphy both in his Bibliography (Murphy, 1971a, p. 60) and in his recent edition of the work (1971b, p. 3). But Wieruszowski argues that the book must have been written 'after 1140'. See Wieruszowski, 1971a, p. 335 and note. For a discussion and illustration of the five-part system of composition, see Murphy, 1974, pp. 220–6.

As well as laying down general rules, the *dictatores* were concerned from the first to indicate how their recommendations should be applied in practice. This they achieved by supplementing their handbooks with *dictamina*, or collections of model letters, the point of which was to illustrate their precepts being correctly put to use. This method was again pioneered by Adalbert of Samaria, who included at the end of one of his theoretical treatises an appendix of forty-five *formulae* or model letters as exemplifications of his rules.[1] The same pattern was immediately taken up by such *dictatores* as Hugh of Bologna and Henricus Frankigena, both of whom were writing in the 1120s (Haskins, 1929, pp. 178, 180). Thereafter a large number of similar *dictamina* appeared throughout the twelfth century, culminating in two highly-publicised contributions to the *genre* by Boncompagno da Signa (*c.* 1165–1240), who was arguably the most original – and unquestionably the most boastful – of the Bolognese masters teaching at the start of the thirteenth century. His first treatise, completed in 1215, was entitled *The Old Rhetoric*, and included a final section of model letters designed for the use of 'noblemen, cities and peoples' (Paetow, 1910, pp. 76–7). His other *Dictamen*, which he issued in 1235, was imposingly entitled *The Newest Rhetoric of All*, and offered the student an almost bewildering array of models, all arranged in sections according to the rules governing the correct subdivision of formal letters. Turning to Book V, for example, we find a comprehensive exposition of all the possible 'Forms of exordium' (p. 262). These include twelve different opening paragraphs to be used for writing to the Pope, five for writing to a cardinal, two for writing to a bishop and four for writing to the Emperor, together with model openings for letters to city senators, *podestà*, consuls, professors, schoolmasters and so on through an exhaustive list of all the people to whom a city official or a private citizen might ever have occasion to write in a formal style (pp. 262–73).

It was through the medium of these models or *formulae* that the *dictatores* first moved on from the idea that they were merely inculcating formal rhetorical rules, and began to concern themselves self-consciously with the legal, social and political affairs of the Italian City Republics. This development occurred in two main ways. By the middle of the twelfth century, it became usual for the letters included in treatises on the *Ars Dictaminis* to focus on issues of immediate practical interest to the students taking the course. Hitherto, since the main intention had simply been to illustrate the rhetorical rules in action, the *dictatores* had tended to allow the subject-matter of their examples to remain remote or even

[1] See Haskins, 1929, pp. 174, 177. For a similar group of letters see Adalbert's *Precepts*, pp. 43–74.

fanciful in character.[1] Now they began to make a systematic effort to ensure that the content of their models should have a more obvious value and relevance for their pupils in their personal lives or future careers. One of the earliest examples of this trend is provided by an anonymous *Dictamen* issued by a Florentine master in the 1150s. This includes several model letters for a student to send to his family, assuring them of his continued academic progress and asking them for more money (Wieruszowski, 1971a, pp. 336–9). It also includes two letters of specific political advice, the first indicating the best way of persuading a community to raise a contingent of knights and archers, the second explaining how to approach the magistrates of another city about the need to punish one of their citizens for having robbed someone from one's own community (Wieruszowski, 1971a, pp. 340–1, 343). This tendency for the *dictatores* to use their *Formulae* as vehicles for offering advice about the problems of city life became highly developed in the course of the next century. By the time we come to Mino da Colle's treatise on *The Arts of Letter Writing* in the 1290s, or Giovanni de Bonandrea's teaching at Bologna after 1302, we find them devoting the whole of their attention in their *dictamina* to the special needs and problems of students, teachers, merchants, judges, priests, administrative officials and all the other leading classes of citizens in the City Republics (Wieruszowski, 1971b, pp. 360, 365–6; Banker, 1974, pp. 155–7).

The other important extension of the *Ars Dictaminis* occurred in the early thirteenth century. It first became customary at that time to combine the teaching of letter-writing with the so-called *Ars Arengendi*, the art of making formal public speeches. This meant that the *dictatores* began to append lists of model orations to their theoretical treatises in addition to the usual lists of model letters. The earliest leading rhetorician to offer an exposition of the two arts together was Guido Faba (*c.* 1190–1240), a pupil and rival of Boncompagno's at Bologna, whose collection of *Speeches and Epistles*, first issued in the 1230s, included a considerable number of exemplary orations as well as letters (Kantorowicz, 1941, pp. 256, 275). After this the combination of the two arts rapidly became the orthodoxy, a change reflected in such well-known handbooks as Brunetto Latini's *Rhetoric* and Giovanni de Bonandrea's *Brief Introduction*, both of which were in widespread use by the end of the century (Banker, 1974, p. 157). This further development in the use of rhetorical examples had an obvious practical significance, especially in a society which conducted the whole

[1] See Wieruszowski, 1971a, p. 336 and 1971b, pp. 364–5. For a good example of a *Dictamen* of this character, see the list of models from Hugh of Bologna, *Rules of Letter-Writing* given in Murphy, 1974, p. 217.

of its legal, political and diplomatic business through the medium of formal speeches and debates. It enabled the *dictatores* to make a covert but systematic contribution to the discussion of most of the important public questions of the day. The outcome of combining the *Ars Arengendi* with the *Ars Dictaminis* was thus that the teaching of rhetoric, and the self-image of the rhetoricians, began correspondingly to assume an even more public and political character (Kantorowicz, 1943).

Once the study of rhetoric came to embody so much incidental political content, it became a short step from giving an exposition of the *Ars Dictaminis* to offering a direct commentary on civic affairs. This step was duly taken by a number of *dictatores* and their pupils in the first half of the thirteenth century, when they began to deploy their characteristic concern with model letters and speeches in a variety of new and more openly propagandist contexts. The effect was to bring about the emergence of two distinctive new *genres* of social and political thought.

The first of these was a new style of city chronicle (cf. Hyde, 1966b). The cities had of course produced a number of annalists in the course of the twelfth century, but these had invariably been clerics whose interests had tended to be confined to illustrating the workings of divine providence in political and especially in military affairs (Fisher, 1966, pp. 144, 156–61) This somewhat threadbare tradition started to undergo a radical transformation in the opening decades of the thirteenth century, when a number of lawyers, *dictatores* and other lay exponents of the rhetorical arts began for the first time to concern themselves with the histories of their cities. The outcome was the emergence of an entirely new form of civic historiography, more rhetorical in manner and more self-consciously propagandist in tone than anything which had previously been attempted (Wieruszowski, 1971d, p. 613).

One of the earliest examples of this development is Boncompagno da Signa's account of *The Siege of Ancona*. This describes an incident from Barbarossa's campaign of 1173, and was probably written between 1201 and 1202 (Hyde, 1966a, p. 287). Although Boncompagno presents himself in his Preface in the orthodox guise of a city chronicler, it is clear that his motives and methods as an historian are entirely derived from his background as a teacher of the *Ars Dictaminis*. This is evident in the first place from the way in which he chooses to organise his account of the siege. He presents his story not in the traditional form of a narrative, but rather in the manner of a rhetorical exercise, nearly half the account being given over to a sequence of model speeches put into the mouths of the leading protagonists. The same background and preoccupations as a *dictator* are even more apparent in Boncompagno's choice of theme. His main concern is clearly to exploit the familiar conventions of the city chronicle in such a way as to furnish himself with a more direct medium than that of the *Dictamen* for the expression of his political beliefs. The consequence is that the formal orations around which he organises his narrative are all blatantly propagandist in character, designed to advertise their author as a purveyor of useful political advice as well as to inculcate the characteristic ideology of the City Republics. One of the orations is devoted to encouraging the whole body of the citizens to take up arms on their own behalf, another to stressing the need for the cities to come to one another's aid, and another to celebrating the ideal of Republican liberty (pp. 24, 40, 43). The speech in praise of liberty in fact makes up the centrepiece of Boncompagno's account. It is spoken by an elderly citizen, who addresses the assembled people of Ancona at the moment when the Emperor's emissaries are offering to raise the siege if a suitable ransom is paid. The people are undecided: food is short and they cannot be sure of victory (p. 23). Then the old man speaks. He reminds them that they are 'descended from the nobility of ancient Rome', and that 'up to this moment' they have always been prepared 'to fight for the preservation of liberty' (p. 24). He exhorts them to 'hold fast and fight like men, since glorious triumph is gained in the greatest battles' (p. 26). And he ends by denouncing 'effeminacy and pusillanimity', warning them that they will gain 'eternal opprobrium' if they voluntarily allow their liberty and their city to be taken away from them (pp. 26–7).

This new type of chronicle was soon imitated and developed by a number of other rhetoricians, most notably by Rolandino of Padua (*c.* 1200–76), who had been a pupil of Boncompagno's at Bologna (Hyde, 1966a, pp. 198, 287). Rolandino wrote an ambitious *Chronicle of Padua* in the early 1260s, taking as his theme the rise and fall of Ezzelino da Romano as overlord of the city. The work is entirely rhetorical in construction, being punctuated at every significant point with letters and speeches in the typical manner of the *Ars Dictaminis*. When Ezzelino is born, Bishop Gerardus marks the occasion with a model speech on the ideal of godly government (pp. 41–2). When Ezzelino first develops his ambitions, he enunciates them in a model letter (p. 49). When the *podestà* of Verona is expelled by Ezzelino in 1230, he presents a model oration to the people of Padua denouncing the rule of tyrants (pp. 55–6). And when the Archbishop of Ravenna arrives in 1256 to lead the Papal crusade against Ezzelino, he makes a model speech exhorting the Paduans to fight for the recovery of their liberty (p. 106). As these examples indicate, Rolandino is also concerned, even more stridently than Boncompagno, to exploit the familiar format of the city chronicle in order to deliver a direct political message. The whole of his *Chronicle* is in fact designed as a celebration of Republican liberty – the need to treat it as the key political value, the need to fight for it when it is jeopardised. This controlling ideological purpose is manifest from the very beginning, when Gerardus, speaking at the birth of Ezzelino, is made to exalt liberty and argue that 'tyrants are not to be held in any reverence' (p. 42). The same theme is reiterated in the oration spoken by the deposed *podestà* of Verona, who is made to claim that the overthrowing of his Republican regime is 'against all reason and the will of God' (p. 56). The same commitment is repeated once again at the climax of the narrative, when the Archbishop of Ravenna is made to demand in his speech to the Paduans that they must 'fight to defend the liberty of their fatherland' with such 'vigour and courage' that 'the fame of their victory spreads throughout all the world' (p. 107).

The other *genre* of political writing which arose directly out of the *Ars Dictaminis* was that of advice-books intended for the guidance of *podestà* and city magistrates. The earliest known example is an anonymous Latin treatise entitled *The Pastoral Eye*, which was written according to Muratori in 1222 (p. 93). But the best-known as well as the most extended contribution to the *genre* at this formative stage in its development was John of Viterbo's account of *The Government of Cities*, which he completed in the 1240s after serving as one of the judges to the *podestà* of Florence (Hertter, 1910, pp. 43–72).

The appearance of these treatises marks a dramatic extension of the *Ars Dictaminis*. Their authors are no longer content to offer their views about the conduct of affairs in an oblique form. They abandon any pretence that their essential concern is to offer instruction in the rhetorical arts, and instead present themselves directly as the natural political advisers of rulers and cities. Nor are they content to write simply for students who might later expect to become magistrates. Instead they address their treatises directly to the magistrates themselves. This new approach soon began to be widely copied, and later came to exercise a pervasive influence on the development of Renaissance political thought. The pattern of topics covered in these early advice-books can still to some extent be discerned even in the most sophisticated of the later contributions to the same *genre*, such as Machiavelli's *The Prince*. One specific instance of this continuity is provided by the discussion at the end of *The Pastoral Eye* as to whether a *podestà* should always act with strict justice, or whether he should sometimes temper his judgments with clemency on the one hand or severity on the other (pp. 124–5). John of Viterbo considers the same dilemma, devoting three of his longer chapters to the question of whether a *podestà* 'should want to be feared rather than loved' or 'loved far more than feared' (p. 262). He observes that 'those who want to be feared' argue that 'with severity and cruelty' they 'are able to keep a city more readily in peace and tranquillity, while 'those who want much more to be loved' reply that 'it is nothing but a vileness of the soul' to insist that clemency should always be ruled out (pp. 262–3). His own solution, stated more emphatically than the similar conclusion in *The Pastoral Eye*, is that 'those who want to be feared for excessive cruelty are utterly in the wrong', for 'cruelty is a vice', and 'is therefore a sin' which cannot possibly have any place in good government.[1]

But the most important way in which these early advice-books helped to set a pattern for the later 'mirror-for-princes' literature was in the emphasis they placed on the question of what virtues a good ruler should possess. *The Pastoral Eye* ends with the figure of Justice mounting an 'invective' against the habitual vices of *podestà*, and exhorting them 'to follow the right way and never deviate from it' (pp. 125–6). The same theme is taken up at much greater length by John of Viterbo in two of the major sections of *The Government of Cities*. The first lists an impressive range of vices which the *podestà* is counselled to avoid, beginning with drunkenness, pride and anger and ending with venality and the taking of gifts (pp. 235–45). The other section – prefaced by the observation that 'it is not sufficient to abstain from evil without also doing good' – proceeds to enumerate 'the virtues which the magistrate ought above all to cultivate'. He must first of all fear God and honour the Church, and thereafter govern all his actions according to the four cardinal virtues, which are listed – in a manner later typical of Renaissance moralists – as prudence, magnanimity, temperance and justice (pp. 245–53).

While these advice-books represent a new and influential departure, however, they remain largely derivative from, and basically dependent on, the existing conventions of the *Ars Dictaminis*. This can be seen most clearly in their extensive use of model speeches and letters as a way of making their main political points. When John of Viterbo opens his discussion by considering the problem of selecting a new *podestà*, the form his advice takes is that of a model letter to be sent by the city to a suitable candidate (p. 222). When he goes on to counsel prospective *podestà* about the best way of responding to such invitations, he produces two further model letters, one designed for refusing the post and the other for accepting it (p. 222). Finally, when he comes to advising incumbent *podestà* on the proper conduct of their government, both he and the author of *The Pastoral Eye* provide a sequence of model orations suitable for delivery on all formal occasions. There are speeches for the *podestà* to

[1] *The Government of Cities*, p. 264. Cf. the similar account in *The Pastoral Eye*, p. 124.

make to his Council, speeches for the councillors to offer by way of reply, speeches for the outgoing *podestà* to deliver to his successor and speeches for the new *podestà* to make in response.[1] While the focus is more overtly political than anything in the earlier traditions of rhetorical writing, these writers still view the structure of civic government entirely from the perspective of a teacher of the rhetorical arts.

THE EMERGENCE OF HUMANISM

While there is undoubtedly an important element of continuity between the earliest books of advice to *podestà* and the later development of a rhetorical political style amongst the Renaissance humanists, it would be misleading to imply that there is any simple line of descent to be traced from the first to the second of these traditions of thought. This would be to overlook the influence of a new and self-consciously humanist form of rhetorical theory which was imported into Italy from France in the second half of the thirteenth century, and which had the effect of interrupting and transforming the prevailing conventions of the *Ars Dictaminis* (Kristeller, 1965, p. 4).

The changes which overtook the study of rhetoric in Italy at this time were based on the idea that the subject should be taught not merely by the inculcation of rules (*artes*) but also by the study and imitation of suitable classical authors (*auctores*). Hitherto the curriculum of the *Ars Dictaminis* had generally been conceived, as Paetow puts it, as nothing more elevated than a business course (Paetow, 1910, p. 67). The overwhelming emphasis had been placed on learning the rules of composition; little space had been left for the more 'humanist' assumption – in vogue at the same time in the French Cathedral schools – that one should also make a study of the ancient poets and orators as models of the best literary style (Haskins, 1929, p. 170; Banker, 1974, p. 154). This severely practical approach was especially emphasised at Bologna under Boncampagno da Signa. He explicitly attacked the French method of teaching rhetoric through the medium of *auctores* as 'superstitious and false' (Wieruszowski, 1971c, p. 594). He made it a proud boast at the start of one of his own manuals, *The Palm*, that 'I do not recall that I have ever read Cicero' as a guide to rhetorical technique (p. 106).[2] And he made it abundantly clear from his

---

[1] See *The Pastoral Eye*, pp. 96–7, 99–100, 100–1; and *The Government of Cities*, pp. 230, 232, 280.

[2] It is obvious from the context that what Boncompagno means is that he has never read over Cicero's works with his students, not that he has never read Cicero's works himself, as Paetow and Murphy both appear to assume (cf. Paetow, 1910, p. 77 and Murphy, 1974, p. 254). It is arguable that Murphy is altogether too dismissive of Boncompagno's stature and

own writings that he thought of the subject entirely in practical terms. One of his handbooks, *The Myrrh*, is wholly devoted to stating the rules for drawing up wills; another, *The Cedar*, is similarly concerned entirely with the correct procedures for drawing up local statutes and ordinances (Paetow, 1910, p. 76).

Although Boncompagno's approach became the orthodoxy, the alternative and more humanist tradition of rhetorical instruction was never completely extinguished. It survived even in Italy in some of the Grammar schools, and it continued to flourish in France throughout the thirteenth century (Wieruszowski, 1971c, p. 423 and 1971d, pp. 601–4). Despite the ascendancy of scholasticism, one of the major centres for this type of study remained the University of Paris (Rand, 1929, pp. 256, 266). Here the leading *dictator* was John of Garland, who taught the *Ars Dictaminis* continuously from 1232 until his death twenty years later. His method of instruction was firmly anchored to the relevant classical texts, with entire poems and orations being taken as instances of good rhetorical style (Paetow, 1910, pp. 17, 85). But the leading centre of rhetorical teaching in the humanist manner was Orleans. Here the chief exponent of the *Ars Dictaminis* was Bernard of Meung, who began his career around the year 1200. He too insisted on a close association between rhetoric and Latin literature, and established a tradition of instruction founded not on the explication of rhetorical rules, but rather on the discussion of Cicero's *On Invention* and the pseudo-Ciceronian treatise *On the Theory of Public Speaking* (Haskins, 1929, p. 191; Banker, 1974, p. 154).

During the second half of the thirteenth century, a number of leading Italian *dictatores* were educated in France, imbibed this very different approach to the subject, and returned to propagate these new methods of teaching in the Italian Universities. One of the first to follow this path was Jacques Dinant. He began by studying rhetoric and Latin literature in France, and came to Bologna as an instructor in the *Ars Dictaminis* towards the end of the thirteenth century (Wilmart, 1933, pp. 120–1). The treatise on the *Ars Arengendi* which he went on to produce at this time in connection with his teaching was almost entirely modelled on the pseudo-Ciceronian *Theory of Public Speaking* (Wilmart, 1933, pp. 113–14; Banker, 1974, p. 154). But the most important pioneer of this approach was Brunetto Latini (*c.* 1220–94). He went to live in France in 1260 after the victory of the Sienese at Montaperti led to his exclusion from his native Florence (Carmody, 1948, p. xv). During his exile he encountered Cicero's rhetorical writings for the first time, as well as making a study of

significance. For a different emphasis, Cf. Paetow, 1910, pp. 74–9 and Wieruszowski, 1971c, p. 426 and 1971d, p. 594.

his theoretical treatises on the rhetorical arts (Wieruszowski, 1971d, p. 618). After his return to Florence in 1266, this led him to introduce a far more literary and classical flavour into his own writings on the *Ars Dictaminis*. He not only produced the first Italian version of three of Cicero's major public speeches, but went on to translate and supply a commentary to his treatise *On Invention*, which he described as the greatest work on rhetoric ever written (Davis, 1967, pp. 423, 432; East, 1968, p. 242).

This method of studying the *Ars Dictaminis* through the medium of classical *auctores* soon became established as a new orthodoxy. This happened even in Bologna, hitherto the centre of the most practical and even philistine approach to the rhetorical arts. As early as the 1270s Fra Guidotto of Bologna translated *The Theory of Public Speaking* into Italian and used it as a manual of instruction in the *Ars Dictaminis* (Wieruszowski, 1971b, pp. 370–1). During the same decade Bono da Lucca made it the central principle of his teaching at Bologna that the entire study of rhetoric should be 'drawn from the Ciceronian fount' (Wieruszowski, 1971b, p. 364). The new movement reached its zenith early in the fourteenth century, with the appearance of the classic treatise embodying the new humanist approach, the *Brief Introduction to the Art of Letter-Writing* by Giovanni di Bonandrea (1296–1321) (Murphy, 1971a, p. 63). This was almost entirely derived from Cicero's *On Invention* and *The Theory of Public Speaking*, and according to Banker it immediately gained for its author 'the pre-eminent position in rhetorical instruction' not merely in Bologna but throughout the Italian universities (Banker, 1974, p. 159).

As soon as the teaching of rhetoric came to be founded on the study of classical examples and authorities, a further important intellectual development began to take place in the Italian universities. A number of students who had started by learning the *Ars Dictaminis* simply as a part of their general legal training began to become increasingly interested in the classical poets, orators and historians whom they were called upon to examine as models of good rhetorical style. They began, that is, to treat these writers not simply as masters of various stylistic tricks, but as serious literary figures worthy of study and imitation in their own right.[1] The resulting efforts of these early fourteenth-century lawyers to study the classics for their literary value rather than merely for their use may be said to entitle them to count as the first of the true humanists – the first writers amongst whom 'the light began to shine', as Salutati later put it, amidst the general darkness of their age (Wieruszowski, 1971c, p. 460).

[1] See Ullman, 1941, p. 218 and Wieruszowski, 1971d, p. 620. This connection between the *Ars Dictaminis* and the emergence of humanism suggests an answer to the question put by Weiss as to why so many of the earliest humanists should have been lawyers. cf. Weiss, 1947, pp. 4–6.

As Salutati noted in his panegyric on these earliest exponents of the revival of letters, the two centres in which the rays of humanism first shone most brightly were the cities of Arezzo and Padua. There is little direct evidence about the earliest stirrings of humanism in Arezzo, since the works of Geri, the leading poet and scholar of the time, have almost all been lost (Wieruszowski, 1971c, p. 460). But there can be no doubt about the intrinsic merits as well as the great historical importance of the so-called circle of 'pre-humanists' at Padua in the early years of the four-teenth century (Weiss, 1947, p. 6). The first significant figure in this group was the judge Lovato Lovati (1241–1309), of whom Petrarch himself remarked in his book *On Memorable Matters* that he was 'easily the greatest poet our country had seen' up to that time (p. 84). His major contribution was to revive the tragedies of Seneca and make a special study of their metrical effects (Weiss, 1951, pp. 11–23). Amongst the younger members of his circle there were several poets and scholars of note, including Rolando da Piazzola, who wrote extensively in Latin verse, and Ferreto de Ferreti, whom we have already encountered as the author of one of the earliest celebrations of the *signori* and their cause (Weiss, 1947, pp. 7, 11–12). But the most important of Lovati's disciples was undoubtedly the lawyer Alberto Mussato (1261–1329), who attained a position of promi-nence in Paduan politics, as we have already seen, in the course of the long struggle against Cangrande of Verona. Mussato was the author of two histories of his own time, both inspired by Livy's and Sallust's accounts of Republican Rome. The second and more ambitious of these, the *History of the Achievements of the Italians after the Death of the Emperor Henry VII*, he was still writing in exile at the time of his death in 1329 (Hyde, 1966a, pp. 297–8). But the most remarkable of his works was *Ecerinis*, a play in Latin verse which Weiss has characterised as 'the first secular drama written since classical times' (Weiss, 1947, p. 10). This was modelled on the tragedies of Seneca, and was written in 1313–14 (Hyde, 1966a, pp. 298–9). It is recognisably the work of a humanist poet and rhetorician, and its quality is such that Mussato has even been hailed as 'the father of Renaissance tragedy' (Ullman, 1941, p. 221).

As well as marking the first beginnings of the revival of letters, this movement had a considerable influence on the development of Renaissance political thought. This can be discerned in two main ways. The first is that the works of these pre-humanist *literati* were often strongly political in themselves. There are clear signs of this motivation in the *duecento* poets of Arezzo. The best example is the work of Guido d'Arezzo, who wrote an attack on the Florentines in the 1260s for deserting their civic ideals, and especially for encouraging the destructive play of faction, claiming that these faults served to explain their disastrous defeat at Montaperti in 1260 (Rubinstein, 1942, p. 218). But the most wholehearted attempt to employ the new literary culture in the service of the City Republics was made by the pre-humanists at Padua, and in particular by Alberto Mussato, who clearly saw himself as a politician and propagandist as much as a scholar and poet. The whole purpose of his *Ecerinis*, as he explains himself in his Introduction, is 'to inveigh with lamentations against tyranny' and to celebrate the value of fighting for liberty and self-government (p. 5). The play takes as its theme the rise and fall of Ezzelino as tyrant of Padua – with copious allusions to the more immediate threat posed by Cangrande to the freedom of the city. The drama opens with an account of Ezzelino's demonic parentage, and proceeds to portray in horrifying detail the 'savage tyranny' of his rule, marked by 'prisons, crosses, torments, deaths and exile' (p. 37). The climax comes with the recapture of Padua from the tyrant, after which the Chorus celebrates 'the killing of the savage madness of tyranny and the regaining of peace' (pp. 50, 59). The value of the play as political propaganda was immediately recognised by the hard-pressed city of Padua. Mussato was ceremonially crowned with laurel by the commune in 1315 – the first of many such Renaissance coronations of great poets – and a civic decree was enacted requiring the play to be read aloud annually before the assembled populace (Weiss, 1947, p. 1; Rubinstein, 1965b, p. 63).

The other way in which the emergence of this new literary culture helped to shape the growth of political theory was less direct but of far greater significance. The new classical influences served to enrich and strengthen both the existing *genres* of political writing which had already arisen out of the study of rhetoric earlier in the thirteenth century, helping them to become more sophisticated in presentation as well as more explicitly propagandist in tone.

This development was partly a matter of purely literary confidence. This can be observed in the first place in a number of city chronicles composed in the latter part of the thirteenth century. One important example is provided by the historical section of Brunetto Latini's major work, *The Books of Treasure*, which he composed in French during his exile in the 1260s (Carmody, 1948, p. xvii). Latini's book takes the traditional form of an encyclopedia, but in content it is manifestly the work of a *dictator* of the new school, combining extensive citations from Plato, Seneca, Sallust, Juvenal and especially Cicero with its more conventional information and advice. A further example is the *Chronicle* of Florence composed early in the fourteenth century by Dino Compagni, a lawyer and politician who had received an early training in the *Ars*

Dictaminis (Ruggieri, 1964, pp. 167–9). Covering the climacteric years between 1270 and 1312, Compagni presents his story with notable literary skill in an appropriately rhetorical style, interspersing his narrative with set speeches, ironic apostrophes and dramatic lamentations on Florence's loss of liberty (e.g., pp. 5, 24, 78, 92, 259). Finally, the same classical influences can also be discerned in the remarkable history and description of Milan written by Bonvesin della Riva in 1288 and entitled *The Glories of the City of Milan*. Bonvesin was a teacher of rhetoric by profession, and while his book is in many ways unique, it is unquestionably a product of the literary background we have sketched, containing many elaborate 'exclamations' and alliterative apostrophes in the highest rhetorical style (e.g., pp. 123, 174–6).

The same growth of literary assurance can also be detected in the other *genre* established earlier in the thirteenth century, that of handbooks addressed to *podestà* and city magistrates. The best example is provided by the third and final section of Latini's *Books of Treasure*, which is entitled 'The Government of Cities' (p. 317). This takes the form of a conventional advice-book, with much of the material being drawn directly from John of Viterbo's treatise of the same name. As well as the usual model speeches and letters,[1] however, Latini adds a great deal of Ciceronian rhetorical theory and Aristotelian moral philosophy in the newly fashionable classical style.[2] The effect is to imply a much closer set of connections than the earlier mirror-for-princes literature had managed to suggest between 'the sciences of speaking and of governing well', which Latini artfully yokes together in his opening chapter (p. 17). He now feels able to insist – with copious allusions to Cicero – that 'the chief science in relation to the government of cities is that of rhetoric, that is, the science of speech' (p. 317; cf. Davis, 1967, p. 423). The impact of this new assurance was such that Latini soon came to be regarded – as Giovanni Villani records in his *Chronicle* a generation later – not merely as 'a consummate master of rhetoric' but also as 'a great philosopher', since he was 'the first who taught refinement to the Florentines and the art of speaking well and ruling the Republic according to proper political rules'.[3]

---

[1] The final section of Book III of the *Books of Treasure* includes a model letter to be sent to a prospective *podestà*; two possible replies – one for refusal and the other for acceptance; various model speeches for the *podestà* to deliver on first arriving; a model speech to be made at the outbreak of war; and a model speech of farewell. See pp. 396–7, 398–9, 401–4; 419–20.

[2] The opening sections of Book II of the *Books of Treasure*, on 'the nature of the virtues and vices according to the *Ethics*' (p. 175) is wholly a paraphrase of Aristotle (see Davis, 1967, p. 423). The opening sections of Book III, which are 'concerned with speaking well' (p. 317) are wholly a paraphrase of Cicero's *On Invention*. See East, 1968, p. 242.

[3] See Villani, *Chronicle*, Bk. VIII, section 10, vol. 1, p. 174. Davis, 1967, p. 423 translates the final phrase as 'ruling . . . according to the science of politics.' The original reads 'secondo la politica'.

But the most important development to be observed in these treatises and chronicles lies in the increasingly systematic character of the political arguments they advance. As we have seen, they were writing at a time when the City Republics were confronting the rapid advance of the *Signori* and an accompanying loss of confidence in their elective systems of government. Faced with the possible extinction of an entire political tradition, they responded by furnishing the first full-scale defence of the characteristic political values of the City Republics. Drawing on the literary and rhetorical background we have sketched, they proceeded to develop an ideology devoted not merely to upholding the central value of Republican liberty, but also to analysing the causes of its vulnerability and the best methods of attempting to ensure its continued life. It is the structure of this ideology which we must next turn to analyse.

THE RHETORICAL DEFENCE OF LIBERTY

The starting-point for all these writers is provided by the ideal of liberty, taken in its traditional sense to mean independence and Republican self-government. It is misleading to argue – as Witt and others have done – that no attempt was ever made to vindicate the superiority of Republican liberty over monarchical forms of government before the work of the Florentine humanists at the end of the *trecento* (Witt, 1971, pp. 175, 192–3). A century earlier than this, we already find Bonvesin della Riva asserting in his account of Milan that 'the city deserves to be commended for its liberty', and even maintaining – a trifle optimistically in view of the recent arrival of the Visconti – that although 'many tyrants from outside the city have tried to occupy it', they have always been successfully repulsed (p. 155). Mussato exhibits a similar concern for the Republican values of Padua at the start of his *History of the Italians*, where he contends that after the deliverance of the city from the tyranny of Ezzelino, the return of the Republic brought 'the most honest and the most upright' form of government the citizens had ever enjoyed (cols 586, 588). He later reiterates the same contention in the course of a highly rhetorical 'invective against the people of Padua' in Book IV, in which he attacks his fellow-citizens for permitting Vicenza to be lost, and proclaims that his own concern has always been 'to uphold the liberty of our native city' (col. 614). But the most unequivocal expression of a preference for Republican liberty over any other form of government is pronounced by Latini in his *Books of Treasure*. He briskly asserts at the start of Book II that 'governments are of three kinds, the first of kings, the second of aristocracies and the third of peoples, of which the third is far better than the others' (p. 211). And later he mounts an invidious comparison between Republics and Monarchies in his section on 'the government of cities'. Any city government based on 'submitting to the rule of kings and other princes' is said to involve 'the selling of offices to those who bid the highest figure, with scant regard for the good and profit of the townspeople'. This is entirely different from 'the type of city government found in Italy', where 'the citizens, the townspeople and the community select their own *podestà* or *signore*', with the result that 'the people of the city and all their dependents gain the greatest possible benefit' (p. 392).

These writers are not content, however, simply to insist on the value of Republican liberty in the face of the engulfing despotisms of their time. They also go on to ask why the *signori* are managing to advance so successfully, so that the traditional constitutions of the City Republics are everywhere being threatened and undermined. The basic answer, they all agree, is that the free cities are dangerously weakened by internal factions. Bonvesin singles out 'the corrosion of envy' and the resulting lack of any 'civic concord' as the first 'special defect' in the government of Milan (pp. 170, 174). He concludes his description of the city with a fierce rhetorical 'exclamation' against its 'lack of quietude', denouncing its leading citizens for 'bending all their power against their own people', trying 'to dominate them in the manner of a vile tyrant' and 'imitating the crime of Lucifer' by encouraging them to fight amongst themselves (p. 175). Compagni similarly insists at the start of his *Chronicle* that the 'struggles for office' amongst the 'proud and quarrelsome' Florentines have been the root cause of the conflicts which 'have undone so noble a city' (pp. 3, 5). And the same point is even more forcefully made by Latini, who laments the fact that 'warfare and hatred' have by now 'multiplied so greatly amongst the Italians' and have 'led to such divisions in almost every city between different factions of the townsfolk' that 'anyone who now succeeds in winning the love of one side automatically wins the hatred of the other' (p. 394; cf. also p. 45).

A second reason these writers give for the loss of civic liberty is the increase of private wealth, which some of them even treat as the root cause of political factiousness. The belief underlying this diagnosis – that the pursuit of private gain is inimical to public virtue – has been subjected to a detailed analysis by Hans Baron in his study of 'Franciscan poverty and civic wealth' (Baron, 1938b). Baron treats the dislike of increasing luxury in late thirteenth-century Italy essentially as 'the consequence of Franciscan influence' (pp. 2, 4). He first sees this outlook being reinforced by a stoic suspicion of opulence, and a corresponding sense that one ought to concentrate on 'stiffening national power through simplicity in civic life' (p. 15). This is said to have developed for the first time in Florence – and specifically in the works of Boccaccio – in the second half of the fourteenth century. He then sees this tendency to denigrate the acquisition of riches being superseded in the early years of the fifteenth century, especially in the works of such leading 'civic humanists' as Leonardo Bruni and Francesco Barbaro (pp. 18–20). They not only argued that no connection can be made between the growth of private opulence and the decline of public morality; they even went on to suggest that the possession of private wealth might constitute one of the most valuable means for an active citizen to lead a virtuous public life.

There are several features of this analysis which are perhaps somewhat questionable. The idea that increasing wealth may serve as a positive blessing can scarcely be an invention of the *quattrocento* 'civic humanists', since we already find the same contention being advanced with almost vulgar fulsomeness by Bonvesin, whose account of the greatness of Milan is replete with exclamations and statistics about the excellence of the city's 'glorious prosperity' and 'abundance of all good things' (pp. 92, 171; cf. Hyde, 1965, pp. 327–8, 337). Nor can the distaste for luxury which is undoubtedly exhibited by a majority of Italian moralists at the end of the thirteenth century – in contrast with Bonvesin's outlook – be attributed exclusively to the influence of what Baron calls 'Christian spirituality'.[1] It is evident on the contrary that the fears which are voiced by such writers as Compagni, Mussato and Latini are already the expression of stoic rather than Franciscan beliefs, and are based in particular on Sallust's highly relevant explanation of the collapse of the Roman Republic into the despotism of the Empire. Compagni traces the disruption of Florentine government in the 1290s not merely to 'pride and rivalry for office', but also to the fact that 'the minds of the false *popolani*' had been 'corrupted to do wrong for the sake of gain' (p. 139). Latini similarly treats it as an axiom that 'those who covet riches destroy the virtues', and cites Juvenal to the effect that 'wealth breeds bad habits' (p. 299). And Mussato draws extensively on stoic authorities in seeking to account for the final 'captivity and death' of the Paduan Republic at the hands of Cangrande in 1328 (cols 766, 768). While he does not underestimate the contribution made by 'internal faction' and 'lethal ambition', he mainly follows Sallust in emphasising the baleful effects of 'morbid cupidity', 'the lust for money', and the accompanying loss of civic responsibility.[2] He traces the origins

---

[1] This is what Baron says (1938b), pp. 5 and 15. But at p. 4 he cites Latini's suspicion of wealth, and characterises this view as that of the 'Medieval stoics', a concession which appears somewhat inconsistent with his general case.

[2] Mussato, cols 586–7, 716. Rubinstein, 1957, pp. 169–70, 172–3, shows that Mussato's account is actually a paraphrase of Sallust's at this point.

of Padua's downfall to the moment when her leading citizens began 'to turn to usury', and so allowed 'sacred justice to be supplanted by the growth of their avarice'. This in turn caused the city to be 'won over to the ways of fraud and deceit', thus ensuring that 'good acts became turned into evil and selfishness'. The final and inescapable result was that 'the reins of the whole government were snapped' and the liberty of the city was forfeited (col. 716).

Following this diagnosis of the two major threats to the maintenance of Republican liberty, the other main concern of all these writers is to suggest how the traditional ideals of the City Republics may most effectively be preserved. The basic answer they give is a very simple one: the people must set aside all personal and sectional interests, and learn to equate their own good with the good of their city as a whole. Compagni defends this ideal in reporting a speech he himself made on being appointed one of the Priors in the Florentine government of 1301. The chief appeal he makes to his fellow-citizens is 'to love one another as dear brethren' and to treat 'the love and the good of your city' as the highest good of all (pp. 92–3). Bonvesin similarly calls on the Milanese in one of his 'exclamations' to place the good of their city above all factional loyalties, and to recognise that 'only in peace will you flourish' (p. 174). And Latini constantly reverts to the same theme throughout his *Books of Treasure*. When speaking of Aristotle's views on 'the government of a city' in Book II, he begins by emphasising that 'if each man follows his own individual will, the government of men's lives is destroyed and totally dissolved' (p. 223). When discussing the outlook of various other ancient philosophers later in Book II, he praises both Plato and the stoics for reminding us that 'we are not born just for ourselves', and that 'we ought to consider the common profit above everything else' (p. 291; cf. also pp. 224, 267). Finally, when he turns in Book III to give his advice to the rulers of cities, he insists that just as the people 'should concern themselves night and day with the common good of their city', so their governors must be sure 'never to do anything which is not for the manifest profit of the city as a whole' (pp. 392, 418).

This is obviously to beg the central question, however, of how to attain such a unity between the interests of a city and those of its individual citizens. To this the writers we are considering give an answer which, when developed by the humanists of the Italian Renaissance, supplied the foundations for one of the major intellectual traditions concerned with the analysis of virtue and corruption in civic life. We may say that, in the evolution of modern political theory, there have been two main approaches to this theme. One stresses that government is effective whenever its institutions are strong, and corrupt whenever its machinery fails to function adequately. (The greatest exponent of this outlook is Hume.) The other approach suggests by contrast that if the men who control the institutions of government are corrupt, the best possible institutions cannot be expected to shape or constrain them, whereas if the men are virtuous, the health of the institutions will be a matter of secondary importance. This is the tradition (of which Machiavelli and Montesquieu are the greatest representatives) which stresses that it is not so much the machinery of government as the proper *spirit* of the rulers, the people and the laws which needs above all to be sustained. And it is this second viewpoint which the early rhetorical writers may be said to share – and which they may indeed be said to have introduced for the first time into early modern political thought.

This commitment is reflected in each of the major topics they consider in discussing the practical question of how the common good is to be secured. They begin by treating with special seriousness the problems of how to promote men of virtue to serve as leaders of the people. The radical answer they characteristically give is that the traditional nobility must be by-passed, and men from all classes of society made eligible, the only condition being that they should possess sufficient largeness of vision to oppose the rule of any sectional interests. This is the scale of values Compagni claims to be supporting in his defence of the Florentine Priorate overthrown in the *coup* of 1301. He denounces the 'Black' nobility for factiousness, and insists that the 'White' *popolani* were all genuine patriots 'disposed to the common good and the honour of the Republic' (p. 126; cf. Becker, 1966, p. 678). Latini expresses the same outlook, laying a special emphasis on the underlying assumption that the only criterion of true nobility must be the possession of virtue. He begins his 'comparison of the virtues' in Book II of his *Books of Treasure* by speaking of 'those who delight in the nobility of their lineage and boast of their great ancestors' (p. 294ff.; cf. Davis, 1967, p. 434). To this he immediately opposes the characteristically stoic belief that all such pretensions are absurd, since 'true nobility, as Horace says, is nothing but virtue' (p. 296; cf. Holmes, 1973, p. 128). He insists that even though a man may have inherited a great name, 'there is no nobility in him if he leads a dishonest life' (p. 296). And conversely, he maintains that 'one ought not to consider a man's power or his lineage' when thinking of choosing him as a *podestà* or a magistrate, since the only relevant considerations ought to be 'the nobility of his heart and the honourable character of his life' (p. 393). The same assumptions are echoed by Dante in the fourth book of *The Banquet*, and it may be significant in this connection that Dante was actually a pupil of Latini's, whom he addresses in the *Inferno* as his master, speaking with admiration of what he had learned from him (p. 159; cf. Davis, 1957, pp. 74, 86). Dante begins his extensive discussion of nobility by citing the belief – which he takes to be the opinion 'of almost everyone' – that the sole criterion of nobility is 'the possession of ancient wealth' (p. 240). This he dismisses on the grounds that riches 'are naturally base', and are thus 'foreign to the nature of nobleness' (pp. 276, 279). He also considers the view that anyone is noble 'who is a son or grandson of any worthy man, although he himself be of nought' (p. 258). This he regards as an even more disgraceful mistake, since such a man 'is not only base' but 'the very basest' for failing to follow the good examples available to him (p. 259). His own conclusion, which he finally reaches after twenty chapters of elaborate distinctions, is simply that 'wherever virtue is, there is nobleness' (p. 322). As in the case of Latini, the radical outcome of the argument is thus the suggestion that the quality of nobility – which is said to give a man a title to serve as a leader of the people – is taken to be a purely personal property, an individual attainment rather than the possession of families which happen to be ancient or rich.

The other major concern of these writers is to consider what advice should be given to *podestà* and other magistrates once they have duly been elected and installed in office. This is the point at which they reveal most clearly their sense that what matters most in good government is not the fabric of institutions, but rather the spirit and outlook of the men who run them. They scarcely offer any analysis of the administrative structure of the City Republics; they concentrate all their attention on the question of what attitudes a magistrate must adopt in order to ensure that the common good of his city is constantly pursued.

It is true that this final theme is of little concern to Compagni, since it lies outside the scope of his essentially historical interests. Nor does it greatly occupy Bonvesin, whose talents are mainly descriptive, and who contents himself with the pious hope that 'the prayers of wise men' may induce God to bring peace to Milan and an end to factiousness (pp. 171, 176). With the mirror-for-princes writers, however, including Latini, John of Viterbo and the anonymous author of *The Pastoral Eye* it is no exaggeration to say that the ambition to supply their rulers and magistrates with practical advice on how best to conduct themselves provides the central theme of all their very similar treatises.

The outcome of this concern is in part a straightforward restatement of the classical typology of the cardinal virtues, together with the injunction that every ruler, as Latini demands, 'must ensure that his government embraces all these virtues and avoids all the vices' (p. 417). It is important in this connection that Latini was writing in the first generation which possessed a Latin translation of Aristotle's *Nicomachean Ethics*. He was able to draw heavily on this source in order to furnish a more elaborate analysis than any of his predecessors of the qualities every good ruler ought to possess. He must have prudence, 'the first virtue', which includes foresight, care and knowledge (pp. 231, 243). He must have temperance, which is said to involve honesty, sobriety and continence (pp. 248, 253–4). He must have fortitude or strength, enabling him to attain 'magnificence in war and peace' as well as constancy and patience 'in the face of assaults from adversity' (pp. 259, 260). And finally, he must have a sense of justice, a highly complex quality which is taken to include liberality, religiousness, pity, innocence, charity, friendship, reverence and the desire for concord (pp. 271, 291–2).

Latini and his predecessors are more distinctive, however, when they turn to consider which vices ought especially to be avoided in the conduct of good government. The first point Latini makes is that no ruler must ever be content merely to appear to possess the virtues of rulership. This is first argued in Book II in 'the comparison of the virtues' and later repeated in Book III in the course of the main discussion of 'the government of cities'. A ruler who wishes to maintain his power, Latini contends, 'must actually be as he wishes to seem', for he will be 'grossly deceived' if 'he tries to gain glory by false methods or faint words' (p. 303; cf. pp. 394, 417). A second vice Latini counsels the ruler to avoid is the sin of parsimony and avarice. John of Viterbo had already spoken of these failings (p. 240) as 'the mother of all evils', and Latini agrees that every ruler has a duty to ensure that his officials are paid 'in such a way that he cannot be blamed for avariciousness' (p. 413). Next, Latini devotes particular attention to an issue which, as we have seen, Machiavelli was later to make notorious, and which the author of *The Pastoral Eye* as well as John of Viterbo had already discussed at length. As Latini presents it, the argument is 'between those who prefer to be feared rather than loved, and those who wish to be loved rather than feared' (p. 414). His own answer, again following his predecessors in the mirror-for-princes *genre*, is that any ruler who indulges in 'fierce pains and sharp torments' will be making a prudential as well as a moral mistake (p. 414). He not only endorses Cicero's maxim to the effect that 'the greatest thing in a governor is clemency and pity, so long as this remains connected with what is right'; he also warns us (again citing Cicero) that 'fear will not long keep you your signory', whereas 'nothing helps one more to retain one's power than being loved' (pp. 302, 415). Finally, and most important of all, he follows both *The Pastoral Eye* and John of Viterbo in concluding that the highest duty of any ruler must always be to serve as a model of probity, avoiding at all costs the temptations of fraud and deceit. This is said to apply even in time of war, for 'one should place no credence in those who say that one ought to purchase victory over one's enemies by trickery as well as force' (p. 268). And in time of peace the maintenance of 'a proper faith in God and towards one's fellow-men' is said to be the greatest virtue of all, and 'the sum of all the others', since 'without good faith and loyalty there can be no upholding of what is right' (p. 394).

This concentration on the issue of political virtue was destined to become one of the most characteristic features of later Renaissance political thought. Two and a half centuries later, Machiavelli devoted his most notorious chapters in *The Prince* – the chapters on 'how a prince should govern his conduct towards his subjects' – to a consideration of precisely the same range of themes (p. 90). Like Latini and his predecessors, Machiavelli first asks whether the prince must actually possess, or only appear to possess, 'the qualities deemed to be good' (p. 91). Then he asks whether princes should be generous or parsimonious, cruel or compassionate, and finally whether they should always seek to honour their word (pp. 92, 95, 99). Again like the earlier writers, Machiavelli agrees that the central question at issue is how a prince can best hope to 'keep his state', and how far a life of political virtue will in fact be conducive to this end. The sole difference between his account and those we have just examined is that, whereas Latini and his predecessors insist that the dictates of prudence and virtue will always turn out to be the same, it is at this point that Machiavelli introduces his crucial disjunction between the pursuit of virtue and the achievement of success in political affairs.

3

Scholasticism and liberty

The previous chapter attempted to trace the process by which the traditional study of the *Ars Dictaminis* gradually evolved in the course of the thirteenth century into a political ideology capable of defending the City Republics and their threatened liberties. This chapter will be concerned with the way in which, shortly after this time, the same ideological needs began to be met in a contrasting but no less influential style through the introduction into Italy of the themes and methods of scholastic political thought.

THE RECEPTION OF SCHOLASTICISM

The role of scholasticism in the development of Renaissance political theory has been much debated. Ullmann and others have recently argued that scholasticism 'ushered in humanism', and have even claimed to find a direct line of descent running from the political theories of Marsiglio to those of Machiavelli (Ullmann, 1972, p. 268; cf. also Wilks, 1963, p. 102). By now it will be evident, however, that this is to trace a misleadingly straightforward path, since it overlooks the crucial contribution made to the emergence of humanism by the earlier traditions of rhetorical instruction we have just examined. Nevertheless, the suggestion constitutes a valuable corrective to the usual belief – expressed for example by Hazeltine – that scholastic legal and moral philosophy made no contribution at all to 'the great intellectual awakening' associated with the humanists, since its practitioners remained entirely 'aloof from the spirit and purpose of the Renaissance' (Hazeltine, 1926, p. 739). As the present chapter will attempt to show, the belated yet brilliant flowering of scholastic studies in the Italian universities in fact made a contribution of fundamental importance to the evolution of Renaissance political thought.

The foundations of scholasticism were first laid with the gradual rediscovery of the main corpus of Aristotle's philosophical works. A considerable number of Aristotelian texts, often preserved in Arabic translations, began to filter into Europe through the Caliphate of Cordoba early in the twelfth century (Haskins, 1927, pp. 284–90). Due to the efforts of such scholars as Bishop Raymond of Toledo, these soon started to appear in Latin translations, a process which rapidly led to the transformation of the liberal arts courses in most of the leading universities of northern Europe (Knowles, 1962, pp. 188, 191). The first Aristotelian texts to be popularised in this way were the logical works, but by the middle of the thirteenth century the moral and political treatises had also been made available. A partial translation of the *Nicomachean Ethics* was issued by Hermannus Alemannus in 1243. A full translation of the same text was produced by the Dominican William of Moerbeke later in the same decade. And finally, the first Latin translation of the *Politics*, again by William of Moerbeke, was completed soon after 1250 (Knowles, 1962, pp. 191–2).

Aristotle's moral and political theory at first appeared not merely alien but threatening to the prevailing Augustinian conceptions of Christian political life.[1] Augustine had pictured political society as a divinely ordained order imposed on fallen men as a remedy for their sins. But Aristotle's *Politics* treats the polis as a purely human creation, designed to fulfil purely mundane ends. Furthermore, Augustine's view of political society had merely been ancillary to an eschatology in which the life of the pilgrim on earth had been seen as little more than a preparation for the life to come. Aristotle by contrast speaks in Book I of the *Politics* of the art of 'living and living well' in the polis as a self-sufficient ideal, never hinting at any further purposes lying beyond it which need to be invoked in order to invest it with its true significance (pp. 9–13).

It is thus a fact of overwhelming importance for the development of a modern, naturalistic and secular view of political life that the initial feelings of hostility – and condemnation – which greeted the rediscovery of Aristotle's moral and political writings were not allowed to stand. Instead an attempt was made to effect a reconciliation between the Aristotelian vision of the self-sufficiency of civic life and the more otherworldly preoccupations characteristic of Augustinian Christianity. This movement originated at the University of Paris, where the issues were most eagerly debated by the new teaching orders in the Church. It is true that the Franciscans, and especially Bonaventure, continued to oppose any such syncretic tendencies, but their rivals the Dominicans soon began to devote themselves to the elaboration of an entire philosophical system erected on the twin foundations of Greek and Christian thought (Gilson,

[1] For a valuable discussion of the contrasts between Augustinian and Aristotelian conceptions of political life, see Wilks, 1963, pp. 84–117.

1955, p. 402). The leading pioneer in this development was Albert the Great (c. 1200–80) who was teaching at the University of Paris throughout the 1240s (Gilson, 1955, p. 277). The greatest exponent of the new approach was his pupil St Thomas Aquinas (c. 1225–74) who began to lecture at Paris in the early 1250s, returning there again between 1269 and 1272 (Gilson, 1924, pp. 2–3). By the time of his death two years later, Aquinas had completed all but the third section of his massive *Summary of Theology*, a complete Christian philosophy founded on what Knowles has characterised as a 'thorough acceptance' of Aristotelian moral and political thought (Knowles, 1962, p. 264).

Discussing *The Politics* in his *Theology* and in his unfinished treatise on *The Rule of Princes*, Aquinas naturally sought to adapt Aristotle's views on law and civil society to the predominantly feudal and monarchical arrangements prevailing in northern Europe. It was obvious, however, especially to such theorists as Marsiglio of Padua, that Aristotle's own preoccupations were in fact more closely related to the problems of small-scale City Republics such as those of Northern Italy. So it is not surprising to find that, although the Italian universities played no part in the recovery of Aristotle's works, his moral and political philosophy soon came to exercise a powerful influence on Italian political thought (Kristeller, 1961, p. 36).

The influence of the *Politics* in Italy was disseminated through two main channels. First of all, the Roman lawyers at Bologna, possibly under the influence of the new law-schools in France, began to incorporate the concepts and methods of Aristotelian political theory into their glosses and commentaries. One of the earliest leading jurists to employ this scholastic approach was Bartolus of Saxoferrato. As well as reinterpreting the ancient law-books, as we have seen, in such a way as to vindicate the independence of the City Republics, Bartolus wrote a series of political tracts which are heavily reliant on Aristotle's *Politics* both in doctrine and style of argument. This dependence is especially marked in the *Tract on City Government*, but it is also evident in the *Tract on the Guelfs and Ghibellines* and in the famous *Tract on Tyranny*. It seems important to emphasise this point, since it is arguably underestimated even by the leading authorities on Bartolus's works. Ullmann, for example, speaks of the Roman law as furnishing 'the exclusive basis' of Bartolus's legal and political philosophy (Ullmann, 1965, p. 214). And Woolf even declares that Bartolus never regarded Aristotle as 'in any sense a particular authority' (Woolf, 1913, pp. 385–6). Such claims are potentially misleading, however, for Bartolus in fact quotes Aristotle repeatedly throughout his political works, in which the main aim – as Bartolus himself indicates – is to deploy an

Aristotelian theory of political society in order to diagnose and seek to remedy the internal weaknesses of the Italian City Republics.

The other way in which the influence of Aristotle's moral and political theory began to filter into Italy was through direct contact with the scholastic curriculum being taught at the University of Paris. An increasing number of Italian students were attracted to Paris after the middle years of the thirteenth century. Some of them – like Aquinas himself – remained there to study and teach, but others returned home to propagate the tenets of scholasticism, still virtually unknown in the Italian universities. One of the earliest political writers to follow this path was Remigio de Girolami (d. 1319). He studied for the Arts Degree at Paris in the 1260s, where he almost certainly attended Aquinas's lectures. Thereafter he returned to his native Florence, and taught for many years as *lector* in the Dominican school attached to Santa Maria Novella, where the young Dante may well have been one of his students (Davis, 1957, pp. 74, 81). As well as writing voluminous sermons and commentaries, Remigio produced two political tracts of a thoroughly Thomist and Aristotelian character, both of which he addressed to his fellow Florentines in the wake of the *coup* of 1301. The first, written in 1302, was entitled *The Common Good*; the other, completed two years later, was called *The Good of Peace* (Davis, 1960, pp. 668, 670). A second Dominican moralist who followed the same line of intellectual development was Ptolemy (or Bartolommeo) of Lucca (d. 1327). He too studied at Paris in the 1260s, and he tells us himself in his *Ecclesiastical History* that he 'very frequently had discussions' with Aquinas (col. 1169). Ptolemy later returned to Italy, where he was eventually appointed Bishop of Torcello in 1318. His major political work, probably written between 1300 and 1305, boldly took the form of a continuation of Aquinas's unfinished account of *The Rule of Princes*. Aquinas was assumed throughout the later Middle Ages to have written the whole of this treatise, but in fact Ptolemy was the author of most of the second and the whole of the third and fourth books (p. 270). Finally, the most important political philosopher who helped to import the tenets of Aristotelianism into Italy at this time was of course Marsiglio of Padua. The son of a Paduan lawyer, initially educated at the local University, Marsiglio moved to Paris at an unknown date, stayed there to teach and rose to become Rector of the University in 1312 (Gewirth, 1951, p. 20). As we have seen, his major political work, *The Defender of Peace*, was completed in 1324. We have already considered the second of the two Discourses into which the book is divided, in which Marsiglio seeks to defend the liberty of the City Republics against the encroachments of the Church. We must now consider the more secular and purely political doctrines of the opening Discourse, in which Marsiglio[1] describes the internal workings of the City Republics, seeks to diagnose the causes of their chronic weaknesses, and in the process develops a theory of popular sovereignty more overtly and systematically Aristotelian than any which had hitherto been advanced.

THE SCHOLASTIC DEFENCE OF LIBERTY

As with the rhetorical writers we have already discussed, the fundamental political commitment of all these scholastic theorists was to an ideal of political independence and republican self-government. Marsiglio opens his *Defender of Peace* by lamenting that 'the Italian natives' of his own day are being 'deprived of the sufficient life', since they are being forced to experience 'the harsh yoke of tyrants instead of liberty' (p. 4). Bartolus expresses a similar outlook in his *Tract on City Government*. He begins by noting that the first regime to be established 'in the city of Rome after the expulsion of the kings' was a republican system 'founded on the body of the people' (p. 417). Then he makes it clear that the same form of government is the one most suited to the Italian cities of his own time. He concedes in Aristotelian vein that 'the question of what constitutes the best kind of rule' cannot be settled without knowing 'the grade of magnitude' of the polity involved, and he admits that 'in a really large polity' it may be necessary to institute the rule of kings (pp. 418, 419, 420). But he is sharply critical of Aquinas's assumption that monarchy is always the best form of government. He thinks there is no doubt that 'in smaller-scale cities the most appropriate type of rule is government by the whole body of the people' (p. 419). And he instances the city of Perugia (where he spent much of his professional life) as a place where 'the government is at peace, and the city grows and flourishes' due to the excellence of its Republican institutions.[2] The same commitment, involving the same

[1] The first Discourse of *The Defender of Peace* has often been attributed to John of Jandum, one of Marsiglio's teachers at Paris, rather than to Marsiglio himself. (See for example Lagarde, 1948, pp. 31–3 and the references given in Gewirth, 1948, pp. 267 and note.) There are good internal reasons for doubting this ascription, since the arguments of the first Discourse are widely at variance with those of John of Jandum's known political works. (See Gewirth, 1948, pp. 268 et seq.). If my interpretation of *The Defender of Peace* is valid, moreover, it may be said to supply a further reason for doubting John's authorship. I take Marsiglio's main aim in the first Discourse to be that of analysing and seeking to vindicate the form of popular sovereignty embodied in such Italian City Republics as his native Padua. If this is correct, it seems highly unlikely that John of Jandum – who scarcely knew this milieu – can have been the author of the first Discourse. It seems far more likely that Marsiglio – who witnessed his native city pass from Republicanism to tyranny within four years of completing *The Defender of Peace* – must have been the author of the entire treatise.

[2] Cf. also Bartolus's insistence at the start of his *Tract on Tyranny* that, just as tyranny is the worst form of government, so rule by the people (*directe regimen*) is normally the best (p. 322). For a useful discussion of the ways in which the Italian jurists of the fourteenth century in general supported an ideal of active citizenship, see Riesenberg, 1969, pp. 246–7.

criticism of Aquinas, is reiterated by Ptolemy in his continuation of *The Rule of Princes*. Aquinas had started this treatise by distinguishing between 'regal' and 'tyrannical' types of rule, as a preface to his claim that while tyranny is the worst kind of government, hereditary monarchy is the best (pp. 225, 233). Ptolemy prefers to distinguish between 'despotic' and 'political' forms of rule, defining a 'political' regime as one in which the government is 'conducted according to law' and 'on behalf of the main body of the people' (p. 283). This leads him to reverse Aquinas's preference, since it prompts him, as he says himself, 'to include "regal" within the category of "despotic" regimes', and to argue that an elected form of 'political' system ought always to be preferred (p. 391). He admits it may not always be possible to establish such a free and self-governing type of regime, since 'some areas of the world are more suited to servitude than to liberty' (p. 287). But he maintains that in any country where the people 'have virile spirits, courage in their hearts and confidence in their intelligence', such a 'political' system not only constitutes the best but the most natural form of rule (p. 381). He concludes by boasting that this is why 'this type of regime flourishes above all in Italy', a country in which the people prize their liberty so highly that – as he approvingly but rather optimistically asserts – 'no one is able to wield perpetual power or to rule in a tyrannical way' (p. 381).

This preference for Republicanism is underpinned by a new vision of ancient Rome and its history, a vision barely hinted at by the earlier rhetorical writers. The scholastic theorists now begin to think of the Republican period rather than the Empire as the age of Rome's greatest excellence. As a consequence they adopt a new attitude towards the leading figures of the later Republic, especially Cato and Cicero. Previously these men had tended to be seen purely as stoic sages, and hence as models of aloofness from the turmoil of political life. Now they are praised instead as great patriots, as paragons of civic virtue who saw that the liberty of the Republic was in jeopardy and attempted to preserve it from the onrush of tyranny.

Hans Baron has popularised the belief that before the early *quattrocento* there was no expression of a theoretical preference for Republicanism in Italian political thought, and hence no appreciation of Cicero's 'civic doctrine' or his commitment to Republican political values.[1] It is arguable, however, that the main elements in this humanist historical consciousness

---

[1] See Baron, 1966, p. 121. For other expressions of the same belief, see for example Rubinstein, 1942, 1958, p. 200; Holmes, 1973, p. 129; Witt, 1971, p. 171. Baron himself was originally more tentative (and hence more historically accurate) in his early article on 'civic spirit'. See Baron, 1938a, esp. p. 84.

were in fact formed with the arrival of scholastic political theory in Italy nearly a century before.[1] Marsiglio already thinks of Cicero not as a stoic sage but rather as a prudent public official, whose behaviour at the time of the Catilinarian conspiracy he finds especially commendable (pp. 56–7). Remigio praises both Cato and Cicero for their patriotic Republicanism in his discussion of *The Common Good*, and shows a corresponding distrust for Julius Caesar and his vision of Empire (p. 68; Davis, 1960, p. 666). Bartolus reminds us in his *Tract on City Government* that it was under the Republic, not the Empire, 'that the city of Rome grew to greatness' (p. 420). And Ptolemy of Lucca devotes several chapters of his *Rule of Princes* to expressing his admiration for the Roman Republic and his corresponding suspicion of the Empire which superseded it.[2] He refers to Cato with approval for having opposed the coming of the principate, and for rallying his fellow-citizens in an attempt to preserve their Republican heritage (pp. 284–5). He admires the Republican system of annual election to all major offices, and praises the consuls 'for having governed the people in a "political" way' (p. 353). He singles out both Cato and Cicero for 'the example they give of love of one's country', and exhibits a marked hostility towards Julius Caesar, whom he accuses of 'usurping the supreme power' and 'converting a genuinely "political" regime into a despotic and even tyrannical principate' (pp. 313, 362).

While they express a strong preference for Republican liberty, these writers are all acutely aware of the prevailing tendency for the free institutions of the City Republics to become swallowed up by the rule of tyrants. Marsiglio begins by voicing the lament – later repeated in almost the same words by Machiavelli – that Italy is 'battered on all sides because of strife and almost destroyed, so that it can easily be invaded by anyone who wants to seize it' (p. 4). And Bartolus in his *Tract on City Government* agrees that 'Italy today is full of tyrants', whom he blames for having established a form of government so degenerate that Aristotle had not even envisaged it (pp. 418, 427). The result is 'a completely monstrous state of affairs' in which 'there are very many tyrants, each of whom is

---

[1] As Davis, 1967, p. 427, has already observed, some elements of this outlook can be found even earlier, in Latini's account of the fall of the Roman Republic in his *Books of Treasure*. Latini regards the Catilinarian conspiracy as the beginning of the end of Roman liberty (p. 44). He accordingly glorifies Cato's attack on Caesar's alleged complicity in the plot, treating it as one of his main examples of great rhetoric in action (pp. 348–51). And he praises Cicero not merely as 'the most eloquent man in the world' but also as a great patriot who 'by his great wisdom' as consul 'managed to overcome the conspiracy' which Catiline had directed against the freedom of the people (p. 44). Davis has used this and other evidence, in a sequence of valuable articles, to challenge Baron's thesis about the originality of *quattrocento* 'civic humanism'.

[2] This counterexample to Baron's general thesis is the only one acknowledged by Baron himself. See Baron, 1966, pp. 55, 57.

strong in a different region, while none is strong enough to prevail over the others' (p. 418).

One of the main concerns of these theorists is thus to ask why the system of government they so much admire should have proved so vulnerable to the coming of the despots. They scarcely pay any attention to the idea – so prominent in the rhetorical writings we have examined – that the growth of private wealth may have served as a corrupting political force. They tend on the contrary to support the view which is often taken to have been developed for the first time in the early *quattrocento* – the view that private wealth, as Bartolus puts it, 'tends to promote virtue', since 'it tends to promote magnanimity, which is a virtue, as St Thomas himself agrees' (vol. 9, p. 117). They strongly agree with the rhetorical writers, however, that the most dangerous weakness in the City Republics is their extreme factiousness, their continual discord and lack of internal peace. And they deploy their Thomist and Aristotelian sources in such a way as to make this familiar point in a novel and far more emphatic style.

The basic contention they all advance is that the attainment of peace and concord, *pax et concordia*, represents the highest value in political life. One of Remigio's tracts, as we have seen, is actually entitled *The Good of Peace*, and opens with the claim that 'peace is the chief aim and the greatest good of the people' (p. 124). Marsiglio similarly stresses the centrality of peace in the title of his great work, which begins with an elaborate apostrophe to 'tranquillity or peace' as the condition most of all commended to us by Christ and his Apostles (pp. 3–4). Bartolus endorses the same outlook at several key points in his political works. He starts his *Tract on City Government* by arguing that 'the basic aim' in government must always be 'peace and unity', and he repeats in his *Tract on Tyranny* that 'the main aim in a city', and hence the main duty of a just ruler, must always be 'to maintain the citizens in peace and quietness' (pp. 325, 418).

D'Entrèves in his analysis of *The Defender of Peace* expresses some surprise that Marsiglio should have taken this ideal of peace as his starting-point (D'Entrèves, 1939, p. 50). This ceases to be surprising, however, as soon as we recall the Aristotelian roots of Marsiglio's thought, together with his interest in explaining the loss of liberty in the City Republics of his own day. Aristotle had already laid it down, and Aquinas had already repeated, that the preservation of peace provided 'the means to uphold the good and safety of the people'.[1] Marsiglio simply reiterates this assumption at the start of *The Defender of Peace*, arguing that good government

---

[1] This is Aquinas's way of putting the point in the section of *The Rule of Princes* which he actually wrote, p. 226.

and 'sufficiency of life' must essentially be seen as 'the fruits of peace and tranquillity' (pp. 3, 5). The reason he makes this contention so central to his argument is because he takes it to explain why the liberty of the Italian City Republics is everywhere being threatened and lost. He assumes that, just as the fruits of peace are good government, so the fruits of the negation of peace must be tyranny, since tyranny is the negation of good government (pp. 3–5). Now the negation of peace or 'opposite of tranquillity' is a state of 'discord and strife' (p. 4). So he concludes that the key to explaining why the *Regnum Italicum* is 'sorely beset by all kinds of hardships and troubles' must lie in examining the causes of her chronic discord and factiousness, which are currently preventing her from enjoying the 'sweet fruits of peace' (p. 4).[1]

The consequence of this Aristotelian belief in a direct relationship between faction and tyranny is that all the scholastic theorists tend to treat the problem of civil discord as the main danger to the liberty of the City Republics. They are conscious of two main ways in which such discord arises. One of these, which Marsiglio particularly stresses, is when a division of power is established within the ruling Council of a city. This had increasingly happened in practice with the election of *Capitani del Popolo* as a means of challenging the exclusive jurisdiction of *podestà* in the latter part of the thirteenth century. As Marsiglio indicates, the danger inherent in any such development is that the ordinary citizen is given 'no more reason for appearing before one ruler than before the other or others'. The result is not merely confusion but injustice, for 'if he appears before one of them, ignoring the others', he may find himself absolved by one but 'convicted by the others for contempt' (p. 82). This can only lead to 'the division and opposition of the citizens, their fighting and separation, and finally the destruction of the state', since no one will be able to agree on who ought rightly to be obeyed (p. 83).

But the chief danger these writers emphasise is the prevalence of faction and discord amongst the citizens themselves. Remigio laments in his tract on *The Common Good* that St Paul's prophecy about an age of strife has been 'clearly fulfilled in these times by modern man, and above all in Italy'. There the people not only 'neglect the common good', but 'incessantly lay waste and destroy villages, cities, provinces and the whole country with their inordinate hostilities' (p. 59). Marsiglio similarly

---

[1] If this analysis of Marsiglio's concept of *pax* is correct, it is misleading of Rubinstein to claim that in early *trecento* political thought the concepts of *pax et concordia* were always viewed as 'the most desirable effects of just government' (Rubinstein, 1958, p. 187). Marsiglio's argument seems rather to be that just government is the effect of which *pax* is taken to be the precondition. For a full analysis of the role of peace in Marsiglio's political theory, see Gewirth, 1951, pp. 94–115.

emphasises that where 'men's contentions and injuries toward one another' are not 'avenged or measured by a standard of justice', the result is sure to be 'the fighting and separation of the assembled men and finally the destruction of the state' (p. 64). And Bartolus devotes the whole of his *Tract on the Guelfs and Ghibellines* to analysing the problem of endemic faction in the City Republics. He concedes, with an appeal to the authority of Aquinas, that it may sometimes be legitimate to promote a faction if the aim is 'to disrupt a tyranny' and to 'attain a just government' (p. 415). But he argues that where such parties are 'not for the public good' but are merely formed 'in order to remove another party from government', then 'their formation must be straightforwardly illicit', since they constitute the greatest danger to good order and peace (p. 415).

The main question for all these writers is thus to ask how faction and discord can be avoided and peace secured. Here they agree in general terms with the answer given by the rhetorical theorists we have already examined. They insist, that is, that all sectional interests must be set aside, and the good of each individual citizen equated with the good of the city as a whole. The aim is to ensure, as Marsiglio repeatedly demands, that 'the common benefit' is 'aimed at and attained' at all times (p. 72; cf. pp. 5–6, 42). While this is a familiar commitment, however, they often express it in a novel and dramatic style by introducing a deliberate ambiguity into the scholastic analysis of the concept of 'the common good'. The clearest example is provided by Remigio's adaptation of Aquinas, the effect of which is to produce a political doctrine which Kantorowicz has characterised as 'Thomist proto-Hegelianism' (Kantorowicz, 1957, p. 479). Aquinas had laid it down at the start of *The Rule of Princes* that 'a regime cannot be considered right and just unless it is established for the common good of the people' (p. 224). Remigio manages with a barely visible sleight of hand to convert this doctrine into a fierce demand for civic loyalty, since he treats the idea of acting 'for the good of the city' (*pro bono communis*) as interchangeable with the idea of acting 'for the good of the members of the community' (*pro bono communi*) (Rubinstein, 1958, p. 185). He then employs this strongly 'corporationist' commitment, as Davis calls it, as the governing assumption of his argument in *The Good of Peace* (Davis, 1960, p. 670). The specific question he raises is whether it is justifiable, in order to maintain peace between cities, to overlook injuries done to individual citizens (Davis, 1959, p. 107). He considers the case of someone's property being seized by the citizens of another city, and asks what kind of redress should be sought in such circumstances. The answer he gives is that, since the welfare of the city is of so much greater importance than the rights of any individual member, it may be necessary in such a situation to overlook the injury altogether if the only alternative is a breach of the peace between the two cities involved.[1]

As in the case of the rhetorical writers, however, the announcement of this general commitment still leaves the central question begged. How is such a unity between the good of the city and the good of its individual citizens in practice to be established? It is when we come to the treatment of this problem that we find a complete contrast between the scholastic theorists and the writers we have already considered. As we have seen, one of the most characteristic moves made by the rhetorical writers at this point was to focus on the concept of 'true nobility', the aim being to determine the range of qualities we ought to look for in our rulers if we wish to ensure that they are genuinely devoted to the common good. The scholastic theorists by contrast exhibit much less interest in this theme. And when they do consider it, they tend to offer a strongly contrasting point of view. This is evident in Marsiglio's chapter on the election of rulers, but the clearest instance is provided by Bartolus's discussion of the concept of nobility at the end of his commentary on the Code (vol. 6, pp. 114f.) This takes as its starting-point Dante's claim that virtue constitutes the only true nobility (p. 116). Bartolus concedes that this may be a correct account of what he calls 'spiritual' or 'theological' nobility. A man may be noble 'in the sight of God' simply 'because he is virtuous and is thus saved' (p. 118). But he maintains that, although one should be 'reverent towards the memory of so great a poet', there are two points at which Dante's analysis is nevertheless mistaken (p. 117). He thinks first of all that Dante exaggerates when he insists on divorcing nobility from inherited wealth. As we have seen, Bartolus believes that wealth is capable of promoting virtue. He also believes that 'anything which tends to promote virtue tends to promote nobility'. So he concludes, in line with such conservative moralists as Da Nono, that there must be at least some connection between the possession of riches and the achievement of nobility.[2] His other argument is that Dante's account is oversimplified, since it fails to recognise that the concept of nobility is in part a legal one. A woman may attain nobility through marriage, while a man may become a noble simply because 'a prince may choose out of his grace or by the law

---

[1] Pp. 134–5. For the same general commitment, see for example Ptolemy, *The Rule of Princes*, p. 364 and Bartolus, *Tract on Tyranny*, p. 327. As Rubinstein has shown, the idea that 'the ruler' and 'the common good' should be the same is also central to the iconography of Lorenzetti's famous fresco on 'good government' at Siena. See Rubinstein, 1958, esp. p. 181. The same commitment recurs in other treatises by Remigio as well, notably in *The Common Good*. For discussions of this theme – together with extracts from Remigio's treatise – see Egenter, 1934 and Minio-Paluello, 1956.

[2] See Bartolus, vol. 6, p. 117. The authorities he cites at this point are Aquinas and Aristotle in the *Nicomachean Ethics*, Bk. IV. For Giovanni da Nono, see Hyde, 1966b, pp. 107–9, and for his views on nobility see Hyde, 1966b and Hyde, 1966a, pp. 64–5.

to confer a patent of nobility upon him' (p. 118). (This happened to
Bartolus himself when the Emperor Charles IV made him a count in
1355 – Sheedy, 1942, p. 105.) It follows according to Bartolus that we
must be prepared to recognise not merely 'godly' but also 'civil' nobility,
'which has been invented by us to be similar to, and an imitation of, godly
nobility' (p. 118). But this in turn means that we cannot simply equate
nobility with virtue, as Dante wishes us to do. For this is to overlook the
obvious fact that genuine titles of civil nobility may sometimes be acquired
or inherited by people who are not intrinsically worthy of them. As
Bartolus concludes, we cannot avoid accepting the son of a king as a noble,
'even though he may be reprobate and infamous', since 'that which someone possesses by birth can never be taken away from them' (p. 118).

But the main contrast between the scholastic theorists and the earlier
rhetorical writers lies in the type of political advice they think it most
appropriate to give. It is clearly assumed by the scholastic theorists – and
in the case of Remigio it is explicitly stated – that the arts of rhetoric are
of marginal significance in political life, since they offer little more than a
training in the techniques of 'verbal adornment' (Davis, 1965, p. 431; cf.
McKeon, 1942, p. 23). So the scholastic writers spend little time on the
favourite rhetorical pursuit of advising rulers and magistrates on how best
to speak, write and generally comport themselves in the most persuasive
style. They tend instead to devote their main attention to the machinery of
government. They present themselves less as moralists than as political
analysts, pinning their hopes less on virtuous individuals than on efficient
institutions as the best means of promoting the common good and the rule
of peace.

The main danger to peace which they isolate is, as we have seen, the
prevalence of faction. So the major reforms they propose are all designed
to minimise the risk of factious disturbances. It seems important, especially in the case of *The Defender of Peace*, to stress the centrality of these
practical interests. One reason is that Marsiglio's first Discourse has often
been discussed – for example by Lagarde (1948) and Wilks (1963) – in virtual isolation from the circumstances in which it was composed. As soon as
we focus on its immediate political context, however, it becomes evident
that Marsiglio was not merely writing an abstract work of constitutional
thought. He was also advancing a concrete set of political proposals which
– while he undoubtedly believed them to be valid for all times – were
manifestly intended in the first instance to resolve the specific problems
of the Italian City Republics. A further reason for wishing to emphasise
these more immediate concerns is that this enables us to gain a truer
measure of Marsiglio's achievement. A number of commentators who

have treated the first Discourse simply as a general theory have felt prompted to complain – as Lagarde does – at the 'feebleness' of Marsiglio's constitutional ideas (Lagarde, 1948, pp. 199–200). As soon as we uncover the context in and for which he was writing, however, it becomes possible to vindicate a more positive sense of Marsiglio's originality. What we in fact find – in Bartolus as well as in Marsiglio – is not merely a conventional diagnosis of faction as the main threat to the liberties of the City Republics; we also find a new and radical answer to the question of how these liberties might best be secured.

As we have seen, one aspect of the central problem of faction which Marsiglio particularly emphasises is the danger of allowing power to become divided within the ruling councils of cities. It is accordingly one of the leading aims of his first Discourse to suggest a means of avoiding this difficulty. The solution he proposes is simply that magistracy must never be divided. He thinks that experience shows it to be impossible, 'if civil justice and benefit are to be conserved', for 'any city or state to have a plurality' of governors or magistrates who are 'not subordinated one to another' (p. 82). So he insists that even though the government may consist of 'several men', it must be 'numerically one government with respect to office', thus ensuring a 'numerical unity' in 'every action, judgment, sentence or command forthcoming from them' (p. 81; cf. Gewirth, 1951, pp. 115–25).

But the type of factiousness which, as we have seen, the scholastic theorists fear most of all is the formation of rival parties by hostile groups of citizens. So the main question they raise is how this is to be avoided. The very radical solution which Bartolus as well as Marsiglio proposes is that 'the ruler' should be the whole body of the people, so that no such internecine fighting can in principle arise. It is sometimes suggested that in asking for a single and unified 'human legislator', Marsiglio is 'clearly thinking' (as Wilks asserts) 'in terms of the universal Roman Emperor' (Wilks, 1963, p. 195). But this seems insensitive to the essentially civic context of Marsiglio's political thought. It is evident from his own way of putting the point that Marsiglio is mainly thinking in terms of the Italian City Republics. He not only equates the figure of the legislator with 'the people or the whole body of citizens, or the weightier part thereof',[1] but goes on to add that the will of the legislator must be 'expressed by words in the general assembly of the citizens', which he regards as the most authoritative forum for discussing all legal and political affairs (p. 45). The

[1] For a full discussion of Marsiglio's concept of 'the weightier part', see Gewirth, 1951, pp. 182–99. For the relations between the concept and the civic context of Marsiglio's thought, see Gewirth, 1951, esp. pp. 27–9 and 187.

same populist commitment, as well as the same civic concerns, are even more clearly revealed in Bartolus's political works, especially his *Tract on City Government*. The most appropriate form of rule in any city other than the very largest, he maintains, must always be 'a popular regime' in which 'the whole jurisdiction of the city remains in the hands of the people as a whole' (p. 420).

The way in which Marsiglio and Bartolus go on to defend this central thesis involves them in a fundamental reappraisal of prevailing scholastic assumptions about popular sovereignty. Aquinas had laid it down in his *Summary of Theology* that, although the consent of the people is essential in order to establish a legitimate political society, the act of instituting a ruler always involves the citizens in alienating – rather than merely delegating – their original sovereign authority. Both Marsiglio and Bartolus argue the contrary case. Marsiglio insists that the 'whole body of citizens' remains the sovereign legislator at all times, 'regardless of whether it makes the law directly by itself or entrusts the making of it to some certain person or persons' (p. 45). This has sometimes been taken to be the expression of a uniquely radical defence of popular rule. Gewirth, for example, draws a firm distinction at this point between Marsiglio's doctrine and that of the civil lawyers, who are said to have avoided any suggestion that 'the active, continuing control of the laws and the ruler' should be lodged at all times with the body of the people (Gewirth, 1951, p. 253). This contrast, however, seems somewhat overdrawn. It is true in general that the civil lawyers reject any idea of inalienable popular sovereignty, but this is not true of Bartolus, who clearly endorses Marsiglio's more radical point of view. He makes the point most unequivocally in his defence of 'those cities which *de facto* recognise no superior in temporal affairs, and so possess *Imperium* in themselves' (vol. 6, p. 669). The legal position of the citizens in such a city, Bartolus contends, is that 'they constitute their own *princeps*', so that any 'right of judgment' held by their rulers and magistrates 'is only delegated to them (*concessum est*) by the sovereign body of the people' (vol. 6, p. 670).

Aquinas had further suggested in the *Summary of Theology* that, since the people always alienate their sovereignty in the act of setting up a government, it follows that all rulers must be genuine sovereigns who are *legibus solutus*, unfettered by any formal obligations to obey the positive laws. The same contention was generally advanced by the civil lawyers in discussing the *Lex Regia*, as well as by close disciples of Aquinas such as Egidio Colonna (*c.* 1243–1316), who lays it down in his *Rule of Princes* that 'if we are speaking of positive law, it is far better for a people to be governed by the best king than by the best laws' (p. 533). Again, however, both Marsiglio and Bartolus argue the contrary case. As Marsiglio insists, even if the people agree to transfer the right to exercise their sovereignty to a supreme ruler or magistrate, such an official can never become 'the legislator in the absolute sense, but only in a relative sense and for a particular time'. The ultimate authority must remain at all times in the hands of the people themselves, who can always check or even remove their rulers if they fail to act in accordance with the strictly limited powers entrusted to them (pp. 45, 88). Bartolus endorses the same conclusion in his commentary on the Digest, as well as spelling out in greater detail the limitations to be imposed on all rulers and higher magistrates. No ruler, he contends, can 'remit any sentences' or 'suspend the execution of any judgment' or 'alter any laws and ordinances' or 'make any statutes contrary to those agreed by the whole body of the people'. No action, in short, can be initiated even by our highest magistrates unless they have first 'gained the authority of the people or at least a majority of their ruling Council' (vol. 6, p. 670).

Bartolus and Marsiglio both assume that the people will in fact wish as a matter of convenience to delegate their sovereign authority to be exercised on their behalf by a *pars principans* or 'ruling part'. This in turn raises a further difficulty to which they finally address themselves. If the citizens constitute the legislator, while the *pars principans* conducts the actual government of the city, the problem is how to ensure that the actions of the *pars principans* are in fact kept fully under the ultimate control of the sovereign body of the people.

Both theorists answer this question in exactly the same way. They each propose three constraints to be imposed on all rulers and magistrates to prevent them from ignoring the will of the people and so degenerating into tyrants. The first is summarised by Marsiglio in the form of the rule that 'for the sufficiency of civil life it is absolutely better for the commonwealth that each monarch be named in a new election rather than by hereditary succession' (p. 71). Bartolus endorses the same requirement, adding the proviso in his *Tract on Tyranny* that no election which is made 'in fear' should be regarded as valid, since 'jurisdiction must always be voluntarily transferred' (p. 323). The danger they both have in mind is that, as Marsiglio phrases it, 'non-elected kings rule less voluntary subjects', since they are more readily able to forget that their true status is merely that of elected officials who have been appointed as administrators of the law 'for the common benefit' (p. 32). Hence it follows, he adds, 'in accordance with truth and the manifest views of Aristotle', that some process of election must always be preferred in order to ensure 'a more certain standard of government' (p. 33).

The second constraint they both impose is that no ruler must ever be allowed more than the minimum possible discretion in administering the law. The problem they have in mind here – a very familiar one in the City Republics – is emphasised by Bartolus in particular at the end of his *Tract on Tyranny*. It is not enough to elect someone who appears to be a suitable ruler if he is then allowed to govern according to his own discretion. This is to leave open the possibility that he may turn into 'a silent or hidden tyrant', since he may be able after his election 'to gain so much power that he is able to conduct the business of the city in any way he likes' (p. 326). The solution, as Marsiglio agrees, is to ensure that all civil judgments 'be made according to the law' rather than 'according to the discretion of the judge', so as to ensure that the business of government is preserved as free as possible from any intrusions of 'ignorance and perverted emotion' (p. 40). The general rule is later incapsulated by Marsiglio in the form of a characteristic appeal to the authority of Aristotle. 'As he said in the *Politics*, Book V, Chapter 6: "the fewer things the rulers control", that is, without law, "the longer must every government endure, for they", that is, the rulers, "become less despotic, they are more moderate in their ways and are less hated by their subjects" ' (p. 43).

The final constraint discussed by Marsiglio and Bartolus takes the form of a complex system of checks to be imposed on all magistrates and ruling councils to ensure that they remain responsive at all times to the wishes of the citizens who elected them. Marsiglio raises the issue in the course of replying to possible objections to his theory of popular sovereignty (pp. 54–5). As Previté-Orton originally observed, the result is a general account of the constitutional procedures actually in operation in the surviving City Republics of Marsiglio's own time (Previté-Orton, 1935, p. 149). A very similar system is outlined by Bartolus in much greater detail in his commentary on the Code.[1] He envisages a pyramidal structure of government with its foundations in the will of the people. The basis of the system is provided by the *Parlamentum* or general council elected by all the citizens. This assembly then elects a smaller council convened by the 'rector' or supreme magistrate. And this group in turn appoints as many officials as are needed to carry on the more technical aspects of government (p. 37). The aim is to devise a system which will at once be efficient and answerable. Its efficiency is guaranteed by the fact that the actual running of the city's affairs is placed in the hands of a number of administrative experts. Its responsiveness is assured by the fact that the

---

[1] See *Works*, vol. 9, pp. 36ff. Ullmann, 1962, presents a full analysis of Bartolus's ideal system of government at pp. 715–26. He notes both the 'very great agreement' between Bartolus's and Marsiglio's theories at this point, and the fact that Bartolus offers the more precise and detailed account. See pp. 726–33. I am much indebted to this important article.

ultimate power to elect and remove both the rector and the ruling council remains with the *Parlamentum*, which as Bartolus strikingly remarks may be equated with 'the mind of the people' (vol. 9, p. 37; cf. Ullmann, 1962, pp. 717, 720–1).

The theory of popular sovereignty developed by Marsiglio and Bartolus was destined to play a major role in shaping the most radical version of early modern constitutionalism. Already they are prepared to argue that sovereignty lies with the people, that they only delegate and never alienate it, and thus that no legitimate ruler can ever enjoy a higher status than that of an official appointed by, and capable of being dismissed by, his own subjects. It was only necessary for the same arguments to be applied in the case of a *regnum* as well as a *civitas* for a recognisably modern theory of popular sovereignty in a secular state to be fully articulated. This development was of course a gradual one, but we can already see it beginning in Ockham, evolving in the conciliarist theories of d'Ailly and Gerson, and finally entering the sixteenth century in the writings of Almain and Mair, passing from there into the age of the Reformation and beyond.

As well as exercising this long-term influence, the theories of Marsiglio and Bartolus also had an immediate ideological significance in the Italian City Republics of their own time. They not only provided the fullest and most systematic defence of Republican liberty against the coming of the despots; they also suggested an ingenious way of arguing against the apologists for tyranny in their own terms. As we have seen, the main defence of the late *duecento* despots and their successors took the form of claiming that, while the preservation of Republican liberty tended to involve political chaos, the rule of a single *signore* could always be guaranteed to bring peace. Even Aquinas endorses this scale of values in *The Rule of Princes*. He maintains that 'all cities and provinces which are not ruled by a single person become riven by factions and waver about without ever attaining peace'. And he adds that 'as soon as they come to be governed by a single ruler, they rejoice in peace, flourish in justice and enjoy an abundance of wealth' (p. 227). It is against this orthodoxy that the defence of Republican liberty mounted by Marsiglio and Bartolus needs to be understood. They concede that the fundamental value in political life is the maintenance of peace. But they deny that this is incompatible with the preservation of liberty. The final word they leave with their contemporaries is thus that it may be possible for the people to enjoy the blessings of peace without having to incur the loss of their liberty: the key to bringing this about is said to be to ensure that the role of 'the defender of peace' is discharged by the people themselves.

Further Reading

(1) *Dante.* Gilson, 1948, provides an excellent general account of Dante's thought. D'Entrèves, 1952, surveys the development of his political ideas. For a contrasting analysis, see Limentani, 1965. Dante's theory of monarchy is discussed in Kantorowicz, 1957, Chapter 8, and his theory of Empire in Davis, 1957.

(2) *Bartolus of Saxoferrato.* Vinogradoff, 1929, includes a sketch of the Roman-law background. For Bartolus's theory of *Imperium* and its intellectual context, see Riesenberg, 1956 and Keen, 1965. For his theory of popular sovereignty see Ullmann, 1962. The best general account of Bartolus's political thought is still the one given by Woolf, 1913.

(3) *Marsiglio of Padua.* Lagarde, 1948 and Gewirth, 1951, contain the fullest surveys of Marsiglio's political ideas. For a briefer account see D'Entrèves, 1939, Chapters 3 and 4. The intellectual context of Marsiglio's thought is discussed in Wilks, 1963 and in Rubinstein, 1965b, the latter being an exceptionally valuable article.

PART TWO

The Italian Renaissance

4

The Florentine Renaissance

Writing his dialogues on *The Civic Life* in the mid 1430s, Matteo Palmieri proudly emphasised the position of cultural pre-eminence attained by his native Florence in the course of his own lifetime. 'Every thoughtful person must thank God for having been permitted to be born into this new age, so full of hope and promise, which already rejoices in a greater array of nobly-gifted talents than the world has seen in the course of the previous thousand years' (pp. 36–7). Palmieri was of course thinking primarily of the achievements of the Florentines in painting, sculpture and architecture – the achievements in particular of Masaccio, Donatello and Brunelleschi. But he also had in mind the remarkable efflorescence of moral, social and political philosophy that occurred in Florence at the same time – a development initiated by the humanist Chancellor Salutati, further extended by such leading members of his circle as Bruni, Poggio and Vergerio, and later taken up by a number of young writers whom they clearly influenced, including Alberti, Manetti, Valla and Palmieri himself.

A great deal of attention has naturally been paid to the question of why such a concentrated study of moral and political issues should have arisen in Florence during this particular generation. The answer which has had the greatest impact on recent scholarship has been the one proposed by Hans Baron in his study of *The Crisis of the Early Renaissance*.[1] He sees the development of political ideas in early *quattrocento* Florence essentially as a response to the 'struggle for civic liberty' which the Florentines were forced to wage with a series of belligerent despots throughout the first half of the fifteenth century (Baron, 1966, pp. 28, 453).

The first phase of this conflict began when Giangaleazzo Visconti, the Duke of Milan, declared war on Florence in May 1390 (Bueno de Mesquita, 1941, p. 121). Giangaleazzo had already succeeded in making himself

[1] See Baron, 1966. Since I disagree with so many of his specific findings, it is important to begin by emphasising the great importance of Baron's pioneering works on the early *quattrocento* humanists. I am greatly indebted not merely to his technical discussions about the dating of their works, but also to his analysis of their doctrines and his salutary insistence on the centrality of their contribution to Renaissance political thought.

lord of all Lombardy in the 1380s. This he had achieved by intervening in the wars of the Carraresi in 1386, as a result of which he managed to gain control of Verona, Vicenza and Padua by 1388 (Baron, 1966, p. 25). He then turned his attention to isolating and encircling the Florentines. He first moved against them from the west, taking Pisa in 1399 and accepting the surrender of Lucca soon afterwards (Bueno de Mesquita, 1941, p. 247). Next he threatened them from the south, capturing Siena in September of 1399 and Assisi, Cortona and Perugia in the course of the following year (Buena de Mesquita, 1941, pp. 247–8). Finally, he attacked them from the north, winning a decisive victory over the Bolognese, their last remaining allies, at the battle of Casalecchio in June 1402 (Bueno de Mesquita, 1941, p. 279).

A miracle saved Florence at this most perilous moment, since Giangaleazzo died of a fever just as he was preparing to strike at the city itself in September 1402 (Bueno de Mesquita, 1941, p. 298). It was not long, however, before the Florentines found themselves confronting a further and far more protracted threat to their traditional liberties. The aggressor on this occasion was Giangaleazzo's son, Duke Filippo Maria Visconti of Milan. He began, very much in the manner of his father, by securing northern Italy, seizing Parma and Brescia in 1420 and incorporating Genoa into the Duchy of Milan in the following year (Baron, 1966, p. 372). Then he started to move in the direction of Florence, beginning with the capture of Forli and its neighbouring towns in 1423 (Baron, 1966, p. 376). This prompted the Florentines to declare war, so precipitating a conflict which lasted almost without interruption until 1454, when Cosimo de Medici finally succeeded in negotiating a peace which included an acknowledgment by Milan of its willingness to recognise – and if necessary to defend – the independent status of the Florentine Republic.

According to Baron's analysis, this political background supplies the explanation for the two most striking facts about the discussion of social and political issues in early *quattrocento* Florence. The events just described are taken in the first place to explain why so many Florentine writers became so deeply immersed in questions of political theory throughout this period. The 'lonely stand' taken by Florence against the despots, and in particular 'the Florentine–Milanese confrontation' of 1402, is said to have acted as a catalyst which served to precipitate this new and more intense awareness of political affairs (Baron, 1966, pp. 444–6). The same events are also held to account for the particular direction taken by Florentine political speculation at this time, especially the concentration on Republican ideals of liberty and civic involvement. Baron treats the crisis of 1402 as the cause of 'a revolution in the politico-historical outlook of the Florentines', arguing that 'the defence of Florentine independence against Giangaleazzo' exerted 'a profound influence' on 'the strengthening of Florentine republican sentiment' (Baron, 1966, pp. 445, 448, 459). The final significance of 'the political crisis of Italy' in the opening years of the fifteenth century is thus said to be that it gave rise to 'a new type of humanism' – a humanism rooted in 'a new philosophy of political engagement and active life' and devoted to the celebration of Florence's republican liberties (Baron, 1966, p. 459).

This thesis about the emergence of 'civic humanism', as Baron calls it, has gained wide acceptance. Martines, for example, contends that Baron 'has demonstrated' that 'the birth of civic humanism was to a large extent a function of the Florentine experience with Giangaleazzo Visconti' (Martines, 1963, p. 272). Becker agrees that Baron has 'argued persuasively' for such a connection 'between cultural developments and Florentine public life' (Becker, 1968, p. 109). And Baron himself has recently noted the 'wide assent' accorded to his claim that the wars against Milan 'finally determined the emergence in *quattrocento* Florence of a politically minded, community conscious Humanism' (Baron, 1968, p. 102).

Nevertheless, there are two factors – both central to an understanding of Renaissance humanism – which must lead us to question Baron's account. The first is that, in treating the crisis of 1402 as 'a catalyst in the emergence of new ideas', Baron has underestimated the extent to which the ideas involved were not in fact new at all, but were rather an inheritance from the City Republics of medieval Italy (cf. Baron, 1966, p. 446). The other problem is that, in emphasising the special qualities of 'civic' humanism, Baron has also failed to appreciate the nature of the links between the Florentine writers of the early *quattrocento* and the wider movement of Petrarchan humanism which had already developed in the course of the fourteenth century. The main aim of this chapter will accordingly be to investigate these two issues in turn, attempting to relate them to a somewhat broader outline of the evolution of political ideas in the Florentine Renaissance.

THE ANALYSIS OF LIBERTY

The first major difficulty with Baron's thesis about 'civic humanism' can be expressed at its simplest by saying that it underestimates the extent to which the Florentine writers of the early *quattrocento* were following in the footsteps of the medieval *dictatores*.[1] One important element of con-

---

[1] I owe an obvious debt at this point to P. O. Kristeller's seminal essays on the development of humanism. He originally made the crucial observation that 'the humanists, far from representing a new class, were the professional heirs and successors of the Medieval rhetoricians,

tinuity between these two groups, as Kristeller in particular has emphasised, is that they generally received the same form of legal training, and subsequently went on to occupy very similar professional roles, acting either as teachers of rhetoric in the Italian universities or more usually as secretaries in the employment of cities or the Church. This certainly describes the career of Coluccio Salutati (1331–1406), the elder statesman amongst the Florentine humanists of the early fifteenth century. He began by learning the *Ars Dictaminis* at Bologna under Pietro de Muglio, and subsequently put his professional skills to work as Chancellor of several Tuscan cities, first at Todi in 1367, then at Lucca in 1370 and finally at Florence from 1375 until his death (Donovan, 1967, p. 195; Ullman, 1963, pp. 9–10). The same story can be told about all three of his closest disciples – Bruni, Vergerio and Poggio Bracciolini. Leonardo Bruni (1369–1444) studied law and rhetoric as well as Greek in Florence during the 1390s, entered the Papal Curia as a secretary in 1406, returned to Florence after 1415 and eventually served as Chancellor of the Republic from 1427 until his death (Martines, 1963, pp. 165, 167). Pier Paolo Vergerio (1370–1444) followed much the same path, beginning with a training in the civil law at Florence in the 1390s and going on to join the Papal Chancellery as a secretary in 1405 (Robey, 1973, p. 34; Baron, 1966, p. 130). And Poggio Bracciolini (1380–1459) similarly studied the civil law at Bologna as well as Florence in the 1390s, after which he began a long term of office as a *dictator* in the Papal Curia in 1404 (Martines, 1963, pp. 123–4). Finally, the same pattern can be traced in the careers of many of the younger generation of humanists who came under the direct influence of the Salutati circle, including Alberti, Manetti and Palmieri. Leon Battista Alberti (1404–72) studied canon law at Bologna in the 1420s, gained a doctorate there in 1428 and became a Papal Secretary in 1434 (Grayson, 1957, pp. 38–43). Giannozzo Manetti (1396–1459) received a legal and humanist education in Florence, served for more than twenty years on various committees and councils of the Republic, subsequently joined the Papal Curia and ended his career as secretary to the king of Naples (Martines, 1963, pp. 179–84, 190–1). And Matteo Palmieri (1406–75) followed a similar but even more successful public career in Florence, acting as an ambassador on eight different missions as well as holding office in the city over sixty times in a career spanning nearly half a century of legal and administrative work (Martines, 1963, p. 192).

The most important similarities, however, between the medieval

the so-called *dictatores*'. For this remark see Kristeller, 1956, p. 564 and for further amplification see pp. 262, 560–1. The implications of Kristeller's work for the criticism of Baron's thesis have been most tellingly spelled out by Jerrold Seigel, 1966, p. 43 and 1968, pp. 204–5.

dictatores and the Florentine humanists of the early fifteenth century derive from the range of topics they chose to consider in their moral and political works. Like their predecessors, the humanists basically concerned themselves with the ideal of Republican liberty, concentrating their main attention on the question of how it comes to be jeopardised and how it can best be secured.

It is of course important not to exaggerate the resemblances between the early *dictatores* and the later humanists. If we turn first to consider what arguments the early *quattrocento* writers tend to present in discussing the dangers to liberty, we find that while they often raise the same questions as their predecessors, they generally arrive at a strongly contrasting set of answers. Unlike the *dictatores*, the humanists no longer place any great emphasis on the dangers of faction. The reason for this change of perspective is perhaps to be sought in the fact that, with the promulgation of a new constitution in 1382, following the revolt of the Ciompi four years earlier, Florence moved into an unusually stable period of oligarchic domination which lasted for well over a generation (Bec, 1967, p. 34). If we glance as far forward as the 1430s, we do find the fear of faction reviving again in such treatises as Palmieri's *Civic Life* (pp. 110–13). But if we focus on the earlier generation of humanists, we encounter a much more complacent sense that the constitutional difficulties of the Republic may actually have been resolved. Bruni in particular strikes an excessively optimistic note in the *Eulogy* of Florence which he composed between 1403 and 1404.[1] He not only glosses over any surviving evidence of factional antagonisms, but even feels able to boast that 'we have succeeded in balancing all the sections of our city in such a way as to produce harmony in every aspect of the Republic' (p. 259; cf. Witt, 1976, esp. p. 264).

One effect of this increased confidence is that, in most of the political writings produced by Salutati and his circle, one of the major issues

---

[1] This is Baron's suggested dating, but – as with the dating of Bruni's *Dialogue* – the issue remains a subject of learned debate. Seigel, wishing to minimise the significance of the crisis of 1402 in the formation of 'civic humanist' thought, has sought to re-establish the traditional assumption that the *Eulogy* was written before the crisis of 1402, and probably in 1400-1. (See Seigel, 1966, esp. pp. 19–23.) Baron, who remains strongly committed to the theory that Bruni's views were decisively shaped by the crisis of 1402, continues to insist that the *Eulogy* cannot have been composed earlier than the summer of 1403, and was probably finished as late as 1404. (See Baron, 1967 and esp. 1955, pp. 69–113.) The issue does not seem to me – either in this case or in the similar case of Bruni's *Dialogues* – to be one of great historical importance. It is true that Baron has been able to offer powerful arguments for dating the composition of both works to the years immediately following the crisis of 1402. It would be a mistake to suppose, however, that this helps to sustain the theory that Bruni's writings of these years contain a number of new ideas which could only have been developed as a result of the crisis of 1402. As I shall shortly attempt to show, when considering Bruni's relationship to earlier Italian political thought, there are many similar ideas to be found in a number of humanist and pre-humanist works which were unquestionably written long before 1402.

discussed by all the earlier *dictatores* comes to be virtually ignored. The prevalence of faction had caused the earlier theorists to feel that any blinkered pursuit of one's own individual interests will be certain to be inimical to the maintenance of the common good. As we have seen, this led them to agonise most of all over the question of how to reconcile the rights of individual citizens with the welfare of the community as a whole. With writers like Bruni, however, we arrive at the more familiar and complacent sense that this is a problem which can largely be left to look after itself. When Bruni praises the initiative of Florence's merchant classes in his *Oration* of 1428, he clearly implies that as long as each individual pursues his own affairs 'with industry' and 'quickness in matters of business', we may safely assume that the ultimate effect of such enlightened self-interest will be beneficial to the Republic as a whole (p. 4).

Another long-standing source of alarm about the preservation of political liberty had been the expectation that the growth of private wealth might prove to be a corrupting force in political life. We have already encountered this fear in such writers as Latini and Mussato, and it welled up again in Machiavelli and Guicciardini in the following century. Again, however, the humanists of the early *quattrocento* scarcely seem disturbed by this possibility at all. They tend on the contrary to glory in the opulence as well as the activities of Florence's merchants, whose tireless wanderings, as Bruni tells us in his *Oration* of 1428, have even taken them as far afield as Britain, 'which is an island situated in the ocean almost on the edge of the world' (p. 4). They normally make a point of emphasising, moreover, that this restless pursuit of gain is a positive blessing to the Republic. The treatise *On Avarice and Luxury* which Poggio wrote in 1428–9 contains a defence of the view that 'money is the nerve of life in a commonwealth, while those who have a love of money are the very foundations of the commonwealth itself' (pp. 12–14; cf. Garin, 1965, pp. 43–4). The same sentiments frequently appear in Palmieri's account of *The Civic Life*, as well as in the dialogue on *The Family* produced by Alberti in the early 1430s.[1] Alberti is admittedly more cautious, and reminds us that 'nothing is so detrimental to our gaining fame and honour as avarice' (p. 166). But even he agrees that wealth is particularly conducive to 'gaining and preserving happiness', and he makes a special point of insisting that 'the riches of private citizens are most useful' in relation to the public good, since they can be applied 'to supply our country's needs', especially 'when the fatherland is in dire straits' (pp. 147–8).

While the early *quattrocento* humanists remain relatively unmoved by

[1] For the date of Alberti's *The Family*, see Baron, 1966, p. 348. For Palmieri on wealth, see pp. 118–21, 128–31, 146–7, etc.

these traditional fears about the preservation of liberty, they go on to emphasise a quite different source of danger which their predecessors had barely recognised. They argue that the main threat to the integrity of the Florentine Republic lies in the fact that its citizens are no longer prepared to fight for their freedom against the encroachments of tyranny, but are willing instead to place the defence of their liberties in the wholly un-reliable hands of hired mercenary troops.

As a background to this new anxiety, we need to consider the changing conditions of civic as well as military life in fourteenth-century Florence. The growing complexity of mercantile affairs made it increasingly difficult for most of the richer citizens to keep up their traditional obligations of military service.[1] During the war against Siena in the 1260s the city had been able to put into the field as many as eight hundred fully equipped militia cavalrymen (Bayley, 1961, p. 8). But by the time of the campaign against Lucca some eighty years later their numbers had dwindled to a mere forty (Bayley, 1961, p. 15). Meanwhile there was a natural tendency to repose an increasing trust in mercenary cavalrymen, over two thousand of whom were in regular employment with the Republic by the middle of the fourteenth century (Bayley, 1961, p. 15). It was not long, however, before the Florentines discovered that such stipendiary troops were capable of being as much a menace to the independence of their city as a means of defending it. An early foretaste of this danger occurred at the siege of Pisa in 1362. The hired Florentine soldiers suddenly demanded double pay, and when this was refused three of their Captains immediately withdrew, taking with them over a thousand fighting men (Bayley, 1961, p. 12). An even more dangerous defection of the same kind occurred at the start of the war against Milan in 1424, when one of the leading *condottieri*, Niccolo Piccinino, deserted with his entire army from Florence to Milan, thereby bringing the Republic to a state of virtual collapse (Bayley, 1961, p. 57).

The humanists responded to this new threat of political blackmail by producing a series of increasingly virulent tirades against the employment of mercenaries. One of the earliest and most eloquent appeared in the book of letters *On Familiar Matters* which Petrarch began to compile from his correspondence in the 1350s (Wilkins, 1961, pp. 87–8, 206). He complains that 'our armies are full of thieves and robbers' who 'prey more frequently upon their allies than their enemies'. They 'run away more readily than they fight', their bearing 'is less martial than effeminate', and 'while they

---

[1] Some recent scholars have doubted whether this decline was in fact as sudden as has usually been supposed. See Mallett, 1974, p. 13, and Waley, 1969, p. 135. Cf. also Mattingly's insistence (Mattingly, 1961) that the attacks mounted by the humanists on the mercenary system were inaccurate.

love the name of war they hate war itself', since their only real concern is with getting their pay (pp. 151–2). Salutati takes up the same complaint in a letter of 1383 about the conduct of affairs in Florence. He laments the ignominious fact that the city is no longer defended by its own citizens, but is given over into the hands of men 'who can scarcely be called men at all', who have no interest in the liberty of the Republic, but are merely greedy for booty and the pursuit of their 'licentious crimes'.[1] By the time we come to Alberti, discussing the issue over a generation later in his *Momus*, we find him treating the problem with an almost resigned irony. Momus, who personifies the darker side of human nature, is pictured early in his satanic career attempting to suborn the military men of the age. But he very soon finds himself frustrated: he discovers that their corruption is already complete (cf. Tenenti, 1974).

The solution proposed by the early *quattrocento* humanists took the form of reviving the ideal of an armed and independent citizenry – the ideal commended by Aristotle in Book III of the *Politics*. They maintain that Florence must be defended as well as governed by men who are ready to offer not merely their political skills but if necessary their lives in order to maintain the Republic and its liberty. We find these values being voiced by Salutati as early as the 1360s,[2] but the fullest statement of the ideal is owed to Leonardo Bruni, who constantly reverts to it throughout his political works. He insists at the end of his *Eulogy* of Florence that every citizen must be prepared 'to bear arms for the preservation of liberty' (p. 260). He concludes his tract of 1422 *On Military Service* by attacking 'the love of money' as a reason for fighting, arguing that 'the aim of a soldier must be to acquire glory, not wealth' (pp. 387–8). And he holds up for our admiration many examples of prominent citizens who have proved themselves willing to risk their lives for the safety of the city. He begins his *Life of Dante* by mentioning as especially praiseworthy the fact that the young poet 'fought valiantly for his country' at 'the great and famous battle of Campaldino' (p. 83). He includes in his *Eulogy* an account of a victory won by the Republic against Volterra in the good old days of the mid thirteenth century, and praises the citizens for having 'acted by themselves without the help of any foreign auxiliaries, fighting on their own behalf and contending as much as possible for glory and dignity' (p. 255). And in the *Oration* he wrote in 1428 for the funeral of Nanni Strozzi, the Florentine general killed in action against the Milanese, one of the main aims of his panegyric – which is largely derived from Thucydides

---

[1] Salutati, *Epistolario*, ed. Novati, vol. II, p. 85. All citations from Salutati's correspondence refer to this edition, except where it is specifically noted that Rigacci's edition is being used.
[2] See for example Salutati, *Epistolario*, I, 26–7.

– is to illustrate 'what a great difference there is between foreign soldiers and those fighting for the love of their city' (p. 6). When describing how Strozzi and his men were fatally ambushed, he first emphasises how the mercenaries amongst them 'at once yielded, thinking nothing of more importance than their safety'. Their craven behaviour is then contrasted as strongly as possible with the gallant bearing of Strozzi himself. 'Willing to put the love of his country before his own safety', he at once hurled himself into the battle, and 'for a time managed to check the onrush of the enemy' before falling mortally wounded (p. 6).

Discussing the dangers to political liberty, the early *quattrocento* humanists thus arrive at a set of conclusions which contrast markedly with those of their predecessors. If we now turn, however, to consider their analysis of the concept of political liberty itself, we encounter a number of striking resemblances between their views and those of the theorists we have already discussed.

The humanists begin by defining the concept of liberty in a traditional and well-established way. They habitually use the term to denote both independence and self-government – liberty in the sense of being free from external interference as well as in the sense of being free to take an active part in the running of the commonwealth. It is misleading of Hans Baron to describe this view as part of 'a new ideology' which was 'generated' in the course of 'the long wars against tyranny' in the first half of the fifteenth century (Baron, 1966, pp. 28–9, 418–19). The analysis the humanists give is in fact an extension of various themes which, as we have already seen, can be found in diplomatic negotiations, city chronicles and other forms of political propaganda dating back at least as far as the middle of the thirteenth century.[1]

The first aspect of this traditional definition of 'liberty' which the humanists adopt is the idea of preserving the integrity of the surviving City Republics against any further inroads by the *Signori*. Salutati furnishes a splendid proclamation of this commitment in the official letter he wrote in 1390 in response to Giangaleazzo's declaration of war. The peroration declares that 'we shall now take to arms for the defence of our own liberty as well as the liberty of others, whom you are gravely oppressing with the yoke of your tyranny, hoping that the eternal justice of the Divine Majesty will guard our liberty and take note of the misery of

---

[1] The dependence of the so-called 'civic humanists' on these earlier writings has been very properly emphasised by Rubinstein, 1968, esp. p. 449, and more recently by Struever, 1970, p. 117. For the discussion of 'liberty' – in both the senses I have indicated – throughout the fourteenth century in Florence, and especially during the constitutional crisis of the 1370s, see Brucker, 1962, esp. p. 73 and Becker, 1962, esp. pp. 395–6.

Lombardy, not preferring the ambition of a single mortal man to the liberty of so many peoples' (col. 817). During the ensuing wars against Milan, this image of Florence as a watchdog of political independence was constantly invoked by Salutati and his followers, and especially by Leonardo Bruni, one of whose chief boasts in his *Eulogy* of Florence was that 'our citizens rejoice very greatly in the liberty of all peoples, and are thus the absolute enemies of all tyrants' (p. 245). Bruni went on to supplement this claim by recalling the many occasions on which the Florentines had willingly 'faced dangers for the safety and liberty of other peoples' (p. 256). He praises the Republic for 'saving the people of Lucca and ovecoming the Pisans' in the previous century, and insists that 'the whole of Italy would have fallen under the power' of Giangaleazzo in the previous decade if Florence had not 'stood up for the liberty of Italy', withstood his onslaught 'with the greatest prudence and force', and so 'liberated the whole of Italy from the danger of servitude' (pp. 256, 258).

The other traditional sense of 'liberty' which the humanists continue to celebrate is the idea of maintaining a free constitution under which every citizen is able to enjoy an equal opportunity of involving himself actively in the business of government. Bruni sometimes refers to this as 'the true liberty', and it is one of his proudest claims about the constitution of Florence that it does in fact serve to secure this value. He first makes this point at the end of his *Eulogy*, arguing that the sovereignty of the City's popular Council ensures that 'the people and their liberty dominate everything', with the result that 'the maintenance of liberty is nowhere as well assured' as in Florence (pp. 260, 262). But his main discussion of the ideal occurs in his *Oration* on Strozzi, which opens with a renewed tribute to the Florentines and the excellence of their government. The overriding merit of Florence's constitution is said to be that 'it makes it equally possible for everyone to take part in the affairs of the Republic'. This in turn is said to guarantee that 'everything is directed to the greatest possible extent towards maintaining the liberty as well as the equality of all its citizens'. They are free to criticise as well as to control their government, since 'no one has to stand in awe of anyone else's power or capacity to do them harm'. And they are free from any danger of being enslaved by a tyrannical regime, since the involvement of all the citizens ensures 'that the control of the city is always prevented from falling into the hands of one or a few people' (p. 3).

The next and connected point at which the humanists continue to endorse the views of the earlier *dictatores* about the concept of political liberty is in the unequivocal preference they express for Republicanism over any other form of government. Hans Baron is again somewhat misleading in his treatment of this theme. He assumes that an enthusiastic adherence to 'the Medieval idea of Imperial Monarchy' constituted one of the 'traditional convictions' of Italian political theorists throughout the period before the start of the fifteenth century (Baron, 1966, pp. 160, 242). He is thus led to speak of a complete 'cleavage' between this background and 'the new outlook' attained by the 'civic humanists' of the early *quattrocento*, whose 'criticism of Imperial monarchy' is said to place them in sharp contrast 'to these features of the previous century'.[1] As we have seen, however, the repudiation of the Empire, together with the belief that a Republican form of government is the one best suited to the *Regnum Italicum*, can be found as early as Latini's political writings in the 1260s, as well as in Mussato's chronicles, Bartolus's commentaries and Ptolemy of Lucca's treatise on government in the first half of the next century. It would thus be more accurate to think in terms of the so-called 'civic humanists' drawing on a considerable reservoir of anti-monarchical feeling in attempting once again to vindicate the special merits of Republicanism at the start of the fifteenth century.

The first 'civic humanist' to mount an explicit attack on the value of monarchy was Salutati, who issued a public letter on this theme as early as 1376, complementing it with a further letter in praise of Republican liberty in 1392 (II, 386–93; cf. Witt, 1969, pp. 452–5). Bruni enthusiastically supports the same position in his *Oration* on Strozzi, which includes an explicit attack on 'those who prefer a monarchical form of government'. Bruni's main argument is that kings cannot hope to be well served, since 'good men are a source of greater suspicion to them than bad men, the reason being that virtue in anyone other than themselves is always threatening to them' (p. 3). Alberti repeats the same contention in his dialogues on *The Family*, in the course of discussing the business of 'good management'. He insists that 'in princely courts the good are always outnumbered by hypocrites, flatterers and envious men', with the result that 'only rarely is virtue well rewarded' by princes or kings (p. 245). The obvious moral, as Bruni had already declared in his *Oration*, is that 'the popular form of government' should be treated as 'the only legitimate form', on the grounds that it not only 'makes possible true liberty and equality before the law for the whole body of the citizens', but also 'enables the cultivation of the virtues to flourish without any suspicions being aroused' (p. 3).

---

[1] See Baron, 1966, pp. 49, 58, and Witt, 1969, p. 450, arguing that 'a conception of Republicanism based on the psychological importance of liberty' is found no earlier than in Salutati's political works.

It is true, however, that in Bruni's commendation of Republican political life there is at least one original – and extremely influential – element. This is his view of the supposed connections between the freedom and the greatness of commonwealths. The special merit of a Republic, as he contends in his *Oration*, is that 'the hope of rising to public honours, of building up a career by one's own efforts, is the same for everyone' (p. 3). The significance of this equality lies in the fact that men are said to 'rouse themselves and raise themselves up as soon as the hope of honour is held out to them, whereas they collapse into idleness as soon as it is withdrawn' (pp. 3–4). This in turn means that 'as soon as a capacity for rising to honours and pursuing power is made available to a free people', we may expect this factor, more than anything else, 'to have the effect of calling forth their talents' (p. 4). The closest possible connection is thus held to exist between the promotion of a competitive and *engagé* ethos amongst the citizens and the maintenance of a strong and effective commonwealth. This belief emerges most clearly at the end of Bruni's *Oration*, where he observes that 'it is not at all surprising' that Florence 'is so outstanding for its talents and industry', since 'this hope of honour is in fact held out, and these energies are in fact released, amongst all the citizens of our city' (p. 4). Soon afterwards the same moral was drawn with no less complacency by Poggio Braccioli ni in a letter addressed to Filippo Maria Visconti in 1438. Poggio begins by assuring the Duke that 'the possession of liberty', together with the ability of all the citizens 'to act together in its cause', means that the people of Florence 'are raised up and excited' to an unusual degree 'to engage in the cultivation of the virtues'. And he ends by arguing that this is why none of 'the many famous and magnificent cities in Italy' has ever been able to surpass Florence 'either in talents or learning or wise studies or civic prudence or good customs or the virtues' (pp. 183–4).

While this account of the relationship between freedom and power is a novel one, it clearly arises out of two assumptions which we have already seen to be prominent in the writings of the medieval *dictatores*. The first is the claim that the promotion of a healthy and uncorrupt form of political life depends less on perfecting the machinery of government than on developing the energies and public spirit of the citizens. We have already observed this belief in a number of thirteenth-century books of advice to *podestà*, and it still underlies a work such as Bruni's *Eulogy* of Florence. When Bruni discusses the greatness of the Republic, he continues to attribute it to the fact that 'there has been no desire for leisure on the part of the citizens', who 'have not thought it right to live a life of tranquillity', but have 'continually exerted themselves on the city's behalf', opposing themselves to its enemies 'and dedicating themselves to upholding its traditional liberties' (p. 252).

The other familiar assumption the humanists continue to accept is that a citizen's worth must be measured not by the length of his lineage or the extent of his wealth, but rather by his capacity to develop his talents, to achieve a proper sense of public spirit, and so to deploy his energies in the service of the community. Like their predecessors, the humanists incapsulate this value in the proposition that virtue constitutes the only true nobility. Perhaps the finest statement of this commitment occurs in the debate about the concept of nobility written by Buonaccorso da Montemagna (c. 1392–1429), a young Professor of Law at Florence who appears to have been in close touch with the city's humanist circles (Mitchell, 1938, p. 176; cf. Baron, 1966, p. 420). Buonaccorso's *Controversy about Nobility* was completed in 1428, and translated into English some twenty years later by John Tiptoft, the Earl of Worcester, at that time a student of Latin and Greek at Florence (Mitchell, 1938, p. 177). (It is worth citing from Tiptoft's version, since it constitutes one of the earliest humanist treatises to appear in the English language.) The *Controversy* – or *Declamation*, as Tiptoft prefers to call it – takes the form of a debate between two young men who are both anxious to marry Lucretia, the daughter of a Roman nobleman 'full of riches, honour and friendship' (p. 215). Lucretia tells her father she will accept whichever suitor proves himself to be 'more noble' (p. 217). Each accordingly makes a speech in praise of his own nobility. The first, Cornelius, delivers a brief oration in which he boasts of 'the high glory' of his famous ancestors and his own 'abundance of riches' (pp. 217, 221). The other, Gaius, then presents a far longer and more imposing (though somewhat priggish) speech assailing Cornelius's account of nobility for having 'set it in blood and riches' (p. 226). True nobility, he replies, 'rests not in the glory of another man, or in the flitting goods of fortune, but in a man's own virtue' (p. 226). He repeats Dante's claim that the possession of great wealth cannot be relevant, since 'honest poverty may take away no part of virtue' (p. 232). He also agrees with Dante's view that the idea of nobility as 'a thing of inheritance' must be 'a vain supposing', since a man of ancient lineage with no virtues of his own ought in fact to be regarded as especially 'shameful and abominable' for having failed to follow the example of his 'worshipful ancestors' (pp. 229–31). The final characterisation of the truly noble man is thus that he must be a person of upright character who can claim to possess 'a certain excellence in virtue and manhood', and whose achievements can be seen to reflect his own 'labour and desert' (pp. 232, 234).

A few years later the same themes were taken up by Poggio Bracciolini in his dialogue *On Nobility*, after which the equation between virtue and nobility became a humanist commonplace, repeated by Alberti, Landino and Platina and even emblazoned as a reminder to the young gentry of England on the arms of Trinity College, Cambridge. Poggio's dialogue on the subject opens with a remarkable survey of different attitudes towards nobility in Italy, Germany, France, England and Spain, but after this the discussion settles down into a repetition of the familiar stoic argument about the importance of individual self-development. The 'vulgar opinion' that nobility 'consists in the goods of fortune' is first discarded on the grounds that this would be to associate nobility with ignoble things (p. 72). And the conventional belief – which, as we have seen, Bartolus had partly endorsed – that the possession of nobility is essentially a matter of being born into a family 'famous for its great deeds' is similarly dismissed with the observation that many of the greatest Romans 'were born of unknown rustics, but later attained nobility through their own virtues and achievements' (p. 78). The climax of the dialogue is thus reached when it is proclaimed once again that 'the palm of nobility must be due to virtue alone' (p. 80). The truly noble man is perceived, as in Buonaccorso, as a highly active and ambitious individualist, a man who cultivates 'honesty and valuable skills' which he then devotes to his own glorification and the service of the commonwealth (p. 83).

The final point at which the early *quattrocento* humanists may be said to build on earlier views about the concept of political liberty is in their historical philosophy, and especially in the preference they express for the freedom of the Roman Republic over the despotism of the later Empire. Here again Hans Baron speaks somewhat misleadingly when he repeatedly asserts that this 'Republican interpretation of Roman history' constitutes one of the 'novel elements in the historical thought of the Renaissance'.[1] It is true that such an interpretation scarcely makes any appearance in the writings of the earlier *dictatores* – though even here Latini constitutes an important exception to the rule. We have already observed, however, that all the main elements of a Republican view of ancient Rome and its history can be found in the treatises of Remigio, Ptolemy, Bartolus and other scholastic writers of the early fourteenth century. The somewhat ironic truth – in view of their continual denigration of all scholastic thought – is that when Salutati, Bruni and their followers discuss the history of Rome, what they are basically doing is ratifying and extending this essentially scholastic interpretation of the facts.

---

[1] See Baron, 1966, p. 64. See also pp. 6, 47–8, 54, 75, 460. See also Ferguson, 1958, p. 25 and Baron, 1958, p. 26. Pocock, 1975, p. 56 follows Baron in speaking of Salutati's attack on Julius Caesar as a 'revolutionary' change of attitude.

This comes out most clearly in Bruni's *Eulogy*, which corroborates Salutati's thesis that Florence was originally founded not by Julius Caesar, as had always been patriotically supposed, but rather by Sulla's veterans in the last years of the Republic (Baron, 1966, p. 63). Since Florence is so famous for her Republican liberties, Bruni regards it as obvious that 'this colony must have been established at the time when the city of Rome flourished most greatly in its power and liberty' (p. 247). He concedes that 'this liberty was undermined, not long after the establishment of the colony, by the most atrocious crimes' (p. 245). But he insists that 'such a splendid Roman colony' can only have been set up when 'the liberty of the people had not yet been stolen from them by any Caesar, Antony, Tiberius or Nero' (p. 235). This praise of the Roman Republic is matched by an active hostility towards Julius Caesar which again repeats the views of Bruni's scholastic predecessors. Caesar is treated in the *Eulogy* as the pivot around whose career the liberty of the Roman Republic swings into the tyranny of the Empire. Before him came Camillus, Scipio, Marcellus and Cato, all 'most sacred and deserving men' (p. 246). Then came Caesar himself, whose 'many and grave vices', including 'the proscription of innocent citizens' are said to have 'overshadowed his great and many virtues' (p. 247). And after Caesar the government fell into the hands of a group of men 'who were not redeemed from their vices by any virtues at all' – including the loathsome Caligula, 'who wished that the Roman people had only a single neck' (pp. 246–7).

The only point at which Bruni and his followers may be said to extend the analysis offered by the earlier scholastic theorists is in the explanation they offer for the greatness of the Roman Republic and the decadence of the Empire. Bruni treats the history of Rome as the clearest evidence for his belief that a people is bound to achieve greatness as long as there is freedom to take part in the business of government, and bound to fall into corruption as soon as this liberty is taken away from them. He first alludes to the rise and fall of Rome as the best proof of this theory in his *Eulogy* of Florence, where he notes that 'after the Republic was transferred into the hands of a single man, famous and talented minds (as Tacitus says) can be found no more' (p. 247). But his main development of the thesis occurs at the start of his *History of the Florentine People*, which he mainly composed between 1414 and 1420 (Ullman, 1946, p. 218; Wilcox, 1969, pp. 3, 67–98). The opening Book consists of a synoptic survey of the history of Italy from the origins of the Roman Republic to the campaigns against Frederick II in the middle of the thirteenth century. The organising principle of the discussion is the idea that the growth and collapse of Roman hegemony is basically to be explained in terms of the attainment and loss of political liberty. The triumphant progress of the Republic is taken to illustrate the fact that 'when the pathway to greatness is opened up, men raise themselves up with greater ease, whereas when it is closed off to them, they fall back into idleness' (p. 13). Conversely, the corruption and decline of Rome is said to date 'from the very moment at which the liberty of the people was removed, and they fell under the rule of the Emperors' (p. 14). With the coming of the principate 'the people handed over their liberty', and 'with the loss of their liberty came the waning of their strength' (pp. 14, 18). As in Gibbon, so in these remote humanist predecessors, the decline and fall of the Roman Empire is basically attributed to the excesses of absolute power which inevitably set in as soon as the 'public spirit' of the citizens began to be lost.

THE RECOVERY OF CLASSICAL VALUES

So far we have examined the ways in which the themes of pre-humanist and scholastic political theory were taken up and developed by the so-called 'civic humanists' at the start of the fifteenth century. Next we need to broaden our perspective and consider the links between these Florentine writers of the early *quattrocento* and the wider movement of humanism which had already arisen in the course of the fourteenth century.

We have already observed the beginnings, in early *trecento* Arezzo and Padua, of a literary movement that can properly be called 'humanist' – a movement rooted in the teaching of rhetoric and increasingly devoted to the study and imitation of classical history, poetry and moral philosophy (cf. Kristeller, 1956, p. 544). We next need to note that, after the middle of the fourteenth century, this movement gathered momentum and confidence in two ways which in turn had a profound effect on the Florentine humanists of the early *quattrocento* period.

One important development took the form of a rapid growth of sheer information about the ancient world. The humanists began to institute systematic searches, especially in monastic libraries, for further writings by their favourite classical authors, looking in particular for additional texts by Cicero, whom they regarded (in Petrarch's phrase) as 'the great genius' of antiquity.[1] These treasure-hunts rapidly yielded a series of important discoveries (Kristeller, 1956, p. 262). The full text of Cicero's *Familiar Letters* was recovered by Salutati from the Cathedral library at Milan in 1392 (Baron, 1966, p. 493). The histories of Tacitus and Thucydides, as well as a number of Plutarch's *Lives*, were rediscovered and made available for the first time in centuries (Kristeller, 1961, pp. 14–17).

[1] See Petrarch, *On his own Ignorance*, p. 79.

Bishop Landriani found a complete manuscript of Cicero's *Making of an Orator* in the library at Lodi in 1421 (Murphy, 1974, p. 360). And Poggio Bracciolini made a series of spectacular discoveries in the northern monasteries which he visited while attending the Council of Constance between 1414 and 1418 (Murphy, 1974, pp. 357–8). Searching at St Gallen in 1416, he recovered a complete version of Quintilian's rhetoric for the first time since the ninth century (Clark, 1899, p. 128). And two years later, evidently at Langres, he came upon the poems of Statius and Manilius, the philosophy of Lucretius, and several orations by Cicero previously thought to have been lost (Clark, 1899, pp. 126n., 128).

The most important development, however, was that in consequence of acquiring so many new texts, and so coming to recognise how far they had originally been written in – and for – a very different kind of society, the humanists gradually began to adopt a new attitude towards the ancient world. Hitherto the study of classical antiquity – which had ebbed and flowed throughout the Middle Ages – had failed to generate any feeling of radical discontinuity with the culture of Greece and Rome. A sense of belonging to essentially the same civilisation continued to persist, and nowhere more strongly than in Italy, where the legal code of Justinian was still effectively in force, the Latin language was in daily use on all formal as well as learned occasions, and most of the cities continued to inhabit the sites of ancient Roman settlements. As Panofsky has emphasised, the effect of this continuing sense of familiarity was that, in all the *rapprochements* with the classical tradition which took place throughout the Middle Ages, we never find any effort being made to approach the culture of the ancient world on its own terms (Panofsky, 1960, pp. 110–11). Instead we always encounter what Panofsky has called a 'principle of disjunction' – a disjunction between the employment of classical forms and the insistence that they carry messages of contemporary significance. Panofsky offers many examples of this tendency from the Romanesque period of arts and architecture, in which classical elements of decoration were generally applied in a thoroughly eclectic manner, while Greek and Roman figures tended to appear as 'barons' and 'damsels' in medieval landscapes, often engaged in Christian rituals and invariably dressed in wholly anachronistic styles (Panofsky, 1960, pp. 85–6, 102). A similar outlook, as we have already seen, also affected the medieval study of ancient rhetoric and philosophy. When the *dictatores* of the thirteenth century began to shift their attention away from the inculcation of rules, and called instead for a study of 'the best authors', they fell upon the oratorical writings of Cicero with intense enthusiasm. But they never made any attempt to determine

Cicero's own sense of the proper aims and purposes of rhetorical instruction. They merely fitted his oratorical texts into the existing framework of
the traditional *Ars Dictaminis*.

Towards the end of the *trecento*, however, we come upon a completely
changed attitude. As Panofsky sums it up, 'the classical past was looked
upon, for the first time, as a totality cut off from the present' (1960, p. 113).
A new sense of historical distance was achieved, as a result of which the
civilisation of ancient Rome began to appear as a wholly separate culture,
one which deserved – and indeed required – to be reconstructed and
appreciated as far as possible on its own distinctive terms.

One striking symbol of this change can be seen in the new attitude
adopted towards the physical remains of Imperial Rome. Throughout the
Middle Ages there had been a trade in marble torn from the ancient
buildings, some of which had found its way as far afield as Westminster
Abbey and the Cathedral at Aachen (Weiss, 1969, p. 9). By the start of
the fifteenth century, however, under the promptings of such writers as
Flavio Biondo in his *Rome Restored*, such vandalism came to seem almost
sacrilegious, and the archaeological investigation and preservation of the
ancient city began to be undertaken for the first time (Robathan, 1970,
pp. 203–5, 212–3). But the most important symptom of the new outlook
was of course the development of a non-anachronistic classical style. This
was first achieved in sculpture and architecture in early *quattrocento*
Florence: Ghiberti and Donatello began to imitate the exact forms and
techniques of ancient statuary, while Brunelleschi made a pilgrimage to
Rome to measure the precise scale and proportions of the classical buildings, his intention being – as his contemporary biographer Antonio
Manetti expressed it – to 'renew and bring to light' a truly Roman instead
of merely a Romanesque style (Panofsky, 1960, pp. 20, 40). Within a
generation a similar transformation had overtaken the art of painting:
Mantegna began to introduce an exact classicism into his frescoes, and the
same values were soon adopted and developed in Florence by Pollaiuolo,
Botticelli and a long line of their pupils and followers (Panofsky, 1960,
pp. 174–6).

The crucial point for the purposes of the present argument is that the
same story can be told about the revolution engineered by the humanists
in the study of ancient rhetoric and philosophy in the course of the fourteenth century. The hero of this story is Petrarch. He finally succeeded in
overcoming the disjunction between the classical foundations of the *Ars
Dictaminis* and the practical purposes it was mainly designed to serve.
Rejecting all attempts to fit Cicero's writings into the pre-established
traditions of instruction in the rhetorical arts, he sought to recover – in

the genuinely historical spirit characteristic of the Renaissance – what Cicero himself had taken to be the special value of an education founded on a combination of rhetoric and philosophy. The outcome of this enquiry, as Seigel has phrased it, was that 'Petrarch transformed Medieval Italian rhetoric by rediscovering its classical roots and scope, thus enabling practising rhetoricians to remake themselves in something like the Ciceronian image'.[1]

Petrarch first of all rediscovered Cicero's sense of the proper goals of education. As Cicero had stated his ideal in the *Tusculan Disputations*, the aim of education is not merely to produce a man with a certain range of technical skills, nor even a man capable of attaining all the virtues and 'right-minded states'. The ambition must rather be to cultivate 'the single virtue' (*virtus*) which has been 'found to outshine the rest'. Cicero even maintains that 'it is from the word for man (*vir*) that the word virtue (*virtus*) is derived'. So he insists that this special quality of *virtus* is the one we must seek above all to acquire, not merely 'if we wish to prove possessors of virtue' but also 'if we wish to be men' (pp. 195, 197). The fundamental aim of all education is thus taken to be the development of the *vir virtutis* – the truly manly man, the person whose character can be summed up simply by saying (as Shakespeare makes Antony say of Brutus) 'This was a man.'[2]

Petrarch also rediscovered the lofty place Cicero assigned to the study of rhetoric and philosophy in helping to shape the *vir virtutis* or man of true manliness. This theme is taken up in particular in *The Making of an Orator*, Cicero's longest and most important rhetorical work. The true *vir* must first of all be a man of wisdom. So Cicero makes the study of moral philosophy central to the training of his character. But he must also be capable of putting his wisdom to use, relating his philosophy to his life and fulfilling himself as a citizen rather than merely as a sage. According to Cicero, this means that rhetoric must be accorded a no less central place in his education. The special value of the subject is said to be its 'power of driving the hearers forward in any direction in which it has applied its weight' (I, p. 45; Cf. also I, 23–7). The indispensable role it is thus said to play is that, by uniting wisdom with eloquence, it enables a knowledge of the truth to be effectively communicated, and so allows the most salutary doctrines of the philosophers to exercise their proper influence on the conduct of public affairs.

[1] See Seigel, 1968, p. 222. See also pp. 31–2, 61, 215, 224. I am much indebted to Seigel's fine account of Petrarch's Ciceronianism and its influence. See also the valuable discussion of the same themes in Whitfield, 1943, esp. pp. 47, 104–5, 195.
[2] See *Julius Caesar*, V, v, 75. For an account of these ancient ideals of education, see Marrou, 1956, esp. pp. 98–9.

The key to interpreting the humanism of Petrarch and his successors lies in the fact that, as soon as they recovered this authentically classical perspective, they turned themselves into fervent advocates of the same Ciceronian ideals. The outcome was a transformation of existing views not merely about the proper aims and content of education, but also about the nature of man, the extent of his capacities and the proper goals of his life. It is this transformation which the rest of this chapter will attempt to analyse.

THE CONCEPT OF 'VIRTUS'

The first and fundamental move the humanists made was to spell out the sequence of assumptions underlying the Ciceronian concept of *virtus*: first that it is in fact possible for men to attain this highest kind of excellence; next that the right process of education is essential for the achievement of this goal; and finally that the contents of such an education must centre on the linked study of rhetoric and ancient philosophy.

One immediate effect of adopting this classical scale of values was that the humanists arrived at a positively jubilant sense of the value of their own rhetorical studies. It now seemed to them unquestionable that rhetoric and philosophy must be regarded as the key cultural disciplines (cf. Seigel, 1968, p. 61). They thus succeeded in bringing to birth a doctrine that was subsequently to prove almost embarrassingly long-lived: the doctrine that a classical education not only constitutes the only possible form of schooling for a gentleman, but also the best possible preparation for an entry into public life.

Petrarch himself presents this argument in his treatise *On his Own Ignorance*, a defence of humanist studies written in 1367 in response to the sneers of four young students of scholastic philosophy who had said of him that he was 'a good man, but uneducated' (Wilkins, 1961, p. 210). Petrarch insists in reply that it is not enough to learn 'what virtue is' from studying Aristotle. Aristotle's analysis may well involve 'penetrating insight', but 'his lesson lacks the words that sting and set afire'. The crippling effect of this limitation is that, since he is unable to urge his readers 'towards love of virtue and hatred of vice', he is also unable to bring his theories into any direct contact with practical life (p. 103). The only way to overcome this weakness is to study rhetoric, and especially the rhetoric of Cicero, from whose genius, as Petrarch confesses, 'I can hardly tear myself away' (p. 85). It is only when we have learnt how to unite wisdom with eloquence, how to 'stamp and drive deep into the heart the sharpest and most ardent stings of speech', that we can hope to discharge the really vital task of philosophy – that of arguing in such a way that our hearers are not only instructed in the virtues but incited to the performance of virtuous acts (p. 104). These views about the unity of theory and practice were then taken up by all the Florentine humanists of the early fifteenth century. Salutati praises Petrarch in a letter of 1374 both for stressing the importance of rhetoric and for 'excelling so greatly in eloquence' himself (1, 179). Bruni devotes much of his *Dialogue* to affirming the need for a union between philosophy and rhetoric, and points to Petrarch and Cicero as the two great examplars of such a synthesis. He begins by lauding Cicero as the man 'who carried philosophy from Greece to Italy, and nourished it with the golden river of his eloquence' (p. 54). And he ends with a fine tribute to Petrarch as 'the man who restored the *studia humanitatis*, at a time when such studies were extinct, and showed us the way to gain learning for ourselves' (p. 94).

Within a generation this belief in the importance of eloquence had come to be an article of faith as well as a defining characteristic of the humanists. The praise this prompted them to lavish on the study of rhetoric tended in consequence to become prodigiously high-flown. A good example is provided by the *Oration in praise of Oratory* delivered by Bartolommeo della Fonte (1446–1513) at the start of his first lecture-course as Professor of Rhetoric at Florence in November 1481 (Trinkaus, 1960, pp. 91–4). The mastery of oratory, he assured his audience, is indispensable 'in our domestic affairs as well as in our public activities' (p. 96). The man who is able to join wisdom with eloquence has at his disposal the power 'to punish the wicked, to care for the good, to embellish his native land and to benefit all mankind' (pp. 96–7). It is thus obvious that 'the study of eloquence' gives rise to 'greater advantages in public and private affairs' than any other discipline (p. 95). We must think of it, in short, as nothing less than 'the mistress of the whole human race' (p. 99).

A second effect of recovering the Ciceronian ideal of *virtus* was to give rise to a new sense amongst the humanists that the precise details of a young man's education – the question of what exactly he should be made to learn, and in what exact order of priorities – must be treated as matters of the highest importance. We find this belief reflected in the fact that, by the start of the fifteenth century, a number of humanists began to set up their own schools to ensure that the right subjects were properly taught. The pioneer of this development was Giovanni di Conversino, two of whose pupils became amongst the most influential of humanist educators: Vittorino da Feltre, who established a famous school at Mantua in 1423, and Guarino da Verona, who taught at Ferrara for over thirty years until his death in 1460 (Hay, 1961, pp. 154–5). Another sign of the same outlook was the emergence during this period of a distinctive new *genre* of moral and political thought – a *genre* of advice-books concerned not so much with supplying direct counsel to *podestà* and princes, but rather with offering guidance about the best form of education to be given to those who might subsequently find themselves discharging these important roles. The earliest treatise of this character was the brief but extremely influential handbook *On Good Manners* produced by Pier Paolo Vergerio in 1402 (Baron, 1966, p. 494). The basic assumption of Vergerio's discussion is that if we receive the right kind of instruction 'in grave and liberal studies' early in life, this provides us with the best guarantee of being able to 'attain and practice *virtus* and wisdom' in our subsequent careers (pp. 96, 102). He accordingly treats with a new and special seriousness the question of what exact curriculum should be followed if the aim is to ensure that a true *vir virtutis* is duly produced. He thinks that a knowledge of history must be given 'first place'; that moral philosophy comes 'next in importance'; and that 'the third branch of study' must be rhetoric, 'the formal study by which we attain the art of eloquence' (pp. 106–7). Within a generation this outlook had come to be embodied in a growing list of humanist guides to the correct education of princes and gentlemen. We find the same assumptions in Maffeo Vegio's book on *The Education of Children*, again in Guarino's account of *The Right Order of Teaching and Learning*, and above all in Aeneas Sylvius Piccolomini's educational works, including his influential letter of 1445 to the king of Hungary on the education of prices, as well as his treatise of five years later on *The Education of Children* (Garin, 1965, p. 76; Woodward, 1963, p. 180).

A further effect of reviving the ideal of the *vir virtutis* was that it led the humanists to adopt a new and distinctive answer to the perennial question of what entitles a man to regard himself as truly well-educated. This involved them in rejecting a dichotomy central to the pedagogic theory and practice of the high Middle Ages. Hitherto it had generally been assumed that two different systems of education needed to be maintained, one suitable for gentlemen and the other for 'clerks'. This belief continued to be held almost universally in northern Europe throughout the fourteenth century. It is still embodied, for example, in *The Canterbury Tales*, even though Chaucer was of course writing a generation after Petrarch. One of the pilgrims described in the *Prologue* is a young scholar from Oxford, while another is a young squire. The former spends all his time reading Aristotle's philosophy, but the latter is wholly preoccupied with practising the ideals of chivalry and learning the arts of war. As soon as we turn, however, to the educational writings of the early *quattrocento* humanists, we find these distinctions being deliberately obliterated. One of the earliest treatises to reflect this development is Vergerio's advice-book *On Good Manners*. This opens with a dedication to Umbertino of Ferrara, in which the young *signore* is accorded the highest praise because 'you had before you the choice of training in Arms or in Letters' and 'to your great credit you elected to become proficient in both alike' (pp. 103–4). The ideal now being held out for imitation is that of the so-called 'Renaissance man', the man who aims at nothing less than universal excellence. He is no longer allowed to think of himself as a specialist either in the arts of government or scholarship or war. He is only permitted to regard his education as completed when it is possible to say of him – as Ophelia says of Hamlet – that he has succeeded in combining 'the courtier's, soldier's, scholar's eye, tongue, sword'.[1]

But by far the most important consequence of adopting the ideal of the *Uomo universale* was that it prompted the humanists to reject the entire Augustinian picture of human nature. St Augustine had explicitly laid it down in *The City of God* that the idea of pursuing *virtus*, or total human excellence, was based on a presumptuous and mistaken view of what a man can hope to achieve by his own efforts. He himself argued that, if ever a mortal ruler succeeds in governing virtuously, such a triumph can never be ascribed to his own powers but 'only to the grace of God'. He was careful to add, moreover, that even when God 'has granted virtue' to such a ruler in response to his prayers, he will still be sure to 'fall short of perfection in righteousness' due to his fundamentally corrupted nature (Vol. II, p. 245).

One effect of this immensely influential argument was that, in all orthodox discussions about man's nature and capacities throughout the Middle Ages, the possibility of aspiring to the attainment of *virtus* ceased to be mentioned, just as the representation of the concept is wholly absent (so Panofsky assures us) from medieval art (Panofsky, 1960, p. 177). It is of course accepted that a man of saintly disposition may be capable of attaining a number of individual virtues, and thus of avoiding most of the grosser forms of vice. It is always assumed, however, in line with St Paul's teachings in *Corinthians*, that *virtus generalis* is possessed by God alone and personified only by Christ.[2] Any suggestion that it may be open to men to imitate such pre-eminent excellence is automatically ruled out, as Innocent III was to argue in his famous treatise *On the Misery of Man*, by 'the sinful condition of human existence' (p. 31).

[1] *Hamlet*, III, i, 159.
[2] See 1 Corinthians, 1, 24. For this reference and a discussion of its implications see Mommsen, 1959b and 1959c. My own accounts of the Augustinian attack on *virtus* and the humanist recovery of the concept are greatly indebted to Mommsen's analysis, and to the development of its themes in the opening chapter of Mazzeo, 1967. See also Menut, 1943, pp. 308–21.

These values are deliberately reversed by Petrarch and his followers. We must be careful, however, not to confuse this return to a classical view of human nature with a reversion to paganism – a confusion which has often been held to run through Burckhardt's celebrated account of 'the recovery of antiquity' in his *Civilization of the Renaissance*. There is no doubt that Petrarch was a fervently Christian writer, and bequeathed to the early *quattrocento* humanists an essentially Christian view of how the key concept of *virtus* should be analysed. This can be seen very clearly in his treatise *On his Own Ignorance*. He assumes that the attainment of *virtus* is essentially a matter of acquiring all the individual virtues, and he stresses that these must include not merely the cardinal virtues praised by the moralists of antiquity, but also the fundamental virtue of Christian faith. He continues to insist that 'the two things without which there can be absolutely no happiness' are 'Faith and Immortality', and he summarises his outlook by equating wisdom with piety (pp. 65, 75). The same assumptions are repeated by all the early *quattrocento* humanists. Perhaps the clearest of the many accounts in which they develop a similar view of *virtus* is the one given by Alberti in his second dialogue on *The Family*. His discussion opens with a warning from the father of one of the young men taking part in the debate to 'remember that the time you do not employ in acquiring *virtù* is lost' (p. 137). The analysis of what it means to attain *virtù* then proceeds by way of itemising all the individual virtues it is necessary to cultivate in order to live a perfect social life. First we need the virtues that 'hold men together in human society', the greatest of which are 'justice, equity, liberality and love'. Then we need a further range of virtues to sustain us against the adversities of life, including 'firmness, stability, constancy, strength and scorn for transitory things' (p. 141). So far the analysis might be said to be essentially Aristotelian, since it is evidently rooted in the belief that the four cardinal virtues are justice, wisdom, temperance and fortitude. It is only completed, however, with the addition of two further claims, both of which reflect an unequivo- cally Christian scale of values. The first is that we must never congratulate ourselves on acquiring any of these 'great and excellent virtues', since we must recognise that this ability has been 'instilled in our souls' by God (p. 140). The other is that no one can in consequence be said to be following a truly virtuous life unless his 'excellent deeds' are performed not merely with 'manly firmness', but also with 'a love of righteousness' and a constant desire to commend himself to his Maker (p. 142).

It would be misleading, however, to conclude that Petrarch and his disciples were nothing more than orthodox Christian moralists. Although they fitted their accounts of the *vir virtutis* into a Christian framework, there is no doubt that their restoration of this classical ideal involved them in a sharp rejection of prevailing Augustinian assumptions about man's fallen nature. The force of this rejection can be seen as early as 1337, when Petrarch started to write the first version of his treatise *On Famous Men* (Wilkins, 1959, p. 283). He devotes no attention at all to the customary medieval pantheon of worthies and saints. His heroes are entirely taken from the ancient world, and the reason he gives in almost every case for singling them out is that they are said to have succeeded in attaining true *virtus*. There is a life of Camillus which praises him for 'his rigid *virtus*'; a life of Marcellus which speaks of 'the *virtus* through which he gained his glory'; and a long life of Scipio which broaches a favourite humanist theme, the idea that the mere vigour and 'fury' of a barbarian like Hannibal can never be expected to match the kind of *virtus* Scipio displayed in his final and overwhelming campaign against Carthage (pp. 31, 133, 158). The pervasive assumption throughout the lives is that true *virtus* can indeed be attained, and that any man worthy the name must strive above all to attain it.

This anti-Augustinian view of man's nature and capacities recurs even more markedly amongst the humanists of early *quattrocento* Florence. They start by insisting that men do in fact have the power to attain the highest excellence. It is at this point that, by way of underlining this commitment, they invent one of the most characteristic *genres* of Renaissance moral thought – the *genre* devoted to extolling 'the excellence and dignity of man'. The most famous example is of course the oration on this theme composed by Pico della Mirandola in 1484 (p. 217). Thirty years before this, however, Giannozzo Manetti had already produced a very similar treatise in the form of a point-by-point rebuttal of Innocent III's deeply pessimistic vision of *The Misery of Man* (Trinkaus, 1970, p. 177). Manetti's immensely confident reply closes on a note later sounded repeatedly throughout the Italian Renaissance: a note of almost strident confidence in man's 'unmeasurable dignity and excellence' and in 'the extraordinary endowments and rare privileges' of his nature (pp. 102, 103).

The next claim the Florentine writers stress is that, since men are capable of attaining such excellence, they have a duty to make the pursuit of *virtus* the main aim of their lives. Salutati announces this commitment as early as 1369, assuring a correspondent of that year that 'others can glorify wealth, dignities and power', but 'I always reserve my admiration for *virtus* itself' (1, 79). Manetti takes up the same theme in his treatise on *The Dignity of Man*, alluding to Cicero's idea of a connection between the true *vir* and the pursuit of *virtus*, and ending with the injunction, 'Let your chief aim be *virtus*' (p. 102). And Alberti summarises the outlook underlying these demands when he concludes his first dialogue on *The Family* by proclaiming that *virtus* itself 'is nothing else than perfect and well-developed nature' (p. 80).

Finally, the humanists turn this view of man's capacities into an urgent patriotic plea. Having come to regard the Roman Republic as the greatest repository of *virtus* in the history of the world, they bewail the fact that the modern *Regnum Italicum* has fallen away so gravely from its pristine heights, and call upon their fellow-countrymen to restore the ancient glories of their native land. This demand – often expressed as a hope – is already central to Petrarch's discussion of *virtus*, and is beautifully embodied in his famous *canzone* 'My Italy', which includes the verse (in Edward Dacres' fine seventeenth-century translation):[1]

> Virtue 'gainst fury shall advance the fight
> And it i' the combat soon shall put to flight;
> For the old Roman valour is not dead,
> Nor in the Italians' breasts extinguished.

Salutati takes up the same battle-cry in a public letter of 1377 addressed to the people of Rome, in which he asks them to 'recall the ancient *virtus*' and resist the tyrannical attempts of the Papacy 'to bring about the desolation of Italy'.[2] And Bruni in his *Eulogy* agrees that ancient Rome exhibited 'more instances of *virtus*' than 'all the other Republics of all time', and goes on to express the much more sanguine hope that some of this spirit may have been born again in Florence, which he praises 'not only for its splendour and nobility', but 'also for its *virtus* and the things it has achieved' (pp. 244, 251).

THE POWERS OF THE 'VIR VIRTUTIS'

To assert that men are capable of reaching the highest excellence is to imply that they must be capable of overcoming any obstacles to the attainment of this goal. The humanists willingly recognise that their view of human nature commits them to just such an optimistic analysis of man's freedom and powers, and in consequence go on to offer an exhilarating account of the *vir virtutis* as a creative social force, able to shape his own destiny and remake his social world to fit his own desires.

They begin by reverting to the classical belief that the human predic-

---

[1] Dacres produced this version in the course of his 1640 translation of Machiavelli's *The Prince*, which ends by citing these lines. I have adopted the Dacres version from George Bull's translation of *The Prince*, p. 138. For the original verse, see Petrarch, *Il Canzoniere*, ed. Scherillo, p. 279.
[2] For this letter see Salutati, *Epistolae*, ed. Rigacci, vol. II, pp. 141, 143.

ament is best envisaged as a struggle between man's will and fortune's wilfulness. The Romans had worshipped the goddess Fortuna as the daughter of Jupiter himself (Patch, 1922, p. 133). They always conceded her a great power over human affairs, portraying her with a wheel on which the fates of men are kept turning by her sheer caprice. They insisted, however, that her sway is not inexorable, since she can always be wooed and even subdued by a man of true *virtus*. It was this classical apposition between *virtus* and *fortuna* – with the accompanying belief that fortune favours the brave – that the Renaissance moralists revived. One of the most brilliant sketches of the outlook on life they were thus led to adopt has been given by Burckhardt in discussing the character of Alberti in *The Civilization of the Renaissance* (Burckhardt, 1960, p. 87). Born under the slur of illegitimacy, the constraints of poverty, the indignity of exile and the threat of ill-health, Alberti treated all these blows of fortune as nothing more than a series of challenges, setting his will to overcome them one by one. The outcome was that he succeeded by his great *virtus* in totally subduing the onslaughts of Fortuna, snatching the highest prize of immortal fame and glory away from her envious grasp.

The recovery of this classical dramatisation of the human condition again represents an almost Pelagian departure from the prevailing assumptions of Augustinian Christianity. St Augustine's definitive attack on Roman polytheism in Book IV of *The City of God* had actually focussed (after discussing Jupiter and the minor deities) on the twin goddesses of Virtus and Fortuna (Vol. II, pp. 65, 71). He found two cardinal errors underlying the transformation of these forces into objects of worship. One was the fact that the deification of fortune involved denying the beneficent power of God's providence. St Augustine continually insists in his reply that it is by 'divine providence' that 'human kingdoms are set up', a process that can never happen 'rashly or at random', since it is God himself, and 'not Fortuna, the goddess of luck' whose will is involved (II, pp. 125, 135). The other mistake is taken to lie in failing to appreciate that, since the whole world is in fact governed inexorably by God's providence, there can be no question of carving out one's own fate in the manner presupposed by the classical idea of a combat between *fortuna* and *virtus*. The truth is that, if men prove capable of achieving greatness, this is only because God has willed it: the power involved 'is not a goddess, but the gift of God' (II, p. 71).

Both these claims were destined to become pervasive assumptions of medieval moral and political thought (Pocock, 1975, pp. 39–43). As late as the fourteenth century, we still find them being unequivocally endorsed by the Florentine *dictatores*, and even by Dante in his political works. When Latini discusses 'the goods of Fortune' in his *Books of Treasure*, he insists on the equation between fortune and providence, repudiating the classical contention 'that fortune is blind' on the grounds that 'we must rather believe what wise men say, that it is God by whom the powerful are thrown down and the feeble lifted up' (p. 279). When Dante speaks in his *Monarchy* of the means by which the Romans 'gained sway throughout the world', he is adamant that the providence of God and not the will of men is the fundamental determinant of events. The belief that the Romans 'owed their supremacy simply to armed force' is stigmatised as 'a superficial view', since it fails to recognise 'the convincing marks of divine providence' lying behind their rise to power' (p. 29). And when he later discusses the power of fortune in the seventh Canto of the *Inferno*, he still upholds the same essentially Boethian idea of Fortuna as a heavenly instrument, a 'general minister and guide' ordained by God to dispose of 'the goods of the world' (p. 73).

When we come to Petrarch and his successors, however, we encounter a deliberate attempt to reconstruct the classical image of man's predicament which Augustine had tried to obliterate. The humanists first of all revert to claiming that, where man's capacity for action is limited, the controlling factor at work is nothing more than the capricious power of fortune, not the inexorable force of providence. Alberti furnishes perhaps the clearest evidence of this crucial conceptual shift. When he speaks in his *Three Dialogues* of Fortuna's terrible powers, he addresses her as the 'supreme goddess', claiming that she alone 'sends the Gods to heaven' and 'uses her lackeys, when she wishes, to depose them' (p. 33). And when he discusses the role of Fortuna in his dialogues on *The Family*, he again portrays her as the major force guiding and interrupting human affairs. He not only acknowledges how far 'we know through experience' that Fortuna affects our lives; he also describes her engulfing powers in the same figure of speech later made famous by Machiavelli in *The Prince*, speaking of 'the waves of the times and the impetuous flood of fortune' as the major obstacles to our happiness (pp. 106, 143).

This sense of fortune's capricious tyranny sometimes induced in the humanists a mood of extreme pessimism. We encounter this tone above all in Poggio, and especially towards the end of his life, when he even wrote a treatise entitled *The Misery of the Human Condition*, bewailing 'the license and power of fortune over human affairs' (p. 89: cf. Trinkaus, 1940, pp. 84–92). But the main effect of reverting to this classical picture of the human predicament was to generate amongst the humanists a new and exciting sense of man's ability to struggle against the tide of fortune, to channel and subdue its power, and in this way to become, at least to some extent, the master of his own fate.

One important reflection of this optimism can be seen in the novel and striking emphasis the humanists begin to place on the concept of the freedom of the will. This emerges most clearly in their treatises on the dignity of man. Hitherto most discussions of man's excellence, and his unique place in the universe, had tended to concentrate on the fact that he is the possessor of an immortal soul. The beginnings of a new attitude can first be discerned in Petrarch's account of *The Remedies of Both Kinds of Fortune* (Trinkaus, 1970, pp. 179, 190–3). After this the humanists increasingly shift their ground towards an acceptance of Petrarch's contention that, alone of all creation, man may be said to have the capacity to control his own destiny. One of the main reasons Manetti gives for wishing to commend the dignity of man is his ability to mould his own fate by 'the many operations of intelligence and will' (p. 193). And one of the central themes of Pico della Mirandola's *Oration on the Dignity of Man* is the idea of the individual's free and creative powers. Pico begins by imagining that, when God created man, He addressed him and explained his unique position in the universe. All other beings, God is said to have revealed, are 'limited and constrained within the bounds of laws prescribed by us'. Man alone is 'constrained by no limits' and endowed with his 'own free will'. And the reason God gives for having placed humanity 'at the world's centre' in this way is the desire that men should be able 'with freedom of choice' to create and mould their own characters (p. 225).

The same commitment is reflected in the confidence with which the humanists begin to deny that everything in the world is providentially ordained. This soon becomes evident in their approach to writing history, as Green has recently observed in his study of the Florentine chroniclers of the fourteenth century. The idea of equating Fortune with Providence and treating it as a lawlike force – which we still encounter in Compagni – begins to give way to a sense that Fortune amounts to little more than chance, and to a corresponding sense that human responsibility and choice play a far greater role in the flux of events than earlier historians had supposed.[1] Soon afterwards the same outlook begins to appear in a number of humanist discussions of religious belief. A strong sense of man's freedom clearly underlies Pico's devastating attack on the alleged science of astrology, and is fully explicit in a work such as Alberti's dialogue *On Religion*, in which the idea that 'fate or destiny' constitutes 'the source of our sorrows' is firmly rejected on the grounds that 'men are themselves

---

[1] See Green, 1972, esp. pp. 57–9. Cf. also Gilmore, 1956, p. 59. For Compagni's equation between Fortune and Providence, see pp. 74, 150, 234, etc.

the cause of their own afflictions' (pp. 29–30: cf. Garin, 1965, pp. 108–11).

The humanists summarise all these assumptions in the form of a doctrine which Garin has characterised as 'the typical motif of the Renaissance': the claim that it is always open to men to exercise their *virtus* in such a way as to overcome the power of *Fortuna* (Garin, 1965, p. 61; cf. Kristeller, 1965, pp. 59–60). One of the finest statements of this central theme occurs in the Preface to Alberti's dialogues on *The Family*. He begins by raising the question of why so many ancient families 'which were once most happy and renowned are now extinct'. Many people, he notes, believe that this is due to the power of Fortune, 'with her fickleness and caprices'. They imagine that she is capable of taking 'large families of virtuous men', who are 'adorned with great dignity, fame, praise, authority and refinement' and throwing them 'into poverty, solitude and misery' (p. 27). His own view, however, is that such explanations often 'blame Fortune unjustly' (p. 28). He insists on the far more heroic and typically humanist view that 'most of the time men are themselves responsible for whatever good or ill befalls them' (p. 28). So he concludes that it is only when great families have lost their *virtus* that Fortune proves able to conquer them. The moral is that as long as we retain our 'manly *virtù*', it will always be possible, 'even though invidious Fortune oppose us', to continue to reach for 'the highest pinnacle of glory' and to perform 'the greatest and most sublime deeds' (p. 32).

This emphasis on man's creative powers came to be one of the most influential as well as characteristic doctrines of Renaissance humanism. It first of all helped to foster a new interest in the individual personality. It came to seem possible for man to use his freedom to become the architect and the explorer of his own character. This in turn helps to explain the growing psychological complexity of much sixteenth-century literature, as well as the passion for introspection which was later to prompt Montaigne to devote the whole of his creative energies to the investigation of his own nature. The same outlook also helped to popularise a new view of man's relationship with his environment. The idea began to gain ground that man might be able to use his powers to bring about a transformation of the physical world. At one level this gave rise to the dramatic conception of the *magus*, the benign magician who employs his occult arts in order to uncover the secrets of nature. This Faustian figure is the real hero of Pico's *Oration on the Dignity of Man*, in which he is hailed as a true philosopher and urged to bring forth 'the miracles concealed in the recesses of the world, in the depths of nature, and in the storehouses and mysteries of God' (p. 249). At a more mundane level, the same emphasis on man's natural creativity gave rise to the no less influential doctrine of the moral significance of work. We are accustomed to think of this as a Puritan legacy, but it is arguable that part of the attraction of the Puritan glorification of labour at the end of the sixteenth century arose out of the fact that it resonated with a similar doctrine propagated by the Renaissance humanists over a century before. Manetti already assumes that the special dignity of man is closely connected with his capacity for work. He declares that 'without activity there is no pleasure' and adds that 'just as some toil is involved in every activity, just as surely do we find pleasure equal to and even greater than the labour in any one of our pursuits' (p. 95). The same gospel is preached even more fervently by Alberti in his dialogues on *The Family*. We are instructed to 'abhor idleness and laziness', and assured that we can never hope 'to achieve honours and dignity' without 'the loving study of excellent arts, without assiduous work, without striving in difficult manly tasks' (p. 138). As with Manetti, the praise of man's powers culminates in a recognisably Puritan creed: on the one hand we are warned that 'there is nothing that gives rise to dishonour and infamy as much as idleness'; and on the other we are reminded that 'man was not born to lie down and rot in idleness, but to stand up and act' (pp. 138, 139; cf. Garin, 1965, pp. 43-4).

Having argued that it is possible to aspire to the highest excellence, the humanists conclude their account of the *vir virtutis* by explaining why it is also appropriate for men to devote their lives to the pursuit of this goal. This leads them to describe the kinds of reward a man of true *virtus* should expect to receive from the full exercise of his noblest capacities. It is a remarkable measure of the extent to which men were by this time felt to possess God-like qualities that the humanists express this sense of what is due to a *vir virtutis* in precisely the same language later used in the Authorised Version of the Bible to describe what is due to God: in each case what is said to be owed to such unsurpassable excellence is the tribute of honour, glory and praise.

Once again this perspective involved a direct attack on the assumptions of Augustinian Christianity (Lida de Malkiel, 1968, p. 89). St Augustine had roundly declared in *The City of God* that 'the love of praise is a vice', that the quest for honour is 'a pestilential notion' and that 'there is no true virtue where virtue is subordinated to human glory' (Vol. II, pp. 207, 209, 243). The reason given for these judgments is that such a worldly scale of values reverses the proper priorities of Christian life. 'If the passion for glory is stronger in the heart than the fear or love of God', this inevitably makes it a great 'foe to pious faith'. The only salvation lies in ensuring that 'the passion for glory should be surpassed by the love of righteousness' (II, p. 211).

This warning against worldliness again became one of the most powerful voices in later Christian moral thought. If we turn to Innocent III's discussion of *The Misery of Man*, for example, we encounter the strongest possible denunciation of the figure of 'the ambitious man', the man who 'lays violent claims to honours' because of his 'unbridled vanity' and 'morbid desire to dominate' (p. 49). And even in such later treatises as Aquinas's account of *The Rule of Princes*, we still find essentially the same scale of values being upheld. Aquinas regards it as a grave mistake to think of 'worldly honour and glory' as a 'sufficient reward for those in kingly office' (p. 241). Citing St Augustine's attack on the pursuit of 'worldly and fleeting honour', he continues to insist that good rulers 'must carry out their duties not out of ardour for empty glory but out of love of eternal blessedness' (pp. 243–4).

The moral and political writings of Petrarch and his successors again offer a completely contrasting point of view. As with the discussion of *virtus*, however, it is important not to confuse their classical perspective with a purely pagan outlook on life. They continue to insist on the fundamental Christian doctrine that the vices are to be avoided simply because they are evil, and the virtues pursued for no other reason than that they are good in themselves. As Alberti insists in *The Family*, we must learn to dismiss 'ugly subterfuges' as 'improper for a man', and to follow the pathway of virtue simply because it 'has its own great reward' and hence 'makes itself praised perforce' (pp. 41, 301).

Such saving clauses, however, to the effect that virtue constitutes its own reward scarcely amount to more than priggish asides. They do nothing to hinder the development of the full-blooded humanist belief that the appropriate goal for a man of *virtus*, and the fundamental reason for devoting oneself to a life of the highest excellence, is the hope of acquiring the greatest possible amount of honour, glory and worldly fame. One of the most formative moments in the history of this idea occurred in 1341, the year in which Petrarch finally achieved his long-standing ambition of being crowned as 'a great poet and historian' at Rome (Wilkins, 1943, pp. 155, 158–9, 171). His response, after receiving the laurel wreath, took the form of a speech on the vocation of the poet, in the course of which he declared that the highest aspiration for a man of letters must be to make himself 'worthy of glory' and thus to gain 'immortality for his name' (Wilkins, 1943, p. 174). During the next generation this attitude was developed in the hands of Petrarch's followers into a full-scale ideology connecting the nature of man, the aims of education and the proper goals of human life. One of the finest summaries of the resulting outlook is again to be found in the pages of Alberti's dialogues on *The Family*. Alberti begins with the assumption that 'Nature has instilled a great desire for praise and glory in everyone who is not completely listless and dull of mind' (p. 84). This leads him to argue that the principal aim of education must be to guide young men 'in the ways of honour and praise', leading them in 'the path of virtue and honour' and showing them that this is also 'the path to glory and fame' (pp. 40, 81). The value of this training is of course said to be that it produces the fully manly man, the true *vir virtutis* who finally comes to prize 'the beauty of honour, the delights of fame and the divineness of glory' above everything else in life (p. 202).

The swaggering figure of the Renaissance gentleman continued to be held up as an ideal, in spite of Machiavelli's scepticism, at least until the end of the sixteenth century (cf. Bryson, 1935, pp. 1–14). And a number of assumptions about his education have remained with us ever since. University students in the twentieth century are still described as pursuing 'honours', and at the end of their course they are characteristically rewarded with glory, proceeding to their degrees *cum laude* or even *summa cum laude*. Apart from such quaint survivals, however, the ideology surrounding the *vir virtutis* was largely swept away, at least in northern Europe, by the middle of the seventeenth century. With his bristling code of honour and his continual thirst for glory, the typical hero of the Renaissance began to appear slightly comical in his wilful disregard for the natural instinct of self-preservation – an instinct stoutly defended by Falstaff in his famous denunciation of 'honour' for urging men into battle without showing them how to 'take away the grief of a wound'.[1] After this unashamed dismissal of the central ideal, it was not long before the entire structure of assumptions about virtue, honour and glory began to collapse – undermined by Rochefoucauld's ironic disbelief and Hobbes's rival theory about the universality of self-interest (cf. Hirschman, 1977, esp. pp. 9–12).

THE HUMANISTS AND THE RENAISSANCE

So far we have considered the extent to which the efflorescence of social and political theory in early *quattrocento* Florence can be seen as an outgrowth of two earlier intellectual traditions: that of the medieval *dictatores* and that of the Petrarchan humanists of the later fourteenth century. This is not to say, however, that the writings of the Renaissance

---

[1] *Henry IV*, Pt. I, V, i, 134.

humanists can be adequately explained simply by treating them as a continuation and development of these existing strands of thought. The caveat is important, since the suggestion that a smooth line of descent can be traced from the *dictatores* to the humanists sometimes seems to underlie Kristeller's influential account of the evolution of Renaissance culture. He speaks, for example, of the 'continuity of thought which connects the Middle Ages with the Renaissance', and declares that 'the period of the Renaissance' must to a large extent be regarded as 'a direct continuation of the Middle Ages' (Kristeller, 1956, pp. 38, 359, cf. Seigel, 1966, p. 43).

Kristeller's approach has of course proved an extremely fruitful one. It prevents us from accepting the traditional but misleading picture of the Renaissance as a period of sudden and explosive cultural change (cf. Ferguson, 1948, pp. 195–252). This remains a necessary corrective, for while it is a commonplace to speak of the isolation of the Renaissance from its medieval roots as the main defect of Burckhardt's classic analysis, it is remarkable how far a similar set of assumptions continues to underlie a great deal of recent scholarship on Renaissance thought. Hans Baron, for example, still insists on marking a sharp break 'around 1400', claiming that while a writer like Salutati is still in some ways 'strongly medieval', the appearance soon afterwards of a work like Bruni's *Eulogy* shows us that 'the threshold between the medieval and the Renaissance has been crossed'.[1] A further merit of Kristeller's viewpoint is that it serves to assign a precise and non-anachronistic meaning to the term 'humanism'. Previously this concept had generally been used with uncontrollable vagueness to refer to a supposed 'new philosophical movement' characteristic of the Renaissance (cf. Kristeller, 1956, p. 574). Kristeller has decisively punctured this myth by showing – as we have already seen – that most of the so-called 'humanists' were in fact professional teachers and exponents of the rhetorical arts, and were thus concerned with an aspect of Italian civic culture which was neither novel nor essentially philosophical in character (cf. Kristeller, 1962a and Campana, 1946).

It is arguable, however, that one effect of this approach has been to give rise to an oversimplified explanation of *quattrocento* moral and political thought. It has become fashionable in the first place to lay a somewhat exaggerated emphasis on purely 'internal' explanations of the rise of humanism. Seigel appears to assume, for example, that once we have established the close dependence of the humanists on earlier intellectual traditions, we have thereby shown that 'civic sentiment and direct political

[1] See Baron, 1966, pp. 8, 105, 449. Germino, 1972, p. 1, similarly speaks of 'a profound break in the continuity of Western political speculation' in the Renaissance, and Pocock, 1975, p. 52, claims to find a 'decisive break' around the year 1400.

involvement were not determining elements in early humanism' (Seigel, 1966, p. 10). And Robey has similarly argued in his study of Vergerio that, since Vergerio's 'vindication of the Roman Republic' can allegedly be attributed to a 'predominantly literary inspiration', it follows that we must view with 'a certain scepticism' any suggestion about 'the possible relations between the humanist movement and the political circumstances' of early *quattrocento* Florence (Robey, 1973, pp. 24, 33).

It seems misleadingly one-sided, however, to suppose that an 'internal' history of humanism can hope to serve as a sufficient explanation of its development, and thus that the sort of 'external' explanations favoured by Baron can be altogether ruled out. It is of course true, as we have already seen, that most of the arguments propounded by the so-called 'civic humanists' about the concept of political liberty had already been sketched by a number of earlier scholastic as well as pre-humanist writers in the course of the previous two centuries. But we still need to ask why it happened that these particular arguments were revived in one particular generation – and with such particular intensity – at the beginning of the fifteenth century. Even if we reply (as Seigel does in the case of Leonardo Bruni) that the early *quattrocento* humanists were merely deploying a traditional set of literary skills in the hope of commending themselves to the rulers of the Florentine Republic, we still need to ask what made it rational for them to assume that these were the appropriate skills to display if their aim was in fact to attract the attention of the Florentine government as a prospective employer of their talents (cf. Seigel, 1966, p. 25). The answer it seems most plausible to give is that, in reviving and extending the available traditions of Republican political theory, they may in part have been prompted by a patriotic desire – or by a wish to seem to have the patriotic desire – to celebrate and defend the liberties of Florence against the continuing threat of domination by Visconti Milan (cf. Holmes, 1969, p. 101).

There is another and more important point at which Kristeller's account of the relationship between the humanist movement and the intellectual life of medieval Italy has tended to give rise to an oversimplified understanding of Renaissance political thought. As we have seen, two distinct intellectual traditions had arisen in the Italian universities in the later Middle Ages, each of which had evolved its own approach to learning by the start of the fourteenth century. One tradition had grown out of the indigenous and already venerable study of the rhetorical arts. The other had developed out of the scholastic curriculum, first imported into Italy from northern Europe in the latter part of the thirteenth century. Now there is no doubt – as Kristeller has shown – that there are strong lines of continuity between the medieval rhetoricians and the *quattrocento* humanists. But it would be highly misleading to imply that there are any similar connections to be traced between the humanists and the exponents of scholastic philosophy. It is evident on the contrary that the humanists crystallised their identity as a self-conscious intellectual movement in part at least out of a growing hostility towards the increasing popularity of scholastic studies. So it is arguable that the development of the humanist movement arose at least as much out of a reaction against, and a conscious rejection of, this newer intellectual orthodoxy as it did out of a capacity to deepen and extend the existing traditions of instruction in the Italian universities.[1]

Kristeller and his followers have not of course failed to emphasise the hostility of the humanists to the rise of scholasticism in Italy. But they have perhaps tended to underestimate its substantive significance. They have generally claimed that, as the exponents of a form of instruction which had always enjoyed a central position in the Italian universities, the humanists were merely expressing a conservative resentment at the possibility that the growth of scholasticism might threaten their own position and prestige. They accordingly responded by assuring their students that the traditional curriculum centred on the rhetorical arts was 'more humane' (*humaniora*) and more suited to a truly educated man than the pursuit of fashionable scholastic quiddities (Kristeller, 1956, pp. 563, 572). As Kristeller has argued, this suggests a purely superficial clash between the humanists and their scholastic rivals. So he dismisses 'the humanist attack' as little more than a case of 'departmental rivalry', and insists that it went with an undiminished willingness to leave scholasticism unchallenged within its own intellectual sphere (Kristeller, 1956, pp. 263–4, 577). For all their 'noisy advertisement', he maintains, the humanists were never concerned to 'deny the existence or the validity' of scholastic studies, and showed themselves quite prepared to settle into 'a long period of peaceful co-existence' with scholasticism, in which 'both traditions developed side by side' (Kristeller, 1956, pp. 563, 574, 576, 577)

There is of course a valuable corrective embodied in this insistence on what Kristeller describes as a widespread tendency 'to exaggerate the opposition of the humanists to scholasticism' (Kristeller, 1956, p. 561). It has sometimes been assumed that, with the triumph of humanism, the study of scholastic philosophy was all but outlawed from the Italian universities (e.g. Lecler, 1960, II, p. 12). Kristeller has done much to reveal that such an impression is little more than a reflection of successful

---

[1] This point, and its implications for Kristeller's account of the rise of humanism, has been very well brought out by Gray, 1963.

humanist propaganda. The presence of such major figures as Pomponazzi and George of Trebizond is enough to indicate that Aristotelian philosophy continued to flourish and develop throughout the later *quattrocento*, while the writings of a humanist like Manetti serve to reveal how far it was possible to combine a classical outlook with the pursuit of a number of essentially scholastic interests (cf. Seigel, 1968, pp. 226–41, Monfasini, 1976, esp. p. 156).

This perspective begins to become misleading, however, as soon as we are asked to suppose that scholasticism and humanism simply 'co-existed as different branches of culture' throughout the Renaissance (Kristeller, 1956, p. 580). This underestimates the growing confidence with which the humanists were in fact willing to invade scholastic fields of study, to denounce their rivals for continuing to follow benighted methods, and so to insist with increasing imperialism on the need for the special techniques of humanism to be put to use throughout the entire spectrum of the intellectual disciplines. It seems essential for this range of considerations to be given much greater prominence if a satisfactory explanation for the rise of a distinctively humanist moral and political theory is to be reached (cf. Weisinger, 1945a).

The humanists first of all launched a direct assault on scholasticism at the methodological level, focussing in particular on the scholastic approach to the interpretation of the Roman Law. They based this attack on their key belief that all the texts of the ancient world should be studied and appraised as far as possible in their own terms. This commitment made them highly critical of Bartolus and his followers, whose very different methods had become established as an orthodoxy throughout the Italian law-schools in the course of the fourteenth century. As we have seen, the cardinal principle of Bartolist interpretation was the claim that the ancient law-books should be analysed in just such a way as to make them speak as directly as possible to contemporary legal and political experience. This wilfully anachronistic approach in turn caused the humanists to treat the entire school of Post-Glossators with withering scorn. One of the earliest and most vitriolic of their denunciations occurs in a letter from Lorenzo Valla to his fellow humanist Pier Candido Decembrio, in which Valla comments on Bartolus's own treatise on tokens of honour. Valla pronounces it 'completely unworthy' that books of this kind should have 'so many admirers' when they are 'so utterly ignorant' and 'so extra-ordinarily ineptly written' (1, p. 633). He begins by ridiculing Bartolus, Baldus, Accursius 'and all that tribe of men' for writing 'in a barbarian language' which is 'not the language of the Romans at all', as a result of which they sound like so many honking geese (1, p. 633). And he ends by adding that, when it comes to questions of historical meaning and context, Bartolus shows an even more scandalous lack of understanding, since 'he corrupts the laws to be interpreted with his perversity', he 'asserts many other things without foundation', and he lays himself open to censure at literally thousands of points (1, pp. 635–6, 643; cf. Kelley, 1970, p. 41).

This rejection of scholastic methodology played a key role in helping to establish a genuinely historical jurisprudence. Valla's insistence on the need to treat Justinian's Code as an artifact from an alien culture was reiterated in Italy by Crinito and especially Poliziano, and adopted soon afterwards with particular enthusiasm in France, where the pioneering works of Budé and Alciato helped to popularise a purely historical approach to the law, a method later extended by Le Douaren, Connan, Baudouin and the formidable Cujas. (Kelley, 1966, pp. 186–7; cf. Kisch, 1961). As we shall later see, this movement was to have a profound impact on the development of sixteenth-century social and political thought. The recognition of the ancient law-books as the product of a wholly different society helped to lay the foundations for a comparative study of different legal systems. And this in turn provided Jean Bodin with the historical materials as well as the intellectual perspective out of which he was able to fashion his 'science' of politics.

As well as impugning their methodology, the humanists went on to denounce the characteristic preoccupations of their scholastic rivals. The key principle they brought to bear at this point was their insistence that philosophy must show itself to be of some practical use in social and political life. This in turn led them to repudiate the scholastic approach to the study of philosophy in two distinct ways. First they challenged the Schoolmen for engaging in largely trivial enquiries, paying far too little attention to the central question of how we ought to behave. As Petrarch complains in his treatise *On his own Ignorance*, the scholastics are always prepared to tell us many things which, 'even if they were true', would 'not contribute anything whatsoever' to enrich our lives. But they are quite content to remain in complete ignorance of such vital concerns as the question of 'man's nature, the purposes for which we are born, and whereunto we travel' (pp. 58–9). This attack on what Petrarch regarded as the 'arrogant ignorance' of the Schoolmen was reinforced by all the early *quattrocento* humanists (p. 116). One of the most biting of their criticisms, as one might expect, again came from Lorenzo Valla. Having agreed to deliver an oration *In Praise of St Thomas Aquinas*, Valla proceeded to turn his title into a sneering irony, arguing that while we must concede the Angelic Doctor his saintly virtues, we cannot avoid noticing that 'the holy man's knowledge' was 'for the most part of trifling consequence', since he devoted himself almost entirely to 'the petty reasonings of dialecticians' without ever seeing that such preoccupations are mere 'obstacles in the way of better kinds of knowledge' (pp. 22, 23, 24; cf. Gray, 1965).

The other charge the humanists make is that, even when the Schoolmen concern themselves with social and political issues, they merely reveal their incapacity to deal with them. They remain content to develop their usual range of distinctions in their usual barbarous style. So they fail to recognise the fundamental need for philosophy to be combined with the pursuit of eloquence if it is to have any hope of persuading our wills and thus coming to exercise a beneficial influence on political life (Gray, 1963, p. 505; cf. Struever, 1970, pp. 60–1). As Petrarch tells us in *His Own Ignorance*, 'I snarl at the stupid Aristotelians' when they 'consume their time in learning to know virtue instead of acquiring it'. For this leads them to miss the crucial point that (as he puts it in a famous epigram) 'it is better to will the good than to know the truth' (pp. 105, 107). Again this line of attack was carried on with renewed vigour by the early *quattrocento* humanists. Salutati, for example, dismisses the logic of the Schoolmen on the grounds that it merely 'proves in order to teach', while declaring that the study of the humanities is able to discharge a far more useful function, since it 'persuades in order to guide' (Emerton, 1925, p. 358). And Bruni in a similar style devotes much of the first part of his *Dialogue* to assailing 'the arrogance joined with the ignorance' of the scholastics, who 'try to propagate philosophy while knowing nothing of letters' and in consequence 'utter as many solecisms as they do words' (p. 56).

These denunciations again played a positive role in helping to crystallise some of the most characteristic values and attitudes of the humanists. We can now see, for example, how it happened that, in spite of their strong literary bent, the humanists left a legacy of increasing interest in the experimental sciences and the practical arts. With their rejection of scholastic abstractions, they became increasingly anxious to maintain that all knowledge ought to be 'for use' – an outlook which may be said to reach its apotheosis in the work of Francis Bacon. Some of the later humanists were even prepared to maintain that this touchstone should be applied to the most abstract philosophical enquiries previously monopolised by the Schoolmen. The most dramatic instance is provided by the logical writings of Pierre Ramus (1515–72), who set himself to dismantle the entire fabric of Aristotelian logic on the grounds that it was not properly 'designed for use', and proceeded to elaborate a new and purportedly more 'natural' set of logical categories 'which may be put to use in teaching, learning or practising any discipline or art' (cf. Gilbert, 1960, p. 135).

The same animus against the alleged remoteness of scholastic studies also helps to account for some of the characteristic emphases of humanist social and political thought. It helps in the first place to explain the growing belief that a life devoted to pure leisure and contemplation (*otium*) is far less likely to be of value – or even to foster wisdom – than a life in which the pursuit of useful activity (*negotium*) is most highly prized. As Hans Baron has stressed, this argument was first wholeheartedly embraced by the Florentine humanists of the early fifteenth century (cf. Baron, 1966, pp. 121–9). Dante had still thought of wisdom as a purely intellectual rather than a moral virtue, and had made it his highest aim in *The Divine Comedy* to be led by Beatrice towards a contemplation of the divine (Rice, 1958, p. 30). Petrarch had reacted even more strongly against the alleged value of *negotium*, in spite of the fact that his great hero Cicero had warmly espoused it. He composed a treatise in 1346 in praise of *The Life of Solitude*, and later addressed a strong rebuke to Cicero in his letters *On Familiar Matters* for having wished in his older years 'to give up the *otium* appropriate to your age and profession' in order to return to a life of politics with its 'involvement in so many useless quarrels'.[1] When we come to the early *quattrocento* humanists, however, we find an increasing emphasis on the belief that a life of wisdom must include prudent action as well as contemplation, and a corresponding insistence that a life of pure *otium* can never be appropriate even for a poet or a sage (cf. Rice, 1958, p. 30). One of the earliest and most pointed expressions of this new scale of values can be found in a letter written by Vergerio in 1394 (p. 436). He imagines himself to be Cicero, replying to Petrarch's expressions of disgust at his desire to keep up his involvement in political affairs. He makes Cicero insist that, since it is always a man's duty to strive 'to be held dear first by his own country and thereafter by all mankind', this makes it entirely justifiable for him to have wished 'to remain at all times engaged in *negotium*' (p. 439). Within a generation this explicit rejection of the Aristotelian belief that a life of *otium* constitutes the highest state of being had come to be one of the most strongly entrenched humanist values. When Bruni, for example, wrote his *Life of Dante* some thirty years later, he treated it as one of the poet's finest qualities (which he blames Boccaccio for having overlooked in his biography) that he managed to retain his usefulness as a citizen even in the midst of his most intensive studies. This proves, Bruni adds, that it is a 'false opinion' of 'ignorant persons' to hold 'that no one is a student save he who buries himself in solitude and ease'. The truth is, he concludes, that 'to estrange and absent oneself from society is peculiar to those whose poor minds unfit them for knowledge of any kind' (p. 84).

[1] See Petrarch, *On Familiar Matters*, pp. 226–7 nd cf. *The Life of Solitude*, p. 109.

Finally, this reaction against the pure speculation of the scholastics, with their consequent lack of concern for civic life, also helps to account for the special emphasis which the early *quattrocento* humanists place on the importance of addressing their writings to the whole body of their fellow citizens. This again represents a radical departure from the intellectual traditions they had inherited. As we have already seen, the tendency even amongst their closest intellectual forebears, the early *dictatores*, had always been to address their treatises not to the citizens at large, but rather to *podestà* and other elected magistrates. Something of the same outlook can still be seen in Salutati, who composed *A Treatise on Tyrants* as late as 1400 in which he consistently adopted the ruler's point of view, stressing the dangers inherent in any justification of tyrannicide and even defending Julius Caesar against the charge that he had ruled as a tyrant.[1] When we come to Salutati's followers, however, we find them exhibiting a strong interest in reaching a different and much wider kind of audience. Bruni begins the second part of his *Dialogue* (p. 78) with an implied rebuke to Salutati for continuing to endorse a monarchical point of view, and later makes it a proud boast in his *Oration* that the Florentines 'hate the haughtiness and disdain of powerful men with great vehemence' and 'look for *virtus* as well as probity in every citizen' (p. 3). And Alberti offers perhaps the most confident summary of the new outlook in his dialogues on *The Family*. He scorns the idea of acting as an adviser to princes, arguing that they are 'idle, do not practice any honourable profession' and are in any case barely educable, since they habitually 'give in to all their appetites' (p. 259). He instead puts his trust in, and addresses himself wholeheartedly to, the entire citizen-body of Florence, advising the heads of ordinary households on how to 'attend to affairs of state', how to 'bear the burden of public office', and how to ensure that they 'preserve the tranquillity' and 'safeguard the welfare' of the Republic of which they are both the rulers and the ruled (p. 186).

The outcome of this attack on scholasticism, with the self-definitions it entailed, was that the humanists finally came to adopt a new vision of history, together with a remarkably assured sense of their own historical importance. This again involved them in questioning one of the key assumptions of Augustinian Christianity (cf. Mommsen, 1959c). St Augustine had viewed the march of history essentially as a linear development, a gradual unfolding of God's purposes for the world. The humanists by contrast revert to the claim originally advanced by Aristotle in Book V of *The Politics*, and reiterated by Polybius and Cicero, that the course of

[1] See pp. 81, 91–3, 94–100; cf. also Witt, 1969, pp. 434, 439–40.

human events can be shown to proceed in a series of recurring cycles. They derived this insight not merely from their ancient authorities, but also from their conviction that a golden age in antiquity, at first blotted out by an intervening period of scholastic obscurantism, had now begun to revive once again with their own recovery of the glories of the classical world. So we find Salutati commenting with approval, as early as 1379, on the text at the beginning of Ecclesiastes which assures us that 'there is nothing new under the sun' (Emerton, 1925, p. 304). He admits that 'nothing returns in precisely the same form', but he points out that 'we see daily some image of the past renewed', and he predicts that 'everything that now is shall return again' (Emerton, 1925, pp. 303, 305).

With this new vision of the past, the humanists acquired a correspondingly elevated sense of their own position in the ever-changing cycle of events. They first of all invented the concept of the 'middle' ages – which they also thought of as the 'dark' ages – to describe the period lying between the achievements of classical antiquity and the restoration of its grandeur in their own time. This too involved them in reversing a prevailing assumption about the correct way of dividing up the past. Previously the ancient world had been very widely regarded as an age of benighted ignorance, with the ending of the dark being signalled by the coming of Christ, 'the light of the world'. But the humanists now equated the coming of the dark, in spite of the Incarnation, with the waning of classical culture in early Christian Europe – again a markedly Gibbonian rather than a Christian view of events.

This new perspective can already be found in Petrarch, especially in the letter he wrote in 1359 explaining why he eventually decided to bring his study *Of Famous Men* to a close in the period shortly after the collapse of the Roman Republic (cf. Mommsen, 1959a, pp. 111, 118). He had no desire, he said, to proceed beyond that point, since it was followed by an era of 'so much darkness' and so few notable men (cf. Mommsen, 1959a, pp. 118, 122). The same vocabulary and implications were soon adopted with even greater polemical force by a number of early *quattrocento* humanists. Bruni devoted the first part of his *Dialogue* to lamenting the fact that 'the glorious heritage' of the ancient world had been 'so much despoiled' by the subsequent onset of darkness and barbarity (pp. 58, 62). Giovanni Andrea Bussi (1417–75) consciously bracketed off this intervening period of obscurantism, labelling it with deliberate condescension 'the middle age' (Edelman, 1938, p. 4). And Flavio Biondo became the first historian to exploit the underlying idea that the past can be divided into three distinct periods when he came to sketch the argument of his *Decades* in the early 1440s (Hay, 1959, pp. 102, 116–17). The outcome was the first self-conscious history of 'medieval' Europe – the first survey to be organised around the now familiar assumption that the millennium following the fall of Rome in 410 can be treated as a self-contained unit of historical time.

It is characteristic of the humanists, moreover, that they not only saw this period of darkness as coming to an end in their own time, but also perceived themselves to be the agents mainly responsible for this splendid transformation of the world (Weisinger, 1943, pp. 563, 567). They expressed this confidence in the form of two metaphors, both of which have become permanently embedded in our ways of thinking about the *quattrocento* and its significance. One stresses the idea of a rebirth, a return to life, a Renaissance in the study of arts and letters. Valla speaks, for example, in the Preface to his book on *The Elegancies of the Latin Language* of the humane studies being 'roused up in our own time and coming to life once again' (*reviviscant*) after being 'in a state of degeneracy for such a long time' (p. 14). The other favourite metaphor speaks of witnessing the dawn, seeing an end to the darkness and a return to the light. Petrarch writes in exactly these terms in his account of *His Own Ignorance*, speaking of those who, like himself, have begun to 'enjoy the light' and no longer feel obliged to 'stagger on in darkness' by stumbling after scholastic pedantries (p. 96). Bruni similarly speaks in his *Oration* of Florence's achievement in having 'brought back to light' (*in lucem revocavit*) a knowledge of Latin letters, thereby 'recovering and reviving a form of study which had previously been almost dead' (p. 4). And Salutati seems to have been echoing general opinion when, in a letter of 1406, he cited Poggio's view that the man who deserved to be credited more than anyone else for having 'called back into the light' (*redacta ad lucem*) an understanding of humane letters was Petrarch, whose greatest claim to fame was taken to be his unique achievement in having been 'the first to encourage these studies by his own labour, industry and vigilance' (IV, p. 161; cf. Weisinger, 1944, pp. 625–6).

Once the humanists became confident that they had brought the dark ages to an end and initiated a true Renaissance, it was only necessary to take a short step in order to reach the further and even more daring conclusion that the light they had kindled might be capable of shining more brightly than ever before. Bruni already felt able at the end of his *Dialogue* to express the hope that 'our Florentine authorities' on the liberal arts 'may now be able to become the equal or even the superiors of the ancient sages' (p. 96). A generation later, Benedetto Accolti went on to suggest with even greater assurance in his *Dialogue on the Pre-eminence of the Men of his Age* that the grandeur of the ancient world had by that time been matched (cf. Baron, 1966, p. 347). And once it became possible to look back on the achievements of the *quattrocento* as a whole, this belief in the superiority of the 'moderns' over the 'ancients' began to be held as an article of faith. When Vasari surveyed the artistic splendours of the Italian Renaissance in the 1550s, it seemed to him obvious that, in the work of such masters as Michelangelo, the finest attainments of antiquity had been 'gloriously surpassed' (cf. Panofsky, 1960, p. 33). And when Louis le Roy (1510–77) came to write his *Considerations* on the history of his times in 1567, he expressed an even broader faith in the new 'peak of perfection' attained 'in the course of the past hundred years', claiming that 'things previously covered in the darkness of ignorance have not merely been brought to light again', but that 'many other things have come to be known which were entirely unknown in the ancient world' (Weisinger, 1945b, p. 418. Cf. also Gundersheimer, 1966, pp. 115–16).

5

The age of princes

Francesco Guicciardini, writing his *History of Italy* at the end of the 1530s, divided the later Renaissance into two distinct and tragically opposed periods of political development. As the opening of the *History* explains, the line of demarcation falls in 1494, the year in which 'French troops, summoned by our own princes, began to stir up very great dissensions here' (p. 3). Before this fatal moment 'Italy had never enjoyed such prosperity, or known so favourable a situation' (p. 4). The long years of conflict between Florence and Milan had finally come to an end in 1454, after which 'the greatest peace and tranquillity reigned everywhere' (p. 4). With the coming of the French, however, Italy began to suffer 'all those calamities with which miserable mortals are usually afflicted' (p. 3). When Charles VIII invaded in 1494, he forced Florence and Rome into submission, fought his way as far south as Naples and allowed his vast armies to pillage the countryside. His successor Louis XII mounted three further invasions, repeatedly attacking Milan and generating endemic warfare throughout Italy. Finally, the greatest disaster of all came when the Emperor Charles V decided in the early 1520s to contest the French control of Milan, a decision which converted the whole of the *Regnum Italicum* into a battlefield for the next thirty years (Green, 1964, pp. 94–9).

One trend, however, continued uninterruptedly throughout these periods of fluctuating fortune: the extension and consolidation of increasingly despotic forms of princely rule. Sometimes – as in Naples and Milan – this merely involved the imposition of new and more powerful masters rather than new styles of government. But in cities with active Republican traditions – such as Florence and Rome – the outcome was a protracted conflict between the advocates of Republican 'liberty' and the exponents of allegedly 'tyrannical' practices.

For an account of this struggle in Rome we can scarcely do better than follow the analysis given by Machiavelli in his Chapter on Ecclesiastical Principalities in *The Prince*. As he begins by observing, the fatal weakness of the early *quattrocento* Popes had been their inability to contain the rival factions of the 'Roman barons' led by the Orsini and the Colonna (p. 75). Both these families had devoted themselves to fomenting popular disturbances, their main ambition being to prevent the Papacy from gaining any control over the city's government. The Colonna backed a Republican uprising in 1434, forcing Eugenius IV to abandon Rome for nine years, while a similar plot by the Republicans in 1453 terrorised the final years of Nicholas V's pontificate (Armstrong, 1936, pp. 169, 174). But as Machiavelli goes on to relate, the situation changed dramatically in the latter part of the fifteenth century. First came Sixtus IV, 'a spirited Pope', who attacked the Republican cliques and began to restore his temporal authority throughout the Papal States (p. 75). Next came Alexander VI, whom Machiavelli admiringly congratulates for having shown 'more than any other pontiff who ever lived' how far the prestige of the Papacy could be enhanced by the unhesitating application of 'money and armed force' (p. 75). And finally came the brilliant reign of Julius II, who 'did everything for the aggrandisement of the Church' and 'succeeded in all his enterprises' (p. 76). He 'found the Church already great', with 'the Roman barons destroyed and, as a result of Alexander's vigour, the factions wiped out'. But he also 'improved on all these things', turning the Papacy into a despotic principality and a formidable military power in precisely the ways Machiavelli believed to be essential for the eradication of corruption in political life (p. 76).

A similar but more insidious extension of 'tyrannical' practices occurred in Florence during the same period. The beginnings of this transformation can be traced back as far as 1434, when Cosimo de Medici returned from exile and started to build up a ruling political oligarchy under his own leadership.[1] A further move towards the establishment of a *signoria* was made in 1458, when a new Council of a Hundred – far more open to electoral manipulation than the traditional large councils – was given power to advise and legislate on a wide variety of financial as well as political affairs (Rubinstein, 1966, pp. 113–16). But the most decisive step in the direction of a Medicean despotism was taken in 1480, when Cosimo's grandson Lorenzo *Il Magnifico* helped to set up a new and permanent Council of Seventy, mainly staffed by his own supporters, which was then assigned almost complete executive control over the affairs of the Republic (Rubinstein, 1966, pp. 199–203). As one of Lorenzo's opponents declared in the 1480s, the outcome of all these 'reforms' was the creation of a

[1] See Rubinstein, 1966, pp. 11–18. Although my information in this paragraph is taken from Rubinstein's book, it should be noted that he is concerned to question the traditional assumption – which I am inclined to accept – that these developments can be interpreted as deliberate steps towards the establishment of a *signoria*.

regime in which 'no magistrate dared, even in the smallest matters, to decide anything' without first assuring himself of Lorenzo's agreement (Rubinstein, 1966, p. 225).

This is not to say that the Florentines signed away their ancient constitutional rights without a struggle. After the premature death of Lorenzo in 1492, two serious attempts were made to exclude his successors from power and to re-establish the old traditions of Republican liberty. The first of these *coups* took place in 1494, when Lorenzo's son Piero was forced into exile immediately after his undignified surrender of the city to the French (Rubinstein, 1966, pp. 229–35). The second upheaval occurred in 1527, when the Medici were again driven from power and the restoration of the Republic was once again proclaimed.

These challenges were not enough, however, to check the inexorable movement towards *il governo d'un solo* in Florence. The Republic of 1494 collapsed ingloriously in 1512, when the Medici regained control with the aid of Spanish troops (Schevill, 1936, p. 369). And the final attempt to set up a popular regime in 1527 ended even more swiftly in defeat. The Medici Pope, Clement VII, managed to conclude a treaty with the Emperor Charles V in 1529, binding him to turn his armies against the rebellious Florentines (Schevill, 1936, p. 487). After holding out with conspicuous bravery for more than a year, the Republic was finally forced to capitulate, and it was left to Clement VII to settle its affairs. He thereupon appointed the youthful and illegitimate Alessandro de Medici to be *gonfaloniere* of Florence for life, and in 1532 went on to invest his heirs and successors with the lordship of the city in perpetuity. So the Florentine Republic finally dissolved into the Grand Duchy of Tuscany, and suffered the government of an increasingly effete succession of Medici Dukes for the next two hundred years (Schevill, 1936, p. 514).

The final triumph of the *signori* almost everywhere in Italy helped to bring about a number of important developments in the character of Renaissance political thought. One of the most obvious changes was a marked diminution of interest in the values which had helped to underpin the traditional Republican concept of citizenship. To Bruni and his successors it had seemed obvious that the idea of *negotium*, or complete involvement in civic affairs, should be taken to represent the highest condition of human life. But to Pico, Ficino and the other leading philosophers of the later *quattrocento* it seemed no less obvious that a life of *otium*, or contemplative withdrawal, ought above all to be prized (Rice, 1958, p. 58). So they dethroned the writings of Cicero from the position of pre-eminence assigned to them by the earlier 'civic' humanists, and proclaimed instead – in Ficino's words – that the dialogues of 'the divine

Plato' must be regarded as 'the first and greatest' philosophical treatises of the ancient world (vol. 2, pp. 116, 117).

One effect of this change of allegiance was that the sort of interest in politics which the early *quattrocento* humanists had displayed came to be regarded as a lesser and even a vulgar form of intellectual pursuit. This attitude is clearly reflected in Pico's *Oration on the Dignity of Man*, in which he pours scorn on those who focus their careers 'on profit or on ambition', and boasts that he himself has 'relinquished all interest in affairs private and public' in order to devote himself 'entirely to leisure for contemplation' (p. 238). A more radical consequence of abandoning the value of *negotium* was that the idea of involving oneself in any meaningful way in the business of government eventually came to seem a complete impossibility. This later spirit of scepticism is best illustrated by Francesco Doni (1513–74), writing in the generation after the final collapse of the Florentine Republic. He continually emphasises that nothing at all can be done to reform the corruption of the world, and insists that this apparently cynical stance must be seen as nothing more than the cultivation of 'a good ignorance' (cf. Grendler, 1966, pp. 243–6).

A further change of outlook which came with the age of princes was that those who continued to devote their main attention to the study of politics began to address their treatises to a quite different type of audience (cf. Gilbert, 1939, p. 456). As we have seen, the earlier 'civic' humanists had normally felt able to assume a context of Republican institutions, and to direct their advice and exhortations to the whole body of the citizens. When we come to the humanists of the later Renaissance, we almost always find them presupposing a context of princely rule, even when it is evident – as in the case of Patrizi and Machiavelli – that their own personal preference would have been for a Republic. We find in consequence that they tend to overlook the figure of the individual citizen, and to concentrate all their attention on the far more imposing and influential figure of the prince.

This is not to say that these were the first theorists to compose books of advice intended specifically for *signori* and princes. We have already observed the emergence of such a *genre* in fourteenth-century Padua, where Ferreto Ferreti wrote in praise of the della Scala almost as soon as they seized power in 1328, and where Pier Paolo Vergerio wrote his fragment *On Monarchy* between 1394 and 1405 (Robey, 1973, p. 17). A similar tradition developed soon afterwards in Milan, especially after Giangaleazzo Visconti began to emphasise the absolute character of his rule, forbidding the use of the term *popolo* and insisting that all the citizens must be referred to as his *subditi* or subjects (Hay, 1961, p. 105). The

Milanese humanists quickly responded with a series of dutiful panegyrics on the excellence of princely rule. Uberto Decembrio (c. 1350–1427) dedicated four books *On Public Affairs* to Filippo Maria Visconti in the 1420s, while his son Pier Candido Decembrio (1392–1477) wrote a *Eulogy in Praise of the City of Milan* in 1436, intending the work as a direct reply to the *Eulogy* on the Florentine Republic composed by Leonardo Bruni some thirty years earlier (Cosenza, 1962, pp. 607–9; Baron, 1966, pp. 69, 425).

Nevertheless, it would still be true to say that the heyday of such eulogies and advice-books came in the latter part of the fifteenth century. The *genre* even developed an additional dimension during this period. A number of treatises began to be written less for princes than for their courtiers, the aim being to supply them with instructions about their education, their deportment and their role in relation to their prince. One of the earliest examples was Diomede Carafa's tract on *The Perfect Courtier*, which he completed while attached to the Neapolitan court in the 1480s (Cosenza, 1962, p. 419). But the most celebrated and influential work of this character was *The Book of the Courtier* by Baldesar Castiglione (1478–1529), a series of dialogues which were drafted between 1513 and 1518, first printed ten years later, and eventually became established as one of the most widely-read books of the sixteenth century (Mazzeo, 1967, p. 132).

But the main recipients of advice-books were the princes themselves, and it is evident that most of the humanists conceived their treatises with specific rulers in mind. Thus Francesco Patrizi (1412–94) dedicated his elaborate discussion of *The Kingdom and the Education of the King* to Pope Sixtus IV in the 1470s (Cosenza, 1962, p. 1345). Bartolomeo Sacchi (1421–81) wrote his tract on *The Prince* for one of the Gonzago dukes of Mantua in 1471 (Baron, 1966, p. 437). Diomede Carafa (1407–87), as well as writing advice for courtiers, produced a memorandum on *The Office of a Good Prince* for Ferdinand of Naples in the 1480s (Gilbert, 1939, p. 469). And Giovanni Pontano (1426–1503), who served as Ferdinand's secretary for more than twenty years, originally brought himself to the attention of the king by presenting him with a treatise on *The Prince* in 1468 (Cosenza, 1962, pp. 1461–2).

By far the most famous of these advice-books was of course Machiavelli's *The Prince*, which he completed at the end of 1513 and dedicated some two years later 'to the magnificent Lorenzo de Medici' (p. 29).[1]

[1] There is now general agreement that, as Machiavelli himself implied in a letter to Francesco Vettori of December 1513, a complete draft of *The Prince* was written between July and December 1513. For the letter to Vettori see Machiavelli, *Letters*, pp. 139–44. For the suggestion that the dedication was inserted between September 1515 and September 1516, see

Machiavelli had a special reason for wishing to offer himself as an adviser to princes in 1513, in spite of the fact that his whole career up to that point had been spent as a public servant under the restored Florentine Republic (Ridolfi, 1963, pp. 15, 131–2). The Republic had collapsed, as we have seen, in the previous year, the Medici had returned to power and Machiavelli had suddenly found himself deprived of his office and livelihood. He urgently needed to commend himself to the city's new masters, and he rather optimistically hoped (as his letters to Vettori make clear)[1] that if he could somehow persuade the Medici to read his book, he might be able to win his way back into the political employment which he craved. The book failed in its avowed purpose, but it succeeded in making a contribution to the *genre* of advice-books for princes which at the same time revolutionised the *genre* itself.

THE HUMANIST IDEAL OF PRINCELY GOVERNMENT

Although the political theory of the later Renaissance presents us with a sharp change of focus, it would be misleading to imply that the resulting literature of advice-books for princes and courtiers represented a wholly new departure in humanist political thought. There was nothing unfamiliar about the idea of offering practical counsel to political leaders about the conduct of their affairs. This had always been the aim of the older tradition of advice-books intended for *podestà* and city magistrates, and this tradition had in turn made use of the far more ancient conceit of holding up a 'mirror' to princes, presenting them with an ideal image and asking them to seek their reflection in its depths.[2] Nor was there anything unfamiliar about the assumptions underlying the advice which the humanists of the later Renaissance went on to offer to the princes of their age. As we turn to analyse their works, the first point which needs to be emphasised is the extent to which they continued to draw on the values and attitudes which the 'civic' humanists of the earlier *quattrocento* had already articulated.

Their hero was still the *vir virtutis*, and they continued to insist that the right ambition for this heroic character should be that of winning for himself the greatest possible degree of honour, glory and fame (cf. Kontos, 1972, pp. 83–88). The later humanists even placed an increasing emphasis on these already familiar beliefs, since they typically viewed the

Bertelli, 1960, p. 9. For a recent survey of the debate surrounding the dating of *The Prince*, see Geerken, 1976, p. 357.
[1] See Machiavelli, *Letters*, pp. 101–7, 139–44.
[2] For a discussion of the elaborate imagery of the *speculum*, the 'mirror-for-princes', see Shapiro, 1975, esp. pp. 41–4.

prince as a man capable of achieving *virtus* to an unsurpassable extent. Patrizi proclaims in one of his chapter-headings that 'the king must establish glory for himself by his deeds', and never doubts that the attainment of glory must be seen as 'the very greatest reward for the exercise of *virtus*' (p. 399). Castiglione exhibits an even stronger commitment to the same scale of values, especially in Book IV of *The Courtier*, in which he considers the relationship between the courtier and his prince. He first announces that the courtier's chief ambition, and 'the end to which he is directed', must be that of furnishing his ruler with sound political advice (p. 288). He then declares that the aim of this counsel must be to ensure that the prince seeks 'honour and profit', strives for 'the pinnacle of glory', and succeeds in consequence in making himself 'famous and illustrious in the world.'[1] Throughout the dialogues it is always assumed that, although it may be wrong 'to seek false glory and what is not deserved', it is no less wrong 'to rob oneself of a deserved honour and not to seek that praise which alone is the true reward of virtuous labours' (p. 99).

These values are no less clearly endorsed by Machiavelli in *The Prince*. He insists that princely conduct must be *onesto* as well as *utile*, and accordingly demands that all princes must take as their model 'some historical figure who has been praised and honoured', keeping 'his deeds and actions before them' at all times (p. 90). He points to Ferdinand of Aragon as a contemporary ruler worthy of imitation, singling him out at the start of his Chapter on 'How a prince must act to win honour' on the grounds that 'from being a weak king he has risen to being, for fame and glory, the first king of Christendom' (p. 119). Conversely, he expresses contempt for Agathocles of Sicily, in spite of his remarkable achievements, on the grounds that the criminal methods he invariably employed 'can win a prince power but not glory' (p. 63). And when he turns at the end of *The Prince* to address himself directly to the Medici, his main concern is still to offer them the assurance that 'nothing brings a man greater honour' than the founding of a new principality – thus reminding them that if they succeed in bringing 'new laws and new institutions' to Italy, they will also gain for themselves the richest prize in political life (pp. 133–6).

A second element of continuity between the mirror-for-princes theorists and their predecessors lay in their analysis of the forces opposing the *vir virtutis* in his quest for honour, glory and fame. They all agree that the chief responsibility for the collapse of our best-laid plans must be

---

[1] See Castiglione, pp. 290, 319–21. Cf. the discussion of Book IV in Ryan, 1972. For Carafa's similar account of the relationship between the courtier and his prince, see *The Perfect Courtier*, pp. 77–80, 94–5.

attributed to the capricious and potentially overwhelming power of fortune. It is of course admitted, as Pontano puts it in his treatise *On Fortune*, that although the goddess is 'devoid of reason', she is sometimes 'capable of contributing to a man's happiness' (pp. 519, 543, 549). But the main emphasis is usually placed on the power of fortune to do us unexpected and often irreparable harm. This theme is nowhere treated with greater bitterness than in Castiglione's *Book of the Courtier*. So constantly does he inveigh against fortune for 'uplifting to the skies whom she pleases' and 'burying in the depths those most worthy of being exalted' that *The Courtier* eventually had to be placed on the Index for the heresy of attributing so much importance to a pagan deity (cf. pp. 1–2, 14, 30, 285; Cartwright, 1908, II, p. 446).

The same belief is again repeated – and with characteristic vehemence – in Machiavelli's *Prince* (cf. Flanagan, 1972, pp. 127–35). He begins, like Pontano, by conceding that it is possible to attract the favourable attentions of fortune, and acknowledges that men are sometimes permitted to 'achieve great things' in this way. He lays it down as an axiom in his opening chapter that there are two main ways of gaining a principality, either by the exercise of *virtù* or by the gift of fortune (p. 33). And later he includes a special section on 'new principalities acquired with the help of fortune' in which he takes the case of Cesare Borgia as the most instructive example of a man who 'acquired his state' entirely through 'good fortune' (pp. 53–4). Machiavelli's main emphasis, however, is always on the goddess's unstable character, and the consequent folly of relying for any length of time on her support. He devotes his penultimate Chapter to ruminating on 'How far human affairs are governed by Fortune', and he likens her at that point to 'one of those violent rivers which, when they are enraged, flood the plains' and allow 'no possibility of resistance' (p. 130). Similarly, he concludes that the moral to be drawn from Cesare Borgia's career is that a prince should always rely on his own *virtù* rather than the favours of fortune in seeking to 'maintain his state'. Having acquired his power entirely 'through the good fortune of his father', Cesare was peculiarly liable to lose it as soon as his luck deserted him. This duly happened with alarming suddenness, so that 'what he instituted was of no avail', and he ended his life as a prey to 'the extraordinary and inordinate malice of fortune' (pp. 54–5).

Having emphasised the role of fortune in human affairs, the mirror-for-princes writers go on to ask what qualities a ruler needs to possess in order to ensure that fortune's power is controlled and minimised. The answer they suggest again reveals their dependence on the scheme of concepts already outlined by the earlier *quattrocento* humanists. They all agree that, as Patrizi declares, 'it is only by means of *virtus* that a prince can hope to overcome the malice of fortune and achieve the goals of 'honour, glory and fame' (p. 228). As in the case of the earlier humanists, Patrizi has two main claims in mind at this point. One is that a prince who acquires true *virtus* 'will never be dominated in his affairs by fortune' since he will always be able to remain steadfast even in the most adverse circumstances (p. 280). The other is that, since 'good fortune is always the companion of bravery', a prince who possesses *virtus* will also have the best chance of enlisting the support of the capricious goddess in the conduct of his affairs (p. 280). The concept of *virtus* is thus taken to represent the key quality which a prince needs above all to cultivate if he is to 'maintain his state'. As Pontano emphasises in his tract on *The Prince*, '*virtus* is so much to be honoured' that all rulers must 'rouse themselves to follow it' in all their public acts (pp. 1034, 1042). *Virtus* is 'the most splendid thing in the whole world', more magnificent even than the sun, for 'the blind cannot see the sun' whereas 'even they can see *virtus* as plainly as possible' (p. 1044).

Once again we find Machiavelli reiterating the same doctrines in *The Prince*. He insists first of all that a man of true *virtù* can never be totally overwhelmed even by the most evil fortune. Although he concedes in his chapter on 'How far human affairs are governed by fortune' that the goddess may well be 'the arbiter of half the things we do', he still contends that this leaves 'the other half or so to be controlled by ourselves' (p. 130). He is also a firm believer in the adage that *Fortes Fortuna Adiuvat* – that fortune favours the brave. He points out that 'being a woman, she favours young men, because they are less circumspect and more ardent, and because they command her with greater audacity'. And he ends by declaring with a characteristic flourish that, 'because fortune is a woman' the aim of the man of *virtù* must be 'to beat and coerce her' until she becomes submissive to his will (p. 133).

For Machiavelli, as for the other humanists, the concept of *virtù* is thus used to denote the indispensable quality which enables a ruler to deflect the slings and arrows of outrageous fortune, and to aspire in consequence to the attainment of honour, glory and fame. This emerges very clearly in his chapter on 'Why the Italian Princes have lost their states' (p. 128). He issues a warning to all new princes that, if they wish to achieve the 'two-fold glory' which comes from establishing a new principality and securing it, they need above all to recognise that 'the only sound, sure and enduring methods' to employ are 'those based on your own actions and *virtù*' (p. 129). The same commitment recurs even more strongly in the final chapter of *The Prince*, in which Machiavelli issues his 'Exhortation' to the Medici 'to liberate Italy from the barbarians' (p. 133). He begins by assuring them that since their 'illustrious House' possesses 'fortune and *virtù*', it follows that no one could be better fitted to 'lead Italy to her salvation' (p. 135). And he ends by quoting the stanza from 'My Italy' in which, as we have already seen, Petrarch had appealed to his fellow-countrymen to prove that their *virtus* had not been lost, and that they might be capable of resurrecting the glories of ancient Rome in modern Italy (p. 138).

Finally, most of the mirror-for-princes writers continue to endorse the familiar humanist assumption that, since the right kind of education is of crucial importance in shaping the character of the *vir virtutis*, there must be a close connection between the provision of the best educational and the best political advice. Machiavelli constitutes something of an exception to this rule, since he only glancingly mentions the question of the ruler's 'intellectual training' – perhaps because he genuinely believed (as he sometimes seems to imply) that the best education for a prince would simply consist of memorising *The Prince* (cf. p. 89). But in most of the other advice-books for rulers and courtiers there is a continuing emphasis on both the central claims we have already seen to be characteristic of humanist educational treatises. First of all, there is a strong endorsement of the belief that no absolute distinction should be drawn between the type of education suitable for gentlemen or princes and the type of education suitable for 'clerks'. One of the most influential discussions of this theme is contained in the opening Book of Castiglione's *Courtier*. There the French are repeatedly castigated for 'thinking that letters are detrimental to arms', and for their barbaric assumption that 'it is a great insult to call anyone a clerk' (pp. 67, 69). Castiglione's own view is that although 'the principal and true profession of the courtier must be that of arms', he should also be a man of high cultural attainments, 'conversant not only with the Latin language but with Greek as well', and 'more than passably learned' in 'those studies which we call the humanities' (pp. 32, 70). The other familiar issue these writers discuss is the nature of the curriculum to be followed by aspiring princes and courtiers alike. The fullest account is given by Patrizi in the second Book of *The Kingdom and the Education of the King*. He begins by stressing the importance of acquiring suitable tutors for young princes, and goes on to outline a detailed course of instruction of a typically humanist kind. This starts with Grammar, 'the foundation of all the other disciplines', continues with the study of the best ancient authors, and concludes with an extensive account of 'what the king must know of mathematics' as well as a discussion of the import-ance of music and bodily exercise (pp. 69–75, 78–86). The outcome is to make it the strenuous duty of the prince to offer himself as a model of 'the Renaissance man' to the rest of his subjects.

So far we have considered the extent to which the mirror-for-princes writers of the later Renaissance continued to endorse the values and concepts already articulated by the earlier *quattrocento* humanists. It remains to analyse the ways in which the changing character of their audience prompted them to introduce a number of new elements into their moral and political thought.

They tended in the first place to differ sharply from most of their predecessors in their views about the purposes of government. The 'civic' humanists, as well as the authors of advice-books for *podestà* and city magistrates, had all committed themselves to the claim that the preservation of liberty and justice must be taken to constitute the main values in political life. By contrast, the mirror-for-princes theorists developed an argument which, as we have seen, had already been canvassed by the earliest defenders of 'despotic' and 'tyrannical' regimes. They contended that the essential business of government consists of maintaining the people not so much in a state of liberty as in security and peace. This new sense of priorities can be observed most clearly in the final section of Castiglione's *Book of the Courtier*. One of the characters in the dialogue attempts to protest at the strong emphasis being laid by the other speakers on the virtues of tranquillity and obedience. He declares that 'since liberty has been given to us by God as a supreme gift', it is altogether wrong 'that one man should have a larger portion of it than another', a situation 'which happens under the rule of princes, who for the most part hold their subjects in the closest bondage' (p. 304). He is quickly assured, however, that such a view of political life amounts to nothing more than a plea that we should be allowed 'to live as we like' instead of living 'according to good laws' (p. 305). And once this convenient equation between a state of equal liberty and of sheer license has been insinuated into the debate, the other speakers feel able to conclude with renewed confidence that the true office of a good ruler must be 'to establish his people in such laws and ordinances that they may live in ease and peace' and 'may worthily enjoy' a condition of undisturbed tranquillity (pp. 310–11).

The same shift in priorities is no less clearly marked in Machiavelli's *Prince*. He mentions the 'ancient liberty' of Republics only to remark that this tends to make them less amenable to princely government (p. 49). He repeatedly asserts that the chief duty of a ruler must be to attend to his own 'security and strength', while ensuring at the same time that his subjects are 'stabilised and made secure' (pp. 113, 114). And he even characterises his own aim in writing *The Prince* as an attempt to draw up a set of rules such that anyone who follows them 'will appear to have been long-established and will quickly become more safe and secure in his government than if he had been ruling his state for a long time' (p. 128).

The mirror-for-princes writers generally go on to argue that, since these values can be secured most readily under the rule of a prince, it follows that monarchy must be regarded as the best form of government. It is true that Machiavelli and Patrizi both refuse to draw this alleged corollary. Machiavelli in particular prefers to hold in tension two contrasting views about the rival merits of princely and popular regimes. On the one hand he stresses, both in *The Prince* and later in *The Discourses*, that in conditions of advanced political corruption it will always be necessary – in a Republic no less than a principality – to rely on the strong rule of a single man in order to restore the pristine *virtù* of a commonwealth. But on the other hand he implies in *The Prince*, and later states as explicitly as possible in *The Discourses*, that his own personal preference will always be for a life of political liberty, and hence for a Republican form of government.

The more usual line of argument, however, was that no one who is genuinely concerned about the values of security and peace can possibly continue to uphold the traditional preference for the liberty of Republics. We already find this implication being drawn with great confidence as early as Vergerio's fragment *On Monarchy* – which is subtitled 'the best form of government'. Vergerio begins by contending that the main purpose of government is to ensure the avoidance of faction and the maintenance of 'safety, security and the defence of innocence' (p. 447). He then argues that 'the government of the multitude' brings nothing but 'tumultuousness', with the ceaseless interplay of parties, the continual plundering of property and the perennial threat of civil war (p. 448). So he regards it as obvious that 'monarchy is to be preferred to the rule of the people' (p. 447). He not only insists that princes 'are far better' at 'removing all seditions and tumults amongst the citizens', but even maintains – in an apparently deliberate confusion of the traditionally opposed categories – that 'with a good king who is just and clement' we are assured in effect of 'true liberty' because 'we are assured of peace' (pp. 447, 449). In the course of the *cinquecento* this way of contrasting the security of *regna* with the seditiousness of *communitates* became an accepted commonplace amongst the humanists – as it had been for a long time amongst scholastic writers. When, for example, Giovanni Rondinelli looked back in 1583 on 'the old days' of the Florentine Republic, he felt convinced that the city had been 'filled with towers, castles and quarrelling factions' throughout the era of popular regimes, and that the finest achievement of the Medici had been to bring about the end of these disturbances by imposing the *Pax Medicea*, the peaceable rule of their own princely government (cf. Cochrane, 1965, p. 12).

The other major change introduced by the mirror-for-princes theorists into their inherited political vocabulary centred on their analysis of the key concept of *virtus*. So far we have seen that they agreed with their humanist predecessors in defining the concept heuristically as the quality which enables a man to combat the power of fortune and attain the goals of honour, glory and fame. If we now turn, however, to investigate the nature the qualities they had in mind in applying the term, we find that their interest in the *virtus* of rulers rather than ordinary citizens prompted them to incorporate two significant new emphases into their accounts.

The first of these was the suggestion – adapted from Aristotle's *Politics* – that the qualities which deserve admiration in a prince may be different from those which deserve admiration in a private citizen. This makes it somewhat misleading to claim, as some scholars have done, that 'political virtues were deemed identical with private virtues' by these writers (cf. Anglo, 1969, p. 190). If we look, for example, at Patrizi's discussion of *virtus* in *The Kingdom and the Education of the King*, we find him maintaining quite unequivocally that 'the virtues of the ruler are one thing, the virtues of the people are another' (p. 95). He declares that there are many qualities, especially those which go with 'a modest outlook', which 'warrant the highest praise in ordinary citizens', but are quite inappropriate in princes (pp. 95–6). He concedes that 'citizens ought to strive to acquire *virtus*', but he makes it plain that he regards this as a relatively passive quality, one which includes the cultivation of 'obedience and goodwill' and of 'gratitude for the benefits they receive from their kings' (pp. 371, 392).

The same dichotomy is even more sharply drawn by Machiavelli in *The Prince*. The *virtù* of the ruler is treated as an astonishingly creative force, the key to 'maintaining his state' and enabling him to fight off his enemies. The chief merit of the people is taken by contrast to lie in their characteristic tendency to benign passivity. Machiavelli assumes throughout that 'the people ask only not to be oppressed', and scarcely troubles in consequence to assign them a speaking part in the drama of political life. He insists that as long as their ruler 'does not rob the great majority of their property or their honour', they will 'remain content' and largely pliable (p. 102). And he counsels the 'wise prince' to strengthen these habits of loyalty by devising 'ways by which his citizens are always and in all circumstances dependent on him', the aim being to ensure that 'they will always be faithful to him' in times of necessity (p. 71). The prince is invariably portrayed by Machiavelli as a figure in movement, but the activity of the people is said to be confined to 'the restlessness of a few', who 'can be dealt with easily and in a variety of ways' (p. 102).

The second new element which the later humanists introduce into their discussions of *virtus* is a tendency to explain the meaning of the term by reference to an increasingly heroic list of individual moral qualities. Although Machiavelli dissociates himself as sharply as possible from this move, it is generally assumed in the more conventional advice-books that the possession of *virtus* can be equated with the possession of two particular groups of the conventional virtues.

It is first of all claimed that no one can be accounted a man of true *virtus* unless he displays all the leading Christian virtues as well as the 'cardinal' virtues singled out by the moralists of antiquity. This aspect of the analysis is simply a reiteration of the arguments we have already found in the writings of Petrarch and the early *quattrocento* humanists. One of the fullest restatements of this commitment is supplied by Patrizi in *The Kingdom and the Education of the King*. He asks himself at the beginning of Book VI 'What is *virtus*?', and he observes that Plato supplies us with the essence of the answer when 'he states that there are four principal virtues' (pp. 235, 237). These are then itemised and discussed at considerable length. First comes the virtue of prudence or wisdom, which is taken to include reason, intelligence, circumspection and sagacity (pp. 237–50). Next comes the virtue of temperance, which goes with modesty, abstinence, chastity, honesty, moderation and sobriety (pp. 254–70). The third cardinal virtue is fortitude, a simpler and more self-evident property which is said to be 'the virtue appropriate above all to great men' (p. 275). And finally there is the over-arching virtue of justice, which Patrizi divides into its divine, natural and civil aspects, agreeing with Plato that it must be regarded as 'the greatest good of all' (pp. 314–19). But the elaboration of this Platonic typology by no means brings us to the end of Patrizi's analysis. He next goes on to endorse with great emphasis the orthodox humanist assumption that all these virtues will be in vain unless they are supplemented and strengthened by the fundamental Christian qualities of piety, religion and faith. He defines piety as 'the idea of God', and argues that religion is 'the inseparable companion' of this virtue, since 'it is concerned with the worship of the divine' (pp. 346–50). But he insists that the greatest virtue of all is Christian faith, which 'gives forth such splendour that all the other virtues of kings and princes become obscure without it' (p. 358). Unless our rulers cultivate this quality, Patrizi concludes 'their wisdom will be in vain and lying', their temperance will be 'sad and ashamed', their fortitude will be 'cowardly and torpid' and their administration of justice will amount to 'nothing more than the shedding of blood' (p. 358).

The other virtues these writers emphasise are those which they take to be especially appropriate for kings and princes to cultivate. This preoccupation had scarcely surfaced in the writings of the 'civic' humanists, since their main concern had been to analyse the *virtus* of the citizen-body as a whole. There was a clear precedent for this interest, however, in the earlier advice-books intended for *podestà* and city magistrates, and it was essentially their approach which the mirror-for-princes writers now began to take up and develop in a more elaborate style.

They begin by declaring that all rulers must seek to acquire the related virtues of liberality and magnificence. These are 'amongst the greatest virtues of all', as Patrizi asserts, 'in the case of kings and princes' (pp. 304, 308). Pontano devotes two special treatises to extolling these qualities, the underlying assumption in each case being that a prince who exhibits parsimony or avarice is sure to cheat himself of attaining the highest prizes of glory and fame. The tract *On Liberality* insists that 'nothing is more undignified in a prince' than a lack of generosity, and repeatedly (and somewhat misleadingly) praises Ferdinand of Naples as a model of liberal patronage (pp. 10, 45, 55). The tract *On Magnificence* similarly explains that a reputation for creating 'noble buildings, splendid Churches and theatres' is an indispensable adjunct of princely glory, and again singles out Ferdinand of Naples for 'the magnificence and majesty' of the public buildings he commissioned (pp. 85–7).

The second princely virtue was said to be clemency. This contention led the mirror-for-princes theorists to take up a question which, as we have seen, had invariably been debated by the authors of advice-books for *podestà* and city-magistrates: whether it is better for a ruler to seek to be feared or loved. As in the case of their predecessors, all these writers answer that, as Castiglione puts it, the prince must always aim to be 'not only loved but almost adored by his subjects' (p. 317). It is true that there was an element of disagreement at this point, for it was sometimes suggested – for example by Patrizi – that it may occasionally be appropriate and impressive for a ruler to behave with marked severity (p. 325). But even Patrizi concedes that this is a dangerous course to adopt, since severity 'readily degenerates into savagery', and 'there is no vice more shameful, detestable or inhuman' than cruelty in a prince (p. 325). It was generally agreed, moreover, as Pontano affirms at the start of his treatise on *The Prince*, that 'those who want to rule ought to display two qualities above all, the first being liberality and the second clemency' (p.

1026). The value of clemency, Pontano goes on, can scarcely be exaggerated, for 'whenever we recognise this quality in anyone, we admire and honour him in everything, we consider him as a god' (p. 1026).

Finally, the prince was exhorted to remain at all times the soul of honour, always giving his word freely and never breaking his promises. It is true that these qualities were envisaged less clearly than liberality and clemency as distinctively princely virtues. They tended to be seen as part of the more general code of conduct which the humanists had evolved for the guidance of Renaissance gentleman, a code in which the ideas of 'swearing upon one's honour' and 'giving one's word as a gentleman' had already come to be regarded – as in Castiglione's *Courtier* – as synonymous with the most unvarnished telling of the truth (cf. pp. 117, 138, 290). There is ample evidence, however, that this was a value which the ruler, as the leading exponent of the code of honour, was expected to display with exceptional scrupulousness. Patrizi lays it down with great emphasis in one of his chapter-headings that a king 'is never to engage in deceit, never to tell a lie, and never to permit others to tell lies' (p. 138). Pontano agrees in his treatise on *The Prince* that 'nothing is more disgraceful' than a ruler 'not keeping his word', and insists that 'if the situation should arise, it is absolutely required that he should keep his faith even with his enemies' (p. 1026). It is evident, moreover, from a number of contemporary memoirs that a prince who duly displayed these qualities was always accorded the highest admiration and praise. This emerges very clearly, for example, from the fine account of Duke Federigo of Urbino's career given by Vespasiano da Bisticci (1421–98), a Florentine bookseller who composed a notable series of *Lives of Illustrious Men of the Fifteenth Century*. The first quality he cites in his imposing list of Federigo's 'eminent virtues' is 'his good faith, in which he never faltered' (p. 85). Vespasiano reports that 'all to whom he gave his word bear witness that he never broke it', and adds a number of anecdotes to show that the Duke treated all his promises as 'inviolable', whether they were 'under obligation or free', and whether they were given in writing or merely by word of mouth (p. 86).

MACHIAVELLI'S CRITIQUE OF HUMANISM

So far, in considering Machiavelli's *Prince*, we have concentrated on the extent to which it can be shown to embody the values and preoccupations characteristic of the mirror-for-princes *genre* as a whole. It seems essential to begin by adopting this perspective. This makes it possible in the first place to identify a common misunderstanding of the relationship between

The Prince and the more conventional political literature of its age. It is often claimed that Machiavelli's book is entirely *sui generis*, that it is 'not to be placed in any category', and even that it 'completely ignores the concepts and categories' in terms of which the other political theorists of his generation were accustomed to express themselves.[1] It will by now be evident, however, that the format, the presuppositions and many of the central arguments of *The Prince* make it a recognisable contribution to a well-established tradition of later *quattrocento* political thought. A second reason for adopting this perspective is that, in setting out the main assumptions of the mirror-for-princes writers, we are also placing ourselves in the best position to observe how far Machiavelli may have had the further intention to question or even to ridicule some of their values. It is of course evident – and we have Machiavelli's own assurance on the point – that he saw himself as a self-conscious critic of several key elements in the existing literature of advice-books for princes (cf. p. 90). But it is only when we have grasped the precise intellectual context within which he was writing that we can hope to recognise the points at which, and the extent to which, he was in fact concerned to challenge and repudiate his own humanist heritage.

There are two main sections of *The Prince* in which Machiavelli is clearly concerned to mount a direct attack on the political theories of his contemporaries. He first denounces them for failing to emphasise the significance of sheer power in political life.[2] As we have seen, it had generally been assumed that, as long as the prince devotes himself wholeheartedly to a life of virtue, this will enable him to attain the highest goals of honour, glory and fame. Machiavelli insists by contrast that this naively overlooks the extent to which the maintenance of a successful government depends on an unflinching willingness to supplement the arts of persuasion

---

[1] For these contentions see Plamenatz, 1963, vol. I, p. 7, and Berlin, 1972, p. 160. This remains the usual textbook view of Machiavelli's political thought. As the above quotations reveal, moreover, the same assumptions continue to recur in the writings of distinguished historians of ideas. This is in spite of the fact that the investigation of the links between *The Prince* and the humanist literature of advice-books for princes first began to be undertaken a considerable time ago. For an interesting (though overstated) chapter-by-chapter series of parallels between Machiavelli and other humanists, see Allan Gilbert, 1938. For a partly contrasting discussion of the same theme, see Felix Gilbert, 1939. This latter article is of great value, and I am much indebted to it.

[2] This point is particularly emphasised by Gilbert, 1965, esp. p. 154. (Gilbert's whole book is of exceptional value, and I am particularly indebted to it.) Wood has argued (1967, p. 171) that Machiavelli even redefines the concept of *virtù* in order to make it stand for 'a pattern of behaviour most distinctively exhibited under what might be described as battlefield conditions'. It is arguable – as Hannaford has pointed out – that this unduly neglects the political overtones in Machiavelli's use of the term (Hannaford, 1973). But there is no doubt (as the final section of this chapter will attempt to indicate) that Machiavelli does in effect redefine the concept, and that part of his redefinition involves him in laying an exceptionally strong emphasis on the military prowess of the prince.

with the employment of effective military force. It is this aspect of princely government – ignored in a self-consciously civilised manner by most of his contemporaries – that Machiavelli restores with great polemical emphasis to the pages of *The Prince*, insisting on the need (in Wolin's apt phrase) for 'an economy of violence' (cf. Wolin, 1961, pp. 220–4).

It is necessary, however, to exercise a certain caution in making this point. It is sometimes suggested that, with the publication of Machiavelli's political theory, 'it is possible to date the beginning of a new view of warfare' (Walzer, 1966, p. 273). This arguably overestimates the novelty of Machiavelli's insistence on the need to construe the concept of *virtù* in part as a military quality. It would certainly be mistaken to think of him as the first writer to introduce this doctrine into humanist political thought. For the willingness to fight on behalf of one's *patria*, the readiness to employ violence in its cause, had always been treated by the earlier 'civic' humanists as an indispensable aspect of the *virtus* of the true citizen. Nor would it be accurate to think of Machiavelli as the first writer to carry over these assumptions about the inescapability of force into the more rarified atmosphere of the mirror-for-princes literature. Bartolomeo Sacchi – who had served as a professional soldier under Piccinino in his youth – had already insisted in his treatise on *The Prince* in 1471 that a ruler must always be prepared to combine diplomacy with coercion, and must always ensure in consequence that he is backed by a fully trained army of his own citizens (cf. Bayley, 1961, p. 234).

There is no doubt, however, that Machiavelli places an exceptionally strong emphasis on the role of sheer force in the conduct of government. He devotes three central chapters of *The Prince* to discussing military affairs, arguing that 'the main foundations of every state' are constituted by 'good laws and good arms' (p. 77). He begins with the very strong contention that 'where there are good arms, good laws inevitably follow' (p. 77). And he summarises his advice by insisting, with characteristic exaggeration, that the prince 'should have no other object or thought, nor acquire skill in anything, except war, its organisation and its discipline' (p. 87). He also discusses a related topic which, as we have seen, had always been stressed by the earlier *quattrocento* humanists: the folly and danger of employing mercenary troops. He offers it as an absolute rule that 'if a prince bases the defence of his state on mercenaries he will never achieve stability or security' (p. 77). And he adds that there is 'little need to labour this point, because the present ruin of Italy has been caused by nothing else but the reliance placed on mercenary troops' (p. 78). The solution he proposes – again in line with the views of earlier humanists – is that every prince must devote himself to building up a citizen militia, and must 'assume personal command and captain his troops himself' (pp. 78, 84). Unless this is done, Machiavelli grimly concludes, 'no principality is secure; rather, it is dependent on fortune, since there is no *virtù* to defend it when adversity comes' (p. 87).

The other point at which Machiavelli challenges the prevailing assumptions of the mirror-for-princes writers is in discussing the role of *virtù* in political life. As we have seen, two main contentions about the idea of *virtù* had arisen out of the humanist tradition of moral and political thought: first, that *virtù* is the quality which enables a ruler to attain his noblest ends; and secondly, that the possession of *virtù* can be equated with the possession of all the major virtues. As a result, the leading theorists of princely government had all gone on to furnish the same fundamental piece of political advice: that if a ruler wishes to 'maintain his state' and achieve the goals of honour, glory and fame, he needs above all to cultivate the full range of Christian as well as moral virtues. It is precisely this central conclusion that Machiavelli denies. He agrees that the proper goals for a prince to aim at are those of honour, glory and fame. But he rejects with great vehemence the prevailing belief that the surest way of attaining these ends is always to act in a conventionally virtuous way.

While it is clear what position Machiavelli is attacking at this pivotal point in his argument, the exact nature of the position he wishes to defend is a little obscured by his love of paradox. Sometimes he seems to be saying that, while princes have a duty to act virtuously, they must recognise that in order to act as virtuously as possible they should not attempt to act virtuously all the time. He sometimes seems, that is, to be pointing to an irony which is often underlined by Renaissance moralists: the irony that (as Hamlet expresses it) it is often necessary to 'be cruel only to be kind'.[1] Machiavelli first gestures at this line of thought in discussing the virtue of liberality. He points out that since the desire to appear generous often leads princes to impose gratuitous burdens on their people, a prince who is not afraid to act parsimoniously may discover that 'in time he will be recognised as being essentially a generous man' (p. 93). The same paradox is even more clearly invoked in his ensuing discussion of clemency. He begins by observing that 'Cesare Borgia was accounted cruel', but he immediately adds that 'this cruelty of his reformed the Romagna, brought it to unity, and restored order and obedience' (p. 95). The moral of the story is said to be that a prince who is confident enough to start out by 'making an example or two' will eventually 'prove more compassionate' than a ruler who fails to put down 'disorders which lead to murder and rapine' simply in order 'to escape being called cruel' (p. 95).

[1] *Hamlet* III, iv, 178.

The heart of Machiavelli's message, however, consists of two somewhat different – though scarcely less paradoxical – claims about the role of the conventional virtues in relation to the attainment of princely honour, glory and fame. The first is that nothing matters so much as the keeping up of appearances. It is even hinted that, as long as this can be done successfully, nothing else matters at all. The aim of the prince, we are repeatedly told, is to be 'judged honourable' and to be 'universally praised' (p. 101). It is thus essential, especially if he is not in fact a virtuous man, that he 'should be so prudent that he knows how to escape the evil reputation attached to those vices which could lose him his state' (p. 92). This in turn means that he must be willing to become 'a great liar and deceiver', taking advantage of the fact that 'men are so simple' that 'the deceiver will always find someone ready to be deceived' (p. 100). The indispensable talent is the ability to counterfeit virtue: the prince 'need not necessarily have all the good qualities', but he must 'certainly appear to have them' at all times (p. 100).

The prince is comfortingly assured, moreover, that this talent is not difficult to acquire. The reason is that although 'everyone is in a position to watch' his behaviour, 'few are in a position to come in close touch' with him (p. 101). As a result, his policies will normally be appraised not by their intrinsic qualities but rather by their 'appearances and results' (p. 101). The implication, conveniently for the prince, is that if he succeeds in maintaining a sufficient degree of remoteness and majesty, he 'will always be judged honourable and will be universally praised' even if his methods are not in fact honourable at all (p. 101).

Machiavelli's reason for attaching so much importance to the arts of dissimulation and concealment becomes clear as soon as he moves on to his other claim about the role of the virtues in political life. He argues that while it is always essential for princes to appear conventionally virtuous, it is often impossible for them to behave in a conventionally virtuous way. The reason he blandly gives is that 'taking everything into account', the prince 'will find that some of the things that appear to be virtues will, if he practises them, ruin him, and some of the things that appear to be wicked will bring him security and prosperity' (p. 92). It follows that a prince who 'wants to maintain his rule' and to attain the highest prizes of honour, glory and fame must 'learn how not to be virtuous, and to make use of this or not according to need' (p. 91).

Machiavelli makes this self-consciously level announcement of his most heterodox claim in Chapter 15 of *The Prince*, in the course of discussing 'the things for which men, and especially princes, are praised or blamed' (p. 90). The working-out of this doctrine and its implications then occupies him for the next four chapters – the notorious section on 'how a prince should govern his conduct towards his subjects or his friends' (p. 90). Machiavelli begins by stating the conclusion he is concerned to establish: that 'the gulf between how one should live and how one does live is so wide that a man who neglects what is actually done for what should be done learns the way to self-destruction rather than self-preservation' (p. 91). He then proceeds to illustrate this argument by launching an attack on precisely those virtues which the writers of advice-books for princes had always held to be particularly appropriate for rulers to cultivate.

The effect of this attack is deliberately heightened by the fact that Machiavelli continues to make use of all the usual humanist conventions in setting out his own contrasting account of the alleged princely virtues. He begins by reminding us that 'whenever men are discussed', and 'especially princes', it is customary to ask about 'various qualities' which 'earn them either praise or condemnation' (p. 91). He then focusses on the three princely virtues which had always been emphasised in such discussions: 'some, for example, are held to be generous, and others miserly'; 'some cruel, some compassionate'; and 'one man faithless, another faithful' (p. 91). And in turning to offer his own analysis of these attributes, he introduces each part of his discussion with a Latin chapter-heading in the approved humanist style. Thus Chapter 16 is entitled 'De Liberalitate et parsimonia'; Chapter 17 'De Crudelitate et pietate'; and Chapter 18 'Quomodo fides a principibus sit servanda'.[1]

Having set out this canonical list of the so-called princely virtues, Machiavelli proceeds to demolish it point by point. First he considers the virtue of liberality, and assures the prince that 'if your actions are influenced by the desire for such a reputation you will come to grief' (p. 92). Next he turns to the virtue of clemency, and shows that in the case of Scipio this was nothing less than a 'fatal characteristic', one which 'would have spoilt his fame and glory' if the Senate had not managed to check it in time (p. 98). And finally he discusses the virtue of keeping one's word, and tersely concludes that a prince who takes this obligation at all seriously will discover on many occasions that this 'places him at a disadvantage' (p. 100).

Conversely, Machiavelli insists in these chapters that if a prince wishes to 'maintain his state' he will often find it essential, and positively advantageous, 'to act in defiance of good faith, of charity, of kindness, of religion' (p. 101). He illustrates this claim in a similarly polemical vein

[1] The respective headings, that is, are 'Generosity and Parsimony', 'Cruelty and Compassion' and 'How princes should honour their Word'. For the original Latin headings see Machiavelli, *Opere* ed. Bertelli, vol. II, pp. 66, 68, 72. For these translations see *The Prince* (trans. Bull, 1961), pp. 92, 95, 99.

by enlarging on the usefulness of precisely those vices which the mirror-for-princes writers had always counselled the prince to avoid at all costs. Beginning with the quality of miserliness, he points out that 'in our times great things have been accomplished only by those who have been held miserly' (p. 93). Moving on to the vice of cruelty, he argues that this is unavoidable if the prince wishes to keep his subjects 'united and loyal' (p. 95). And finally he emphasises the value of fraud and deceit, stressing that 'contemporary experience shows that princes who have achieved great things have been those who have given their word lightly, who have known how to trick men with their cunning, and who, in the end, have overcome those abiding by honest principles' (p. 99).

It is often claimed that the originality of Machiavelli's argument in these chapters lies in the fact that he divorces politics from morality, and in consequence emphasises 'the autonomy of politics'.[1] But this interpretation appears to embody a misunderstanding of the relationship between his outlook and that of his contemporaries. Machiavelli and the more conventional writers on princely government are in complete agreement, as we have seen, about the nature of the goals which princes ought to pursue. As Machiavelli repeatedly affirms, their aim should be to 'maintain their state', to 'achieve great things' and to seek for the highest goals of honour, glory and fame (pp. 99, 101). The crucial difference between Machiavelli and his contemporaries lies in the nature of the methods they took to be appropriate for the attainment of these ends. The basic assumption of the more conventional theorists was that, if the prince wishes to achieve these goals, he must ensure that he follows the dictates of Christian morality at all times. Machiavelli's basic assumption is that a prince who 'acts virtuously in every way' will rapidly discover that he 'comes to grief among so many who are not virtuous' (p. 91). His fundamental criticism of his contemporaries is thus that they are insensitive to what he sees as the characteristic dilemma of the prince. As he observes with more than a touch of asperity, they want to be able to express their admiration for a great leader like Hannibal, but at the same time to 'condemn what made his achievements possible', especially the 'inhuman cruelty' which Machiavelli frankly sees as the key to Hannibal's glorious success (pp. 97–8). The only way out of this dilemma, he insists, is to accept unflinchingly that, if a ruler is genuinely concerned to 'maintain his state', he will have to shake off the demands of Christian virtue, wholeheartedly embrac-

---

[1] For a discussion of the origins and widespread acceptance of this interpretation, see Cochrane, 1961, p. 115. Cochrane sees Croce as the most influential source of the opinion that Machiavelli's fundamental aim was to vindicate 'the autonomy of politics'; cf. Croce, 1945, esp. p. 59. The most influential interpreter of Machiavelli to adopt this view has been Chabod, 1958, esp. p. 184.

ing the very different morality which his situation dictates. Thus the difference between Machiavelli and his contemporaries cannot adequately be characterised as a difference between a moral view of politics and a view of politics as divorced from morality. The essential contrast is rather between two different moralities – two rival and incompatible accounts of what ought ultimately to be done.[1]

After demolishing the usual scale of values underlying the mirror-for-princes literature, Machiavelli recognises that the next step he needs to take – as he notes without undue modesty – is to 'draw up an original set of rules' for the guidance of new princes (p. 90). The advice this leads him to offer is not presented with complete consistency. Sometimes he seems to be saying that, although the princely virtues may be good in themselves, there is no place for them in political life (p. 100). This leads him to assert that, while the ruler should attempt as far as possible to keep up an appearance of possessing these qualities, he should at the same time abandon them altogether in the actual conduct of his government. This seems in particular to be the logic of the argument about the alleged value of generosity. Although Machiavelli begins by conceding that 'it would be splendid if one had a reputation for generosity', he never seems to suggest that the virtue itself – as opposed to a reputation for possessing it – is one which princes ought to acquire and practise as far as possible (pp. 92–5). He seems on the contrary to be proposing that, although an appearance of generosity ought to be cultivated, the reality ought to be deliberately eschewed. We are first told that 'a prince should try to avoid, above all else, being despised and hated' (p. 95). But we are then warned that 'generosity results in your being both', since the urge to display it only leads to 'a reputation for rapacity, which brings you hatred as well as ignominy' (p. 95). The implication seems to be that the alleged princely virtues of liberality and magnificence ought perhaps to be counted instead amongst the most dangerous of the princely vices.

This highly subversive line of thought culminates in Chapter 17, in which Machiavelli raises a question which, as we have seen, had been prominently debated in the literature of advice-books for *podestà* and city-magistrates: 'whether it is better to be loved than feared, or the reverse' (p. 96). Hitherto this dilemma had invariably been resolved in the same way. Since the inculcation of fear was taken to involve cruelty, and since cruelty was regarded as an inhuman vice, the ruler was always enjoined to make himself loved rather than feared. But Machiavelli insists on the

---

[1] For a recent and extremely eloquent statement of this interpretation of Machiavelli's originality, see the important essay by Berlin, 1972, esp. p. 183.

opposite point of view. Counselling a straightforward avoidance of the conventional virtues at this point, he argues that 'it is far better to be feared than loved if you cannot be both' (p. 96). For the bond of love, he contends, is one which men 'will break when it is to their advantage', whereas 'fear is strengthened by a dread of punishment which is always effective' (pp. 96–7).

The main thrust of Machiavelli's advice, however, does not generally involve him in abandoning the conventional moral norms with so much readiness. He begins his discussion of the princely virtues by acknowledging that 'everyone will agree that it would be most laudable' if a ruler actually possessed and acted on all those qualities which are usually 'deemed to be good' (p. 91). And later he repeats that the prince must not only 'appear to be compassionate, faithful to his word, guileless and devout' but 'should be so' as far as circumstances permit (p. 100). So the most accurate summary of his advice, as he himself intimates towards the end of Chapter 18, is that the prince 'should not deviate from what is good, if that is possible, but he should know how to do evil, if that is necessary' (p. 101). There is a clear allusion at this point to the conventional humanist assumption that the true *vir virtutis* must never engage in such underhand tricks, since he must never depart from the conduct befitting a man of true manliness. Machiavelli begins by observing that, because this frank and manly way of proceeding 'often proves inadequate', it is in fact indispensable for the ruler to become 'half beast and half man', since 'he cannot survive otherwise' (p. 99). He then adds that because it is essential for a prince to know how to make 'a nice use of the beast and the man', it is also essential that he should know which beasts to imitate (p. 99). So the essence of Machiavelli's advice comes to be embodied in the image of the ruler who, being 'forced to know how to act like a beast', learns to model his conduct on both the lion and the fox (p. 99).

This startling conclusion quickly won Machiavelli the reputation amongst Christian moralists of being a man of satanic wickedness. As Macaulay remarked at the start of his famous essay, 'out of his surname they have coined an epithet for a knave' and 'out of his Christian name a synonym for the devil' (Macaulay, 1907, pp. 1–2). The figure of 'the murderous Machiavel' soon became a stock caricature in sixteenth-century drama, and the tendency to strike a note of horrified denunciation in discussing his works – first popularised by Gentillet in his *Anti-Machiavel* of 1576 – can still be found even in a number of contributions to modern scholarship. Butterfield, for example, darkly suggests at the start of *The Statecraft of Machiavelli* that the Elizabethan critics of *The Prince* may not have been as wide of the mark as is sometimes supposed (Butterfield,

1940, pp. 10–11). And Leo Strauss insists in his *Thoughts on Machiavelli* that the doctrines of *The Prince* are simply 'immoral and irreligious', and that their author can only be characterised as 'a teacher of evil' (Strauss, 1958, pp. 9–10, 12, 175).

It must of course be conceded to these traditional interpretations that Machiavelli sometimes likes to affect a self-consciously cool and amoral tone. This is partly a reflection of his own sense of himself as a political expert, capable of offering maxims and reflections suitable for each and every occasion. This in turn means that he sometimes speaks in a purely technical way about issues with obvious moral significance. When he turns in Chapter 8, for example, to consider 'those who come to power by crime', he offers an account of how to become a prince 'by some criminal and nefarious method' while insisting at the same time that there is no need to consider the question of 'the rights and wrongs of this subject' (pp. 61–2). But the main reason for the shocking tone Machiavelli tends to employ lies in his deeply pessimistic view of human nature. He declares that 'one can make this generalisation about men: they are ungrateful, fickle, liars and deceivers, they shun danger and are greedy for profit' (p. 96). So it is hardly surprising that he feels a special obligation to warn the prince that, since men are commonly such 'wretched creatures', he will have to be ready to act in defiance of the conventional pieties if he wishes to remain secure (pp. 96, 101).

Despite his enjoyment of paradox, however, and his undoubted fondness for throwing off shocking asides, it seems something of a vulgarisation of Machiavelli's outlook to label him a preacher of evil. He is far from wishing to take evil for his good, and he seldom says anything to imply that the conventional virtues should not be regarded as admirable in themselves. It is true that he is not completely consistent on this point, and generally prefers to stress the importance of acquiring a reputation for the virtues rather than the virtues themselves. But he is equally capable of insisting without equivocation that 'everyone realises how praiseworthy it is' for a prince 'to be straightforward rather than crafty in his dealings' (p. 99). He often emphasises, moreover, that the conventional virtues ought not to be gratuitously ignored. His main concern is of course with the unfortunate fact that, if a prince possesses 'all the good qualities' and 'always behaves accordingly', he 'will find them ruinous' (p. 100). But he also speaks with disapproval of those princes who never make the least attempt to behave virtuously even in favourable circumstances. His main example is that of Agathocles, the tyrant of Sicily, who 'behaved like a criminal' at 'every stage of his career' (p. 62). Despite the fact that this brought him extraordinary success in the teeth of the most adverse fortune, Machiavelli refuses to hold him up as an example of princely *virtù*, since he argues that such a relentless employment of criminal methods must 'forbid his being honoured among eminent men' (p. 63).

It will by now be evident that the whole of Machiavelli's advice is governed by a highly original sense of what should be taken to constitute true *virtù* in a prince. Hitherto, as we have seen, it had generally been assumed that the possession of *virtù* could be equated with the possession of all the major virtues. With Machiavelli, by contrast, the concept of *virtù* is simply used to refer to *whatever* range of qualities the prince may find it necessary to acquire in order to 'maintain his state' and 'achieve great things'. It is then made brutally clear that, while these qualities may sometimes overlap with the conventional virtues, the idea of any necessary or even approximate equivalence between *virtù* and the virtues is a disastrous mistake.[1] It is true that for Machiavelli a man of completely vicious character, like Agathocles, can never be considered a man of true *virtù*. For *virtù* cannot possibly be equated with viciousness. But it is no less true that Machiavelli expects men of the highest *virtù* to be capable, when the situation requires it, of behaving in a completely vicious way. For the situation of princes is such that *virtù* cannot possibly exclude viciousness. Hence it is that one of the rulers singled out in *The Prince* (and later in the *Discourses*) as a man of pre-eminent *virtù* is the Emperor Severus, of whom we are told in the same breath that he was 'extremely cruel and rapacious' and that he was a prince 'of so much *virtù*' that 'he reigned successfully to the end' in spite of countless difficulties (p. 109). Machiavelli's final sense of what it is to be a man of *virtù*, and his final words of advice to the prince, can thus be summarised by saying that he tells the prince to ensure above all that he becomes a man of 'flexible disposition': he must be capable of varying his conduct from good to evil and back again 'as fortune and circumstances dictate' (p. 101).

---

[1] For Machiavelli's use of *virtù* to mean any quality that helps a prince 'to keep his state', and for the fact that this introduces a 'sharp and decisive' disjunction between *virtù* and the virtues, see the excellent discussion in Hexter, 1964, esp. pp. 956–7. A similar interpretation has been developed by Pocock, 1975, esp. pp. 166, 177.

6

The survival of Republican values

The history of political theory in the later Renaissance offers a striking exemplification of Hegel's dictum to the effect that the owl of Minerva spreads its wings only with the falling of the dusk. As we have seen, the century following the Peace of Lodi in 1454 witnessed the final triumph of princely forms of government almost everywhere in Italy. And yet it was during the same period, in the twilight of the city republics, that incomparably the most original and important contributions were made to republican political thought.

THE CENTRES OF REPUBLICANISM

Of the various centres in which republican ideas continued to be discussed and celebrated throughout the later Renaissance, the one with the most enduring commitment to the traditional values of independence and self-government was Venice. While the rest of Italy succumbed to the rule of the *signori*, the Venetians never relinquished their traditional liberties. They continued to operate the constitution they had originally set up in 1297, which consisted of three main elements: the *Consiglio Grande*, the body responsible for appointing most of the city's officials; the Senate, which controlled foreign and financial affairs; and the Doge, who served with his council as the elected head of the government. It is true that when this rigidly oligarchic system was first imposed, the immediate effect was to generate a series of popular uprisings led by the disenfranchised. But these outbreaks were quickly contained, and after the establishment of the Council of Ten as a secret and permanent committee of public safety in 1335 there were no further disturbances. Venice settled down to an uninterrupted period of freedom and security, becoming the envy of all Italy and earning her unique reputation as the *Serenissima*, the most serene Republic.

The question of how the Venetians managed to combine their political liberty with the avoidance of faction first began to attract the attention of constitutional theorists at the end of the fourteenth century. Pier Paolo Vergerio appears to have been the earliest writer to propose what later came to be accepted as the classic answer to the puzzle. He initially presented his solution in a letter to the Chancellor of Venice in 1394, and subsequently embodied it in his *Fragment on the Republic of Venice* (Gilbert, 1968, p. 468 and note). He based his discussion on Plato's contention in the *Laws* that the soundest and most secure form of government must consist of the three 'pure' forms in combination – the result being an amalgam of monarchy, aristocracy and democracy. He then suggested that the special excellence of the Venetian constitution derived from the fact that it succeeded in fusing together these different systems into a stable form of mixed rule, with the Doge representing the monarchical element, the Senate the aristocratic and the *Consiglio Grande* the element of democracy. He concluded that it was due to this clear understanding of 'what Plato said was best for cities' that the Venetians had been able to live together for such a long time 'in peace and amity', and to govern their affairs with such success that 'there is no more opulent or splendid city in Italy, or even in the whole of the rest of the world' (pp. 103, 104).

This explanation was gratefully taken up by the members of Francesco Barbaro's intellectual circle in Venice in the middle of the fifteenth century. George of Trebizond, who had been brought from Crete to Venice by Barbaro in 1417, wrote to Barbaro in 1451 to explain that the reason for the 'long and happy' life of the Venetian republic lay in its combination of monarchical, aristocratic and democratic features in the finest Platonic style (Gilbert, 1968, pp. 468–9). Barbaro replied with expressions of admiration at George's statement of this important insight. He added that the translation which George had already made of Plato's *Laws* should be supplied with an introduction in which the similarities between Platonic theory and Venetian practice could be developed at greater length. George duly wrote such an essay and dedicated it to the Doge, receiving in return a handsome remuneration for this flattering explanation of Venice's unique political stability (cf. Bouwsma, 1968, pp. 63–4).

The point at which the miracle of Venice's unchanging constitution became of the greatest interest to the rest of Italy was at the start of the sixteenth century. The Florentines in particular began to ask themselves – at a time when their own freedom was being sharply curtailed by the Medici – what made it possible for the Venetians to combine a no less peaceable regime with a far more extensive system of political liberties. The most significant treatise to address this question was the *Dialogue on the Republic of the Venetians* by Donato Giannotti (1492–1573). Giannotti was a friend of Machiavelli's and a fervent republican, who served as Secretary of War to the Ten under the restored Florentine Republic of 1527 and was forced into exile after the final restoration of the Medici in 1530 (Starn, 1968, pp. 21, 26, 39). He drafted his book on Venice while living there in 1526, and first published it when in exile once again in 1540 (Gilbert, 1967, pp. 178–82). He describes the evolution as well as the character of the Venetian constitution, arguing that the combination of liberty and security attained by the Venetians can be attributed to two main causes. One is the balance between the rule of the one, the few and the many which they are able to maintain by combining the rule of the Doge with the Senate and the *Consiglio Grande* (pp. 50ff.). The other is the elaborate system of voting and balloting which they employ in order to ensure that every magistrate is chosen and every political decision made with the object of maximising the common good over any factional advantages (pp. 91–117). It was Giannotti's conclusion that these devices had enabled the Venetians to achieve what one scholar has recently described as 'the mechanisation of *virtù*', and hence the perfection of their government (cf. Pocock, 1975, p. 285).

While the Florentines looked to Venice as a source of practical political wisdom, the Venetians themselves, increasingly aware of their unique stability in the midst of Italy's turmoils, began to analyse and celebrate, with no little complacency, the success of their own constitutional arrangements (Bouwsma, 1968, pp. 95, 111). The first and greatest Venetian theorist to write in this vein was Gasparo Contarini (1483–1542), whose treatise on *The Commonwealth and Government of Venice* was sketched between 1522 and 1525, revised in the early 1530s and first published in 1543.[1] Contarini's book is more purely a panegyric than Giannotti's, revealing less interest in the details of Venice's constitutional machinery and a greater concern to emphasise the sheer genius of Venice's original lawgivers, who 'omitted nothing which might seem to pertain to the right institution of a commonwealth' and thus succeeded in framing a government 'in the highest degree of perfection' (pp. 15, 17; cf. Gilmore, 1973, p. 433). Contarini's is also a more self-consciously conservative work, culminating in the claim that, since it is impossible for anyone to 'blame or find fault with a government so virtuously established', it follows that the main duty of Venice's leading citizens must be to prevent the perfection of their constitution from being altered in any way (p. 147;

[1] For these dates of composition, see Gilbert, 1967, pp. 174–7. The original title of Contarini's book was *De Magistratibus et Republica Venetorum* (Paris, 1543). The title *The Commonwealth and Government of Venice* was supplied by Lewes Lewkenor, who published an English translation of the book in 1599. It is from Lewkenor's version that all quotations have been taken.

cf. Gilbert, 1969). The chief aim of the book, however, is to ask and answer the same question which the admirers of Venice had been considering ever since Vergerio's treatise more than a century before. The question, as Contarini phrases it, is how the Venetians have been able to maintain 'the long continuance' of such a 'sound and quiet safety' at a time when the rest of Italy has been suffering 'so great a misery' (pp. 4–6). The answer he suggests, again in line with the received wisdom, is that their constitution is 'such a mixture of all estates, that this only city retains a princely sovereignty, a government of the nobility and a popular authority, so that the forms of them all seem to be equally balanced', and the dangers of internal conflict are effectively cancelled out (p. 15).

The elaboration of this self-congratulating thesis became the major preoccupation of Venetian political theory throughout the latter part of the sixteenth century (Bouwsma, 1968, pp. 270, 273). The most important of the numerous writers to develop the same argument was Paolo Paruta (1540–98), who presented it in his *Political Discourses*, a work which first appeared in 1599, the year after his death (Monzani, 1852, pp. vii, xxxvi). Paruta discusses the republic of ancient Rome in the first of his two Discourses, that of modern Venice in the second. He traces the process by which the Romans lost their freedom with the coming of the Empire, a decline which he then contrasts in the opening Chapter of his second Book with the unparalleled success of his own native city in combining 'greatness with liberty'. As with all his predecessors, Paruta finds the key to this achievement in the 'form and order' of the Venetian constitution, in which 'all the parts are so well disposed' that all 'domestic discord' is avoided, each aspect of the government being so carefully 'limited and corrected' by the others that 'the public benefit' is invariably secured (pp. 228, 231; cf. Bouwsma, 1968, pp. 270–91).

As well as maintaining its unbroken continuity in Venice, the republican tradition of political theory revived in the early sixteenth century both in Florence and Rome. We have already seen that these cities suffered increasingly despotic forms of government throughout most of the later Renaissance. This trend, however, was to some extent interrupted after the coming of the French in 1494. Both the Medici and the Popes experienced great difficulties in resisting or even negotiating with the invaders, a failure which left an opening for their opponents to challenge the competence of their regimes, and to call for a restoration of popular liberties.

In Rome the most important of these republican insurrections took place in 1511. The occasion was provided by the collapse of the perfidious League of Cambrai which Pope Julius II had engineered three years before. The Pope's intention had been to counterbalance the power of

Venice, but the main effect of his diplomacy was to strengthen the position of the French. They decisively defeated the Venetians at the battle of Agnadello in 1509, and managed as a result to regain control of Milan (Green, 1964, p. 97). When Julius attempted to curb their ambitions by withdrawing from his alliance, Louis XII replied by appealing over his head to a General Council of the Church, which he summoned to meet at Pisa in 1511 and commanded Julius to attend (La Brosse, 1965, pp. 58–9). (It was at this point, incidentally, that the Florentines, menaced by the Pope's armies, tried to persuade Louis XII to convene the Council else-where – an embassy on which Machiavelli served as one of the nego-tiators [Renaudet, 1922, pp. 469–76]). At this juncture Julius fell danger-ously ill, and this together with the failure of his policies provided the signal for what Gregorovius called 'a revolt in favour of lost liberty' at Rome (Gregorovius, 1967, vol. 8, p. 81). It is true that the uprising was unsuccessful, and that Julius's formation of the Holy League in the following year enabled him to regain the initiative in his fight against the French. But in the meantime, as Guicciardini reports in his *History of Italy*, the leader of the anti-Papal faction in Rome, Pompei Colonna, had been able to incite the populace to a serious revolt, rousing them with a fiery speech in which he denounced the 'priestly tyranny' of the Popes and called on his fellow-citizens to 'awake from so deep a slumber' and to fight for their ancient liberties (p. 231).

It was in Florence, however, that the rule of the *signori* was most effectively challenged during this period. As soon as Charles VIII's armies marched into Florentine territory in October 1494, the leader of the Medicean 'despotism', the young Piero de Medici, appears to have panicked (Schevill, 1936, p. 436). He immediately acceded to all the French king's demands, including the surrender of Florence's two major seaports and the disarming of all her border fortresses (Weinstein, 1970, pp. 130–1). When the news of this abject surrender reached the city, a spontaneous revolution broke out. Luca Landucci (c. 1436–1516), whose *Diary* gives an eye-witness account of what happened, reports that the piazza suddenly filled with 'all the citizens' and with 'troops of armed men crying loudly *Popolo e Libertà*' (p. 61). Piero found his way barred by the rebellious *signoria* and learnt that a price of two thousand ducats had been placed on his head (p. 62). After a moment's hesitation he decided to give up without a struggle, and while the mob sacked his palace he rode out of the city with a few followers and into a lifetime's exile (Weinstein, 1970, p. 134).

It is true that the Florentines only managed to enjoy their restored liberties for a short time. As we have seen, the Medici were able to regain control of the city with the help of Spanish troops in 1512. Nevertheless, the intervening period witnessed the revival of a genuinely popular form of government, in which the highest authority was vested in a *Consiglio Grande* with a membership of over three thousand citizens.[1] Furthermore, the return of the Medici in 1512 by no means signalled the end of Florence's commitment to this more traditional type of regime. It was only after the Medici had succeeded in putting down a series of plots against their government in the 1520s, culminating in the last revival of the Republic in 1527, that they were finally able to consolidate their position as hereditary rulers of Florence in the early 1530s.

These last attempts to halt the spread of princely government were largely futile in practice, but they were associated with the most spectacular flowering of Republican political thought. There were two main strands of Republican ideology available to these latter-day protagonists of popular government: one was the fourteenth-century tradition of Italian scholasticism, the leading exponents of which had been such theorists as Bartolus of Saxoferrato, Ptolemy of Lucca and Marsiglio of Padua; the other was the early fifteenth-century tradition of 'civic' humanism, as exemplified by Salutati, Bruni, Poggio and their numerous followers. What we find at the start of the sixteenth century is a revival and an incomparably rich development of both these earlier lines of thought. It is this intellectual movement which the rest of this chapter will attempt to analyse.

THE CONTRIBUTION OF SCHOLASTICISM

The contribution of scholasticism to the flowering of republican political ideas in the later Renaissance has generally been underestimated. Allen, for example, insists that Italian political theory at the end of the *quattrocento* 'owed nothing to the schoolmen', since it had become 'completely detached' from the medieval view of political life (Allen, 1957, pp. 446, 478). And Bouwsma has recently argued that the 'medieval' preoccupations of scholastic philosophy need to be sharply distinguished from 'Renaissance republicanism', a quite separate strand of argument which he in turn equates with the humanist tradition running 'from Salutati to Guicciardini' (Bouwsma, 1968, pp. 1–11, 41). These are orthodox judgments, but they overlook the fact that the traditional liberties of the Italian city republics were defended in the later Renaissance not merely

---

[1] See Gilbert, 1965, pp. 11, 20. See also Weinstein, 1970, p. 248. For an account of the factional disputes which led to the acceptance of a large Council in 1494, see Rubinstein, 1960, esp. pp. 155–59.

by professional humanists, but also by a number of theologians and jurists, whose writings still tended to be couched in an idiom far more closely related to scholastic than to humanist moral and political thought.

If we turn first to Florence, we encounter a systematic attempt to defend the restored republic in essentially scholastic terms in the writings of Savonarola and his disciples after 1494. Savonarola's own political works, in particular those composed between 1494 and 1498, contain a restatement of several arguments we have already met in a number of fourteenth-century Thomists, and especially in the tracts of Ptolemy of Lucca, whose continuation of Aquinas's treatise on *The Rule of Princes* Savonarola sometimes follows word for word.[1]

Fra Girolamo Savonarola (1452–98), a native of Ferrara, originally came to Florence in 1482, after studying at the University of Bologna, and stayed until 1487 (Ridolfi, 1959, pp. 13–16, 25–6). He was recalled by Lorenzo de Medici in 1490, and elected prior of the Dominican priory of San Marco in the following year (Ridolfi, 1959, p. 29). He rapidly became famous as a preacher, the crowds at his sermons becoming so great as early as 1491 that he had to move his services from San Marco to the Cathedral (Weinstein, 1970, p. 99). But it was only after the anti-Medicean coup of 1494 that he finally came into his own as a prophet and a defender of republican political values. From that moment until his trial and execution four years later he was one of the most influential supporters of the restored Florentine republic, and one of the most powerful spokesmen in favour of the city's traditional liberties (cf. Rubinstein, 1960, pp. 155–61).

It is of course obvious that Savonarola was far more than an orthodox preacher of received political beliefs. He saw himself fundamentally as a prophet, a man who perceived God's hand in everything and regarded himself as specially chosen to explain the ways of the Almighty to his fellow citizens. This made him scornful of several assumptions which we have seen to be central to Florentine moral and political theory in the later Renaissance. He was naturally hostile to the humanist emphasis on the alleged ability of fortune to control and overrun men's affairs. He constantly preached that nothing happens except by the will of God, and devoted much of his prophetic fervour to persuading his congregations that Florence was a chosen city guided by God alone (Weinstein, 1970, pp. 141–2). So he violently opposed 'the wicked ones' who persisted in speaking in terms of 'chance or fortune' when they should have been

[1] For a striking instance of a verbal parallel between Ptolemy and Savonarola, see Weinstein, 1970, pp. 292 note and 293 note, comparing Ptolemy's treatise, Book IV, Ch. 8 with a passage from Savonarola's *Compendium Totius Philosophiae*.

thinking only in terms of Godly providence (Weinstein, 1970, p. 280). Similarly, he was contemptuous of the humanist ideal of the *vir* who devotes his *virtus* to seeking the attainment of honour, glory and fame. He insisted that the proper goals of human life are not connected in the least with worldly advancement or display, but only with the cultivation of Christian humility and godliness. So he mounted a puritan attack on the prevailing mores of the Florentines, promoting the notorious 'Burning of the Vanities' in 1497 and 1498, and campaigning successfully for the abolition of several traditional carnivals and the conversion of others into religious festivals (Ridolfi, 1959, p. 128; cf. Schevill, 1936, pp. 271, 446).

Nevertheless, it would be misleading to suggest, as Chabod and others have done, that Savonarola's 'principal theme' was 'one of revolt against the times and the historical situation', and thus that his entire programme was antagonistic to the traditions and aspirations of *quattrocento* Florence.[1] On the contrary, it is evident that even his special prophetic vision of the city's future was closely connected with a number of well-entrenched Florentine myths. Bruni and his followers had already argued that the city had been founded in the period of Rome's greatest freedom – as befitted the guardian of Tuscan liberties – and that her citizens had subsequently fought to maintain their independence, especially against Visconti Milan, in such a way as to give an example to the rest of Italy. As Weinstein has shown, part of Savonarola's success in projecting his own apocalyptic view of Florence's special destiny can be traced to the almost opportunistic skill with which he adapted and applied these prevailing beliefs about the city's historical significance.[2] It is true that, when the French invaded in 1494, he began by proclaiming the doom of the Republic, warning his audiences that 'you have yet to suffer many adversities and much grief' (Weinstein, 1970, p. 139). But he soon turned instead to emphasising Florence's special character as a chosen city, making extensive allusions to the traditional image of the Republic as 'the heart of Italy', the leading exponent of Italian liberties, the centre from which 'the vital spirits are diffused' and 'the voice goes out' to the whole of the rest of the *Regnum Italicum* (cf. Weinstein, 1970, p. 169).

---

[1] See Chabod, 1958, p. 19. This has been the traditional judgment on Savonarola. Cf. also the account in Schevill, 1936, esp. p. 454. This viewpoint has recently been challenged by Weinstein, 1970, an excellent and thoroughly convincing analysis to which I am greatly indebted.

[2] See Weinstein, 1970, esp. pp. 34–6, 139–45. A similar argument was earlier suggested by Gilbert, 1957. Weinstein has acutely observed the way in which Savonarola's prophecies shifted – with some resulting incoherence – from emphasising the doom of the city to giving a no less emphatic account of her role as a chosen vessel of God's highest purposes. Cf. Weinstein, 1970, esp. pp. 67, 141, 169–70.

When we turn to Savonarola's specific constitutional proposals, we find an even closer set of connections between his outlook and certain prevailing assumptions of Florentine political thought. It seems misleading to treat the essence of his political theory, as Pocock has done, as an attempt 'to ground citizenship upon prophecy' (Pocock, 1975, p. 115). For this appears to underestimate the extent to which Savonarola derived his political views from a more familiar and a far more mundane tradition of Dominican political thought, a tradition already familiar to the Florentines through the sermons and other writings produced by such theorists as Remigio de Girolami almost two centuries before.

Savonarola offers his most systematic restatement of this outlook in a brief vernacular treatise, published only a few weeks before his downfall in 1498, entitled *A Tract on the Constitution and Government of the City of Florence* (Weinstein, 1970, p. 289). The tract is in three main sections, the first of which takes up a theme already emphasised by Bartolus as well as Ptolemy of Lucca in their political works. This is the allegation that, although monarchy may in some absolute sense be the best form of government, it is not the best for Italy, and especially not for Florence, where it is essential that a Republican regime should be maintained (pp. 446–50). The reason Savonarola gives for this judgment brings him to the heart of his political message – his message being that Florence should ensure above all that she preserves her traditional liberties. The city must remain a Republic, he argues, because this alone guarantees her citizens the enjoyment of 'true liberty', which is 'more valuable than gold and silver' and 'greater than all other treasures' (pp. 481, 488).

Having singled out the freedom of the Florentines as their 'most precious possession', Savonarola proceeds in the second part of his analysis to ask what tends to jeopardise the preservation of this most vital quality in political life. He spends no time on the old suggestion that an over-active pursuit of private gain may be inimical to the maintenance of a free government. It is a remarkable feature of his argument that he is quite willing to endorse the comfortable assumption that Florence's great wealth should be taken as a sign of God's favour, and that her citizens may expect 'an abundance of riches' as long as they follow God's commands (p. 482; cf. Weinstein, 1970, p. 311). He shows a greater interest in the widespread belief that one of the gravest dangers to political liberty arises out of entrusting the security of one's city to hired mercenary troops. Although he makes no mention of this claim in his *Tract*, he had already alluded in his earlier treatise *On Political and Kingly Government* to the risk of employing soldiers 'who fight not for the love of their *patria* but merely for pay', while the same theme had been taken up by one of his followers, Domenico Cecchi, who published a pamphlet in 1496 denouncing the use of mercenaries and calling for the formation of a citizen militia.[1] But the main threat to liberty which Savonarola singles out is the prevalence of faction and civil strife. He devotes most of the central section of his *Tract* – in the manner of Bartolus and Salutati – to portraying the horrors of tyrannical government, and argues that the main cause of tyranny is always domestic discord, which enables unscrupulous party-leaders to seize control of the government and overturn the liberties of the people (pp. 456–71; cf. Weinstein, 1970, pp. 253, 298).

After discussing these dangers to freedom, Savonarola turns in the final part of his *Tract* to consider, in a no less conventional style, what measures should be taken to ensure that this precious jewel of liberty is continually kept safe. Again he endorses the type of answer already given by such writers as Bartolus and Marsiglio of Padua. He places his entire faith in the efficacy of institutions, arguing in characteristically scholastic style that the only sure solution lies in treating the whole body of the citizens as the supreme authority in all political affairs. He concedes that 'since it is too difficult for all the people to hold meetings every day', it will be necessary to institute a Council consisting of 'a certain number of citizens who enjoy the authority of the entire populace' (p. 474). But he continues to insist that the people merely delegate their powers in establishing such a *Consiglio Grande*, and so concludes that the preservation of liberty depends above all on ensuring that the citizens and their government remain one and the same.

If we turn next to the attack on Papal 'tyranny' which flared up at Rome in 1511, we encounter a similar reliance on the idiom of scholastic legal and political philosophy amongst the defenders of the city's ancient liberties. This can clearly be seen in the case of the most remarkable tract to appear in connection with the crisis, Salamonio's series of seven dialogues entitled *The Sovereignty of the Roman Patriciate*, a work in which an essentially Bartolist theory of inalienable popular sovereignty is presented as the most suitable form of government for the city of Rome.

The author of this work, Mario Salamonio (c. 1450–1532), was a native of Rome and a member of one of the city's most ancient patrician families (D'Addio, 1954, pp. 3, 10). He was educated at Rome University, and subsequently acquired a wide experience of legal and political affairs. He was appointed a member of Pope Alexander VI's commission on the reform of the Roman legal system in 1494, and acted four years later as *Capitano*

---

[1] For the discussion of mercenaries in Savonarola's tract *On Political and Kingly Government*, see p. 582. For a discussion of Cecchi's pamphlet, see Bayley, 1961, pp. 237–8.

del Popolo in Florence (D'Addio, 1954, p. 7). He was present in Rome at the time of the uprising of 1511, and appears to have sided decisively with the Colonna in their attempt to challenge the Papacy's control of the government. Although his book on popular sovereignty was not printed until 1544, it was written in the immediate aftermath of the crisis between 1512 and 1514, and was clearly intended to serve as a theoretical prop to the Republican cause.[1]

Salamonio was of course far more than a mere pamphleteer in favour of the Roman patriciate. He was one of the leading jurists of his age, a famous commentator on the Digest, and a pioneer in seeking to incorporate the historical methods of the humanists into his own legal philosophy. Some of these more academic interests can also be found in the pages of *The Sovereignty of the Roman Patriciate*, in which the first three dialogues are entirely given over to a general statement of the legal theory of *Imperium*.[2] It is only at the beginning of the fourth dialogue that Salamonio turns to consider the more immediate questions posed by the prevailing chaos in Italy and especially in Rome. The transition is effected when the figure of the Philosopher points out that, as Aristotle stresses, the reason for establishing a political society and endowing it with *Imperium* 'is not merely for the sake of living but for the sake of living well and happily' (fo. 34b). This naturally leads the other speakers in the dialogues – an historian, a theologian and a jurist – to consider the prospects and the difficulties of living a full and happy civic life in Italy in their own time. They readily agree with the Historian when he opens the discussion by remarking that they are living in a miserable age, one in which evil habits abound and virtue is scarcely cultivated (fo. 36a). So they proceed to discuss the question of what is preventing them from enjoying a satisfactory civic life, and the further question of what should be done to remedy the manifold corruptions of the age – the two issues which occupy them for the rest of the book.

One of the factors they all take to be inhibiting the achievement of a virtuous civic life is the prevalence of excessive wealth. This fear had been discounted, as we have seen, by the humanists of Bruni's school, and even Savonarola had remained content to endorse a more patriotic sense that the opulence of the Italian cities should be counted as one of their glories. By contrast, Salamonio is one of the first writers to recognise that a

---

[1] Allen is thus mistaken in stating (Allen, 1957, p. 332) that Salamonio was a Spaniard and probably a Jesuit, whose *Sovereignty* was written as well as published in 1544. Cf. the fully documented biographical sketch in the opening Chapter of D'Addio's comprehensive study. (D'Addio, 1954, pp. 3–10).

[2] For an appraisal of Salamonio's theory of *Imperium*, see vol. II, pp. 131–4.

combination of military weakness and enormous wealth had been the main cause of Italy's recent undoing, since it had made her such an irresistible prey to the 'barbarians' in search of easy conquests and massive spoils. He accordingly reverts to the old argument – soon to be reiterated by Machiavelli and Guicciardini – that a good civic life must be founded on the virtue of frugality. One reason for this conclusion is offered by the Theologian, who stresses that 'no one can serve both God and Mammon', and reminds us of Christ's saying that 'it is easier for a camel to pass through the eye of a needle than for a rich man to enter the kingdom of heaven' (fo. 46a). But the chief reason is given by the Philosopher, who argues that 'when riches and rich men are honoured in a city, men of virtue and probity come to be despised' (fos. 45b–46a). Both agree that 'rich men do not esteem the virtues', and thus that the pursuit of riches and the maintenance of a good civic life 'cannot easily be accommodated to each other' (fo. 46a).

But the main blame for the collapse of civic life in Italy is of course attributed to the repeated invasions of the 'barbarians' since 1494. The Historian gives a graphic description of the way in which 'Italy has been oppressed by their invading armies' ever since that time (fo. 40b). They have poured into Venice's land Empire, they have overrun the whole of Tuscany and Emilia, they have even occupied the Papal States (fo. 40b). And the consequences everywhere have been utterly ruinous. There has been pillage and desecration 'without regard for age or sex'; the rivers have run with blood; and the whole of Italy has been given over to 'sinful license' (fos. 40b, 41b).

How then is Italy to save herself, the Philosopher asks, from all this 'iniquity and grief'? (fo. 47a). Some of the answers Salamonio proposes relate to the obvious need for the cities to improve their capacity to defend themselves. This leads the Philosopher to mount the usual attack on 'those who fight with mercenaries', a criticism which is taken up with enthusiasm by all the other speakers (fo. 44b). The Jurist maintains that 'mercenary soldiers spend their whole time in their camps, and are useless in battle', while the Historian cites the recent successes of the French against the Venetians and the Pope as proof of the same point (fo. 45a). The answer, they all agree, is that each city should form its own militia, training its citizens to recognise that 'it is far more noble to fight for one's liberty, one's children, one's hearth and home' than to leave this duty to be performed by mere mercenaries (fo. 44b). The Historian points out that 'the Romans grew great by these arts', and adds that 'the memorable example of Pisa in our own time shows how much difference there is between fighting on one's own behalf and fighting for others' (fo. 44b).

Although the Pisans 'were unable to afford hired troops or the help of allies, they sustained a siege on their own with the greatest fortitude for fourteen years', not only against 'the wealth of Florence', but even against 'the onslaught of the French'. The explanation, he feels convinced, lies in the fact that 'they were fighting for their own liberty' instead of for someone else's pay (fo. 44b).

Salamonio devotes his chief attention, however, to considering how the life of a city can best be regulated in such a way as to ensure that the liberty of its citizens is preserved and their capacity to lead a full and happy life is maximised. He begins with a suggestion which is more humanist than scholastic in inspiration, claiming that 'the city must concern itself with the *virtus* of its citizens', and that 'every ruler must concern himself with *virtus*', offering an example of 'all the moral virtues' to his subjects (fo. 34b, 42a). But his main answer consists of reiterating the same argument which had earlier been developed by Bartolus, Marsiglio and the whole tradition of scholastic legal and political writers in Italy, and which had recently been repeated by Savonarola and his disciples. The key to maintaining a free and happy civic life is said to lie in establishing effective civic institutions, while the key to maintaining these institutions in good order is said to lie in ensuring that the whole body of the citizens retains ultimate sovereignty at all times.

The working-out of this answer takes up the whole of Salamonio's last three dialogues. He first turns in Book V to repudiate the idea that princes have any rights of dispensation in relation to the law, arguing that such an arrangement is no better than tyranny, and that 'everything must be decided by means of the dignity of the law' (fo. 48b). He then seeks to vindicate the more specific claim that the rule of a popular assembly constitutes the best and most suitable form of government for the city of Rome. This is not only claimed – in traditional Bartolist vein – to be in line with the needs of the city and the requirements of natural justice; it is also argued – in the more fashionable idiom of the legal humanists – to be a reflection of the historical rights of the Roman populace. The last two dialogues are then employed to make good this case. The Philosopher begins by asking the Jurist to give an account of 'how sovereignty came to be established' at Rome (fo. 51a). The Jurist replies that there is a very rich literature on the point, and refers to the authority of Giulio Pomponio (1428–97) whose history of the laws and magistracies of the city had been published a generation earlier. According to Pomponio, the Jurist observes, 'it was only because it proved difficult to gather all the people together' that they permitted the exercise of their sovereign authority to be transferred first to the Senate and later to the Emperors (fo. 51b). This analysis is enthusiastically endorsed by the Historian. 'It is absolutely clear from Pomponio's evidence', he agrees, that it was only the difficulty of holding a large meeting of all the citizens that persuaded them to transfer the actual administration of their lawmaking powers to a single individual 'for the sake of the best possible government of the commonwealth' (fo. 52a). Next they consider the famous question of whether the sovereignty of the people may not have been lost with the alleged transference of *Imperium* from the Emperor Constantine to the Pope. The Jurist raises this final doubt, but he is immediately assured by the Historian that 'the very learned Lorenzo Valla' has been able to show that the supposed Donation of Constantine, the pillar of the Papacy's claims to temporal dominion, is in fact a forgery which the Popes have been using to defraud the people of Rome (fo. 52b). The Historian then goes on to point out that even the inscriptions which survive from the period of the Roman principate continue to speak of 'the *Imperium* of the Roman populace', a fact which enables the Philosopher to conclude in triumph that 'no *princeps* can be a true overlord' in Rome, but 'can only be a minister of the people', who are thus said to have retained the ultimate sovereign authority over the city at all times (fos. 55a–b; cf. also fo. 59).

THE CONTRIBUTION OF HUMANISM

Although the contribution of scholastic legal and political ideas to the revival of Republicanism at the start of the sixteenth century was of more significance than is sometimes allowed, it is of course true that the most important works of Republican political theory written at this time were generally cast in a humanist rather than a scholastic mould. The main influence on the evolution of Republicanism during this later period was undoubtedly exercised by the writings of the so-called 'civic' humanists of early *quattrocento* Florence – Salutati, Bruni, Poggio and their various followers. It was essentially the recovery and development of their outlook which gave rise to the last and greatest works of Renaissance political theory, including the Republican treatises of Guicciardini and Machiavelli. It is this tradition of argument which we next need to investigate as a conclusion to our survey of Italian Renaissance political thought.

The beginnings of the revival of Florentine Republicanism can be discerned a whole generation before the anti-Medicean *coup* of 1494. A sense of outrage at the Medici had been growing at least since 1458, when Cosimo had made his first decisive move in the direction of imposing a 'tyrannical' regime. This prompted a number of writers to respond by reviving the ideology of 'civic' humanism. One of the earliest was Francesco Patrizi (1413–92), who composed a major treatise on *The Institution of a Republic* in the 1460s before eventually reconciling himself to writing in the manner of an adviser to princes in his later work on *The Kingdom and the Education of the King*. The same values were kept alive in the 1470s by Alamanno Rinuccini (1419–99), a correspondent of Patrizi's and a virulent enemy of the Medici, who released a deliberately inflammatory tract *On Liberty* in 1479 (Kristeller, 1965, p. 46). And a similar line of criticism was propagated by Donato Acciaiuoli (1429–78) in his commentaries on Aristotle's *Ethics* and *Politics*, as well as in the history of Rome's campaigns against Carthage which he produced in the 1470s (Baron, 1966, p. 437).

But the main efflorescence of Republican political theory occurred in the generation after the return of the Medici in 1512. The defenders of Florence's traditional liberties were animated during this period by three main considerations: the memory of the successful restoration of the Republic between 1494 and 1512; the hope of overturning the government of the Medici once again – a hope which was duly fulfilled in 1527; and the need in the meantime to maintain a spirit of opposition to their allegedly 'despotic' and 'tyrannical' practices. The outcome was the most intensive and influential analysis of Republican political principles to appear in early modern Europe.

The chief forum for the discussion of these ideas was provided by the meetings which took place at the Orti Oricellari, the gardens on the outskirts of Florence owned by Cosimo Rucellai, an aristocratic opponent of the restored Medici regime (Gilbert, 1949, pp. 101, 118). Amongst the leading anti-Medicean theorists who took part in these gatherings was Antonio Brucioli, who was exiled after the failure of the attempted republican *coup* of 1522, and who published his *Dialogues on Moral Philosophy* four years later, a work in which the opening section on 'The Republic' provides an outline of a traditional theory of Florentine liberties (Cantimori, 1937, pp. 88–90; 95–6). But the most important writer to frequent the Oricellari Gardens at this period was Machiavelli. We have seen that, after the collapse of the Republic in 1512, he had at first hoped to find employment with the city's new masters, and had dedicated his tract on *The Prince* to Lorenzo de Medici. It would still be true to say, however, that by background and conviction Machiavelli was basically a Republican, having served as second secretary in the Chancellory of the restored Florentine Republic between 1498 and 1512. When he failed to attract the attention of the Medici after 1512, he readily drifted into the circle of Republican theorists and conspirators foregathering at the

Oricellari Gardens, and appears to have discussed the drafts of his *Discourses on the First Ten Books of Titus Livy* at their meetings. One of the men to whom he dedicated the *Discourses* was Cosimo Rucellai, and his letter of dedication offers thanks to Cosimo for having 'forced me to write what I should never have written of my own accord' (p. 93).

As these circumstances suggest, Machiavelli almost certainly began to compose his *Discourses* only after he came to realise that his hopes of gaining employment under the Medici were misplaced.[1] It seems probable that he started work on the book in 1514, and Felix Gilbert has plausibly suggested that the first stage of composition may have simply taken the form of a commentary on the relevant chapters of Livy, which Machiavelli then worked up into a more systematic treatise by redistributing the material under a series of general headings.[2] It is clear from internal evidence that this process of composition must have been well advanced by 1517. Machiavelli remarks in the middle of his second Discourse that 'if treasure guaranteed victory', then 'a few days ago' the Pope and the Florentines would have defeated Francesco Maria in the war of Urbino (p. 301). The battle which is described as taking place so recently was the one in which Leo X recovered Urbino, and this was fought on 17 September 1517. Finally, it is apparent from similar evidence that the *Discourses* must have been completed before the end of 1519. In his third Discourse Machiavelli refers to Maximilian (who died in 1519) as the reigning Emperor, and in his letter of dedication he asks Cosimo Rucellai (who died in the same year) to be sure to read his book (pp. 94, 490).

Standing somewhat apart from the fervent group of Republicans meeting in the Oricellari Gardens is the more urbane and sceptical figure of Francesco Guicciardini (1483–1540). He managed to survive the change of regime in 1512 far more successfully than Machiavelli, and he subsequently served under both the Medici Popes, Leo X and Clement VII, in a series of important governorships. Nevertheless, his political writings – which exactly span the years between the first restoration of the Medici

---

[1] This claim has been argued most fully by Baron, 1961, from whom I take the details about the internal evidence relating to the dating of the *Discourses*. Baron's thesis involves denying the usual assumption that Machiavelli began work on both *The Prince* and the *Discourses* at much the same time. For Baron's statement of this traditional thesis, see Baron, 1961, p. 231 and refs. there. For his own claim that Machiavelli first wrote *The Prince*, completed it at the end of 1513, and shortly afterwards began work on the *Discourses*, see Baron, 1961, esp. pp. 236, 247. Hexter has sought to argue that the first Discourse cannot have been started before 1515. See Hexter, 1956, esp. pp. 93–5. But this contention has been convincingly challenged by Gilbert, 1965, pp. 230–1. Baron's general argument seems plausible, and most recent commentators have accepted it. See for example Hale, 1961, esp. p. 168, note. Nevertheless, the dating of the *Discourses* remains a subject of learned debate. For two attempts to survey the evidence, see Cochrane, 1961, pp. 133–6 and, more recently, Geerken, 1976, p. 357.

[2] See Gilbert, 1953, p. 147. For a discussion of Gilbert's theory, see Richardson, 1972.

in 1512 and their final return in 1530 – exhibit a consistent if somewhat cautious Republican stance, the sort of outlook one might expect from a member of one of Florence's most prominent aristocratic families. Guicciardini's first political tract was written while he was serving on an embassy in Spain in 1512, and is generally known as *The Discourse of Logrogno*, taking its name from the town in which he happened to be staying when he drafted it (Rubinstein, 1965a). His next important treatise was the *Dialogue on Florentine Government*, which he composed between 1521 and 1523 (Ridolfi, 1967, p. 134). This was followed between 1528 and 1530 by the completion of his *Maxims and Reflections*, a series of brief *aperçus* on men and affairs which he had first sketched in 1512 (Ridolfi, 1967, pp. 206, 310–11). And finally, the last political work he produced before turning to his great *History of Italy* was an unfinished set of *Considerations on the Discourses of Machiavelli* which he probably wrote in 1530 (Ridolfi, 1967, pp. 206–7).

The last important theorist of this group – the man who may claim the somewhat gloomy distinction of being the last theorist of the Florentine Republic – was Donato Giannotti, whom we have already encountered as an expert on the Venetian constitution. Giannotti returned from Venice to his native Florence on the expulsion of the Medici in 1527, and played an important role as an organiser of the civic militia during the long siege of the city between 1529 and 1530 (Pocock, 1975, p. 273). After the final return of the Medici in 1530 he suffered the bitterness of a lifetime's exile, and it was during this period that he composed his account of *The Florentine Republic*, a last and almost nostalgic celebration of the age-old theme of Florentine liberty.

As with all their predecessors, the fundamental ideal to which these theorists give their allegiance is that of political liberty. It is true that this value is sometimes presented – especially in Guicciardini – with a less enthusiastic sense of commitment than in some of the earlier writers we have examined. Guicciardini warns us in his *Maxims* to be wary of 'those who so fervently preach liberty', insisting that 'nearly all of them' have their own interests in mind, and that 'if they thought they would be better off under an absolute government, they would rush into it as fast as they could' (p. 58). Although he defends the importance of liberty in discussing the government of Florence, he tends to do so on sociological rather than strictly on moral grounds (Gilbert, 1965, pp. 98–9). He contents himself with observing, as he puts it in the *Discourse of Logrogno*, that the Florentines have by now become so accustomed to their freedom that 'they are born to it' and regard it as 'proper and natural to the city'

(p. 223). The implication, as he indicates in a characteristically sceptical and pragmatic fashion in his later *Dialogue*, is that it would now be difficult to introduce a different form of government in Florence even if this could be shown to be preferable. Since 'the city has always been free' and is 'naturally attached to liberty', the Florentines are ineluctably committed by their political traditions and 'established conditions' to defending this received value (pp. 97–9).

It was more usual, however, for the importance of political liberty to be upheld in more traditional and less equivocal terms. Patrizi, for example, demands in his chapter 'On Equality between Citizens' in *The Institution of a Republic* that 'everyone must concern himself with liberty' since 'nothing can be of greater importance in civil society than liberty, towards which the spirit of one's whole city should be turned' (fos. 24a, 25a). Similarly, Rinuccini begins his dialogue *On Liberty* by apostrophising 'the love of freedom' as the basis of political life (p. 272). He laments the fact that, although the Italian cities at one time cherished their independence, they now find 'their desire to live a life of liberty' being frustrated by the tyrants (pp. 272–3). And he insists that the kind of 'avidity to maintain their liberty' which the people of Florence at one time displayed must above all be recaptured if they are to have any prospect of living a happy and successful civic life (p. 274).

It is essential to an understanding of Machiavelli's *Discourses* to recognise that he too is basically concerned to uphold the same set of values.[1] It is arguable that this crucial fact has tended to become obscured by the prevailing tendency to insist that there are no important differences between *The Prince* and the *Discourses*, and that the two books are best treated (in Geerken's phrase) as 'interdependent aspects of an organically unified outlook' (Geerken, 1976, p. 357). It is of course true that the *Discourses* contain many references back to *The Prince*, as well as a fuller statement of many of the central themes of the earlier work: there is the same polarity between *virtù* and *fortuna*; the same emphasis on the role of sheer force in overcoming the enmity of fortune; and the same distinctive and revolutionary political morality, founded on the same sharp distinction between *virtù* and the virtues. Nevertheless, it seems misleading to speak without qualification, as Geerken and others have recently done, of the 'fundamental unity' between the two books (Geerken, 1976, p. 357). In *The Prince* the basic value around which Machiavelli organises his advice is that of security: the prince is told above all to 'maintain his

---

[1] It is the achievement of Baron, 1961, and of Pocock, 1975, to have made this clear beyond doubt. See esp. Baron, 1961, p. 228 and Pocock, 1975, p. 316. Although I disagree with their analyses over various points of detail, these are both magisterial surveys to which I am greatly indebted.

state', after which he is to set forth in pursuit of honour, glory and fame. By contrast, the basic value in the *Discourses* is that of liberty: it is this ideal, not that of mere security, which Machiavelli now wishes us to place above all other considerations, including the dictates of conventional morality.

Machiavelli's sense of the centrality of political liberty first becomes manifest early in the opening Discourse, when he describes the growth of freedom in ancient Rome, and argues that 'those who have displayed prudence in constituting a Republic have looked upon the safeguarding of liberty as one of the most essential things for which they had to provide' (p. 115). He repeats the same contention in his chapter on the difficulties of preserving political freedom, insisting that the primary aim of any legislator 'in constituting a Republic' should be 'to foresee all the laws required for the maintenance of liberty' (p. 230). And he adds at the end of the same chapter that the greatness of the Roman Republic can largely be attributed to the fact that its leaders continually introduced 'new institutions in support of the liberties it enjoyed' (p. 232). Later he underpins this belief in the pre-eminent value of liberty with numerous examples. When he mentions his special admiration for the German cities of his own time, the reason he gives is that they 'enjoy freedom and observe their laws in such a way that neither outsiders nor their own inhabitants dare to usurp power there' (p. 244). When he turns in his second Discourse to discuss Rome's administration of her conquered territories, he indicates that his main interest in this topic derives from the fact that such expansionism invariably plays a key role in helping a Republic 'to remain for ever in the peaceful enjoyment of its liberties' (p. 335). And when he examines in greater detail the relationship between the early Roman Republic and its neighbours, he quotes with much approval the opinion of a Roman senator who proclaimed that 'those whose minds are set on liberty, and nothing but liberty', are 'worthy to be made true Romans' (p. 350).

Machiavelli also adopts the same analysis of the term 'liberty' as the earlier Florentine humanists had given. By 'liberty' he means first of all independence from external aggression and tyranny. Thus he equates the moment at which the Florentines 'obtained their freedom' with the moment at which they were able to remove the power of judicial execution from foreign hands (p. 232). Similarly, he speaks of the time when 'the Romans had conquered Africa and Asia, and had reduced the greater part of Greece to subjection' as the time at which 'they had become secure as to their liberty', since they no longer had 'any more enemies whom there were grounds to fear' (p. 162). Secondly, when Machiavelli speaks of 'liberty' he also has in mind the corresponding power of a free people to govern themselves instead of being governed by a prince. He devotes Chapter 16 of his opening Discourse to elaborating a sharp distinction between 'a people accustomed to live under a prince' and a people who have managed to throw off this type of 'tyrannical government' and have thus 'become free' (pp. 153–4). And when he turns in the following chapter to discuss the origins of the Roman Republic, he treats the moment at which the kings were expelled and a representative form of government was established as equivalent to the point at which Rome was able 'both to acquire and to maintain its liberty' (p. 158).

It would scarcely be an exaggeration to say that Machiavelli's pre-occupation with political liberty provides him with his basic theme in all three Books of the *Discourses*. The first Discourse is largely given over to showing how Rome was able to dispose of its kings and grow to greatness under a system of Republican liberty. The main aim of the second is to indicate how the progressive expansion of Rome as a military power helped to sustain the freedom of its people. And the third is devoted to illustrating 'how much the action of particular men contributed to the greatness of Rome and produced in that city so many beneficial results', especially the long continuance of its political liberties (p. 390).

One corollary which the earlier humanists had always drawn from their similar stress on the importance of liberty was that, since this value is best secured under a mixed type of Republican rule, it follows that Republicanism must be the best form of government. This argument is also endorsed by all their intellectual heirs in the later Renaissance. Patrizi begins his account of *The Institution of a Republic* by asking 'Which is better, to be governed by the best of princes, or to live in a free city with the best laws and customs?' (fo. 8a). He replies without hesitation that 'a Republic is preferable to a principality', since 'it can only be judged that life is safer under a Republic than under a prince' (fos. 8b, 10b). Even Guicciardini gives his grudging assent to the same point of view. He insists in his *Maxims* that 'great defects and failings are inherent in popular government', and that a wise man will only admit to preferring a Republi-can regime 'as a lesser evil' (p. 100). Nevertheless, he concedes in his *Considerations* that 'a city is more fortunate under popular government than under a prince's' (p. 106). And he concludes that, if a choice has to be made, his own preference will always be for a mixed form of Republican rule, since this offers the best means of ensuring that 'the protection of liberty' is guaranteed 'against any seeking to oppress the Republic' (p. 71).

Again Machiavelli upholds the same scale of values in the *Discourses*.

This makes it somewhat misleading to suggest, as Cassirer and others have done, that Machiavelli is nothing more than 'a scientist and a technician of political life', dispassionately surveying and classifying its different forms (Cassirer, 1946, p. 156). He is in fact a consistent and even a fervent partisan of popular government. It is true that – in line with his earlier argument in *The Prince* – he concedes that if 'a renaissance is ever to be brought about' in 'a state which is on the decline', this will have to be done 'by the *virtù* of some one person who is then living, not by the *virtù* of the public as a whole' (p. 159). But his general attitude in the *Discourses* towards any form of monarchical government is one of marked hostility. He observes that 'there are and have been any number of princes, but of good and wise ones there have been but few' (p. 252). And he notes that historically the main tendency has been for kings and princes to suppose that 'they have nought else to do but to surpass other men in extravagance, lasciviousness, and every other form of licentiousness' (p. 107). He thus has no hesitation in endorsing the usual Aristotelian claim that a mixed type of Republican regime must be preferable to any of the 'pure' forms of government, including the rule of princes (p. 109). He later goes on, moreover, to make the unequivocal declaration that government by the people 'is better than government by princes', and offers a large number of reasons for holding this belief (p. 256). The populace displays ingratitude to citizens 'much more rarely than do princes' (p. 184). The populace 'in regard to forming a false opinion' always 'makes fewer mistakes than do princes' (p. 499). The populace usually 'makes a far better choice' than a prince 'in the election of magistrates' (p. 255). The populace is in general 'more prudent, more stable, and of sounder judgment than the prince', being 'guilty of fewer faults' and in consequence 'more to be trusted' (pp. 255, 260). And most important of all, 'it is beyond question' that it is only when the populace as a whole is in charge of the government that 'the common good is looked to properly' in that 'all that promotes it is carried out' (p. 275; cf. also p. 154).

There was, however, one important difference of opinion amongst these later Republican theorists about the character of the self-governing regime to which they wished to give their allegiance. This arose in connection with the question of whether the preponderance of political authority should be assigned to the aristocracy or to the body of the citizens as a whole. The traditional answer was that the foundations of a well-ordered Republic should be *largo* rathern than *stretto*, based on an inclusive *Consiglio Grande* rather than the leadership of a small élite (cf. Gilbert, 1965, pp. 60, 156). This suggestion was revived with much emphasis by Giannotti, who lays it down in one of the Chapter headings of Book III of *The Florentine Republic* that 'the Republic ought to be founded on the people', and devotes the rest of the section to arguing in favour of this claim (pp. 104–202). He maintains that 'in a republic which inclines to a principality', the ambitions of the grandees are liable to lead in the end to the destruction of the liberties of the citizen-body as a whole (pp. 105–6). So he concludes that 'a well-ordered Republic' must be based on an extensive *Consiglio Grande*, including all the different ranks of citizens – not just the aristocracy and the middling sort, but the ordinary *popolani* as well, even if their status is such that they are not eligible to serve as magistrates (p. 118). This type of arrangement, in which 'the care of the city is entrusted to all its citizens', will be far more likely to achieve stability, as well as to uphold the crucial value of liberty, than a more restrictively organised form of aristocratic regime (p. 119; cf. Pocock, 1975, pp. 310–13).

The same preference for a *governo largo* is also found in Machiavelli, from whom Giannotti may have taken some of his arguments. Machiavelli discusses the issue in Chapter 5 of his opening Discourse, observing that 'since in every Republic there is an upper and a lower class, it may be asked into whose hands it is best to place the guardianship of liberty' (p. 115). He thinks that if you merely wish 'to maintain the *status quo*', then there may be something to be said for the suggestion – approved in ancient Sparta as well as in modern Venice – that the care of the Republic should be entrusted to the nobility (pp. 116–17). But he insists that if 'you have in mind a Republic that looks to founding an Empire', then the people as a whole must be made the guardians of liberty (pp. 116–17). He later makes it clear, moreover, in discussing the rival merits of Principates and Republics, that insofar as he believes there is a general answer to the question, he is a supporter of 'the masses' against the proponents of oligarchy (p. 252). He points with admiration to the example of 'the Roman populace which, so long as the Republic remained uncorrupt, was never servilely obsequious, nor yet did it ever dominate with arrogance' (p. 253). And he concludes on an uncharacteristically elevated note by insisting that 'not without good reason is the voice of the populace likened to that of God' (p. 255).

Against this preference for a *governo largo*, however, there was ranged a more aristocratic form of Republicanism which insisted on the need for a small and close-knit ruling class to furnish the people with their leadership. Patrizi inclines to this position in discussing 'what kinds of Republic there are' in the fourth chapter of his *Institution of a Republic* (fo. 16a). He is careful to declare that 'the best form of a Republic is one in which all kinds of men are mixed together' (fo. 18b). But he regards it as essential, if it comes to a choice between 'the nobility alone or the plebs alone ruling', 'that 'the government should be in the hands of the nobility rather than the plebs', since they characteristically display a far greater devotion to the common good (fos. 18a–b). As one might expect, the most un-repentant defender of this outlook is Guicciardini, who mounts a sharp attack on Machiavelli in his *Considerations on the Discourses* for attempting to defend the opposite point of view. Guicciardini insists that the body of the people are simply 'not capable of deciding matters of great importance', since they are characterised by 'imprudence and inconstancy, thirst for change, inordinate suspicion' and 'infinite jealousy of all who have wealth or rank' (pp. 66, 106). This means that 'any Republic which leaves the people to decide its affairs soon falls into decay', since it is bound to be 'unstable and always looking for change', as well as 'easily deceived and misled by ambitious men and traitors' (p. 66). Guicciardini concludes that the course of wisdom lies in recognising that 'one should not give the people power in any important matters' (p. 66). Instead one should place the control of the Republic in the hands of the optimates, who are certain to 'rule it with more intelligence and prudence than a multitude', since they are sure to possess 'greater prudence and good qualities' (pp. 64, 71).

Finally, these writers corroborate their preference for Republican 'liberty' by offering a series of highly tendentious reflections on the history of ancient Rome. Here again their comments tend to repeat the judgments already made by the earlier 'civic' humanists of Bruni's school. On the one hand they denounce Julius Caesar with great vehemence as the destroyer of Rome's freedom. Patrizi assails him as 'the usurper of the Republic' and 'an occasion of tyranny' (fo. 90a). And Guicciardini dismisses him in an unwonted burst of passion in his *Considerations* as a 'detestable and monstrous' person who was 'driven by ambition for power' to 'set up a tyranny in a free country' against the needs and wishes of its people (p. 77). On the other hand they idealise the virtue and simplicity of the early Roman Republic and its heroes. Patrizi in particular offers an admiring account of its institutions and the men who set them up, arguing that in any discussion about the structure of a well-ordered Republic 'it is always possible to take Rome as the best example' (fo. 80a).

Once again we find Machiavelli reiterating the same traditional themes. He emphasises that no one should 'be deceived by Caesar's renown', since the truth about his rise to power is that 'he so successfully blinded the masses' that he made them 'unaware of the yoke which they themselves had placed on their necks'. This enabled him to become 'Rome's first tyrant' and ensured that the city 'never again recovered its liberties' (pp. 135–6, 158, 203). Conversely, the large majority of the heroes whom

Machiavelli describes with the greatest reverence lived under the early Roman Republic, in the period before the outbreak of the first Punic war (cf. Wood, 1967, pp. 161–2). His archetype of the civic patriot is Junius Brutus, 'the father of Rome's liberties' (p. 390). His favourite military leader is Camillus, 'the most prudent of all Rome's generals', of whom he observes that his conduct 'deserves the attention of all rulers' (pp. 347, 443). And his ideal of civic virtue is supplied by Scipio, whose pattern of behaviour he urges every private citizen to emulate, expressing the hope that each individual may learn 'to conduct himself in his fatherland rather as Scipio did than as Caesar' (p. 135).

As well as discussing the ideal of liberty, these theorists devote a considerable amount of attention to the no less familiar question of how the freedom of the people under a Republican form of government tends to become jeopardised or lost. They begin by reviving a suggestion which had originally been canvassed by such pre-humanist writers as Latini and Mussato, but had later become submerged under the patriotic outpourings of Bruni and his school: the suggestion that one of the major dangers to the maintenance of freedom and public virtue is constituted by an excessive devotion to the pursuit of private wealth.

Guicciardini's use of this argument, together with his demand that extravagant luxuries must be curtailed, has been characterised by Pocock as 'almost a Savonarolan proposal', a 'transmutation' of a similar puritan outlook into a 'less specifically Christian rhetoric' (pp. 135, 136). We have already seen, however, that in spite of his attack on the 'vanities' of the Florentines, Savonarola had shown himself quite willing to endorse the earlier 'civic' humanist assumption that the great wealth of the city should be treated as a token of its special excellence. By contrast, Guicciardini's sense of outrage at the 'inordinate appetites' of those who pursue riches instead of 'true glory' is more reminiscent of such classical moralists as Sallust and Juvenal, whose feelings of disgust at the gross opulence of ancient Rome had already been cited for their topicality by Mussato and much later by Salamonio.[1] Guicciardini's earliest political treatise, the *Discourse of Logrogno*, includes a similar denunciation of the 'thousand usurpations' and 'thousand dishonesties' which arise in civic life in consequence of an over-active pursuit of gain, and concludes by adding with a characteristic note of weariness that 'this is a malady which it is immensely difficult, perhaps impossible, to extirpate' (pp. 257–8). Nor was this

[1] For Guicciardini's remarks see *The Discourse of Logrogno*, p. 257. For Mussato on the same theme, and for the evidence that Sallust was one of his major sources, see Rubinstein, 1957, pp. 172–5. For Salamonio on Sallust, see his *Sovereignty*, esp. fos. 19a–19b.

merely a fleeting moment of puritan revulsion on Guicciardini's part, for he reverts to the same argument at several points in his *Maxims* almost twenty years later. Again he laments the fact that the prevailing 'style of living' amongst 'the people of Florence' is 'such that everyone wants very much to be rich' (p. 102). And the reason he gives for expressing a certain alarm at this undignified state of affairs is that this makes it 'hard to preserve freedom in our city', since 'this appetite makes men pursue their personal advantage without respect or consideration for the public honour and glory' of the city itself (p. 102).

The same dislike of 'luxurious habits' as a threat to political liberty is expressed with even greater vehemence by Machiavelli in his *Discourses*, only a few years after the argument had been revived by Guicciardini and Salamonio, and popularised by a number of Venetian moralists (Gilbert, 1973, pp. 277–80). Machiavelli declares in his third Discourse that 'wealth without worth' is invariably a cause of civic corruption, and adds that he could easily 'discourse at length on the advantages of poverty over riches', and 'how poverty brings honour to cities', while 'the other thing has ruined them', except that this has 'already been done so often by others' (pp. 452, 477). He makes it clear, moreover, that in referring to these earlier moralists he mainly has in mind such writers as Sallust and Juvenal (cf. Gilbert, 1965, p. 175). This emerges most clearly in Chapter 19 of the second Discourse, in which he discusses the problems that arise when a Republic sets out to acquire new territories (p. 334). He points out that conquests 'do no small harm even to a well-ordered Republic when the province or city it has acquired is given to luxurious habits' (p. 338). And he adds that the nature of the peril involved 'could not be put better than it is by Juvenal in his *Satires*', when he observes that 'the acquiring of foreign lands' familiarised Rome with foreign customs, 'so that, in place of frugality and its other high virtues, "gluttony and self-indulgence took possession of it and avenged the world it had conquered"' (p. 338).

A further and even more familiar danger to liberty which these writers discuss is that of entrusting the defence of one's city to mercenary troops. Giannotti treats this theme in a slightly muted style, doubtless owing to his admiration for Venice, which had always succeeded in combining the use of mercenaries with the preservation of liberty (cf. Pocock, 1975, p. 306). It was more usual, however, to repeat with great emphasis the almost hackneyed claim that the universal tendency to rely on hired troops constituted one of the most damaging scandals of the age. We already find Patrizi lamenting in the 1460s that the prevailing neglect of military training has 'allowed the whole of Italy to become overrun' by her enemies (fo. 282b). And it is not surprising to find an intensification of the same complaints in the period after the shattering return of the 'barbarians' in 1494. Guicciardini, for example, begins his *Discourse of Logrogno* by arguing that hired troops invariably constitute a threat to the stability of popular governments. He is not impressed, moreover, by the apparent counter-example of Venice, since he insists (quite correctly) that in the wars unleashed by the League of Cambrai in 1508 the reliance of the Venetians on mercenaries very nearly cost them their independence (p. 222).

Again Machiavelli develops exactly the same line of thought in the *Discourses*. At one moment he reminds us – in one of his clearest cross-references to *The Prince* – that since he has already 'discoursed at length' in another of his works on 'the futility of mercenary and auxiliary troops', there is scarcely any need for him to go over the same arguments again (p. 339). But he cannot in fact resist the temptation to repeat a lesson which he regards as so peculiarly important. He begins by declaring as unequivocally as possible that 'foreign forces' always 'entail the downfall of civic liberties' (p. 125). Later he explains that this is due to the fact that 'they have no cause to stand firm when attacked, apart from the small pay which you give them', a consideration which 'is not and cannot be sufficient to make them loyal' (p. 218). And throughout his discussion he supplements this claim with a more general attack on the total and ruinous lack of martial spirit amongst his fellow-countrymen. He denounces 'the weakness of modern armies', which 'lack valour as a whole' as well as any effective leadership (p. 326). He mocks the 'idle princes' and 'effeminate Republics' of Italy for engaging in military operations merely 'for the sake of display and not for any praiseworthy reason' (p. 434). And he crushingly concludes his survey by asserting that all 'Italian armies in our day' are 'quite useless', since they 'never win unless they come across an army which happens for some reason to run away' (p. 504).

Finally, most of these writers take up the equally familiar claim that the chief reason for the collapse of Italian liberty lies in the 'corruption' of the people. The writer who furnishes incomparably the richest analysis of this theme is Machiavelli. There is a sense in which the concept lies at the heart of the *Discourses*, for Machiavelli tells us that his main aim in the book is to offer advice to 'those princes and those Republics which desire to remain free from corruption' (p. 142). His fullest discussion of the concept occurs in Chapters 17 and 18 of the opening Discourse, where he makes it clear that what he basically has in mind in speaking of 'corruption' is a failure to devote one's energies to the common good, and a corresponding tendency to place one's own interests above those of the community. This is most clearly indicated in the description he gives of the onset of corruption in ancient Rome, a process which he equates with the increasing propensity of 'the powerful' to propose laws 'for the sake not of their common liberties but to augment their own power' (p. 162). It is this type of development, he claims, which constitutes the gravest threat to freedom. The point is illustrated by a comparison of the behaviour of the Roman people after the expulsion of their kings, when they managed 'forthwith both to acquire and to maintain' their liberty, and their behaviour at the moment when 'the whole of Caesar's stock was exterminated' under the early Empire, when they not only failed to regain their liberty 'but could not even make a start' (p. 158). Machiavelli argues that 'results so diverse in one and the same city are caused by naught else but that in the time of the Tarquins the Roman populace was not yet corrupt, but in the later period was extremely corrupt' (p. 158). So the essence of Machiavelli's doctrine, as he summarises it at the start of Chapter 16, is that 'a people which has become corrupt cannot even for a brief space, no, not even for a moment, enjoy its freedom' (p. 154).

Machiavelli later reiterates the same theme with even greater emphasis in his *History of Florence*, a work which he was commissioned to write in 1520, and which he presented to the Medici Pope Clement VII in 1525 (Gilbert, 1972, pp. 82, 84–5). After giving a panoramic survey of the early history of Italy and Florence in his opening two Books, he turns to offer a more detailed analysis of Florence's fortunes during the period from the second half of the *trecento* to the death of Lorenzo *Il magnifico* in 1492. The increasing corruption of the city throughout this era is his constant theme, and he prefaces each section with a rhetorical introductory chapter designed to illustrate how the *virtù* of the Republic was progressively lost. The opening of Book III complains that the exclusion of the nobility from the government in the course of the *trecento* had the effect of destroying their 'ability in arms' and 'boldness of spirit', and adds that since their growing corruption was never offset by any compensating *virtù* in the populace, the outcome was that 'Florence grew always weaker and more despicable' throughout this time (p. 1141). The opening chapter of Book IV goes on to accuse the populace as well as the nobility of falling into increasing corruption in the first half of the *quattrocento*, arguing that while the people served as 'the promoters of license', the nobles served as 'the promoters of slavery', and neither party showed the least concern for the liberty or general good of the commonwealth (p. 1187). Finally, the opening chapter of Book V completes the story of Florence's demoralisation by explaining how 'a new road was opened to the barbarians' through the loss of military *virtù* suffered by the Florentines in a series of wars 'begun without fear, carried on without danger, and ended without damage' (p. 1233). By the end of the *quattrocento*, 'the vigour that in other countries is usually destroyed by long peace' had been destroyed in Florence 'by the cowardice of those wars', leaving nothing except the 'present abuses' of 'this corrupt world' (p. 1233).

It is sometimes suggested that Machiavelli was 'the first thinker of the Renaissance' to make an extensive study of the role of corruption in political life (Bonadeo, 1973, p. 1). As we have seen, however, a number of earlier humanists – especially Leonardo Bruni – had already concerned themselves with the question of how to ensure that the interests of the community as a whole are properly considered, and not merely the interests of particular groups of citizens. Nevertheless, it is true to say that the humanists of the later Renaissance, and especially Machiavelli, reveal a heightened awareness of the problem, and devote an unprecedented amount of attention to the investigation of its causes.

The main cause Machiavelli isolates – following Bruni's earlier analysis – is the exclusion of the people from playing a sufficiently active role in the business of government. When Machiavelli first raises this issue in Chapter 17 of his opening Discourse, he equates 'corruption' with 'ineptitude for a free life', attributing the growth of this ineptitude to 'the inequality one finds in a city' when a group of oligarchs manages to seize control of its institutions and prevent the rest of the citizenry from helping to operate them (p. 160; cf. Pocock, 1975, p. 209). He later illustrates this danger by considering the history of two institutional developments which finally proved fatal to the liberty of the Roman Republic. One was the extension of the periods during which various magistrates were permitted to hold office. This happened in the case of the Dictators, who eventually helped to make Rome 'servile' by usurping the authority 'of which citizens were deprived' as a result of the increasing length of their rule (p. 194). The same thing happened in the case of the Decemviri, who were given 'unrestricted authority' for a considerable period, as a consequence of which they finally 'became tyrants, and, regardless of everybody and everything, deprived Rome of her liberty' (p. 197). The other equally harmful development, which Machiavelli discusses in his third Discourse, was 'the prolongation of military commands' (p. 473). Although this became increasingly necessary as the Romans conquered further and further afield, it eventually proved destructive of their liberty (p. 474). For 'when a citizen had been for long in command of an army, he won the army over and made it his partisan'. This enabled a series of unscrupulous generals, beginning with Sulla and Marius and culminating with Caesar, to 'find troops to support them in actions contrary to the public good'.

And this in turn meant that the power of the commanders 'in due course led to the downfall of the Republic' (p. 474).

But the most dramatic claim Machiavelli makes about the causes of corruption is that Christianity is very much to blame. There was a hint of a precedent for this allegation in the 'civic' humanist repudiation of *otium* in favour of a more active scheme of human values. But Machiavelli develops this earlier suggestion into a full-scale Gibbonian attack on the Christian religion for its subversion of civic life. He begins by assuming that religious observances help to keep a commonwealth 'good and united', and thus that 'those princes and those Republics which desire to remain free from corruption should above all else maintain incorrupt the ceremonies of their religion' (pp. 142–3). But he insists that religion can only make a positive contribution to civic life if it enables us to glorify the right values, which for Machiavelli are those of 'magnanimity, bodily strength, and everything else that conduces to make men very bold' (p. 278). He believes that Christianity could in principle have performed this function, since it 'permits us to exalt and defend the fatherland' and 'to train ourselves to be such that we may defend it' (pp. 278–9). But he emphasises that in practice the Christian faith has elevated the wrong values, since it has 'assigned as man's highest good humility, abnegation and contempt for mundane things' (p. 278). The effect of espousing this 'pattern of life' has been to make the world weak, and to hand it over 'as a prey to the wicked' (p. 278). So he fearlessly declares that 'if one asks oneself how it comes about that the people of old were more fond of liberty than they are today', we are bound to reply that this is due to 'the difference between our religion and the religion of those days' (p. 277). The 'old religion' glorified the civic virtues and so helped to sustain political freedom; our religion 'has glorified humble and contemplative men' and has thus helped to bring us to our present corrupt state (p. 278).

Machiavelli was not alone in offering this shocking diagnosis; it was soon adopted with evident relish by Guicciardini in his *Maxims*. He agrees that 'too much religion spoils the world, because it makes the mind effeminate, involves men in thousands of errors, and diverts them from many generous and virile enterprises' (p. 104). Like Machiavelli, he goes on to add (somewhat unconvincingly) that in saying this he has no desire 'to derogate from the Christian faith and divine worship' (p. 104). But elsewhere in the *Maxims* he allows himself to denounce the current practice of the Christian religion in a tone of much greater violence than Machiavelli had ever felt able to use. He laments the fact that 'the positions I have held under several popes have forced me, for my own good, to further their interests'. But he adds that 'were it not for that, I should have loved Martin Luther as much as myself', and would have looked forward with unalloyed pleasure to seeing 'this bunch of rascals get their just deserts' (p. 48).

After considering what tends to jeopardise political freedom, the final issue these writers discuss is the question of how these dangers and difficulties may be overcome, so that the traditional ideals of independence and self-government may be most effectively secured. This is not to say that they always remain optimistic about the prospects of success. Patrizi and Machiavelli both recognise that the task may prove impossible in the midst of so much corruption, and thus that they ought perhaps to be addressing themselves entirely to the princes rather than the citizens of their age. Guicciardini tends to strike an even more pessimistic note, and by the time we come to a writer like Trajano Boccalini (1556–1613) at the end of the century, we find the exhaustion of the tradition complete (cf. Schellhase, 1976, pp. 145–7). Boccalini's *Advertisements from Parnassus*, written in 1612–13, is couched in a tone of intense and unrelieved irony at the expense of the very idea of hoping to regenerate the totally corrupted world. The book takes the form of a series of discussions between Apollo and the various princes and philosophers who visit Parnassus. At an early stage in the argument the leaders of the Italian academies report that 'the appetite for learning' has been 'wholly lost' in all parts of Italy. They ask for some remedy 'to preserve them from so great a corruption', but Apollo replies without hesitation that nothing can be done (p. 24). In a later discussion Machiavelli is able to defend himself against the charge of being a pernicious influence by pointing out that the lives of princes are in fact 'a composition of ill words and worse actions' (p. 164). And towards the end of the second Book a climax of irony is reached when 'an eminent virtuoso' tries to present Apollo 'with an elegant oration composed in praise of the present age' (pp. 324–5). This is 'very coldly' received, and the author is handed 'a pair of excellent spectacles' manufactured by Tacitus to help him see the world in its proper light (p. 324). When he looks again he finds the age so full of 'base contrivances' and corruption of all kinds that he cannot bear to contemplate it at all (p. 325; cf. Meinecke, 1957, pp. 71–89).

Before becoming trapped in this sense of complete helplessness, however, the humanists of the later Renaissance devoted much of their attention to reviving and extending a number of traditional arguments about the preservation of liberty. They tend to begin by asking themselves in a new tone of self-consciousness how it is possible to acquire reliable information about the best methods of extirpating corruption and maintaining freedom in political life. The answer they give – which had been implicit in many earlier treatises, but was now stated far more explicitly – is that the key to political wisdom lies in making a systematic study of earlier Republics, especially the Republic of ancient Rome. It is true that Guicciardini, with his habitual scepticism, constitutes something of an exception at this point. The assumption that it might be possible to base a science of politics on the evidence of history struck him as embodying an excessively mechanistic view of human affairs. He responds in his *Maxims* with the utmost sarcasm to those who 'cite the Romans at every turn', claiming that such comparisons are often 'as much out of order as it would be to expect a jackass to race like a horse' (p. 69). And he constantly criticises Machiavelli in his *Considerations on the Discourses* for arguing 'too absolutely' on the basis of a few historical generalisations, and failing to see that there are many judgments and decisions 'which cannot be taken by a firm rule' (pp. 66, 101; cf. Phillips, 1977, pp. 69–73, 88).

The more usual tendency, however, was to endorse the familiar assumption that, as Bodin was later to express it, 'in history the best part of the universal law lies hidden'. Here, as so often, it is Machiavelli who restates the received humanist position with the greatest *éclat* (cf. Kristeller, 1965, p. 28). As he explains in the Preface to his first Discourse, his main aim in writing the book was to 'draw those practical lessons which one should seek to obtain from the study of history' (p. 99). His governing assumption as he sets forth in quest of these lessons is that 'men are born and live and die in an order which remains ever the same' (p. 142). His procedure is accordingly to assume that 'he who would foresee what has to be, should reflect on what has been, for everything that happens in the world has a genuine resemblance to what happened in ancient times' (p. 517). The reason for this, he repeats, is that 'the agents who bring such things about are men', who 'have and always have had the same passions'. This in turn means, as he concludes with his usual confidence, that 'it necessarily comes about that the same effects are produced' (p. 517).

A number of modern scholars have sought to revive Guicciardini's attack on Machiavelli's methodological assumptions at this point, arguing that (as Butterfield puts it) Machiavelli displays a certain 'rigidity' of approach, as well as being 'slavish' in 'his reverence for the statecraft of the ancient world' (Butterfield, 1940, pp. 28, 40). The accusation of rigidity, however, seems rather insensitive, since it ignores the fact that Machiavelli repeatedly qualifies his supposed historical 'rules', conceding and even insisting that 'one never finds any issue that is clear cut and not open to question', and that many accidents occur in politics against which 'it is impossible to prescribe any remedy' (pp. 121, 418). It is arguable, moreover, that to attack Machiavelli for 'slavishly' following the supposed lessons of antiquity is altogether to miss his point. He is not attracted to the statecraft of the ancient world simply because it is ancient. On the contrary, he emphasises in the Preface to his second Discourse that 'the whole truth about olden times is not grasped, since what redounds to their discredit is often passed over in silence, whereas what is likely to make them appear glorious is pompously recounted in all its details' (p. 265). The reason for his interest in ancient – and especially Roman – statecraft is simply that it happens to have been uniquely successful (cf. Gilbert, 1965, pp. 181–2). He urges us to study the Roman Republic not because it represents an aspect of the grandeur of antiquity, but rather for the wholly pragmatic reason that 'there has never been any other city or any other Republic so well adorned', so worthy of imitation and 'so successful' as that of ancient Rome (pp. 104, 270).

Basing themselves in this fashion on the evidence of the past, Machiavelli and his contemporaries next proceed to outline a full-scale programme devoted to securing the value of political liberty. One suggestion they make – arising out of their fears about private wealth – is that freedom and poverty tend to go together. Guicciardini concludes his *Discourse of Logrogno* with the observation that, although free cities need to be rich, their individual inhabitants ought to be kept poor, without any great disparities of wealth of the kind that tend to cause envy and so to promote political disturbances (pp. 258–9). The same suggestion – which would have been anathema to Bruni and his followers – was taken up soon afterwards by several theorists connected with the meetings at the Oricellari Gardens. Brucioli mentions the idea at the end of his dialogue on *The Republic*, while Machiavelli reiterates Guicciardini's doctrine almost word-for-word in his third Discourse (cf. Gilbert, 1965, pp. 151–2). Machiavelli's first proposal for the avoidance of corruption in 'difficult times' is 'to keep the citizens poor', and he later repeats with much emphasis that any institution which 'keeps the citizens poor' will be 'the most useful' one to have 'in a state which enjoys freedom' (pp. 452, 475).

The next proposal made by these writers also represents something of a reversal of the values of earlier 'civic' humanists. As we have seen, Bruni and his followers had mainly concentrated on the question of how to promote the right kind of civic spirit amongst the people and their leaders, assuming that this in turn would serve to maintain the liberty of their city as a whole. By contrast, the later humanists begin to focus on an issue which had previously been considered in detail only by the exponents of a more scholastic approach to the problems of the city Republics and their liberties. They begin, that is, to turn their attention to examining the machinery of government, asking themselves what role is played by laws and institutions in relation to the preservation of freedom.

This helps to explain the appearance of a new and vital element in Florentine political theory at this time: the study and imitation of Venetian constitutional practices. Having raised the question of how to devise laws and institutions for the preservation of liberty, it seemed natural to investigate the case of the Venetian Republic, which appeared to have solved this problem with unique success. As we have seen, the Venetians themselves were prone to argue that they owed their combination of peace and liberty to the stability of their mixed form of Republican government. This in turn meant that, as the Florentine theorists became increasingly excited by the success of the Venetian model, their interest tended to resolve into a demand that Florence should adopt the same Venetian arrangement of a Dogeship, a small Senate of *ottimati* and a democratic *Consiglio Grande*.

The great exception to this rule is Machiavelli. It is true that he is more interested than any of his 'civic' humanist predecessors in 'devising good laws whereby to maintain liberty', and fully accepts the prevailing belief that actual constitutional practices must be studied if we wish to learn the secret of combining liberty with peace (p. 231). When he turns to the discussion of examples, however, he exhibits none of the fashionable admiration for the Venetian constitution at all. He is far more interested in the sort of expansionist Republic 'that looks to founding an Empire, as Rome did' than in the ideal of unchanging serenity which the Venetians were projecting with so much complacency (p. 117). And he insists that unless you are 'content to maintain the *status quo*' in the somewhat languid manner of the Venetians, you must recognise that 'it is necessary to do in all things as Rome did' (p. 117). He accordingly devotes a great deal of his opening Discourse to a description of the 'many institutions essential to the preservation of liberty' which the Romans evolved under the early Republic, taking this to be a subject of far greater and more immediate concern than the investigation of Venetian practices (p. 110).

With most of Machiavelli's contemporaries, however, the desirability of imitating the Venetians became an article of faith. This first produced a visible impact on Florentine affairs immediately after the revolution of 1494, when Savonarola preached a series of political sermons in which he successfully urged his fellow-citizens to endorse the proposed *Consiglio Grande* on the grounds that the same device had proved so successful in Venice (Weinstein, 1970, pp. 151–8). Soon afterwards the Venetian model began to be used by the critics of the restored Republic to justify an aristocratic form of opposition to its populist tendencies. Bernardo Rucellai (1448–1514), the grandfather of Cosimo and the originator of the discussions held in the Oricellari Gardens, attempted to argue at a series of meetings between 1502 and his banishment in 1506 that the resurrection of the traditional *Consiglio Grande* had dangerously overbalanced the Florentine constitution in the direction of a democracy. His own proposal, endorsed by a number of other excluded and disgruntled *ottimati*, was for the addition of a small aristocratic Senate on the Venetian pattern. This reform, it was claimed, would serve as a counterweight to the excesses of popular rule, and would thus help to ensure the stability of the regime (Gilbert, 1968, pp. 475, 477, 483).

This adaptation of the Venetian model as a way of promoting the class-interests of the *ottimati* was adopted with the greatest enthusiasm by Guicciardini. According to his *Discourse of Logrogno*, the basic weakness of the Florentine constitution lies in its exaggerated polarity between its democratic aspect, represented by the *Consiglio Grande*, and its monarchical aspect, represented by the position of *gonfaloniere* for life – a post formally established in 1502 and assigned to Piero Soderini (p. 227). The solution Guicciardini proposes is the introduction of a Senate of some two hundred *ottimati*, an institution which he believes will serve to restore the balance between these two extremes in the approved Venetian style (pp. 234–9). The same argument is later developed at greater length in his *Dialogue on Florentine Government*. The first Book is basically concerned to show that, by diverging in various directions from the norm of mixed government, the Florentines have jeopardised their liberty as well as their security. Under the rule of the Medici the government is said to have been too monarchical; under the restored Republic after 1494 it is said to have become too democratic. Once again the solution to the problem – outlined by Bernardo Nero in the second Book – is taken to consist of introducing a middle link between these two extremes, a solution which is explicitly said to be 'Venetian in conception' and is promised to guarantee the desired combination of liberty and peace (p. 103).

Finally, the same belief that an adaptation of Venice's institutions might save the Florentine republic was later reiterated by Giannotti in both his main political works. One of his chief concerns in his *Dialogue* of 1526 was to furnish a detailed analysis of the Venetian constitution for the guidance of the more radical citizens of Florence. And the governing assumption of the reform-proposals contained in the third Book of his later treatise on *The Florentine Republic* was that, if only his fellow-citizens would imitate the wisdom of the Venetians, they might be able to dispose of their prevailing tyranny for ever, and recover their lost liberties.

Discussing the merits of poverty and the role of institutions, the humanists of the early *cinquecento* may thus be said to have extended and even contradicted a number of previous assumptions about the preservation of political liberty. If we now turn to their major proposals, however, we find them reviving and developing two arguments which had always been central to the humanist tradition, and which they now articulate in their definitive form.

They begin by reiterating the familiar contention that, since mercenary soldiers are useless and dangerous, it follows that any Republic which values its freedom must ensure that it establishes its own system of defence. The Aristotelian figure of the armed and independent citizen, willing to fight for his liberties as well as to legislate on their behalf, is thus brought once again to the centre of the political stage. It is true that Guicciardini, with his accustomed scepticism, is less than fully committed to this argument. He admits at the start of his *Discourse of Logrogno* that a Republic 'must give arms to its citizens', and he agrees that a citizen militia will always be 'incomparably more useful than a mercenary army' (p. 221). But he also expresses the fear that a threat to internal security may be involved if too many citizens are permitted to bear arms (p. 221). And in his later *Dialogue* he adds that, even though a civic militia may well be a valuable institution, this is scarcely a matter of more than academic interest, since there is so little chance of reviving it at such a late and decadent stage in the history of the Republic (pp. 90–3). It was more usual, however, for the long-standing humanist commitment to the ideal of an armed citizenry to be far less equivocally endorsed by these writers. Patrizi, for example, lays it down in his *Institution of a Republic* that 'as many as possible of our youth should be trained in military discipline', and offers a detailed account of how to select 'robust and diligent' young men to ensure that an effective and well-prepared militia will always be available in time of war (fos. 29a, 287b). Giannotti argues in a similar style in the memorandum he drew up in his capacity as secretary of the Ten of War under the restored Florentine Republic of 1527. He rebuts the accusation that a civic militia will always be too inexperienced to constitute an effective fighting force, and goes on to reiterate all the familiar arguments about the need for any self-respecting Republic to provide its own defence as a guarantee of its liberty (cf. Starn, 1972, pp. 289–90).

The same conclusions are fully endorsed by Machiavelli in the *Discourses*. He acknowledges – in a further cross-reference to *The Prince* – that he has already 'said elsewhere that the security of all states is based on good military discipline, and that where it does not exist, there can neither be good laws nor anything else that is good' (p. 491). As before, however, he cannot resist repeating himself. He insists that 'since neither the requisite love nor the requisite enthusiasm can be aroused' except in a citizen army, it follows that 'if one desires to retain a form of state' – whether a Republic or a Principality – it is essential 'to arm oneself with one's own subjects' (p. 218). He praises the founders of the Roman Republic for the pains they took to ensure that their armies were made up of citizens, so ensuring that the people 'might be themselves the defenders of their freedom' (p. 171). And he roundly concludes that 'present-day princes and modern republics which have not their own troops for offence and defence ought to be ashamed of themselves' (p. 168). Like the rest of his contemporaries, he resolutely refused to see that no amount of mustering of the most willing and patriotic citizenry could hope to make the small-scale principalities of Italy any match for the vast national armies which had arisen out of France, Germany and Spain since 1494, and had inexorably set about destroying the civilisation of the Renaissance (cf. Anderson, 1974, pp. 163–8).

Machiavelli's continuing commitment to the ideal of a citizen army went far beyond a mere repetition of these humanist commonplaces. He used his position as Second Secretary to the Republic, together with his personal influence over Soderini, to mount an eloquent campaign in favour of Florence's return to the use of a civic militia. His great opportunity came in 1505, when the mercenaries employed by the city in the interminable assault on Pisa raised a serious mutiny. The leaders of ten companies refused to continue the fight, thereby forcing an ignominious abandonment of the siege (Bayley, 1961, pp. 251–2). Machiavelli's personal response to this combination of treason and incompetence was to draw up a detailed plan for the replacement of the city's hired troops by the re-establishment of a citizen militia (Bayley, 1961, p. 254). A year later, in December 1506, he saw his highest hopes realised: the *Consiglio Grande* gave its legislative support to the idea of reviving the militia, authorising the recruitment of ten thousand men and accepting responsibility for supplying them with arms, uniforms and pay (Bayley, 1961, pp. 260–2). One of the most venerable and cherished projects of humanist political theory was thus converted into an accepted political fact.

It is true that the militiamen recruited from the *contado* under Machiavelli's scheme proved wholly unequal to the task of defending the Republic in 1512. Their attempts to stop the storming and sack of Prato were effortlessly brushed aside by the advancing Spanish infantry, and the Florentines found themselves compelled to surrender immediately in order to avoid incurring a similar fate (Bayley, 1961, p. 276). Nevertheless, Machiavelli's faith in the superiority of civic troops remained unshaken by this *débâcle*. When he came to write his *Art of War* in 1521, he devoted some of the finest passages in his closing Book to defending his concept of a citizen militia against its detractors. The scheme had failed in practice, he claimed, only because it had not been given adequate support – the result being 'an abortion' where it could have been the birth of a really formidable fighting force (p. 725). So he continued to argue that the value of a well-trained citizen army had not yet been disproved, since it had not yet been fairly tested. He ended with the unrepentant boast that the first ruler in Italy to succeed in organising an army of his own citizens according to the rules suggested in *The Art of War* would find it possible 'rather than anyone else' to make himself 'lord of this country' (p. 725).

The other traditional argument which the later humanists emphasised was that, in order to be sure of upholding the value of liberty, what needs to be fostered above all is not so much a structure of effective institutions and laws, but rather a sense of civic pride and patriotism on the part of the people as a whole. This commitment, it was claimed, must be such as to make each individual equate his own good with that of his city, make him devote his best energies to assuring its freedom and greatness, and in this way cause him to place his courage, his vitality and his general abilities in the service of the entire community. This sense of priorities they summarised in typically humanist language by saying that the maintenance of liberty in a Republic is best guaranteed by the promotion of *virtù* in the whole body of its citizens.

The analysis of *virtù* given by these writers thus tends to be couched in somewhat more general terms than in the mirror-for-princes literature. They are not of course interested in the alleged 'princely' virtues, nor are they greatly concerned with the suggestion that the idea of *virtù* may be broken down into a list of component virtues, although they sometimes imply that this can be done. They tend simply to equate the possession of *virtù* with a broad sense of public commitment. This emerges very clearly, for example, from Patrizi's discussion of *virtus* in Book VI of *The Institution of a Republic*. He begins by proclaiming that '*virtus* is the quality by means of which it is possible to maintain a stable and lasting political society' (fo. 196b). He then explains that the man of *virtus* can be recognised by his 'absence of private ambition' and his corresponding willingness to place the benefit of the Republic above his own interests (fo. 196b). Just as 'corruption' tends to be defined by these writers as a failure to devote one's talents to the public good, so they tend to define the idea of *virtù* as a concern to promote the public good above all.

This view is fully endorsed by Machiavelli in the *Discourses*. His analysis of *virtù* in this work is thus somewhat different from his earlier discussion in *The Prince*. Previously he had concentrated on the *virtù* of the prince himself, and had mainly used the term to describe the qualities necessary for successful leadership. In the *Discourses*, by contrast, he is concerned not merely with the *virtù* of individuals, but also with the idea that the same quality may be displayed by the citizen body as a whole. He is also interested in the more abstract and metaphorical suggestion that the commonwealth itself may be capable of *virtù*, just as it may be liable to become corrupt.[1] The outcome is a more collective view of *virtù*, a view which serves to relate the meaning of the term very closely to the idea of 'public spirit' – the phrase actually used by Henry Nevile as a translation of '*virtù*' in his late seventeenth-century edition of *The Works of the Famous Nicolas Machiavel*.

Machiavelli makes his basic meaning clear as early as the Preface to the first Discourse, in which he observes that the men who possess the highest *virtù* are those 'who have gone to the trouble of serving their country' (p. 98). He makes the same point at the end of the third Discourse, where he revives a suggestion which, as we have seen, Remigio de Girolami had already turned into the subject of a special treatise: the suggestion that (as Machiavelli phrases it in his chapter-heading) 'a good citizen out of love for his country ought to ignore personal affronts' (p. 523). Machiavelli underpins these general reflections, moreover, with two sets of examples taken from the history of Republican Rome, both of which are intended to reveal the closeness of the connections between the idea of *virtù* and the idea of discounting one's private ambitions in the name of the common good. One range of illustrations occurs in the discussion of Rome's great men in the third Discourse. We learn that the *virtù* of Manlius lay in the fact that his 'way of behaving was entirely in the public interest, and was in no way affected by private ambition' (p. 469). Similarly, we are told that the greatest proof of Camillus's *virtù* was that, 'having thrice been Dictator', he 'always administered that office to the benefit of the public, not in his own interests' (p. 485). But the most revealing examples are those designed to show that the same quality of *virtù* was possessed by the Roman people as a whole. Their *virtù* was so great, we are told, that 'with all of them love of country weighed more than any other consideration' (p. 428). They remained 'enemies to the very name of king and lovers of glory and of the common good of their country' for over four hundred years (p. 254). And their anxiety to 'maintain their integrity' and uphold the good of their country was so great that all their leaders had to exercise

---

[1] The literature on the changing meanings of *virtù* in Machiavelli is an extensive and valuable one. See in particular Whitfield, 1947, pp. 92–105; Rousseau, 1965, pp. 152–7; Gilbert, 1965, pp. 179–99 (to which I am particularly indebted); Hannaford, 1972, pp. 185–9; Price, 1973, pp. 325–31; and Pocock, 1975, pp. 206–11.

the greatest care 'to avoid the least semblance of ambition, lest it should cause the populace to attack them' (p. 186).

If we turn, however, to the views expressed by Machiavelli and his contemporaries about the significance of *virtù* – the reasons they give for wishing the populace to acquire the quality – we find a much closer resemblance between their outlook and that of the mirror-for-princes writers. The authors of princely advice-books had tended, as we have seen, to offer an heuristic definition of *virtù* as that quality which enables a political leader to 'maintain his state' and pursue the highest prizes of honour, glory and fame. Similarly, the theorists of Republican liberty tend to think of *virtù* as that quality which enables a free people to maintain their freedom and enhance the greatness of their commonwealth. For both groups of writers, the concept of *virtù* is thus used with some consistency to denote those qualities which guarantee success in political life.

This emerges very clearly from the pages of a work like Rinuccini's dialogue *On Liberty*. When the eponymously-named figure of Eleutherius denounces the corruptions of the age, he particularly mentions its lack of *virtus* and 'good arts', its evil magistrates and its blind vices (p. 279). And when he turns in Book II to consider how the values of citizenship might be revived, he makes it clear that he wants above all to see the importance of *virtus* properly inculcated (pp. 294–5). The same scale of values is no less clearly endorsed even by the more cynical Guicciardini. Early in the second Book of his *Dialogue on Florentine Government* the figure of Soderini is made to raise the question of what has brought about the greatness of Florence. He immediately answers that the quality of *virtù* on the part of her leading citizens has served more than anything else to maintain the freedom of the Republic, and has thus turned Florence into a city incomparable 'for its nobility, its grandeur and its generosity' (pp. 93, 95; cf. Pocock, 1975, pp. 248–9).

Again we find Machiavelli endorsing the same conclusions in the *Discourses*. He treats the presence of *virtù* as a way of defining the greatness of Empires and Republics, remarking that 'the world's *virtù* first found a home in Assyria, then flourished in Medea', and 'at length arrived in Italy and Rome' (p. 267). Conversely, he equates the collapse of *virtù* with the onset of political decline, noting that as soon as Sparta 'lost a good deal of its ancient *virtù*' it correspondingly lost 'a good deal of its power and of its Empire' (p. 133). His main account of this relationship between *virtù* and greatness occurs in his discussion of Republican Rome. It was due to the *virtù* of her consuls under the early Republic, he claims, that Rome first 'attained to her highest pitch of greatness' (p. 167). It was due to the same 'outstanding *virtù*' that the Romans next succeeded in subjugating their neighbours (p. 274). And it was due to the fact that what they 'always looked for was *virtù*' in their leaders that they subsequently managed to preserve the greatness of their city for such a long time (p. 260).

Having argued that *virtù* is the key to political success, the next problem these writers confront is that of explaining how this quality can in practice be acquired. As we have seen, the mirror-for-princes theorists had generally answered this question by focusing on the need for rulers and magistrates to be educated in such a way as to follow the virtues in all their public acts. An element of this preoccupation can also be found in several of the later treatises on Republican liberty. Rinuccini discusses the value of a humanist education in the second Book of his dialogue *On Liberty*, while Patrizi offers an unusually extended treatment of the same theme in the second and fourth Books of his *Institution of a Republic*. In Book II he discusses 'the use and value of letters', giving an elaborate account of the need for every citizen to be instructed in grammar, mathematics, music, astronomy and medicine as well as the more usual humanist pursuits of poetry, history and rhetoric (fos. 43b–77a). And in Book IV he adds a description of family life – somewhat in the manner of Alberti – in which he discusses the duty of parents to ensure that their children are properly educated in their civic responsibilities (fos. 133b–148a).

Machiavelli glancingly mentions a number of the same considerations in the *Discourses*. He tells us that many differences in our behaviour are determined by education, and stresses that 'good examples' in civic life 'proceed from good education' (pp. 114, 490). He is prone to argue that the reason why the Italians of his own day are so 'feeble' is due to 'their defective education and to the little knowledge they have of affairs' (p. 479). And he even declares in his discussion of religion at the start of the second Discourse that 'if one asks oneself how it comes about that the peoples of old were more fond of liberty than they are today', one is bound to conclude that this is largely owing 'to the difference between our education and that of bygone times' (p. 277).

But the main answer these writers give to the question of how *virtù* can be acquired is less a legacy from the views of the mirror-for-princes writers, more a conclusion derived from the outlook of the earlier 'civic' humanists. Leonardo Bruni and his followers had already discussed the problem of how to instil in the whole body of the people a sense of public spirit, of civic commitment, of willingness to put the interests of the city above one's own selfish concerns. They concluded, as we have seen, that the solution lies in ensuring that the pathway to honour is kept open to all the citizens, each of whom must be given an equal opportunity to fulfil his highest ambitions in the service of the community. It is essentially this answer which the later theorists of Republican liberty take up and re-iterate. Just as they had argued that the onset of corruption is brought about by excluding the people from playing a sufficiently active role in the business of government, so they claim that the *virtù* of the people is most efficiently promoted by involving them as much as possible in the running of the commonwealth.

It is Machiavelli who – almost in a tone of nostalgia – furnishes the finest restatement of this traditional belief. He first emphasises the crucial importance of political participation in the course of recounting the cautionary tale of the Decemviri in ancient Rome. These citizens were originally assigned 'unrestricted authority' on the understanding that they would use it in order to 'draw up laws for Rome' (p. 197). But by voting them such absolute powers, the people at the same time dealt a fatal blow to their own capacity to retain control of the government, with the result that the Decemviri soon 'became tyrants' and 'deprived Rome of her liberty' (p. 197). The moral for Machiavelli is clear: the people of a free Republic must never hand over any of their powers 'except under certain conditions and for a specified time' (p. 198). The positive commitment underlying these remarks is later made clear when Machiavelli discusses the duties of citizenship in his third Discourse. He considers the danger – highly relevant in Florence at the time – that a rich citizen may be able to 'bring about a tyranny' by 'conferring benefits' and buying support in such a way as to jeopardise the freedom of the city (pp. 481–2). The only way to avoid this dilemma is said to lie in ensuring that it remains more advantageous for every citizen 'to gain favour by his service to the public' than by withdrawing into more private and potentially factious allegiances (p. 482). It is thus Machiavelli's fundamental conviction that a life of political involvement must not only be made available to every citizen on equal terms, but must be made as alluring as possible to men of the highest talents. This alone, he believes, will suffice to ensure that everyone remains content to 'acquire honour and satisfaction' in the service of the community; and this in turn will guarantee that the greatness of individual citizens remains 'helpful, not harmful, to the city and its liberties' (pp. 481–2).

The same emphasis on the need for civic involvement was taken up soon afterwards by Guicciardini in his *Dialogue on Florentine Government*. With his more aristocratic bias, he is less concerned than Machiavelli about ensuring that the citizens as a whole remain in charge of their government. But he is even more anxious to insist that any city which prizes its liberty must take care to enable its leading citizens 'to satisfy their ambitions' in the service of the community (p. 93). It must provide them with 'occasions and freedom to demonstrate and exercise their *virtù*' in such a way as 'to benefit the city' as a whole (p. 93). If they are prevented from following this pathway to 'true honour and glory', there is a grave danger that they may become factious or corrupt, and in either case it will then be easy for an aspiring tyrant to usurp the government. But as long as they are encouraged 'to perform generous and praiseworthy deeds for the benefit and exaltation of their country', this will not only prevent their ambitions from becoming destructive, but will thereby help to ensure that the liberty and greatness of their city are enhanced (p. 93).

With these arguments about the promotion of *virtù*, the humanist defence of Republican liberty comes full circle. For it is claimed by all these writers to be one of the special merits of a Republican form of government that it enables men of the highest *virtù* to pursue the goals of honour, glory and fame in the service of their community. The relations between *virtù* and liberty are thus seen as mutually sustaining: the opportunities offered to men of talent under a free constitution are said to encourage the development of *virtù*; and the *virtù* thus engendered is in turn said to play a vital role in preserving the freedom of the constitution. The exhilarating prospect which is thus held out is that the life of a completely virtuous Republic might actually be without end. As Machiavelli declares: 'Should a Republic be so fortunate as frequently to have men who by their example give fresh life to its laws, and do not merely stop them from going to rack and ruin, but restore their former vigour, such a Republic would last for ever' (p. 467).

THE CONTRIBUTION OF MACHIAVELLI

So far we have concentrated on illustrating the extent to which Machiavelli's *Discourses* can be represented as a relatively orthodox contribution to a well-established tradition of Republican political thought. As in the case of *The Prince*, it seems essential to begin by adopting this perspective. It enables us in the first place to suggest a corrective to the belief that, in the *Discourses* no less than in *The Prince*, Machiavelli's outlook is entirely *sui generis*. It also provides us with a benchmark against which we can now go on to measure the extent to which Machiavelli was in fact concerned to question rather than endorse a number of prevailing humanist assumptions about the ideal of liberty.

There are two key points at which Machiavelli adopts a completely heterodox stance in discussing the concept of Republican liberty. The first is in the fourth chapter of his opening Discourse, in which he challenges 'the view of those who allege that the Republic of Rome was so tumultuous and so full of confusion that, had not good fortune and military virtue counterbalanced these defects, its condition would have been worse than that of any other Republic' (p. 113). Responding to this attack, Machiavelli starts out from the orthodox assumption that one of the main aims in any Republic which values its liberty must be to prevent any one section of the populace from seeking to legislate in its own selfish interests. He then suggests that, if we genuinely accept this argument, we cannot at the same time uphold the conventional view that 'tumults' and civic discords are inevitably damaging to the freedom of a Republic (p. 114). The example in terms of which he seeks to make this point is that of ancient Rome. He begins by noting that in Rome, as in any other Republic, there were at all times 'two different dispositions', that of the plebs and that of their opponents amongst 'the upper classes' (p. 113). He then observes that as long as the plebs were able 'to assemble and clamour against the senate', while the senators in their turn were able to decry the plebs, the net effect was to engineer a tensely-balanced equilibrium which ensured that neither party was able to oppress or ignore the interests of the other (pp. 114–15). He thus concludes that 'those who condemn the quarrels between the nobles and the plebs' under the ancient Republic are 'cavilling at the very things that were the primary cause of Rome's retaining her freedom' (p. 113). For they fail to recognise that, since these conflicts served to cancel out all sectional interests, they served at the same time to guarantee that the only enactments which actually passed into law were those which benefited the community as a whole.

Underlying Machiavelli's line of reasoning is the suggestion that, in emphasising the dangers of civil discord while defending the value of political liberty, most of his contemporaries have simply failed to follow out the implications of their own arguments. As we have seen, they agreed that liberty can only be maintained if *virtù* is promoted, and *virtù* can only be promoted if the citizens remain fully involved in political affairs. But they failed, in Machiavelli's view, to appreciate that the 'tumults' of ancient Rome were a consequence of intense political involvement, and were thus a manifestation of the highest civic *virtù*. So they failed to attain what Machiavelli clearly regarded as a fundamental political insight: that 'all legislation favourable to liberty is brought about by the clash' between the classes, and thus that class-conflict is not the solvent but the cement of a commonwealth (p. 113).

This defence of 'tumults' horrified Machiavelli's contemporaries.

Guicciardini spoke for them all when he declared in his *Considerations on the Discourses* that 'to praise disunity is like praising a sick man's disease because of the virtue of the remedy applied to it' (p. 68; Phillips, 1977, pp. 85–6). This reaction has usually been attributed to the fact that Machiavelli's argument cast such a deep shadow over the fashionable preoccupation with Venetian 'serenity'. Pocock, for example, has even claimed that the *Discourses* as a whole 'are best interpreted as a systematic dissent from the Venetian paradigm' (1975, p. 186). This may well be correct, but appears to underestimate the radical nature of Machiavelli's attack on the prevailing orthodoxy. As we have seen, the belief that all civic discord must be outlawed as factious, together with the belief that faction constitutes one of the gravest threats to political liberty, had been one of the leading themes of Florentine political theory ever since the end of the thirteenth century, when Remigio, Latini, Compagni and above all Dante had all issued fierce denunciations of their fellow-citizens for endangering their liberties by refusing to live in peace. To insist, therefore, on the astonishing judgment that (as Machiavelli expresses it) 'tumults deserve the highest praise' was not merely to sneer at the current admiration for the Venetian constitution; it was also to question one of the most deeply-rooted assumptions in the whole history of Florentine political thought (p. 114; cf. Pocock, 1975, p. 194).

The other point at which Machiavelli sought to undermine the prevailing pieties was in discussing the connections between the pursuit of *virtù* and the requirements of the Christian faith. This relationship was scarcely seen as problematic by the more orthodox defenders of republican liberty. While they agreed that any citizen who possesses the quality of *virtù* will be distinguished by his willingness to place the interests of his community above all other concerns, they never implied that this might lead to any conflicts with the requirements of virtue in the conventional Christian sense. On the contrary, they often made it clear that they assumed a complete compatibility between *virtù* and the virtues. This can be distinctly seen, for example, in Patrizi's discussion of *virtus* in the third Book of his *Institution of a Republic*. He first lays it down that 'all citizens ought to be educated in such a way that they apply themselves earnestly to acquiring *virtus*' (fo. 80a). But he then indicates that, in speaking of *virtus* in these general terms, what he basically has in mind is a traditional list of the cardinal virtues, amongst which he goes on to single out justice above all (fo. 80b).

Machiavelli's attack on these comfortable assumptions takes the form of claiming that, in assuming such a compatibility between *virtù* and the virtues, his contemporaries were once again failing to recognize the implications of their own arguments. He insists that if we are genuinely concerned with the ideal of *virtù*, and agreed that this commits us to putting the interests of our *patria* above all other concerns, then we cannot continue to assume that a man of *virtù* and a man of virtue will necessarily behave in a similar way. For we cannot pretend that such virtues as kindness, truth-telling and the maintenance of justice will always – or even very often – turn out to be compatible with the whole-hearted pursuit of the general good of the community.

Machiavelli presents this dilemma in its starkest form in his chapter dealing with the problems facing a new ruler 'in a city or province which he has seized' (p. 176). Such a leader will naturally wish to avoid having to use cruel or unjust methods, which 'are repugnant to any community, not only to a Christian one, but to any composed of men' (p. 177). But at the same time he will naturally wish 'to hold what he has' and secure his new territories (p. 177). The dilemma which is very likely to arise, according to Machiavelli, is that he will find it impossible to attain his desired ends except by the use of undesirable means. The question he will then be obliged to face is whether he really wishes to shun such methods completely and 'live as a private citizen', or whether he is willing 'to enter on the path of wrong-doing' in the name of maintaining his state (p. 177).

Machiavelli gives his own answer as unequivocally as possible. He has no doubt at all that the goal of maintaining the freedom and safety of a Republic represents the highest, and indeed the overriding, value in political life. So he has no hesitation in concluding that any attempt to employ a Christian scale of values in judging political affairs must be altogether given up. He continues to urge us, of course, to act as virtuously as possible. But he is no less insistent that, if the liberty of our *patria* requires us to tread the path of wrongdoing, we must do so unflinchingly. The point is made with brutal clarity at the end of the final Discourse, where Machiavelli offers us a judgment which, as he says, 'merits the attention of, and ought to be observed by, every citizen who has to give advice to his country' (p. 515). The judgment is this: 'when the safety of one's country wholly depends on the decision to be taken, no attention should be paid either to justice or to injustice, to kindness or cruelty, or to its being praiseworthy or ignominious. On the contrary, every other consideration being set aside, that alternative should be wholeheartedly adopted which will save the life and preserve the freedom of one's country' (p. 515).

For all the many differences between *The Prince* and the *Discourses*, the underlying political morality of the two books is thus the same. The only change in Machiavelli's basic stance arises out of the changing focus of his political advice. Whereas he was mainly concerned in *The Prince* with shaping the conduct of individual princes, he is more concerned in the *Discourses* with offering his counsel to the whole body of the citizens. The assumptions underlying his advice, however, remain the same as before. This becomes clear at an early stage in the opening Discourse, at the point where he is discussing Romulus's original foundation of the city of Rome. Machiavelli feels obliged to mention that Romulus brought about 'the death of his brother and his colleague' in the course of his labours, but immediately adds that 'he deserves to be excused' for these atrocious crimes (p. 133). The reason is that these actions were in fact essential in order to assure the safety of the new city. And Machiavelli's fundamental contention is that no one can reasonably be blamed 'for taking any action, however extraordinary, which may be of service in the organising of a kingdom or the constituting of a Republic' (p. 132). Thus his outlook can be summarised, as he recognised himself, in the form of what he calls the 'sound maxim' that 'reprehensible actions may be justified by their effects, and that when the effect is good, as it was in the case of Romulus, it always justifies the action'.[1]

Throughout the *Discourses* Machiavelli sprinkles his argument with many pieces of advice which reveal his unblinking commitment to this anti-Christian scale of values. He insists – as in *The Prince* – that it is better for a ruler to be feared than loved, and better 'to rely on punishment rather than considerateness' in dealing with his subjects (p. 460). He maintains that, in a situation where a ruler finds a whole city up in arms against his government, the best course of action is to abandon any thoughts of clemency and 'wipe them out' altogether (p. 349). And he repeatedly commends the use of fraud, dissimulation and deceit, even in relation to matters of the highest public importance (e.g., pp. 143, 310, 390, 423). The justification he offers in every case for such 'reprehensible' actions is that they are often unavoidable if the freedom of the commonwealth is to be successfully preserved – a value which is thus allowed to override any rival considerations in favour of clemency, justice or the other conventional virtues of political life (pp. 143, 349, 393).

The outcome of Machiavelli's commitment – as in *The Prince* – is thus that the concepts of *virtù* and virtue cease to have any necessary connection with each other. The idea of *virtù* is simply equated with whatever qualities are in practice needed 'to save the life and preserve the freedom of one's country'. It is then made ruthlessly clear that these qualities stand

---

[1] *Discourses*, p. 132. But this translation is perhaps over-eager to make Machiavelli say that 'the end justifies the means'. The verbs Machiavelli uses – in characteristically epigrammatic juxtaposition – are *accusare* and *scusare*. The action itself accuses, but its outcome excuses (rather than justifies) its performance.

in no very close relationship with the accepted list of Christian and moral virtues (p. 515). As in the case of the analogous discussion in *The Prince*, this is brought out most clearly in Machiavelli's description of two of his favourite heroes of antiquity, Severus and Hannibal. Severus is again singled out for his high *virtù* and his 'great good luck', while Machiavelli assures us in the same breath that he was unquestionably 'a wicked man' (p. 137). And Hannibal's 'outstanding *virtù*' and fame are again celebrated, while Machiavelli reminds us at the same time that his magnificent reputation was achieved by methods which included 'impiety, faithlessness and cruelty' to an extreme degree (pp. 464–5).

Given that this is Machiavelli's moral standpoint in the *Discourses*, there is much to be said for the view that the first of the 'Machiavellians' was Guicciardini, Machiavelli's friend and younger contemporary. Guicciardini's *Maxims* in particular contain many similarly sour reflections on political life. He agrees that 'a truthful, open nature' can 'be harmful' to political success, and argues that 'deception is very useful, whereas your frankness tends to profit others' (pp. 67, 107). He agrees even more strongly that a ruler 'must rely more on severity than on kindness', since 'the wickedness of men is such that you cannot govern well without severity' (pp. 53, 116). And he summarises his advice by warning us in almost theatrically 'Machiavellian' tones that 'you cannot go wrong if you believe little and trust less' (p. 81). Nevertheless, it seems an overstatement to suggest, as Domandi and others have done, that Guicciardini is a more 'Machiavellian' writer than Machiavelli himself (Domandi, 1965, p. 33; cf. also Allen, 1957, p. 498). When Guicciardini discusses Machiavelli's chapter on the problems of new rulers in his *Considerations on the Discourses*, he criticises Machiavelli for showing himself to be so 'extremely partial to extraordinary and violent methods', and for failing in consequence to allow that a new prince might be able to establish his government 'with humanity, kindness and rewards' (p. 92). And although Guicciardini pronounces a number of exceptionally savage judgments in his *Maxims* on the shortcomings of his contemporaries, he is never consistently pessimistic in his appraisal of human nature and its potentialities. Sometimes he is sure that 'men are so false, so insidious, so deceitful and cunning in their wiles, and so avid in their own interests' that they cannot be trusted at all (p. 81). But at other moments he is equally certain that 'all men are by nature inclined towards good rather than evil', and that no one 'would not rather do good than evil, unless other factors induce him to the contrary' (p. 75). Machiavelli by contrast is a consistent, an almost Hobbesian sceptic about the possibility of inducing men to behave well except by cajolery or force. The opening words of the *Discourses* speak of 'the envy inherent in man's nature', and the whole of the work is predicated on the assumption that 'in constituting and legislating for a commonwealth it must needs be taken for granted that all men are wicked and that they will always give vent to the malignity that is in their minds when opportunity offers' (pp. 97, 111–12). While Guicciardini is still prepared to allow a fitful flicker of optimism or self-deception to illuminate his otherwise sombre picture of political life, Machiavelli invariably sees the world of politics as one in which the rational methods of the law-giver must be supplemented at all times with the ferocity of the lion and the cunning of the fox.

THE END OF REPUBLICAN LIBERTY

Perhaps the most central motif of Renaissance humanism, as Garin has emphasised, is the proposition that *virtù vince fortuna* – that *virtù* serves to overcome the power of fortune to control our affairs (Garin, 1965, p. 61). The humanists had always acknowledged the extent of fortune's sway, but insisted at the same time that a man of *virtù* will always find the means to limit and subdue her tyranny. We still find something of the same confidence being expressed by Machiavelli and his contemporaries. Machiavelli declares in the *Discourses* that it is only 'where men have but little *virtù*,' that 'fortune makes a great display' of her powers (pp. 375–6). He even maintains 'that fortune holds no sway' over great men, since 'they do not change, but remain ever resolute' even in the face of her greatest malevolence (p. 488). And he ends his chapter on the influence of fortune by proclaiming in his most elevated tones that, in spite of the goddess's domination of human affairs, men 'should never give up' (p. 372). They should take comfort from the fact that 'there is always hope', even though 'they know not the end and move towards it along roads which cross one another and as yet are unexplored'. And because there is hope 'they should not despair, no matter what fortune brings or in what travail they find themselves' (p. 372).

As the appalling history of sixteenth-century Italy unfolded, however, the later humanists became increasingly worn down by the sense that they were living in an age in which *virtù* and *ragione* were no longer capable of parrying the blows of fortune. The attempts of the Republicans to re-establish a popular government in Rome were finally smashed in 1527, when the armies of Charles V, mutinous and out of control, put the city to the sack and left its fate to be decided by the invading powers (Green, 1964, pp. 153–4). The last Florentine Republic was overwhelmed by the same Imperial armies three years later, after which the Medici finally managed to silence the traditional demands for Republican liberty. Faced with these shattering proofs of fortune's malignancy, the characteristic confidence of the humanists began to falter and collapse into a sense of increasing hopelessness. And with this loss of faith in the power of *virtù*, the great tradition of Italian Republicanism finally came to an end.

The beginnings of this decline can already be observed in Machiavelli, who accepts the ultimately fatalistic view that, in spite of the best efforts of our statecraft, there is an inexorable cycle of growth and decay through which all commonwealths must pass. There are no signs of this deterministic vision of the human condition in *The Prince*, but the *Discourses* begin with a full account of this Polybian theory of inevitable cycles. Machiavelli claims that all commonwealths are originally ruled by princes who, being made hereditary, degenerate into tyrants and so provoke plots on the part of the aristocracy against their leadership. The aristocrats then set up their own governments, which soon degenerate into oligarchies and provoke plots on the part of the masses. They in turn set up democracies, which eventually lead to anarchy and so persuade them to return to the initial position of rule by a prince. This is 'the cycle through which all commonwealths pass' (pp. 106–9). Machiavelli believes, of course, that these inevitable stages of corruption and decline can be staved off by the establishment of a mixed form of Republican regime, since this allows the strengths of the three 'pure' forms of government to be combined without their attendant weaknesses (p. 109). But he later makes it clear that, taking the widest perspective on human affairs, we are bound to conclude that fortune is ultimately in charge. He not only accepts the conventional humanist belief that 'many events happen and many misfortunes come about, against which the heavens have not been willing that any provision at all should be made' (p. 369). He even goes on to assert that 'history as a whole bears witness' to the much more pessimistic claim that 'men may second their fortune, but cannot oppose it', and thus that 'they may act in accordance with, but cannot infringe, its ordinances' (p. 372).

If we move on more than a decade from Machiavelli's *Discourses*, and turn to Guicciardini's *Maxims* and his *History*, we encounter a greatly increased sense of the imbalance between fortune's powers and man's capacities. The *Maxims* begin with some fairly conventional reflections on the fact that fortune 'plays such a large role' in our lives and 'has great power over human affairs' (pp. 45, 49). But it is not long before a note of increasing desperation begins to be audible. Guicciardini admits that 'all cities, all states, all regions are mortal', and that 'everything, either by nature or by accident, ends at some time' in spite of any efforts we may make to prevent this ultimate collapse (p. 89). He accordingly concentrates on trying to offer comfort to those who, like himself, find themselves 'living in the final stages' of their country's existence, arguing that a man who finds himself in such a situation 'should not feel as sorry for his country as he should for himself', since 'what happened to his country was inevitable' at some point, whereas 'to be born at a time when such a disaster had to happen' can only be regarded as a terrible and gratuitous misfortune (p. 89). By the time he came to write his *History* in the closing years of his life, this sense of living in an age of irreversible catastrophe had come to dominate Guicciardini's entire outlook. Abandoning the humanist belief that the main duty of the historian is to furnish his readers with useful precepts and advice, he devotes his entire narrative to recounting the tragedy of Italy's progressive exploitation and collapse. The only general lesson on which he seeks paradoxically to insist is, as Gilbert remarks, 'that of the helplessness and impotence of man in the face of fate' (Gilbert, 1965, pp. 288, 299).

Finally, when we come to a writer like Boccalini, picking his way amidst the ruins of the Republican tradition at the end of the sixteenth century, we encounter a tone of blank despair. The last Book of the *Advertisements from Parnassus* contains a scene in which all 'the chiefest potentates on earth' find themselves arraigned before 'the public censor of politic affairs' to be condemned in turn, in Boccalini's most savagely ironic style, for failing to provide their citizens with the least semblance of sane or effective government (p. 439). The Holy Roman Emperor is accused of scandalous negligence; the French are denounced for sheer madness; the Spanish are told that their government is 'odious to men'; the English are stigmatised as dangerous heretics; the Ottoman Empire is execrated for its 'cruel rigour'; and even Venice is warned that her serenity is being endangered by the excesses of her nobility (pp. 440–7). Each government tries to defend itself, but the justifications they offer merely serve to underline the melancholy conclusion that the age of *virtù* is at an end. Some of them viciously seek to argue that their apparent failings are really evidence of the highest statecraft. Thus the French complain that they have been censured for 'the prime virtues' of their government, while the Ottomans defend their cruelty in strictly Machiavellian terms by insisting that the 'heroical virtues of clemency and mildness' merely serve to endanger 'the tranquillity and peace of states' (pp. 441, 445–6). The more modest nations agree that their conduct is disgraceful, but insist that the evil power of fortune and their own generally adverse circumstances make it impossible even to contemplate any reforms. The Emperor declares that the problems of his government are so intractable that they would have made 'King Solomon himself' appear 'a blockhead' (p. 441). The Spanish admit that their administration is 'faulty and full of danger', but protest that it is not within their powers to suggest any remedies (p. 442). And the king of England simply bursts into tears without trying to justify himself at all (p. 443). The entire age stands condemned as one in which *virtù* can scarcely be recognised, and even when recognised can no longer be pursued.

Further Reading

(1) *Guicciardini*. The standard biography is by Ridolfi, 1967. There is a useful outline of Guicciardini's political ideas in Rubinstein, 1965a, and a very fine account in Gilbert, 1965. For a fuller analysis, see Pocock, 1975. The relationship between Guicciardini's political and historical outlook is well discussed in Phillips, 1977.

(2) *Machiavelli*. Two valuable attempts to survey the vast critical literature have been made by Cochrane, 1961 and Geerken, 1976. The standard biography is by Ridolfi, 1963. The political background of Machiavelli's thought is sketched in Hale, 1961. The background of *quattrocento* political theory is discussed in Baron, 1966, Garin, 1965 and in several of the seminal essays collected in Kristeller, 1961 and 1965. Gilbert, 1965, contains one of the best general accounts of Machiavelli's political ideas. Pocock, 1975, is another fine study, especially interesting on the *Discourses*. Some important studies on special topics: on the dating of *The Prince* and *Discourses*, see Baron, 1961. On Machiavelli as an historian, see Gilbert, 1972. On Machiavelli and the art of war, see Bayley, 1961. On Machiavelli's political morality, see Berlin, 1972, and for two contrasting and influential views see Chabod, 1958 and Strauss, 1958. On the meaning of the key concept of *virtù* in Machiavelli, see especially Whitfield, 1947, Hexter, 1964 and Price, 1973.

PART THREE

The northern Renaissance

7

The diffusion of humanist scholarship

THE MIGRATION OF HUMANISTS

Rabelais tells us that when the young Pantagruel first went to study at the University of Paris, he received a stern letter from his father Gargantua urging him to devote himself with as much energy as possible to a life of scholarship. Gargantua's main purpose in writing was to give an account of the somewhat heroic course of instruction he wished his son to pursue. But he also took the opportunity to offer some appropriately sententious remarks about the great improvements in 'sound learning' which had been achieved in France in the course of his own lifetime. When he was young, 'the times were still dark, and mankind was perpetually reminded of the miseries and disasters wrought by those Goths who had destroyed all sound scholarship'. But now there was light and enlightenment everywhere. The invention of 'the elegant and accurate art of printing' had made it possible to disseminate the new learning so widely that 'the whole world' had become 'full of learned men, of very erudite tutors, and of most extensive libraries'. And the new learning itself had involved a restoration of 'every method of teaching', a revival of 'the study of languages' and a splendid *rapprochement* with the unsurpassed civilisation of the ancient world.[1]

The moment at which this new learning first made its appearance at the University of Paris can be dated with some precision. The earliest scholar who attempted to combine the teaching of Latin and Greek with the study of the humanities appears to have been Gregorio da Tiferna (*c.* 1415–66), who arrived from Naples to take up the first Professorship of Greek in 1458 (Renaudet, 1953, p. 82). His lectures were evidently a sensational success, and he was soon followed by a procession of other Italian humanists, all equally eager to question the University's traditional scholastic curriculum. The first to repeat the challenge was Filippo Beroaldo (*c.* 1440–1504), whose inaugural lecture in 1476 proclaimed that,

[1] Rabelais, *Gargantua*, p. 194. Cf. also Rabelais, *Epistle of Dedication* in *The Five Books*, vol. II, p. 499.

although Paris was already 'the most illustrious centre of all the arts', there was still 'one valuable task' which remained to be performed, and which he proposed to undertake himself. This was to lecture 'on the arts of poetry and the *studia humanitatis*', to reveal 'how closely this kind of study connects with philosophy', and to explain 'how much the study of philosophy can benefit from this connection' (Renaudet, 1953, p. 116 and n.). The next scholar to take up the battle-cry was Girolamo Balbi (*c.* 1450–1536), who came to Paris in 1484 as a lecturer in Greek and the humanities at the Collège de Navarre (Renaudet, 1953, p. 121). But the most decisive campaign in favour of the humanities was waged by Fausto Andrelini (*c.* 1460–1518), who began his teaching career at Paris in 1489 (Cosenza, 1962, pp. 82–3). He stayed for almost thirty years, lecturing indefatigably on Livy and Suetonius as well as on the Latin poets and rhetoricians, and winning high praise from Budé and Erasmus for his classical scholarship (Renaudet, 1953, pp. 123–5). More than anyone else, it was he who ensured that, in spite of the increasingly vocal hostility of the scholastics, the study of the humanities became firmly entrenched in the curriculum by the start of the sixteenth century.

A similar reception of humanist ideas began to take place in England at about the same time (Weiss, 1964, pp. 90–2). The leading pioneer in this case was Pietro del Monte (d. 1457), who arrived in 1435 to take up a post as collector of Papal revenues, and remained for over five years. Del Monte was a considerable scholar in his own right, the author of a discussion of *The Difference between the Virtues and the Vices* which may claim the distinction of being the first humanist treatise to be written in England (Weiss, 1957, p. 25). But his most important role was played as an informal literary advisor to Duke Humphrey of Gloucester, the earliest English patron of humanism. It was Del Monte who persuaded Humphrey to take the novel step of introducing an Italian *dictator* into his household in 1436 (Weiss, 1957, p. 26). The position was given to Tito Livio Frulovisi (*c.* 1400–56), whose main duty was to compose a panegyric on the reign of Humphrey's brother, Henry V. The fruits of this commission were of considerable importance for the development of English human-ism, since Frulovisi responded with a *Life of Henry V* in which the full range of rhetorical techniques – including set speeches by the king on the eve of his major battles – appeared for the first time in the pages of an English chronicle (e.g., pp. 14–16, 66–8). Del Monte also encouraged Humphrey's passion for book-collecting, sending him many volumes from Italy after returning there in 1440, and putting him in touch with other leading scholars – including Bruni and Decembrio – who advised him about the purchase of manuscripts (Weiss, 1957, pp. 46, 58, 62). This enabled Humphrey to assemble a remarkable library, containing not merely the usual works of theology and scholastic philosophy, but also the best translations of Plato, Aristotle and Plutarch, the whole of the extant text of Livy, most of the key works of Cicero, and a large number of modern humanist treatises, including works by Petrarch, Salutati, Poggio, Bruni and Decembrio (Weiss, 1957, pp. 62–5). This aspect of Humphrey's scholarly activity proved to be still more important for the propagation of the *studia humanitatis* in England, especially after he presented some two hundred and eighty of his volumes to the University of Oxford between 1439 and 1444 – thus making available the first major collection of humanist texts for public use (Weiss, 1957, pp. 66–7).

The culture of the Renaissance was further disseminated in England by a number of Italian scholars who came to teach at Oxford and Cambridge in the later years of the fifteenth century. One of the earliest to arrive was the Milanese Stefano Surigone (*fl.* 1430–80), who lectured on grammar and rhetoric at Oxford between 1454 and 1471 (Cosenza, 1962, p. 1726). He was shortly followed by Cornelio Vitelli (*c.* 1450–1500), who received an invitation from Thomas Chaundler to serve as Praelector in Greek at New College in the 1470s, thus becoming the first public teacher of Greek in an English University.[1] Soon after this a number of like-minded propagandists became active at Cambridge. Lorenzo da Savona lectured there in the 1470s, as well as publishing a handbook on rhetoric in 1478 which went through two printed editions before the end of the century (Weiss, 1957, p. 162). And Caio Auberino (*fl.* 1450–1500) combined his duties as an official *Dictator* for the University with the presentation of a similar series of lectures on Latin literature in the course of the 1480s (Cosenza, 1962, p. 163).

This diffusion of Renaissance culture was greatly aided by the fact that the latter half of the fifteenth century was also the first age of the printed book. No group was quicker to perceive the vast potentialities of the new medium than the humanists. The introduction of printing into France provides the clearest example of the way in which they were able to make use of the printing press in order to promote their own interests over those of their scholastic adversaries. The first press to be set up in France was installed in the basement of the Sorbonne in 1470. The moving spirit behind the enterprise was Guillaume Fichet, who emphasised in his *Letter to Robert Gaguin* the significance of 'this new invention lately come out of Germany'.[2] His chief point is that printing 'will vastly contribute to the

---

[1] So says Cosenza, 1962, p. 1903. But this visit is not mentioned by Weiss, 1938, who claims (p. 225) that Vitelli first came to Oxford in 1490.

[2] See Fichet, *Letter*, p. 2. The original is unpaginated, and lacks signature-marks, so I have

restoration of the study of the humanities' (p. 2). During his youth, he observes, 'there were neither orators nor poets' teaching at Paris, with the result that 'the study of Latin had fallen into a condition of almost rustic ignorance' (p. 1). But now 'the muses are being cultivated again', and with the addition of printed books it will be possible to give an even greater encouragement to 'good letters' and 'men of scholarship' (p. 3). Suiting his actions to his words, Fichet proceeded to use his press in order to promote the widest possible distribution of humanist texts and handbooks. Within the first three years he had issued Cicero's *De Officiis*, a complete Sallust, and a considerable number of modern works, including his own textbook on the rhetorical arts, Lorenzo Valla's *Elegancies of the Latin Language*, and the *dictamen* of Gasparino da Barzizza, the first book ever to be printed in France (Renaudet, 1953, p. 84).

Once the doctrines and expositors of the *studia humanitatis* began to percolate through these various channels into northern Europe, this helped to bring about a reciprocal form of intellectual development. An increasing number of scholars from northern universities felt inspired to abandon their scholastic studies, to embrace the humanities, and to seek admission to the universities of Italy in order to pursue the new learning at its source.

It is of course true that large numbers of students from France, England and Germany had gone to Italy throughout the Middle Ages, especially if they wished to take degrees in medicine or law, the two subjects in which the Italian universities had always enjoyed the highest reputation in northern Europe (Parks, 1954, pp. 423–5; Mitchell, 1936, p. 272). We begin to see the signs of a new spirit, however, when we find a number of scholars arriving in Italy with the intention of specialising in one of the traditional disciplines, and then finding themselves lured away by the rival attractions of the humanities. The career of Thomas Linacre (*c.* 1460–1525) provides one of the most important instances of this trend. He first travelled to Italy in 1487 in order to take a medical degree at Padua, but soon went on to study Greek at Rome and the humanities at Florence and Venice, and thereafter continued to divide his time with equal success between the practice of medicine and the pursuit of classical scholarship (Parks, 1954, p. 457). A similar but even more decisive shift of loyalties can be observed in the case of Rudolf Agricola (1444–84). He arrived in Italy in 1469 with the ostensible purpose of reading law at the University of Pavia, but turned almost immediately to the study of

supplied these page-numbers myself. For an account of the relations between printing and the spread of humanism in Germany, see Hirsch, 1971.

rhetoric, and later moved to Ferrara in order to acquire a knowledge of Greek (Spitz, 1963, p. 23). Returning to his native Germany after an absence of ten years, he quickly became famous as a teacher of the humanities, and was later hailed by Erasmus in a letter of 1489 as 'exceptionally highly gifted in all the liberal arts' (p. 38).

The next important development was that a growing number of students from northern universities felt the need to go to Italy specifically in order to improve their knowledge of the *studia humanitatis*. Some of the earliest came from the Sorbonne, where their enthusiasm seems to have been kindled by Gregorio da Tiferna (Renaudet, 1953, p. 186). Robert Gaguin (1435–1501), whom Erasmus was to salute in a letter of 1495 as 'the principal ornament of the University of France', paid two extended visits between 1465 and 1471, while his friend and mentor Guillaume Fichet made a number of contacts with Italian humanists in the course of a lengthy diplomatic mission between 1469 and 1470 (p. 87; cf. Renaudet, 1953, pp. 83, 186). Soon after this a group of young scholars from Oxford began to undertake a similar series of pilgrimages. William Grocyn (*c.* 1449–1519), a pupil of Cornelio Vitelli's, went to study with Poliziano in Florence between 1488 and 1490 (Parks, 1954, p. 462). His friend William Latimer (*c.* 1460–1545) accompanied him on his journey, subsequently moving to the University of Padua in order to perfect his Greek (Caspari, 1968, p. 36). And John Colet (*c.* 1467–1519), who almost certainly started his training under Grocyn, went on to spend three particularly formative years in Italy between 1493 and 1496 (Jayne, 1963, pp. 16, 21). By this time the same route was beginning to be followed by a growing band of scholars from Germany and the Low Countries – a fashion which may be said to culminate in Erasmus's famous tour of Italy between 1506 and 1509 (Nolhac, 1925, pp. 20–52). Two of these visits proved to be of particular importance for the future of German humanism. Willibald Pirckheimer (1470–1530) studied in Italy for nearly seven years in the 1490s, becoming expert in Greek and exceptionally widely read in the humanities (Spitz, 1963, p. 157). And Conrad Celtis (1459–1508), under the inspiration of Agricola's teaching at Heidelberg, left Germany in 1487 for an even more extended stay, working with the librarian of St Mark's at Venice as well as attending the Universities of Padua, Florence and Rome (Spitz, 1957, pp. 3, 11–13).

The significance of these journeys lies in the fact that most of these men returned to teach in their native universities, thus helping to initiate an intellectual revolution which eventually led to the overthrow of scholasticism. Gaguin gained a post at the Sorbonne in 1473, where he lectured with immense success on rhetoric and Latin literature (Tilley, 1918, p.

188). Subsequently he also made a number of important contributions to humanist scholarship, including a partial translation of Livy, a treatise on Latin versification and a chronicle entitled *A Compendium of the Origins and Deeds of the French*, the first history of France to be written in full rhetorical style (Reynolds, 1955, pp. 26–8). Grocyn, Latimer and Colet all came back from Italy to teach at Oxford. Grocyn became the University's first lecturer in Greek in 1491, Latimer was appointed tutor in the humanities at Magdalen College soon afterwards, and Colet delivered his famous series of lectures on the Pauline Epistles 'before the entire University community' between 1498 and 1499.[1] Similarly, Conrad Celtis returned from his travels to become, in Spitz's phrase, 'the arch humanist' of the German Universities, lecturing on the *Ars Dictaminis* at Ingolstadt between 1491 and 1496, and thereafter serving as the first Professor of poetry and rhetoric at the University of Vienna until his death in 1508 (Spitz, 1957, pp. 22, 55, 116).

The eventual outcome of these interactions was the emergence of a new and self-confident humanist culture in France, England and Germany by the beginning of the sixteenth century.[2] The remarkably assured spirit of this northern Renaissance is well summed-up by John Desmarais in the course of a letter published in 1516 as one of the prefatory addresses to More's *Utopia*. Hitherto, he concedes, 'praise for learning has belonged almost exclusively to Greece and Italy'. But now their civilisation has not only been transported to northern Europe, it has even been surpassed. Germany can boast of 'numerous figures famous for learning'; France is distinguished by the genius of Guillaume Budé; and England is now 'pre-eminent' in the humanities, with 'men of such talent as to be able to contend with antiquity itself' (p. 27).

[1] For Grocyn and Latimer, see Caspari, 1968, pp. 35–6. For the claim about Colet's audience, see Duhamel, 1953, p. 493. For the dating of Colet's lectures, see Jayne, 1963, esp. p. 37. Jayne has convincingly challenged the traditional dating, showing that Colet's first lectures on Romans were not given until January 1498, while those on Corinthians were given a year later and the final lectures on Romans in October 1499.

[2] As the following chapters will attempt to show, the bearers of this culture were to a considerable extent in agreement with each other in their moral, social and political philosophies. I shall thus be concerned to suggest that they exhibit a genuine cultural identity which, while naturally of a somewhat loose-limbed character, was nevertheless stronger than any national differences or rivalries. Given this basic contention, it has become necessary to think of some general shorthand term to describe their movement as a whole. I have chosen for sake of the greatest brevity simply to speak of it as 'the northern Renaissance', and its exponents as 'the northern humanists'. This is far from ideal, especially since I shall subsequently argue that a similar series of interactions, giving rise to a similar culture, developed during the next generation in Spain and Portugal. I am not unaware that these countries can scarcely be described as lying to the north of Italy, but no better term than 'northern humanism' has suggested itself as a brief way of indicating the crucial fact that the culture with which I am concerned largely emanated from Italy and subsequently spread across most of western Europe.

It would be misleading to conclude, however, that the development of humanism in northern Europe can simply be explained, as some scholars have suggested, 'immediately and exclusively' in terms of 'the influence of renewed cultural activity in Italy'.[1] There are two main reasons for thinking that this traditional explanation offers an unduly crude interpretation of the facts. One is that – as Simone in particular has emphasised – it is possible to detect a number of Italian cultural influences in northern Europe, and especially in France, as early as the middle of the fourteenth century. The main agent of this diffusion was the Papal Court, which took up residence at Avignon in 1308 and remained there for nearly seventy years. Simone goes so far as to speak of a 'strong current' of Italian ideas radiating outwards from this centre 'to every part of France' in the course of the fourteenth century (Simone, 1969, p. 57). While this sounds somewhat fanciful, there is no doubt that a series of connections can be established between the humanist culture of fourteenth-century Avignon – where Petrarch himself lived for nearly fifteen years – and the much later efflorescence of the *studia humanitatis* at the University of Paris. One direct link is indicated by the career of Guillaume Fichet, who studied at Avignon before going to teach at Paris in 1453, and whose early academic training included a close acquaintance with the works of Petrarch, several of whose writings he translated for his own use (Renaudet, 1953, p. 83; Simone, 1969, p. 148). A further difficulty with the traditional explanation – which Simone tends to overlook – is that many of the elements in pre-Renaissance art and literature which subsequently came to seem most distinctively Italian were in fact imported from France in the late thirteenth and early fourteenth centuries. There are French influences at work in early humanist poetry: the use Petrarch and his imitators made of Provençal themes and techniques has often been pointed out (Nordström, 1933, pp. 160–2). There are similar influences to be traced in some of the greatest works of *duecento* painting and sculpture: both Duccio and Pisano appear to have been heavily indebted to French Gothic models. And there are even French origins, as we have seen, for the distinctive rhetorical culture of Renaissance Italy: the crucial development in the character of the *Ars Dictaminis* at the end of the thirteenth century – the development from the inculcation of rules to the study of classical authorities – seems to have been based largely on imitating the long-standing traditions of

[1] This is the formulation Simone uses (1969, pp. 37–8) as an introduction to his scornful dismissal of this 'romantic' explanation of the northern Renaissance. It seems doubtful, however, whether any historian has ever defended such a simple version of the thesis Simone is concerned to attack. For a more moderate and lucid survey of the attempts which have been made to explain the northern Renaissance largely in terms of a 'transplantation' of Italian values, see Ferguson, 1948, pp. 253–89. For a special study of the historiography of the French Renaissance, see Hornik, 1960.

instruction in the French Cathedral schools (cf. Nordström, 1933, pp. 58–70).

It must also be admitted that, even at the start of the sixteenth century, when the culture of the Renaissance had its greatest impact on northern Europe, the northern humanists were in most cases only receptive to those ideas which to some extent seemed familiar, and thus seemed capable of being assimilated into their own very different range of experiences. This can clearly be seen in the case of their reception of Italian humanist social and political thought (Hyma, 1940, pp. 11–17). As we have already observed, there were two perennial issues which, in the main tradition of Italian political theory, had always been treated with special seriousness: the need to preserve political liberty, and the dangers to liberty represented by the prevalence of standing mercenary armies. But neither of these themes struck any resonating chord with the northern humanists. Given the capacity of their rulers to raise massive national armies, they clearly regarded the alleged problem of mercenaries as little better than an irrelevance. And given the post-feudal and monarchical institutions of France, Germany and England, they evidently found it hard to make sense of the Italian obsession with *libertas*, or to sympathise with the accompanying tendency to argue that Republicanism must be considered the best form of government. We find in consequence that neither of these preoccupations ever receives any extended attention even from the most fervently Italianate of the northern humanists.

These considerations have prompted some historians to deny that the northern Renaissance can be explained even partly in terms of the progressive diffusion of Italian ideas in the course of the fifteenth century. Bush has argued, for example, that 'the real character of English humanism' can be traced as far back as the twelfth century, and that later importations of Italian scholarship 'only ripened and confirmed' this pre-existing culture (Bush, 1939, pp. 47–9, 71). And Nordström has gone so far as to claim that the culture of the Italian Renaissance was little more than 'a straightforward continuation' of a tradition originally 'formed north of the Alps', which found its first and 'most glorious' centre in France, and only appeared much later and in a derivative form in Italy (Nordström, 1933, pp. 12–13).

It seems almost wilfully misleading, however, to deny the obvious fact that the transplantation of Italian humanism to France, Germany and England during the fifteenth century played a major role in determining both the timing and the character of the northern Renaissance (cf. Kristeller, 1962b, p. 14). This was certainly the view of the northern humanists themselves. Erasmus summarises their attitude in a letter to

Cornelius Gerard in 1489. We have been suffering for centuries, he complains, from 'the obstinate growth of barbarism', and living through an era in which men 'turned their backs on the precepts of the ancients'. But now a full knowledge of the humanities has been recovered 'with admirable scholarly application' by 'our good Lorenzo Valla' and his disciples in Italy, as a result of which it has at last become possible 'to bring back into use' all the neglected ancient authors and their works (p. 40). It would of course be possible to dismiss such claims as nothing more than typical humanist self-advertisement. But the fundamental thesis of the following chapters will be that such a response would be mistaken. It will be argued that, although there are many qualifications to be made, the traditional explanation of the northern Renaissance is basically correct: the northern humanists were crucially dependent, both in their technical scholarship and in their more general outlook on social and political life, on the range of concepts and theories already developed by the humanists of *quattrocento* Italy.

HUMANISM AND LEGAL SCHOLARSHIP

One aspect of Italian renaissance culture which became of increasing interest to the northern humanists at the start of the sixteenth century was the technical core of humanism – the attempt to apply detailed techniques of philological and historical criticism to the texts of the ancient world. The resulting story belongs in part to the history of classical scholarship. Celtis and Pirckheimer both became famous in Germany as editors of the Greek and Latin classics, Linacre attained a comparable distinction in England with his translations of Aristotle, and Budé in France achieved a peerless reputation as a Greek scholar with the publication of his *Commentaries on the Greek Language* in 1529 (Sandys, 1964, II, pp. 170, 226–7, 260). As well as concerning themselves with these literary and philosophical manuscripts, however, a number of northern humanists became preoccupied with two rather different sets of texts from the ancient world which, when studied according to the new canons of humanist scholarship, were both destined to exercise a profound influence on the development of sixteenth-century political thought.

They first of all turned their attention to the texts of the Roman law, especially in the form in which they had been definitively codified in the reign of Justinian.[1] As we have already seen, the Italian humanists – and especially Lorenzo Valla – had originally become interested in the law as

---

[1] In this section I am greatly indebted to the brilliant survey of the origins of humanist jurisprudence contained in the opening chapters of Kelley, 1970.

part of their campaign against scholasticism. They wanted to challenge the orthodox scholastic approach to the interpretation of the Civil Code, above all the deliberately unhistorical assumption that the main aim of the jurist should be to adapt the letter of the law as closely as possible to fit existing legal circumstances. Denouncing this methodology as barbarous and ignorant, they sought to insist that a true appreciation of the Code required that its text should be considered in the light of their own historical and philological techniques. The outcome of applying this approach was that the humanists began to make a number of substantive contributions to a new and more historically-minded kind of legal science.

One of their earliest and most devastating *coups* was Lorenzo Valla's proof that the so-called Donation of Constantine was a forgery. The Donation purported to be a legal document granted by the Emperor Constantine to Sylvester, the Bishop of Rome, according to which the Bishop was given supremacy over the four Imperial patriarchs and dominion over the whole of the western Empire. Although some doubts had occasionally been raised about the provenance of the document, the Papacy had not only succeeded in defending its authenticity over many centuries, but had also based its most extensive claims to temporal authority on the alleged character of Constantine's grant. After Valla's study of the document in the 1440s, these claims were utterly discredited. Part of his case was built around the legal contention that the Emperor had no authority to make such a donation, and the Pope no right to receive it. But the two arguments Valla himself regarded as the most decisive were both of a far more detailed and technical nature. The first depended on a piece of philological evidence. According to the Donation, the Emperor agreed to make 'all our satraps' as well as the people of Rome 'subject to the Roman Church' (p. 34). But as Valla scornfully observes, this is glaringly anachronistic: 'who ever heard of anyone being called a satrap in the councils of the Romans?' (p. 35). After amusing himself with this absurdity for some pages, Valla moves on to his second argument, which is based on a simple point about chronology. The Donation speaks of making the Pope supreme over the patriarch of Constantinople. But this is 'an even more absurd' anachronism: at the time when the Donation is supposed to have been drawn up 'there was no patriarch there, no see, not even a Christian city named or founded or even imagined' (p. 39). So Valla has no hesitation in concluding – with much clamour and many exclamations – that the Papacy's claims to temporal dominion have no basis whatever in historical fact.

Valla was also the pioneer in applying the same techniques of criticism to the commentaries on the Roman law (Kelley, 1970, p. 39). His main attack on the jurists appears in the final section of his most important work, the *Six Books on the Elegancies of the Latin Language*. The first five Books are devoted to explaining the correct use of various Latin expressions and constructions, with copious illustrations drawn from the best Roman authors – especially Virgil for poetry and Cicero for prose. The sixth Book then deploys this overpowering classical erudition in order to expose the manifold errors committed by those who continued to write Latin in later and more decadent periods. Many of the most disgraceful contributions to this rising tide of barbarism are shown to have been perpetrated by the jurists. Modestinus is rebuked for having misunderstood the Latin of the *Lex Julia*; Marcus and Ulpian are denounced for having introduced a number of meaningless distinctions into their discussions of legal bequests; and Paulus's legal vocabulary, especially in his account of ancestors and inheritance, is sweepingly dismissed for its failure to conform 'either to reason or to good usage' (pp. 218, 224, 230).

Valla's concept of 'legal humanism' was soon extended by three leading scholars of the next generation. Angelo Poliziano (1454–94), who became Professor of Greek at Florence in 1480, included in his *Book of Miscellanies* a series of five chapters in which Justinian's Code was for the first time analysed according to the new humanist techniques (Kelley, 1970, p. 48). Pietro Crinito (1475–1507), a friend and pupil of Poliziano's, wrote a commentary (now lost) on the section of the Digest dealing with the meanings of legal terms (Kelley, 1970, p. 42). And Giulio Pomponio (1428–97), who had studied under Valla himself at Rome, began to amplify the historical as well as philological aspects of Valla's methodology, producing *A Compendium of the History of Rome* together with an historical analysis of *The Magistrates, Laws and Priests of Rome* (Cosenza, 1962, pp. 1458–9).

The first triumph of legal humanism came when a number of practising jurists – all of whom had hitherto execrated Valla and his disciples – began to acknowledge the justice of Valla's criticisms and to make use of his new techniques. One of the earliest to undergo this conversion was Mario Salamonio. We have already observed the way in which he appealed to Valla's work on the Donation of Constantine, as well as discussing Pomponio's findings on the Roman magistracy, in the course of his dialogues on *The Sovereignty of the Roman Patriciate*. Still more important was the endorsement of the same approach by Andrea Alciato (1492–1550). Alciato originally received a conventional legal education, beginning his studies at Pavia in 1508, moving to Bologna in 1511 and thereafter returning as a practising lawyer to his native Milan (Viard, 1926, pp. 36, 40). But in spite of this background, his essentially humanist allegiances are evident on almost every page of his voluminous legal works. This can be seen most clearly in his mature treatise entitled *The Extra Ornament of the Law*, a series of informal commentaries in twelve books, the first three of which were published in 1536, the next seven in 1544 and the last two in 1551 (Viard, 1926, p. 91). It is true that, as a lawyer rather than a professional humanist, Alciato retains a considerable respect for Bartolus and other leading Post-Glossators, speaking of being 'moved by their authority' even when disagreeing with them (II, p. 319). Similarly, he is at pains to point out that Valla, though no doubt an able philologist, was by no means an erudite student of the law, and was in any case an absurdly hysterical critic of scholastic jurisprudence (II, p. 321). But there is no doubt that, more than any previous jurist, Alciato was sympathetic towards – and indeed saturated with – the culture of humanism. He repeatedly insists on the need for lawyers to have a proper grounding in the *studia humanitatis*; he makes considerable use of Valla's commentaries and emendations; he speaks with admiration of the similar work done by Crinito on the Code; and above all he reserves his highest praise for Poliziano, the man who 'first restored the Digest to light' (II, pp. 294, 303–4, 317; cf. Kelley, 1970, p. 93).

Working with the techniques of the humanists, and adding a far more comprehensive understanding of the law, Alciato was able to develop their somewhat fragmentary insights into a systematic new approach to legal science. He first took up Poliziano's attempt to treat the Code as an historical document, publishing an astonishingly precocious series of *Brief Annotations* on the last three books of the Code in 1515 (Viard, 1926, p. 43). Here he completely abandoned the traditional scholastic method of offering a series of commentaries on existing commentaries. Instead he focused as closely as possible on the text itself, using his knowledge of Greek as well as Latin literature – including Pindar, Hesiod and Thucydides – to elucidate its exact sense, and even offering, in the manner of Valla, a number of conjectural emendations of apparent corruptions in the received manuscripts (II, pp. 98, 102, 115). Next he went on to develop Crinito's work on legal terminology, making an intensive study of the title from the Digest 'On the meanings of Words' in the early 1520s (Viard, 1926, p. 61). And finally he became interested in the problems Pomponio had raised about the history of legal offices, writing a brief treatise on the magistracies of ancient Rome, and including a comprehensive list of all the 'civil and military dignities' established at various times in the eastern as well as the western provinces of the Empire (II, pp. 503–19).

The opening decades of the sixteenth century witnessed the transplantation of these new techniques to northern Europe for the first time. It was in France that the new approach was adopted with the greatest enthusiasm, and it was Guillaume Budé (1467–1540), the leading French humanist, who produced the earliest and greatest manifesto of legal humanism to be published north of the Alps. Budé had travelled to Italy in 1501 and again in 1505, studying with Crinito in Florence and making an examination of the precious notebooks on the Digest which Poliziano had left at his death in 1494.[1] The outcome of these investigations was the publication in 1508 of his fiercely polemical assault on scholastic jurisprudence, the *Annotations on the Pandects*. This contained a brilliant development of both the historical and the philological methods already explored by Valla and his followers. Budé first of all succeeded in discrediting a large number of individual glosses on the Code, showing that they were often based on textual corruptions or anachronistic misunderstandings of key Roman legal terms (e.g., pp. 388–9; cf. Franklin, 1963, pp. 20–1). He also began to question the whole tendency to treat the Code as a homogeneous body of law, demonstrating that its contents had in fact been put together from a number of widely separated periods in the history of ancient Rome (cf. Franklin, 1963, pp. 22–3). The outcome was a challenge to the very foundations of Bartolist methodology, hitherto unquestioned in the law-schools of northern Europe. Instead of treating the Code as *ratio scripta*, 'written reason', and hence as an immediately valid source of law, Budé treated it simply as a text from the ancient world, and hence as an alien document standing in need of interpretation according to the new style of humanist hermeneutics.

The next and most decisive stage in the development of legal humanism was reached when the law schools of northern Europe began to capitulate to the new approach. The first signs of surrender came in 1518, when Alciato was invited to accept a Professorship in France. He began by teaching at Avignon, and moved in 1529 to the University of Bourges (Viard, 1926, pp. 49–63). According to his own proud boast in his *Paradoxes of the Civil Law*, he thus became 'the first man to teach Civil Law in a genuinely classical fashion for over a thousand years' (III, p. 6). Nor was Alciato's triumph short-lived. He succeeded in making Bourges such an internationally famous centre of legal studies that the humanist methods he introduced soon became known simply as the *Mos docendi Gallicus*, the French method of teaching law. And the fame of his teaching quickly attracted a remarkable group of pupils and followers, including Le

[1] The notebooks were actually bequeathed to Crinito. See McNeil, 1975, p. 19. This background to Budé's work makes it somewhat misleading of Franklin (1963, pp. 18–20) to imply that the leading pioneer of legal humanism was Budé himself. Nevertheless, Franklin's discussion is a very valuable one, and I am much indebted to it.

Douaren, Doneau, Baudouin and Cujas, perhaps the four greatest French jurists of the sixteenth century (cf. Kelley, 1970, pp. 101–2).

By this time the methods and discoveries of legal humanism had begun to be taken up with almost equal enthusiasm in Germany. An early and colourful example of this trend is provided by the writings of Ulrich von Hutten (1488–1523), an ally of the humanists and a violent critic of the Church. While studying at Bologna in 1517 Hutten was shown a copy of Valla's exposure of the Donation of Constantine (Holborn, 1937, pp. 81, 85). He promptly carried it back to Germany, produced the first printed edition of the text, and prefaced it with an ironic dedication to the Pope, exhorting him not to surround himself with liars and hypocrites (Holborn, 1937, p. 129). The gesture was not merely popular, it was explosive: Luther himself remarked that when he read Hutten's edition he felt more than ever 'the darkness and deceit of the Romanists' and the need to fight against their lies (Fife, 1957, p. 472).

As in France, however, the real victory of legal humanism came with its acceptance by the jurists and its consequent introduction into the curriculum of the German law schools. The key role in this transformation was played by Ulrich Zasius (1461–1536), who occupied the Chair of Civil Law at the University of Freiburg for over thirty years. Like Alciato, Zasius still continued to operate to some extent within a Bartolist framework, treating the great Medieval jurists with some respect and continuing to cite their authority at important points. But he always laid a very strong emphasis on his admiration for the *studia humanitatis*. He even went so far as to write a hundred-page commentary on the pseudo-Ciceronian *Theory of Public Speaking*, to which he added an introduction praising the rhetorical arts, singling out Erasmus and (in an excess of patriotic zeal) Ulrich von Hutten as the two modern practitioners worthy of comparison with Cicero himself (vol. v., p. 382). In his mature legal writings, moreover, Zasius showed himself an enthusiastic practitioner of the new humanist techniques. One reflection of this commitment was his insistence on the need for an exact philological understanding of the *Code* in place of the old-fashioned preoccupation with glosses and commentaries. As he proclaims near the beginning of his book of *Judgments*, 'when the text itself is expressed to us, we have no need of glosses; where we have the text of the law itself, there we cannot be in doubt' (vol. vi, p. 48). A further sign of the same commitment was his development of the suggestions Pomponio had originally made about the need for an historical approach to the study of legal institutions. In this case, however, Zasius went far beyond the work of his Italian predecessors. He continued to occupy himself with the typically humanist project of attempting to reconstruct a context of Roman institutions as a means of recovering the intentions of Rome's original law-givers. But he also employed the evidence of history to arrive at a much more general theory about the nature of law itself (Kelley, 1970, p. 90). He argued that any legal system will always be the outcome of practice as much as of reason, and thus that it will always be essential in appraising such a system to accept that, as he frequently puts it in his *Judgments*, the voice of custom is 'an authentic instrument' of law, and that 'the authority of custom' has 'very great force' (vol. VI, pp. 477, 535). The special significance of this strongly historicist outlook was that it prompted Zasius to initiate a line of enquiry which was soon to become one of the major battle-grounds of Renaissance legal scholarship. This was the study of the origins and development of fiefs, and the consequent emergence of feudal law in Medieval Europe. With his major treatise on *The Custom of Fiefs*, tracing their foundation, succession and alienation, Zasius thus became one of the earliest civil lawyers to apply the techniques of humanist jurisprudence to the study of a legal system other than that of ancient Rome (cf. vol. IV, pp. 243–342).

This diffusion and development of Italian legal humanism in northern Europe soon began to exercise a profound influence on political as well as legal thought. The achievement of the humanists – in this as in every other aspect of their *rapprochement* with classical antiquity – was paradoxically to increase the sense of historical distance between themselves and the ancient texts which they made it their business to understand. Instead of appearing as 'written reason', and thus as an immediately applicable source of law, Justinian's Code began to appear under the sustained philological gaze of the humanists as little more than a 'battered relic' – a loosely assembled and poorly transmitted series of enactments designed for a long-defunct Empire, with little or no direct bearing on the very different legal and political conditions of early-modern Europe (cf. Kelley, 1970, p. 67). The implications of this extraordinarily unsettling discovery began to be pursued in two quite different directions by a growing band of legal and political theorists in the latter part of the sixteenth century, in each case with important consequences for the subsequent evolution of modern political thought. First of all, it occurred to a number of jurists that the methods employed by the humanists in their studies of Roman and feudal law might equally be applicable to every other known system of law, so that a scientific theory of politics might eventually be established on the basis of a universal and comparative jurisprudence. This became one of the guiding ambitions behind Jean Bodin's *Six Books of the Commonweal*, and the outcome, as we shall later see, was arguably the most original and influential work of political philosophy to be written in the sixteenth century. The other and even more radical effect of dethroning the immediate authority of Roman Law was to suggest the need for a new set of theoretical foundations for the conduct of legal and political debate. Hitherto, the idea of Justinian's Code as 'written reason', together with the high prestige attached to scholastic philosophy, had meant that the concepts of right reason and the law of nature had been used almost universally as touchstones for the analysis of law, obligation and justice. With the attack on Roman Law as *ratio scripta*, however, this degree of consensus about the foundations of political argument began to dissolve. One suggestion which then arose, particularly amongst the jurists themselves, was that since the only indigenous forms of law known to northern Europe were the customary laws of each individual country, it followed that these should be systematised and applied as the only alternative basis for assessing the proper distribution of legal obligations and rights. Given this commitment, the next step was obviously to conduct a series of detailed historical investigations into the precise character of these customary laws, in order to ensure that their provenance and stipulations were fully understood. This in turn meant that discussions about legal and political principles tended to resolve increasingly into discussions about historical precedents. Correspondingly, history became ideology: the conduct of political argument came to be founded to an increasing extent on the presentation of rival theses about the alleged dictates of various 'ancient constitutions.'[1] As we shall later see, this shift in the basis of political argument – with appeals to the laws of nature being supplemented and even supplanted by appeals to the past – came to play a crucial role in the formation of revolutionary ideologies in the later sixteenth century. As with Bodin's concept of a science of politics, we need to begin with the work of the legal humanists if we wish to understand the foundations of this most influential strand in early modern political thought.

HUMANISM AND BIBLICAL SCHOLARSHIP

The other ancient text of major ideological importance which the humanists began to study by means of their new philological techniques was the Bible. This involved them in the first place in adopting a new approach to Biblical exegesis and commentary. The orthodox scholastic method of

[1] For the best sketch of these changes, see Kelley, 1970, Chapters I and II. For an attempt to anatomise the developing uses of history as ideology, especially in the English revolution, see Skinner, 1965. For the best treatment of the whole question of 'ancient constitutions', see Pocock, 1957.

commenting on the Bible had usually taken the form of linking together a sequence of passages with the aim of extracting some more general lesson or tenet of faith (cf. Duhamel, 1953, pp. 495–6). The humanists by contrast sought to recover the precise historical context of each particular doctrine or argument. An early and striking example of their approach is provided by the work entitled *The Sacred History of the Hebrews* by the Florentine humanist Aurelio Brandolini (1440–98) (Cosenza, 1962, p. 337). Brandolini's aim, in the words of his own subtitle, was to offer 'an epitome of the sacred history of the Jews from the volume which they call the Bible and from Josephus' (Trinkaus, 1970, p. 601). He deliberately eschews any attempt to derive allegorical meanings or general morals from the story, dismissing all such scholastic preoccupations as 'petty little commentaries' which merely serve to envelop us 'in the fog of barbarism' (Trinkaus, 1970, pp. 608–9). For Brandolini the Old Testament is fundamentally a chronicle, a work which needs to be approached in historical terms, amplified and if necessary corrected by reference to other authorities, and even rewritten in a more fashionably polished humanist style (cf. Trinkaus, 1970, pp. 602–4).

Amongst the northern humanists the earliest and greatest exponent of this new approach was John Colet. Some two years after his return from Italy in 1496 he delivered his lectures at Oxford entitled *An Exposition of St Paul's Epistle to the Romans*, in which he clearly foreshadowed the overriding concern with the *ipsissima verba* of the Bible which was soon to become such a characteristic feature of the Lutheran Reformation. Colet is not concerned with extracting general doctrines from the text; he makes no mention of any scholastic authorities; instead he concentrates all his attention to trying to elucidate St Paul's meaning by examining the precise historical context in which his words were originally uttered. In the face of these facts it seems almost perverse to maintain (as Rice has done) that Colet's whole outlook in these lectures 'clearly separates' him from 'Renaissance humanism' (Rice, 1952, p. 141). There are at least two points in his exposition where his concern to explain – almost to explain away – St Paul's characteristic emphases seems unequivocally humanist in method as well as in tone. One is his discussion of the passage in which the Apostle maintains that man is nothing and God is all-in-all. Colet's interpretation is based on pointing to the background of civil discord amongst the Romans at the time, and St Paul's consequent anxiety 'to take away arrogance and pride' (p. 58). The other point at which the same approach is even more elaborately used is in the commentary on the famous passage in Chapter XIII enjoining complete political passivity. This too is explained in terms of the prevailing political conditions in

Imperial Rome. The Emperor at the time, Colet points out, was Claudius, 'a man of changeable disposition' who might well have taken the opportunity to destroy the infant Church if its activities had displeased him (p. 94). So St Paul's stress on the need to 'act circumspectly' in the face of such powerful 'enemies and opponents' is said to have been 'opportunely given' in the circumstances (p. 92). Colet concludes that while the doctrine may appear to be an exceptionally stringent one, we are bound to acknowledge, as soon as we know the circumstances in which it was enunciated, that St Paul was exhibiting 'great thoughtfulness and prudence' in offering such cautious advice (p. 95).

A second and ultimately more important innovation which the humanists introduced into Biblical scholarship was the application of their characteristic philological techniques in order to furnish new and more exact translations of the ancient Greek and Hebrew texts. Here again the leading pioneer was Lorenzo Valla, who issued a remarkable series of *Annotations on the New Testament* in 1449 (Trinkaus, 1970, p. 572). Valla's wide knowledge of Greek enabled him in the first place to correct a large number of inaccuracies in the Vulgate translation. But the main significance of his approach lay in his underlying assumption that philology is capable of determining doctrine. A dramatic example is provided by his discussion of the key passage in the First Epistle to the Corinthians where St Paul discusses faith and salvation. According to the Vulgate translation, the doctrine St Paul enunciates is that salvation can only be attained 'by the grace of God with me' – *gratia Dei mecum*. This was generally taken to refer to the capacity of the faithful Christian to co-operate with God in the process of assuring his salvation. Valla insists, however, that what we ought to be saying is 'by the grace of God *which is* with me', since this is the clear and unequivocal sense of the original Greek words. So he concludes that 'those who call this grace with the co-operation of God are saying nothing meaningful at all', for 'Paul is saying that nothing can be attributed to himself, since everything must be referred to God' (vol. 1, p. 868). Although Valla founded his theology on the skills of the grammarian, while Luther was later to rely on the more elevated process of inward illumination, it is remarkable how far the two men nevertheless arrived at similar conclusions (cf. Trinkaus, 1970, p. 868).

Once again these techniques were taken up and developed by the northern humanists at the start of the sixteenth century. A particularly impressive contribution was made by Johannes Reuchlin (1455–1522), a practising German lawyer who became interested in the humanities and taught himself Hebrew as well as Greek (Spitz, 1963, pp. 61–2). In 1506 he published his pioneering work on *The Rudiments of Hebrew*, a grammar of the language combined with a Hebrew–Latin dictionary (Schwarz, 1955, p. 76). One outcome of his studies, as he emphasised himself, was that they made him 'doubtful about the translations' of the Bible, and especially doubtful about the accuracy of the Vulgate (Schwarz, 1955, p. 72). He was able to show that the Greek versions of the Old Testament were based on a misunderstanding of the Hebrew vowel-system, an error which in turn meant that the Vulgate was filled with mistranslations, over two hundred of which he duly pointed out in the pages of his *Rudiments* (Schwarz, 1955, pp. 72–4; 78 n.). This revelation of the results to be gained from trilingual scholarship in turn helped to promote an increasing interest in this vital tool of Biblical humanism. One consequence was the founding of Trilingual Colleges at various leading universities in northern Europe. But perhaps the most imposing outcome was the publication of the first polyglot Bible, an undertaking commissioned by Cardinal Ximenes and produced at the new humanist University of Alcalá between 1514 and 1517 (Lyell, 1917, p. 28). The Old Testament was printed with the Vulgate translation in the centre of the page, the Septuagint Greek on the right, the Hebrew on the left, and the Chaldean paraphrase at the foot of each page of the Pentateuch (Lyell, 1917, p. 28). According to Bataillon, this masterpiece of the printer's art as well as of humanist scholarship was sufficient to establish the fame of Alcalá as a centre of Biblical studies throughout the whole of Europe (Bataillon, 1937, pp. 24–47).

By far the most important of the northern humanists to take up the cause of Biblical scholarship was Erasmus. He appears to have done so under the influence of John Colet, whom he met at Oxford in the course of his first visit to England in 1499 (Smith, 1923, pp. 93–100). After this meeting, as he assured Colet in a letter of 1504, he resolved 'to approach sacred literature full-sail' and to give 'all of the rest of my life' to the study of the holy scriptures (II, p. 86). The first-fruits of this decision appeared in 1505, when he issued the earliest printed version of Valla's *Annotations on the New Testament*, having come upon the manuscript in a monastery library near Louvain in the previous year (Rabil, 1972, p. 58). Erasmus took the opportunity to add an introduction to his edition, in which he not only explained the importance of Valla's work, but also extolled the humanities as the handmaid of theology, and insisted that 'the whole task of translating Scripture is the task of the Grammarian' (p. 312). The climax of Erasmus's Biblical studies came in 1516, when he finally produced his long-awaited edition of the Greek New Testament, together with a new Latin translation in which the errors of the Vulgate were corrected in print for the first time (Huizinga, 1952, p. 91). Again he added an introduction – the *Paraclesis* or Exhortation to the reader – in which he expressed his desire to 'summon all men, as with a trumpet blast, to the most sacred and life-giving study of Christian philosophy', and spoke of his further hope that the Scriptures might soon be 'translated into all languages' and read by everyone (pp. 150, 154; cf. Rabil, 1972, p. 91).

As in the case of Roman Law, the application of humanist techniques to the Bible had a profound impact on the development of sixteenth century political thought. The main channel of influence in this case was provided by the growing number of humanists who devoted themselves to translating the Scriptures. Erasmus's plea for the Bible to be made available in the vernacular was rapidly and very widely answered: by Lefèvre d'Etaples in France, Tyndale in England, Pedersen in Denmark, Petri in Sweden and Luther himself in Germany. With the resulting increase of detailed knowledge of the New Testament, one implication of very great political significance came to be widely perceived: that the prevailing organisation as well as the temporal pretensions of the Papacy were gravely out of line with the original ideals and institutions of the primitive Church. As we shall later seek to show, this discovery in turn helped to promote a revolution in traditional relations between the Church and the temporal authorities over a wide area of northern Europe – a revolution in which the techniques of Biblical humanism may be said to have played the part of the Trojan horse.

8

The reception of humanist political thought

THE HUMANISTS AS ADVISERS

As well as developing the technical aspects of Italian humanism, the northern humanists reveal the deep influence of their *quattrocento* predecessors in their approach to the more general problems of social and political thought. The most obvious evidence of this continuity of outlook is provided by the range of literary *genres* they characteristically employed. They continued to accept the well-established humanist belief that the links between sound learning and sound government are extremely close. So they continued to produce systematic educational treatises, outlining in minute detail the type of training in the *studia humanitatis* to be given to those who might subsequently be expected to play a leading part in the business of government. The two writers who contributed most influentially to this tradition were Sadoleto and Vives, both of whom published their major works in the early 1530s. Juan Luis Vives (1492–1540), by birth a Spanish nobleman, became Professor of the Humanities at Louvain in 1519, where he completed his book *On Education* in 1531 (Noreña, 1970, pp. 57–8, 116). Jacopo Sadoleto (1477–1547), a distinguished Biblical scholar as well as a prominent member of the Papal Curia, issued his somewhat similar account of *The Right Education of Boys* in 1534 (Douglas, 1959, pp. 14–53). Thereafter a large number of works of the same general character continued to appear throughout the sixteenth century, including such celebrated handbooks as *The Schoolmaster* by Roger Ascham (1515–68), who served during the 1540s as tutor to the future Queen Elizabeth.[1] The influence of the *genre* as a whole was immense: it helped to establish a pattern of instruction and an ideal of conduct which remained widely admired for at least the next three centuries.

The northern humanists also made extensive use of the mirror-for-princes *genre*, issuing a large number of treatises in which they discussed

---

[1] For a discussion of some other English educational treatises of the later sixteenth century, see Woodward, 1906, pp. 296–322. To Woodward's list one might add the works of Hugh Rhodes (*c.* 1550), Francis Seager (1557) and Richard Mulcaster (1581).

the education of rulers together with the principles of virtuous government. It is true that surprisingly few works of this nature were written in England, but there is no doubt that some of the most important were produced in France, Germany and Spain in the course of the sixteenth century. In France, Josse Clichtove (1472–1543), a pupil of Lefèvre d'Etaples and a prolific writer on grammar and rhetoric, issued a tract on *The Office of the King* in 1519. In the same year Guillaume Budé, the greatest ornament of French humanism, completed his only vernacular work, *The Education of the Prince*, and presented it to Francis I (McNeil, 1975, pp. 37–8). A similar tradition was kept up during the next generation in Spain and Portugal. Jeronimo Osorio wrote on *The Education and Training of a King* in the 1540s, and Felipe de la Torre dedicated a discussion of *The Education of a Christian King* to Philip II in 1556 (Bataillon, 1937, p. 671). Pedro Ribadeneyra published his anti-Machiavellian tract on *Religion and the Virtues of the Christian Prince* in 1595, and Juan de Mariana issued his treatise on *The King and the Education of the King* in 1599. Finally, the same period witnessed the publication of numerous advice-books for princes in Germany. Jacob Wimpfeling (1450–1528), one of the leading popularisers of early German humanism, wrote *The Epitome of a Good Prince* during the reign of Maximilian (Spitz, 1963, pp. 41–3). Johann Sturm (1507–89), who became famous as the founder of the humanist *Gymnasium* at Strasbourg, and corresponded with Ascham about questions of educational reform, completed his treatise on *The Education of Princes* in 1551. And Erasmus produced perhaps the most influential of all these manuals when he presented his account of *The Education of a Christian Prince* to the future Emperor Charles V in 1516 (Phillips, 1949, pp. 126–7).

A number of humanists also wrote advice-books in which they addressed themselves not merely to kings and princes, but also to their courtiers, nobles, councillors and magistrates. Here again they were drawing on a well-established pattern of Italian political writing, a pattern epitomised by Castiglione's *Book of the Courtier*. One of the most comprehensive treatises of this kind was *The Dial of Princes* by Antonio de Guevara, which was first published in 1529 and translated into English by Sir Thomas North in 1557 (Redondo, 1976, p. 57). Although Guevara's title suggests a work in the mirror-for-princes style, he makes it clear at the start of Book II that his advice is in fact intended for 'great lords' and other servants of princes as well as for princes themselves (fo. 80a). The other leading handbook of this type was *The Book Named the Governor* by Sir Thomas Elyot (*c.* 1490–1546), which first appeared in 1531.[1] Elyot's

---

[1] Lehmberg, 1960, pp. 45–9 accuses Elyot of incoherence in offering his advice to rulers as well

dependence on *The Book of the Courtier* has often been pointed out, although he filters Castiglione's doctrines through a more legalistic and above all a more patriotic sense of the relationship between the study of the humanities and the smooth running of the commonwealth.[1] Both Elyot's and Guevara's treatises proved immensely popular: Elyot's *Governor* went through at least seven editions in its first fifty years, while Guevara's *Dial of Princes* became, according to Meric Casaubon, the most widely-read book (apart from the Bible) in the whole of sixteenth-century Europe (Lehmberg, 1962, p. vii; Grey, 1973, p. ix).

Finally, a number of writers sought to offer their advice not merely to the leaders of society, but also to the whole body of the citizens. It is true that, whereas the Florentine 'civic' humanists had characteristically addressed themselves to this broader audience, this seemed a less obvious ambition in the more hierarchical conditions of northern Europe. Nevertheless, a number of radical humanists, especially in England, trained their attention on the more general problems of reforming the commonwealth rather than merely on the special interests of the ruling classes. The greatest and most original was of course Sir Thomas More (1478–1535), whose *Utopia* was first published in 1516. Many elements of the same outlook later surfaced in Thomas Starkey's *Dialogue between Reginald Pole and Thomas Lupset*, a wide-ranging series of reform-proposals which Starkey completed in 1535 after returning to England from Pole's household in Padua.[2] And the same preoccupation with the good of the community as a whole was further developed in the course of the so-called 'Commonwealth' movement of the mid-sixteenth century, in which the economic and constitutional problems of Tudor England were widely debated by a number of leading preachers as well as humanists, including Latimer, Crowley, John Hales and Sir Thomas Smith.

as to other 'governors', and proposes a conjectural reconstruction of Elyot's process of composition in order to account for this alleged inconsistency in the plan of his work. It is arguable, however, that the explanation is otiose, since it is apparent that Elyot, like Guevara, was following a recognised set of conventions in addressing himself to both these different audiences.

[1] The point was first made at length by Croft in his edition of *The Governor* in 1880. Lehmberg has claimed that Castiglione's *Courtier*, together with Erasmus's *Christian Prince*, were both 'at his side' while Elyot was writing *The Governor*. See Lehmberg, 1960, p. 74. More recently, Major has devoted most of his study of *Elyot and Renaissance Humanism* to tracing the alleged sources of Elyot's political ideas, and has given an elaborate account of the parallels with Castiglione's *Courtier*. See Major, 1964, pp. 60–73.

[2] Elton, 1968, has argued that Starkey (*c*.1499–1538) probably wrote the bulk of his *Dialogue* at Padua in 1533, and only added the final sections in 1535. He also stresses that Starkey's manuscript was never revised, and was almost certainly not presented to Henry VIII as has sometimes been supposed. Starkey's work remained unpublished until the 1870s, when J. M. Cowper edited it and supplied it with the title by which it is generally known. Kathleen M. Burton produced a further edition in 1948, and it is from this version that all quotations have been taken.

As well as employing the same *genres* as their Italian precursors, the northern humanists generally shared their way of thinking about the role of the political theorist in political life. They adopted with enthusiasm the familiar argument that, if philosophers cannot hope to become kings, the next best thing must be for kings to be advised as closely as possible by philosophers. They accordingly tended to see themselves essentially as political advisers – as writers of practical handbooks and purveyors of sage counsels to kings, princes and magistrates (cf. Lehmberg, 1961, p. 89).

Like their Italian predecessors, they tended in consequence to seek careers as secretaries and ambassadors to their rulers. Sadoleto was a leading Papal diplomat, and was made a Cardinal in 1536 as a reward for his services to the Curia. Guillaume Budé acted as a Secretary under Charles VIII, and in 1522 became one of Francis I's Masters of Requests (McNeil, 1975, p. 100). Sir Thomas Elyot was appointed Senior Clerk to the King's Council in 1524, and served after 1531 as ambassador to the court of Charles V (Lehmberg, 1960, pp. 27, 46). And Sir Thomas More, by far the greatest of these political theorists, was also the most successful in the world of political action, becoming Speaker of the House of Commons in 1523, and rising to become Lord Chancellor of England in 1529 (Chambers, 1935, pp. 200, 236).

Perceiving themselves essentially as advisers, many of the humanists prefaced their treatises by discussing 'the problem of counsel' – the difficulty of supplying genuinely useful as well as right-minded political advice (cf. Ferguson, 1965, pp. 90, 107). Those who wrote advice-books for princes and magistrates tended to approach this question largely from the ruler's point of view, focusing on the importance of choosing good councillors and learning to distinguish between true and false friends. They were chiefly concerned about the danger described by Elyot in *The Governor* as 'the mortal poison of flattery' (p. 132). So we find Erasmus in *The Christian Prince* entitling one of his Chapters 'The Prince must avoid Flatterers', and instructing all those in authority to make a special study of Plutarch's essay on 'How to distinguish a friend from a flatterer' (pp. 193, 196). Similarly, we find Budé praising the same essay in his *Education of the Prince*, as well as devoting a series of chapters to explaining 'the need for all great princes and prelates' to recognise the perils which are sure to arise if they fail 'to seek counsel in their affairs', or 'fail to maintain good ministers and faithful servants' (pp. 123, 129, 131, 138).

If we turn, however, to those whose main interest lay in the general reformation of the commonwealth, we find them treating the problem of counsel more as a dilemma for those who might be asked to enter the service of kings and princes. They characteristically considered the question in terms of the favourite humanist debate about the rival merits of *otium* and *negotium* – the life of quiet and contemplation *versus* the life of activity and business. And the immediate answer they always suggested – often in highly satirical style – was that no man of virtue and wisdom should ever abandon a life of scholarship in order to make his career in public affairs.

One reason they often gave was that kings are so readily moved by tyrannical passions that it may prove extremely dangerous to offer them frank advice. The most famous discussion of this danger occurs in Book I of More's *Utopia*. Raphael Hythlodaeus, the traveller recently returned from the island of Utopia, is urged by his listeners to impart the knowledge he has gained to the rulers of Europe. He replies with great vehemence– and with a touch of clairvoyance about More's own future career – that since all kings 'have been from their youth saturated and infected with wrong ideas', it is very likely that anyone who proposes 'beneficial measures' or tries to uproot 'the seeds of evil and corruption' will find himself 'forthwith banished or treated with ridicule' (p. 87). The same complaint is later reiterated with even greater force in Starkey's *Dialogue*. When Lupset tries to persuade Pole at the start of their discussion to 'apply himself to the setting forward of the common weal', Pole at first replies by pointing out that many of the best men who have attempted to do so have found themselves 'banished from their country', while others have been 'put in prison and miserably handled' and some have even been 'put to cruel and shameful death' (pp. 36–7).

But the chief reason for preferring a life of *otium* is said to be that public affairs are well-known to be governed entirely by hypocrisy and lies. This is one of the main themes developed by the so-called *Grands Rhétoriqueurs* in France, a scurrilous group of anti-Court satirists led by Jean Bouchet and Pierre de la Vacherie (Smith, 1966, p. 77). Kings only listen to flatterers, Bouchet proclaims, so honest councillors can only hope to gain a hearing by compromising their honesty. Meanwhile 'good men are overthrown by these wretches, subjects are oppressed by their advice, and everything goes to ruin because they are not suppressed' (Smith, 1966, p. 78). The same argument is presented with no less bitterness in More's *Utopia*. 'There is no chance', Hythlodaeus insists, for a wise councillor 'to do any good' at court, since he will always be forced to work with 'colleagues who would easily corrupt even the best of men before being reformed themselves'. All that can happen is that 'by their evil companion-ship, either you will be seduced yourself or, keeping your own integrity and innocence, you will be made a screen for the wickedness and folly of others' (p. 103). As an example of what he means, Hythlodaeus recalls the occasion when he was encouraged by Cardinal Morton to give his views about the redressing of social injustices in England. The suggestions he made were at first received with ridicule by the Cardinal's retainers, but when the Cardinal made it clear that he himself agreed, they all vied with each other to flatter him and praise the remedies they had just condemned. 'From this reaction', Hythlodaeus grimly concludes, 'you may judge what little regard courtiers would pay to me and my advice' (p. 85).

After a discussion of these preliminary doubts and objections, however, these debates about *otium* and *negotium* were almost always resolved in favour of the idea of involving oneself actively in the business of government. The great exception is More's *Utopia*. No one in the opening dialogue is able to shake Hythlodaeus out of his original conviction that, as he puts it, there is no more than a syllable's difference between service and servitude to kings (p. 55). More's insistence on this unorthodox conclusion contains a double irony. This is partly directed against his underlying acceptance of humanist conventions in *Utopia*, in which he begins by mocking the ideal of counsel but ends by obliquely endorsing it. After Hythlodaeus has repudiated the role of an adviser in Book I, he goes on to give us his account of Utopian communism in Book II, describing the system as worthy of admiration and imitation in almost every respect. He thus provides us in effect with the sound political advice which he began by refusing to offer on the grounds that it would never be heeded. But More's irony is also directed against his own way of life. At the time when he was writing *Utopia* in 1515, he had just made the decision to enter the royal service.[1] He completed the opening Book – the section Hexter has called 'the dialogue of counsel' – immediately after he returned to London from his first diplomatic mission abroad. And he seems to have written Book II – the actual description of the fabulous island – while staying at Antwerp in the course of the embassy itself (Hexter, 1952, pp. 20–1, 100–1). It was thus at the very moment when More had finally decided to seek his fortune at Court that he made Hythlodaeus insist with so much feeling that all such ambitions are absurd, since every courtier will eventually find himself forced to 'approve the worst counsels and subscribe to the most ruinous decrees' (p. 103).

It was far more usual, however, for such discussions to culminate in a denunciation of what Milton was to call a 'fugitive and cloistered virtue', and a corresponding defence of the values associated with the active life. Two main reasons were generally given for this commitment. One was the

---

[1] See Chambers, 1935, pp. 118–20, 157–75. Elton has recently underlined the irony by demonstrating that, in spite of his conventional humanist protestations about his preference for a life of *otium*, More in fact entered the royal service with some eagerness. See Elton, 1972, esp. pp. 87–92.

familiar humanist (and later Puritan) claim that all knowledge ought to be 'for use', and thus that 'the end of all doctrine and study', as Elyot puts it in the closing chapters of *The Governor*, ought to lie 'in good counsel, wherein virtue may be found, being (as it were) his proper mansion and palace'.[1] Perhaps the clearest statement of this viewpoint can be found in the opening discussion between Pole and Lupset in Starkey's *Dialogue*. Lupset begins by berating Pole for living a life of withdrawn scholarship. 'You know right well, Master Pole, that to this all men are born and of nature brought forth: to commune such gifts as be to them given, each one to the profit of other, in perfect civility, and not to live to their own pleasure and profit, without regard of the weal of their country, forgetting all justice and equity' (p. 22). This being so, he goes on, it follows that anyone who allows himself to be 'drawn by the sweetness of his studies' away from the active life 'does manifest wrong to his country and friends, and is plain unjust and full of iniquity' (p. 22). For 'the perfection of man stands not in bare knowledge and learning without application of it to any use or profit of other; but the very perfection of man's mind rests in the use and exercise of all virtues and honesty, and chiefly in the chief virtue whereunto tend all the others, which is, doubtless, the communing of high wisdom to the use of other, in which stands man's felicity' (p. 26). Confronted with this tirade, Pole at first attempts to raise a number of Platonist objections, but eventually concedes that none of them has any real weight. It is beyond doubt, he eventually agrees, that Lupset has established, with sound 'philosophical reasons', that 'every man ought to apply himself to the setting forward of the common weal, every man ought to study to serve his country' (p. 36).

A further reason for accepting this argument was put forward in particular by the mirror-for-princes writers. They all assume that, as Budé declares at the end of *The Education of the Prince*, 'a well-ordered monarchy' is always to be preferred 'to any other kind of government' (p. 202). So they often contend that any man of learning who acts as a councillor to his prince will be performing a service of the highest public importance, since he will be contributing to the 'good ordering' of the monarchy, and will thus be assisting in the preservation of the best possible form of commonwealth. The point is made with great emphasis by Guevara in the opening Book of his *Dial of Princes*. If we furnish our rulers with sound advice, he claims, this will help to ensure that the commonwealth is ruled not merely by just laws, but also by a just king (fo. 50b). And if

[1] For another emphatic endorsement of the idea that 'our study must be attuned to practical usefulness in life' see Vives, *On Education*, p. 284. For a discussion of this element in Renaissance education, and its impact on Elizabethan literature, see Craig, 1950, pp. 87–94. For Elyot's remarks see *The Governor*, p. 238.

we play our part in maintaining such a monarchy, in which 'all obey one virtuous person', whose virtue is in turn encouraged by virtuous councillors, we shall be helping to uphold the best and most godly form of rule, under which 'the people shall profit, the good shall be esteemed and the evil deprived' (fo. 39b).

This still begs the question, however, of why these writers should have thought themselves so peculiarly well-fitted to serve as advisers to princes. The answer is that they not only shared the general humanist confidence in the value of ancient philosophy as a guide to modern life; they also endorsed the more specific claim that the key to political wisdom lies in a proper understanding of the past. History, as Kelley has remarked, was the centrepiece of the humanists' world picture, and served more than anything to provide them with their sense of assurance as men of affairs (cf. Kelley, 1970, p. 21). The grounds for this belief in the practical value of historical studies were spelled out most emphatically by the leading humanist educators, and were nowhere propounded more clearly than in Book V of Vives's *On Education*, the section in which he discusses the relationship between 'studies and life' (p. 226). He begins by laying it down that we may assume 'the essential nature of human beings' to be invariable, since 'changes do not ever take place' in 'the foundations of the affections of the human mind' (p. 232). He then reminds us that these 'affections' also give rise to 'actions and volitions' which in turn produce 'measurable effects' on the course of political life (p. 232). But this means that in studying history we are studying the general causes of events, thus making it possible to 'be warned by the evils which have befallen others' and to gain an insight into 'what we should follow and what we should avoid' in the future (p. 233). Hence it is that Vives regards 'historical knowledge' as 'the nurse of practical wisdom', and concludes – for the same reasons as his *quattrocento* predecessors – that those who have the best understanding of the past may be said to have the best title to act as advisers to princes (p. 233).

It is true that this overwhelming confidence in the possibility of founding a science of politics on the evidence of history was occasionally treated with a certain scepticism even in humanist circles. We have already noted Guicciardini's doubts about Machiavelli's statement of the case, and a much more extreme pyrrhonism was developed by the German humanist Heinrich Cornelius Agrippa (1486–1536), especially in his extraordinary treatise on *The Vanity and Uncertainty of Arts and Sciences*, which he completed in 1526 and published in 1530 (Nauert, 1965, pp. 98, 106). Agrippa begins by training his pessimistic gaze on the *studia humanitatis*, attacking in turn the pretensions of the grammarians, the historians, the rhetoricians and the philosophers. Nowhere is his scepticism more profound than in his survey of the claims usually made on behalf of history. He notes that men 'for the most part' think of history as the teacher of virtue and 'the mistress of life', but he immediately goes on to suggest that there are good reasons for thinking that all such claims are foolish (p. 35). It is not clear in the first place that we can hope to learn from the past at all. For we find on close inspection that all histories are full of errors, either because their authors are straightforwardly ignorant, or else because 'in flattering their own doings' they deliberately 'prefer falsehood before the truth' (p. 38). And even if history is capable of teaching lessons, it is not clear that these will necessarily be lessons in the virtues. Men always assume that 'by the reading of histories a singular wisdom may be gotten', but they fail to recognise that the same sources may just as easily make us experts on the folly of wickedness of mankind (p. 41).

For most of the northern humanists, however, the idea of history as 'the nurse of practical wisdom' remained a key article of faith. All the writers of advice-books for princes and magistrates accordingly urge the study of history on those who are in any way involved in the business of government. Elyot insists in *The Governor* that 'there is no study or science' which is 'of equal commodity and pleasure' (p. 39). And Budé in *The Education of the Prince* develops the same sentiment at considerable length. He assures us that 'the reading of histories' leads to an understanding 'not merely of the past, but also of the present and often the future as well' (p. 55). He thinks this in turn helps our rulers to attain 'prudence' and 'sapience', the two qualities which are said to arise 'out of an understanding of past events' and to be 'more necessary for kings to acquire than anything else' (pp. 65–6, 203). So Budé has no hesitation in endorsing the judgment which Cornelius Agrippa was shortly to ridicule: history, he proclaims, is 'a great mistress', a leader 'even amongst our greatest teachers', and our surest guide to 'an honest and virtuous life' (p. 43).

THE INJUSTICES OF THE AGE

If the humanists saw themselves essentially as advisers, what specific problems and injustices did they think required their expert attention and advice? By no means all of them took a deep interest in this question. Guevara, for example, scarcely raises the issue of social reform, except to make a series of humorous comments on such topics as aristocratic extravagance. Similarly, Budé presents his advice to Francis I without at any point couching his argument in the form of a proposed solution to any recognised social or constitutional difficulty. Nevertheless, it was characteristic of the humanists to think of themselves not merely as advisers to princes, but also as physicians to the body politic. And when they adopted this view of their task, they also tended to exhibit a striking measure of agreement in analysing the ills of their society.

The main argument they developed was one which, as we have seen, had already become central to the whole tradition of humanist political thought. They contended that the gravest danger to political health arises when the people ignore the good of the community as a whole, and concern themselves only with their own individual or factional interests. Erasmus offers a particularly clear statement of this familiar diagnosis at the beginning of *The Christian Prince*. The first precept he lays down is that 'one idea' should 'concern a prince in ruling', just as it should 'likewise concern the people in selecting their prince': that 'the public weal, free from all private interests' should at all times be protected and preserved (p. 140). It is the duty of the prince to recognise that he is 'born for the state' and 'not for his own fancy'; it is the duty of anyone who advises him to ensure that he 'looks not to personal emolument but rather to the welfare of his country'; and it is the basic function of the laws to promote 'the advancement of the commonwealth' according to 'the fundamental principles of equity and honesty' (pp. 141–2; 221).

Judged by these criteria, the humanists generally agreed that they were living in an age which stood in grievous need of reformation. The most celebrated indictment is presented at the end of More's *Utopia*, when Hythlodaeus suddenly exclaims that 'when I consider and turn over in my mind the state of all commonwealths flourishing anywhere today, so help me God, I can see nothing else than a kind of conspiracy of the rich, who are aiming at their own interests under the name and title of the commonwealth' (p. 241). This lack of concern for the public good was widely recognised as the most corrupt and corrupting feature of the age. Starkey, for example, puts the point with no less vehemence in his *Dialogue*, echoing the language More had already employed. Whether we consider princes, lords or other governors, he claims, we find that 'every one of them looks chiefly to their own profit, pleasure and commodity, and few there be which regard the wealth of the commonalty, but under the pretence and colour thereof every one of them procures the private and the singular weal' (p. 86).

As a response to this growing individualism, the humanists first of all issued a series of solemn admonitions to their princes and magistrates. They warned them that this dereliction of their highest duty could only be regarded as morally intolerable. As Erasmus repeatedly proclaims, anyone who governs 'for his own benefit, not for that of his subjects' cannot be considered a genuine prince at all, but only a robber, a 'man-eater' and a tyrant (pp. 161, 170, 174). They were also warned that, if they failed to promote the common good, this would eventually lead to very dangerous practical consequences. Starkey insists throughout his *Dialogue* that 'when they which have rule' devote themselves 'only to their singular weal, pleasure and profit', the outcome is certain to be 'the manifest destruction of all good, public and just common policy' (pp. 61, 70). And Elyot concludes his *Book Named the Governor* on the same ominous note. Citing Cicero as his authority, he argues that whenever our rulers neglect 'the general and universal state of the public weal' in order to promote some 'particular commodity', this always serves to introduce 'a thing most pernicious, that is to say, sedition and discord', which in turn brings the commonwealth into a state of 'extreme dissolution' and decay (pp. 240-1).

As well as issuing these threats, the humanists characteristically sought to apportion blame for this general collapse of civic responsibility. This mainly provided them with an excuse for presenting a series of traditional caricatures of extortionate lawyers, lazy monks and self-seeking priests – a literature of invective and abuse which was soon developed with even greater ferocity by the protagonists of the Lutheran Reformation. The most inventive writer of these satires was of course Rabelais. Gargantua is constantly encountering selfish and gluttonous monks in the course of his travels, and when at the end of the story he arrives at the Abbey of Thelème – an idealised humanist community – he finds a notice on the gateway forbidding entry to lawyers, usurers and all other men of that stamp.[1] A similar genius for satire was displayed by Erasmus in several of his most popular works. His *Praise of Folly* contains a sweeping attack on the lack of public spirit so often shown by lawyers and priests. And even in the more solemn pages of *The Christian Prince* he cannot resist including a series of half-humorous remarks about the 'peculiar form of idleness' to be found amongst those who spend their lives 'in a lazy and sluggish fashion' in Colleges and monasteries (p. 226).

Some of these writers also exhibit a more serious interest in trying to explain the social and economic dislocations of their age. This 'dawning awareness of social process', as Ferguson has called it, was especially marked amongst the English humanists (Ferguson, 1963, p. 11). More's *Utopia* contains a pioneering attempt to discuss the collapse of the 'commonwealth' ideal in a relatively analytical way, and several of his

[1] Rabelais, *Gargantua*, esp. pp. 125-7, 153-4. On Rabelais's 'Erasmian' allegiances, see Febvre, 1947. On Rabelais as a political commentator, and on the humanist orientation of his political thought, see Janeau, 1953.

arguments were later reproduced and developed in Starkey's *Dialogue*. More fixes on two major social groups whom he accuses of undermining the commonwealth by ruthlessly pursuing their own interests at the expense of the public good. First of all he denounces the selfish extravagance of the nobility. They think it essential to their dignity to 'carry about with them a huge crowd of idle attendants who have never learnt a trade for a livelihood' (p. 63). As a result of this absurd pretentiousness they often contribute quite unnecessarily to the growth of unemployment and general misery. For as soon as one of these noblemen dies, his retainers 'are turned out at once' and immediately become an extra and gratuitous burden on the community (p. 63). The other culprits are said to be the landlords, especially those who had recognised that the rearing of sheep was becoming more profitable than the growing of food. 'They are not content', More scornfully exclaims, 'to do no good to their country; they must also do it positive harm'. They 'leave no ground to be tilled; they enclose every bit of land for pasture; they pull down houses and towns' (p. 67). The outcome, in More's famous phrase, is that the sheep are eating the men: in order to satisfy 'the unscrupulous greed of a few', the farmers are being ruined, their labourers are being forced into crime, and the whole community is being impoverished (pp. 65, 67, 69).

This diagnosis was taken up and discussed in greater detail by the radical group of 'Commonwealthmen' in the reign of Edward VI. The Protector Somerset, it has sometimes been argued, may well have been influenced by these theorists, and his fall from power in 1549 may have been due in part to the animosity this aroused amongst the landowning classes (Jordan, 1968, p. 426; 1970, p. 108). The prototype of the angry works of protest the Commonwealth writers produced was *The Complaint of Roderick Mors* by Henry Brinklow (d. 1546), a Franciscan convert to Lutheranism whose book was first published in 1546 (Cowper, 1874, p. v). Another important work of the same character was *The Way to Wealth* by Robert Crowley (*c.* 1518–88), which first appeared in 1550 (Collinson, 1967, pp. 48, 74). But the most remarkable of the Commonwealth tracts was the *Discourse of the Common Weal*, which was evidently written during the second half of 1549, although it remained unpublished until it appeared anonymously in 1581. The question of the authorship of the *Discourse* has never been definitively settled. It has usually been attributed to John Hales (d. 1571), who served as one of the six Parliamentary commissioners appointed in 1548 to investigate the spread of enclosures, and who wrote a number of similar tracts during this period, including a defence of his work as an enclosure commissioner and a memorandum on the 'causes of dearth' (Lamond, 1893, pp. xxv, xlii–xlv). But it now seems more probable that the man who wrote the *Discourse* was Sir Thomas Smith (1513–77), Queen Elizabeth's future ambassador to France and the author of *The Commonwealth of England*, a descriptive account of the English constitution and government which first appeared in 1583.[1] Whatever doubts may remain about the authorship of the tract, however, there has never been any doubt about its importance. Unwin regarded it as 'the most advanced statement of economic thought in Tudor England', and it offers one of the most sophisticated surveys of the political as well as economic philosophy associated with the Commonwealth group (cf. Dewar, 1966, p. 388).

The views of these theorists were closely paralleled in the sermons of a number of radical preachers who rose to prominence during the same period. Their tongues were loosened by the death of Henry VIII and the consequent shift from a lukewarm 'official Erasmianism' to Somerset's full endorsement of the Protestant faith.[2] The greatest of these social critics was Hugh Latimer (*c.* 1485–1555), who is said to have been the main inspiration behind the Commonwealth movement as a whole (Jones, 1970, p. 31). And the most influential of his younger disciples were Thomas Becon (1512–67) and Thomas Lever (1521–77), who both fell under the spell of Latimer's preaching while students at Cambridge, and began to write and preach in a markedly similar style in the early 1550s.

While these men were all radical Protestants, they also tended to be strongly humanist in their education and allegiances – a further proof of the close spiritual connections between humanism and the Puritan movement. Becon and Lever both received their early training at St John's College, Cambridge, recently founded on the advice of John Fisher (1459–1535) to promote the teaching of the *studia humanitatis* within the scholastic citadel of the University (Simon, 1966, pp. 81–2; Bailey, 1952, pp. 2–3). Robert Crowley was educated (like Thomas Starkey) at Magdalen College, Oxford, a leading centre of the humanities ever since William Latimer's appointment there in the 1490s (Cowper, 1872, p. ix). And Sir Thomas Smith was one of the outstanding humanists of his

---

[1] The chief proponent of Smith's authorship has been Mary Dewar, who has sought to substantiate her claim by examining the parallels between the *Discourse* and other works known to have been written by Smith. See Dewar, 1966, esp. pp. 390–4. The result is a powerful case in favour of Smith's authorship, though not perhaps the absolutely 'compelling argument' Dewar has claimed in her biography of Smith. (See Dewar, 1964, p. 54). One leading scholar of the period who has not been convinced has been W. K. Jordan, whose account of the reign continues to accept Hales's authorship. See Jordan, 1968, p. 395n.

[2] On 'official Erasmianism' and its hostility to Protestantism under Henry VIII, see McConica, 1965, pp. 150, 235–8. On the acceptance for the first time under the Protector Somerset of the 'process of Protestantisation' which had been going on in the Universities during the previous reign, see Dickens, 1959, p. 7 and 1965, pp. 44, 50.

generation, an adviser to princes as well as a Professor of Greek at Cambridge, where his learning and eloquence as an expositor of the humanities are said to have dazzled the whole University (Dewar, 1964, p. 13).

This background is strongly reflected in the concern these writers show for the protection of the common good against the encroachments of an uncaring individualism. They constantly complain that, as Brinklow puts it, everyone is 'given to seek their own private wealth only', without recognising that this is always an evil course of action if it is likely to result 'in anything prejudicial to the commonwealth' (pp. 17, 73). Crowley repeats the same attack in *The Voice of the Last Trumpet*, a series of cautionary tales in doggerel verse which he published in 1550. Too many men, he agrees, and especially the merchants, are acting 'only upon hope to climb', and are taking 'no manner pain' for the good of the commonwealth, whereas they ought to be devoting themselves to the good of the community, not merely to their own selfish concerns (pp. 87, 89). The underlying ideal, as Becon expresses it in his massive *Catechism*, is that everyone needs to have 'an eye not so much unto their own private profit, as to the commodity of the country' as a whole (p. 115).

The basic aim of these moralists is thus to identify and denounce the various social groups responsible for undermining this traditional concept of the public good. This partly leads them to repeat the terms of the indictment already drawn up in the opening Book of More's *Utopia*. They are less interested than More in the conduct of the nobility, but they endorse with great emphasis his earlier attack on the landowning classes, assailing them for raising their rents and enclosing arable land in order to turn it into pasturage. Brinklow complains (p. 38) that 'lords' flocks eat up the corn, meadows, heaths and all together', while Becon in *The Jewel of Joy* reiterates More's accusation that the sheep 'which were created of God for the nourishment of man do now devour man' (p. 434). There is an occasional attempt, notably in the more dispassionate *Discourse*, to make a distinction between harmful enclosures 'whereof all the realm complains' and enclosures which (as the Knight in the second part of the dialogue is allowed to point out) may well be 'profitable and not hurtful to the common weal' (pp. 49, 120). But even in the *Discourse* the judicious figure of the Doctor as well as the less temperate Husbandman agree that while 'this feat of enclosing' is always 'profitable to one man', it is commonly 'prejudicial to many', especially where it involves the decay of tillage and the raising of rents (pp. 15, 51–2). If we turn to the radical preachers, moreover, we find the same attack being pursued with an even keener sense of grievance. When Latimer was first invited to preach before King Edward VI, he devoted almost the whole of his opening sermon to exclaiming against 'you landlords, you rent raisers, I may say you step-lords, you unnatural lords' (p. 98). And when Lever delivered his two sermons at St Paul's Cross in 1550, he based much of his second oration on a contrast between the increasingly rare figure of the 'honest gentleman' and the increasingly prevalent blight of 'covetous extortioners' who oppress the people by raising their rents and even by stealing their land (p. 129).

Having reiterated these familiar accusations, the Commonwealth theorists move on to denounce two further social groups for bringing about the worsening economic depression as well as the prevalent social disorders of the age. One significant shift of emphasis is that, whereas More and Starkey had barely mentioned the merchants and other *nouveaux riches* in this connection, these men are now charged with a heavy responsibility. Amongst the radical preachers it is Lever who inveighs most fiercely against these classes. In the two sermons he delivered at St Paul's Cross he singles out the merchants as by far the most selfish and destructive members of the commonwealth. The first sermon attacks them for failing to use their wealth to help the less fortunate, and includes a long tirade against the ungodly practice of lending money at interest instead of giving it freely to those in need (pp. 29, 44). The second concludes that 'these merchants of mischief' are no more than 'crafty thieves', since they deliberately 'make a scarcity and dearth of all things that come through their hands' (pp. 129–30). The same argument is even more bitterly developed by Latimer and his lay followers amongst the Commonwealth-men. They are not quite unanimous on this point, for the figure of the Merchant in the *Discourse* is treated as a decent and essentially respectable character. But they often argue that the merchants are undermining the ideals of the community in a peculiarly insidious way, since they are using their newly-won riches as a means of 'climbing' out of the social positions into which they have been placed by God. Brinklow repeatedly charges them with trying to 'thrust themselves into other men's vocations', thereby demolishing the godly structure of 'degree' which has been ordained in every well-ordered commonwealth (p. 38). And Latimer frequently expresses the same fears in his sermons before Edward VI. He cries out against those who are always 'climbing, climbing' in the social scale, 'some of them far above their degrees', and devotes much of his final sermon to an attack on the figure of 'the covetous man', who is never 'contented nor satisfied' with his proper station in life (pp. 113, 252, 270).

Even more significant is the fact that several of these writers go on to lay the blame for the deepening economic crisis on the shoulders of the government. By the middle of the sixteenth century, many social theorists had come to feel that the problem they most of all needed to be able to explain was, as the *Discourse* puts it, 'the cause' of the 'universal dearth of all things' – that is, the scarcity of goods and the continuing inflation of prices (p. 37). Some observers hit on the bold and plausible suggestion that the king and his advisers had themselves brought on this disaster by their repeated debasements of the coinage.[1] Latimer mentions the possibility that the 'evilness' of debased money 'has made all things dear' in his famous 'sermon on the plough' in 1549, while the same explanation is more elaborately canvassed, and connected with the foreign exchange-rate of English money, in an anonymous tract of the same year entitled *Policies to Reduce this Realm of England unto a Prosperous Wealth*.[2] But the most confident discussion of the theme occurs in the *Discourse of the Common Weal*. The point is taken up at the start of the third dialogue, where the sagacious figure of the Doctor (whose views are said to have been modelled on those of Latimer) offers to tell his questioners 'the one principal cause' of all the prevailing disorders in social and economic life (p. 98). He then argues – against their earlier suggestions – that neither the landlords nor the merchants are basically to blame (p. 101). The fault lies squarely with those evil councillors who have persuaded the crown to engage in 'the debasing or rather corrupting of our coin and treasure' (pp. 69, 104). There can be no doubt, he concludes, that it is this 'alteration of the coin' which represents 'the chiefest and principal cause of this universal dearth', and thus lies at the very heart of the manifold woes of the commonwealth (p. 104).

THE CENTRALITY OF THE VIRTUES

Whether or not they couched their advice in the form of answers to specific social and political grievances, there was widespread agreement amongst the northern humanists about the nature of the advice to be given to their rulers and magistrates. They almost invariably focused on the claim that the key to political success lies in the promotion of the virtues. As with their *quattrocento* predecessors, their basic demand was not so much for a reformation of institutions, but rather for a change of heart.

[1] There were four separate debasements of the English coinage in the course of the 1540s, and it has been estimated that the use of this device brought the crown a total profit of around a million and a quarter pounds. See Jones, 1970, pp. 133–5. Later in the century the most sophisticated economic commentators preferred to emphasise more global causes of the continuing inflation of prices throughout Western Europe, and focused in particular on the alleged effects of the influx of bullion from the New World. For this theory, especially as argued by Jean Bodin, see Saint-Laurent, 1970, pp. 20–30.

[2] For this tract see Jones, 1970, p. 144. It is thus a slight exaggeration for Dewar, 1964, p. 53 to claim that the author of the *Discourse* is alone in suggesting a direct relationship between the debasements of the coinage and the prevailing scarcity of goods.

Some of the most radical of these theorists, especially in England, insisted on the need for the whole body of the citizens to acquire and practise the virtues as a precondition of attaining a 'well-ordered' commonwealth. Arguing in the manner of the original 'civic' humanists, they maintained that 'the civil life', as Starkey puts it in his *Dialogue*, consists of 'living together in good and politic order, one ever ready to do good to another, and as it were conspiring together in all virtue and honesty' (p. 27). Most of the northern humanists, however, were more concerned to offer their advice to princes and other 'governors', and accordingly placed their main emphasis on the need for these leading members of the ruling classes to cultivate the four 'cardinal' virtues singled out by the moralists of antiquity. One of the fullest of these discussions is presented by Elyot in his *Book Named the Governor*. His account appears to be based in part on the analysis given by Patrizi in *The Kingdom and Education of the King*, and develops a similar view of the four major virtues and their role in political life.[1] Elyot starts by considering 'the most excellent and incomparable virtue called justice', which he regards as 'so necessary and expedient for the governor of a public weal that without it none other virtue may be commendable' (p. 159). Next he turns to the virtue of fortitude, a more complex quality which he takes to include 'painfulness' as well as 'the noble and fair virtue named patience' (pp. 183, 187, 189). He then discusses temperance, which he treats in similar vein as a 'companion' of various other virtues, including moderation and sobriety (pp. 209–18). And finally he comes to the virtue of wisdom – which he prefers 'in a more elegant word' to call 'sapience' – which he regards as peculiarly important 'in every governor of a just or perfect public weal', and a quality of even 'more efficacy than strength or puissance' (pp. 218–19).

A further set of qualities which these mirror-for-princes writers emphasised – again following the lead of their Italian predecessors – was the group of so-called princely virtues, the virtues of liberality, clemency and fidelity to one's word. The discussion of these values forms a major topic in all the large-scale treatises produced by the northern humanists on the concept of the perfect prince. Budé especially concentrates on this theme, devoting the last of the three main sections of his *Education of the*

[1] Croft originally pointed to the close similarities between Patrizi's and Elyot's accounts, listing some twenty parallel passages in Appendix F of his edition of *The Governor*, vol. I, pp. 328–32. The same point has recently been made both by Lehmberg and Major. Some scepticism might however be expressed about the extent to which these parallels require us to think in terms of the direct influence of the one writer on the other. Elyot's discussion, like Patrizi's, is highly conventionalised, and might well have been derived directly from classical models, or from a number of other Italian humanist authorities. There may be a certain naiveté embodied in Croft's remark that it is 'curious', in view of the 'very remarkable similarity' between the two works, that Elyot never once cites Patrizi's account. Cf. Croft, 1880, pp. lxv–lxvi.

Prince to considering what he had earlier described as 'the royal virtues worthy of a king's majesty' (p. 108). His analysis mainly proceeds by way of historical examples, with illustrations from the lives of famous Emperors and princes being used to underline the importance of each attribute being discussed (p. 144ff.). The Emperor Augustus is taken as a model of good faith and honesty, two of the 'great virtues' which brought him 'such great glory and renown' (pp. 144, 146). Alexander the Great is cited to illustrate the importance of liberality, a quality which he always displayed in 'great and infinite' measure, while taking care to ensure that 'only those people worthy of his liberality' were rewarded (p. 165). And Pompey is singled out at the end of the book as a paragon of all the princely qualities, a man who 'controlled the violence of avarice with the rein of civility', who 'tempered the fierceness of ambition with the honesty of his will', and who thus attained 'a true pattern of the virtues and properties necessary for all great personages' (pp. 189, 194).

The same preoccupation is even more highly developed in a number of lesser contributions to the mirror-for-princes *genre*. Wimpfeling, for example, devotes almost the whole of his little tract on *The Epitome of a Good Prince* to considering this special range of qualities. He begins by declaring that 'the prince must follow the virtues and good conduct in everything, fleeing from and hating all the vices' (p. 186). And he then goes on to lay a special emphasis on the princely ideals of clemency and magnificence. He insists that 'justice must always be joined with clemency in the prince', and argues that, although the prince 'must never be profuse', he must 'always show himself bountiful and full of liberality' (pp. 187, 189). Similarly, Josse Clichtove devotes over half his brief treatise on *The Office of the King* to the same set of attributes. He begins with clemency, citing Seneca's judgment that this quality represents 'the height of virtue' in a prince (fo. 37a). He then discusses the keeping of one's word, insisting that 'this is one of the main virtues which the prince must diligently exercise', and adding with great vehemence that 'all dissimulation, fraud and the telling of lies must at all times be eliminated' (fo. 43a). And finally he commends the virtue of liberality, arguing that the king must 'not only be bountiful to the poor', but also needs to cultivate 'magnificence', ornamenting his kingdom 'with splendid public buildings' and 'freely giving away fine gifts' (fos. 70a–b).

As well as discussing the princely virtues, a number of northern humanists focused on a further range of qualities which they expected all 'governors' and leading citizens to cultivate. Clichtove gives an account of these properties in the course of describing the virtues of princes, but the fullest treatment of this further theme is supplied by Elyot in the second book of *The Governor*. He lays it down that, when we investigate the concept of gentlemanly conduct, we find that 'there be incident three special qualities' which go to make up the ideal of a gentleman (p. 106). The first is 'affability', the virtue of being 'facile or easy to be spoken unto', which 'is of a wonderful efficacy or power in procuring love' (p. 107). The second is 'placability', the virtue which most of all 'becomes a man noble and honourable', the marvellous value of which 'is best known by the contrary, which is ire, called vulgarly wrath, a vice most ugly and furthest from humanity' (p. 111). And finally the governor, like the prince, must above all be merciful, since 'reason persuades' and 'experience proves' that a man 'in whom mercy lacks and is not found, in him all other virtues be drowned and lose their just commendation' (p. 115).

Finally, the northern humanists characteristically emphasise – far more strongly than most of their Italian precursors – one further virtue which is said to be essential for all rulers to possess: that of godliness. The point is repeatedly made by all the mirror-for-princes writers, but nowhere more strongly or at greater length than in Guevara's *Dial of Princes*.[1] Guevara allocates the whole of his opening Book to explaining 'what excellence is in the prince that is a good Christian', and devotes a special chapter to listing the 'five causes' which should lead all princes to ensure that they are 'better Christians than their subjects' (fos. 1a, 25b). He is mainly concerned to warn them that unless they keep 'the fear and love of the supreme prince' before their eyes at all times, they will find themselves 'in great peril of damnation' (fo 25b). But he ends on a rather more encouraging note by adding as his 'fifth cause' that all governors who have shown 'great confidence in God' have 'always prospered' (fo 26b, cf. Redondo, 1976, esp. pp. 597–602).

The essence of the humanist message, as Erasmus tells us in *The Christian Prince*, can thus be summarised by saying that the aim of government must be to achieve 'the highest degree of virtue', while the duty of the ruler must be to serve as the embodiment of 'virtue in its highest and purest form' (pp. 187, 189). We next need to ask what reasons the northern humanists characteristically gave for assigning such an absolutely central place to the virtues in political life. To recover their answers to this question will be to reach the heart of their moral and political thought.

One highly significant answer was given by those who are sometimes rather

[1] For other examples see Erasmus, *Christian Prince*, esp. pp. 148, 152, 167, 183; Budé, *Education of the Prince*, esp. pp. 18, 32, 41, 69–70, 81–2, Osorio, *Education of the King*, esp. pp. 284, 363, 379, 455, 500.

confusingly known as the Christian humanists – confusingly because all
the humanists were of course Christian, with the possible exception of
Machiavelli. Amongst those who have generally been labelled in this way,
the most important were Erasmus, Colet and More. They were united by
their wish to protest at the widespread assumption that the essence of
Christianity consists of nothing more than a willingness to accept the
sacraments of the Church, to master its theological tenets and to discuss
them in the approved syllogistic style. As Erasmus contemptuously
remarks in *The Christian Prince*, it is absurd to suppose that true Christianity is to be 'found in ceremonies, in doctrines kept after a fashion, and
in constitutions of the Church' (p. 153). A true Christian must rather be a
man who employs his God-given reason in order to distinguish good from
evil, and then uses his best endeavours to avoid the evil and embrace the
good. Colet was the first of the northern humanists to make this point,
presenting it with great force at the beginning of his *Exposition* of St Paul's
Epistle to the Romans. St Paul's teaching, he claims, is that God 'will
render to every man according to his deeds'. This means that as long as
our actions are 'good and righteous', we will always be 'accounted by God
to have lived righteously', even if we possess no knowledge of the law of
God as set forth in the Bible (p. 4). Erasmus soon became the most vocal
protagonist of the same doctrine. 'Who is truly Christian?' he asks in *The
Christian Prince*. 'Not he who is baptised or anointed, or who attends
Church. It is rather the man who has embraced Christ in the innermost
feelings of his heart, and who emulates him by his pious deeds' (p. 153).
The same argument is reiterated in the *Paraclesis*, Erasmus's 'exhortation'
at the start of his edition of the New Testament. There we are told that 'a
genuine race of Christians' would not in the least consist of priests following elaborate ceremonials or learned doctors propounding difficult points
of theology. It would consist of those 'who would restore the philosophy of
Christ, not in rituals or syllogistic arguments, but in the heart and in the
whole of life itself' (p. 156).

For Erasmus and his sympathisers, the pursuit of virtue thus became
of paramount religious as well as moral significance. If a man who embraces the virtues is most conspicuously a Christian, it follows that a prince
and people who work together to create a truly virtuous commonwealth
will also be working towards that greatest of all achievements, the establishment of a genuinely Christian way of life. This is the tremendous hope
underlying Erasmus's repeated demand in *The Christian Prince* that all
rulers and governors must make themselves 'complete in all the virtues'
and see themselves as 'born for the public good' (p. 162). If the prince
attains complete virtue, this will make him fully a Christian; and if he

becomes fully a Christian, this will enable him to lay the foundations of a perfect commonwealth.

By grasping this characteristic commitment of the Christian humanists, it may in turn be possible to cast some light on one of the most puzzling questions about More's *Utopia*: the question of what he may have intended to convey to Christian Europe by stressing the admirable qualities of the Utopians while at the same time emphasising their ignorance of Christianity.[1] When Hythlodaeus first introduces us to the Utopians at the end of Book I, he not only describes their institutions as 'extremely wise', but also as *sanctissima* – as holy in the highest degree (p. 103). He later tells us, however, that when he and his companions first came to Utopia, they discovered that none of its inhabitants had any knowledge of the Christian faith. They knew nothing about the miracle of the Incarnation, and arrived at their religious as well as ethical convictions entirely by the ordinary processes of rational argument (pp. 163–5, 217–19). More thus makes it clear that, in describing the Utopians as extremely holy, what he is praising is simply their achievement of a society in which – as Hythlodaeus puts it at the beginning of his account – 'affairs are ordered so aptly that virtue has its reward' (p. 103). The implication seems inescapable: More is telling us that true holiness consists of living a life of virtue, and thus that the heathen inhabitants of Utopia, far more than the nominal Christians of Europe, have succeeded in establishing a truly Christian commonwealth. The fact that the Utopians are not Christians merely serves, on this interpretation, to intensify More's essentially Erasmian commitment, and to make it resonate with a characteristic note of irony. Erasmus had already insisted that the perfection of Christianity cannot possibly consist in membership of the Church or acceptance of its various dogmas. More presses the argument to its logical conclusion, implying that it may be possible to become a perfect Christian without any knowledge of the Church or its dogmas at all.

As well as equating good actions with the essence of Christianity, the northern humanists characteristically gave a further set of reasons for assigning the virtues such an absolutely central place in political life. They declared that unless corruption is eliminated, self-interest is abandoned, and everyone acts in accordance with the virtues, the two greatest aims of political society will be jeopardised: the leading citizens will be unable

---

[1] The fact that 'the Christian humanists' thought that 'to be a Christian was a way of life', and that this helps us to understand More's *Utopia*, has been well argued by Hexter, 1965, esp. pp. lxviii–lxxvi. Hexter does not mention Colet in this context, and arguably overestimates Erasmus's contribution to the formation of this humanist view of Christianity. But his account of the relationship between these ideas and the interpretation of *Utopia* is entirely convincing, and I am much indebted to it.

to attain their highest goals; and the commonwealth as a whole will be unable to fulfil its fundamental purposes.

To understand this argument, we first need to ask what goals the humanists generally wished their rulers and governors to pursue. The answer is that they tended to endorse the familiar *quattrocento* assumption that the highest ambition for any leading members of a commonwealth should be that of attaining honour, glory and fame. This argument is developed at considerable length in most of the advice-books designed for nobles and magistrates. Elyot, for example, sprinkles *The Governor* with frequent allusions to the importance of winning 'perpetual honour', of 'eschewing reproach for dishonour' and of gaining 'immortal life and perpetual glory' for one's deeds (pp. 185, 200, 205). The same scale of values tends to be presented with even greater fulsomeness by the mirror-for-princes writers. As Budé declares in his *Education of the Prince*, all rulers should recognise their fundamental duty 'to bring honour to honourable things' (p. 87). This means that their Courts should serve as 'temples of honour and nobility', while their main ambition should be that of winning 'honour during their lifetime, with good and honourable fame after their death' (pp. 33, 87). Finally, we find the same assumptions being corroborated no less firmly by the so-called Christian humanists. It is a mistake to suggest, as Hexter has done, that More and Erasmus opposed 'the pursuit of honour' on the grounds that it helped to encourage 'greed, pride and tyranny' (Hexter, 1965, p. lxix). Erasmus in particular lays it down with much emphasis in *The Christian Prince* that 'the main object' of all rulers should be to follow 'the path of right and honour' (p. 163). The prince is instructed to submit himself 'to a rule of honour', to ensure that he is never 'led away from the course of honour by bribes', to learn 'to love morality and loathe dishonour', and above all to recognise that 'you cannot rule others until you yourself have obeyed the course of honour' (pp. 169, 187, 189, 192).

It is partly through their preoccupation with this ideal that these theorists are led to assign such a pre-eminent place to the virtues in political life. For they also maintain, in typically humanist style, that the pursuit of virtue constitutes the sole pathway to honour, so that 'there is no real honour', as Erasmus puts it in *The Christian Prince*, 'except that which springs from virtue and good deeds' (p. 198). One of the fullest statements of this very widespread belief is given in Elyot's *Book Named the Governor*. When he issues his instructions to the tutors of young noblemen at the start of Book I, he advises them to 'commend those virtues' which they wish to inculcate, and to point out 'what honour, what love, what commodity' can be gained 'by these virtues' (p. 20). When he turns at the start of Book II to consider 'what things that he is elected or appointed to be a governor of a public weal ought to premeditate', one of the chief maxims he enunciates is that 'the most sure foundation of noble renown is a man to be of such virtues and qualities as he desires to be openly published' (p. 97). And when he discusses the cardinal virtues in Book III, he is always careful to stress that 'honour and perpetual memory' constitute 'the just reward' of the virtues (p. 184; cf. pp. 192–3).

Most of these writers also consider the role of the virtues in relation to the aims of political society as a whole. As they turn to examine this wider question, it is sometimes possible to catch an echo of the original *trecento* assumption that the main purpose of government ought to be that of ensuring the preservation of the people's liberty. Starkey in particular speaks with admiration in his *Dialogue* of the combination of freedom and harmony to be found in 'the most noble city of Venice', and argues that the gravest threat to any commonwealth lies in the growth of tyranny and the consequent loss of freedom (pp. 163–4). To forestall any such danger in England, he proposes to revive the ancient position of Constable of the kingdom, whose duties would be to 'see to the liberty of the whole body of the realm', to 'resist all tyranny which by any manner may grow upon the whole commonalty', and to call a Parliament if ever there appeared to be 'any peril of the loss of the liberty' of the people (p. 166).

The main tendency, however, was to argue that the fundamental purpose of government is not so much to preserve liberty, but rather to maintain good order, harmony and peace. This had of course been a characteristic commitment of the *quattrocento* mirror-for-princes theorists, and we find the same values being even more strongly underlined by the writers of similar advice-books for the rulers of northern Europe.[1] Perhaps more surprisingly, we also find this viewpoint being endorsed by such leading 'commonwealth' theorists as Starkey and More. More insists in *Utopia* that the aim of all legislation ought to be the maintenance of 'good order', and praises the Utopians for being the most completely 'well-ordered people' on earth (pp. 103, 107). And Starkey similarly acknowledges in his *Dialogue* – in spite of his flirtation with the ideal of liberty – that 'the end of all laws and politic rule is to keep the citizens in unity and peace and perfect concord among themselves', a commitment which leads him to conclude that all 'matters of the common weal' must always be 'referred to this end and purpose: that the whole body of the commonalty may live in quietness and tranquillity' (p. 24).

[1] See for example Wimpfeling, *Epitome*, esp. pp. 184, 187; Erasmus, *Christian Prince*, esp. pp. 164, 198; Guevara, *Dial of Princes*, esp. fos. 174b–176a.

It is due to this Platonic emphasis on the supreme importance of social harmony that all these writers go on to insist once again on the paramount place of the virtues in political life. For they adopt the traditional humanist claim that the key to eliminating faction, overcoming corruption and establishing a well-ordered commonwealth lies in bringing about a triumph of the virtues. Starkey offers a particularly vivid statement of this assumption in the second chapter of his *Dialogue*. 'The end of all politic rule', he declares, 'is to induce the multitude to virtuous living, according to the nature and dignity of man.' Where this is not achieved, and everyone looks 'only to their own singular weal, pleasure and profit', then 'there can be no politic rule or civil order' at all. But where the commonwealth is 'directed in virtue and honesty', and where the people are 'governed virtuously in civil life', the outcome is certain to be a true 'civic order', in which the people are able to live 'quietly and peaceably' with each other in a state of undisturbed tranquillity (pp. 61, 63).

THE QUALITIES OF LEADERSHIP

Underlying this stress on the centrality of the virtues in political life is a potentially radical theory about the qualities required for political leadership. If the possession of virtue is the key to good government, it appears that we ought to nominate only those of the highest virtue to serve as our rulers and magistrates. The radical implication contained in this proposal is of course that we ought not to rest content with the idea of an hereditary ruling class founded on lineage and wealth; we ought instead to seek out the most virtuous members of society, wherever they are to be found, and ensure that they alone are appointed as leaders and governors of the commonwealth.

There is no doubt that this radical suggestion was to some extent endorsed. As we have seen, a number of Italian humanists had already debated the claim that virtue constitutes the only true nobility, and that true nobility, *vera nobilitas*, constitutes the only valid title to rule. One sign of the acceptance of this argument was that several Italian treatises defending this commitment subsequently appeared in translation in northern Europe. Buonaccorso's *Declamation of Nobleness* was turned into English as early as the 1460s, while Giovanni Nenna's very similar *Treatise of Nobility* was translated much later by William Jones (Charlton, 1965, p. 84). Nenna'a analysis is even more unequivocally in favour of equating virtue with true nobility than Buonaccorso's earlier account. As we have seen, in Buonaccorso's *Declamation* the two contestants simply make rival speeches about the idea of *vera nobilitas*, after which we are left to decide for ourselves about the merits of their arguments. But in Nenna's *Treatise* nothing is left to the imagination, for a figure called Nennio steps forward after the two protagonists have spoken in order to tell us the outcome of their debate. He summarises their arguments at great length, noting that one finds true nobility 'in blood and in riches', while the other finds it 'in the virtues of the mind' (fo. 67b). He then declares with some heat that the first of these opinions is 'a cause of pride and ignorance' and of 'insufferable evil' (fo. 80a). So he concludes that true nobility, the only title to 'honour and glory' in the commonwealth, resides entirely 'in the virtues of the mind', which 'set forth a gentleman, and do make him perfectly noble' (fos. 87a, 91b, 96b).

As well as making themselves familiar with such *quattrocento* treatises, many of the northern humanists stated explicitly that they agreed with their conclusions. Elyot, for example, proclaims in Book II of *The Governor* that 'nobility' is simply 'the commendation and as it were the surname of virtue' (p. 106). And Erasmus in *The Christian Prince* points to the radical implications of this doctrine without hesitation. He accepts that when nobility 'is derived from virtue' this is so much more impressive than the kind of nobility which is based on 'genealogy or wealth' that 'in the strictest judgement' only the first can be counted as true nobility at all (p. 151). And he adds that when someone is truly noble in the sense of possessing all the virtues in the highest degree, this means that 'most naturally the power should be entrusted to him', since he excels so much in all 'the requisite kingly qualities' (p. 140). The same arguments recur in a number of specialised treatises on the meaning of *vera nobilitas*. Josse Clichtove, for example, published *A Brief Work on True Nobility* in 1512, maintaining that 'the most outstanding of all the types of nobility is the nobility of virtue' (fo. 5a). And John Heywood (*c.* 1497–*c.* 1580) defended the same conclusion in *Gentleness and Nobility*, a somewhat knockabout verse comedy which he probably wrote in the early 1520s (Cameron, 1941, p. 88). The play introduces us to four characters: a merchant, a gentleman, a ploughman and a philosopher. The merchant begins by observing that he is 'greatly regarded' as 'a wise and noble man' because of his 'great riches' (p. 1). This attitude is decried by the gentleman, who insists that true nobility can only arise out of holding 'great lands by inheritance' (p. 2). The ploughman is then allowed to state the crucial objection to both their claims, putting his argument (pp. 15–16) in the form of a famous rhetorical question:

> 'For when Adam delved and Eve span,
> Who was then the gentleman?'

The radical implications are finally spelled out by the philosopher in the Epilogue: that 'virtue is ever the thing principal' underlying true nobility; and that 'heads, rulers and governors' ought in consequence to be appointed to their high positions solely 'because of their virtue' (p. 35; cf. Hogrefe, 1959, pp. 283–8).

For all their apparent support of these egalitarian claims, however, the northern humanists generally handled the debate about *vera nobilitas* in such a way that any subversive implications of the argument were entirely neutralised, while the argument itself was cunningly deployed in order to support a traditionally hierarchical picture of political life. This stratagem was based on the empirical claim – which at one level was simply a play on words – that while virtue undoubtedly constitutes the only true nobility, it happens that the virtues are always most fully displayed by the traditional ruling classes. As Elyot ingenuously puts it at the start of *The Governor*, 'where virtue is in a gentleman it is commonly mixed with more sufferance, more affability and mildness than for the most part it is in a person rural or of very base lineage' (p. 14). Perhaps the clearest formulation of this widespread and convenient belief was given by Lawrence Humphrey (*c.* 1527–90) in his treatise on *The Nobles, or of Nobility*. Humphrey seems to have relied on – and frequently cites – an earlier account of *vera nobilitas* put forward by Osorio in his *Discourse of Civil and Christian Nobility* in 1552 (Sorrentino, 1936, p. 17). His own treatise – which was first published in Latin in 1560, and translated into English in 1563 – presents a similar analysis of true nobility at the start of the second Book. Humphrey begins by acknowledging that the highest nobility unquestionably resides in 'the inward ornaments and virtues' of the mind (sig. K, 4a). But he immediately goes on to claim that although these virtues are unchanging in themselves, we nevertheless find ('I wot not how') that they invariably 'shine and glitter in a nobleman' more brightly than in anyone else (sig. K, 4b). To some extent the virtues are always 'severed' in 'the rascal rabble', whereas they 'join and throng' in the aristocracy, who are able to 'accomplish more copiously and plentifully than the dregs and dross of men' (sig. K, 5b; sig. L, 2b). Making explicit the pun on which the whole argument is based, we may say that Humphrey's contention is simply that nobles and gentlemen always display the greatest nobility and gentleness.

Virtually all the northern humanists then go on to spell out the more general and deeply conservative message underlying this commitment to the traditional ruling classes. Having admitted that government ought to be placed in the hands of those with the greatest virtue, and having affirmed that those with the greatest virtue happen to be the nobility and gentry, they proceed to draw the pleasingly obvious conclusion: that in order to maintain the best-ordered form of political society, we ought not to tamper with any existing social distinctions, but ought on the contrary to preserve them as far as possible. To put the key doctrine in their own terms, they declare that the maintenance of 'order' presupposes the upholding of existing 'degrees' (cf. Greenleaf, 1964, esp. pp. 53–7).

By far the finest statement of this conviction was of course put into the mouth of Ulysses at the start of Shakespeare's *Troilus and Cressida*.[1] The entire universe, Ulysses begins by saying, bears witness to the importance of 'degree':

> 'The heavens themselves, the planets and this centre
> Observe degree, priority and place'.

The analogy is taken to be exact and inescapable: the social system, like the solar system, cannot hope to survive unless 'degree' is upheld:

> 'How could communities
> Degrees in schools, and brotherhoods in cities,
> Peaceful commerce from dividable shores,
> The primogenitive and due of birth,
> Prerogative of age, crowns, sceptres, laurels,
> But by degree stand in authentic place?'

And the folly of seeking to change the existing system is said to be no less obvious:

> 'Take but degree away, untune that string
> And hark! What discord follows'.

It would be misleading, however, to give the impression, as some scholars have done, that this is to adumbrate 'the Elizabethan world picture', the implication being that the age of Shakespeare should be regarded as the heyday of these assumptions about 'order' and 'degree'. By the time Shakespeare was writing, these static images of the political system had already begun to be destructively challenged by the religious radicals and political revolutionaries of late sixteenth-century Europe. It is arguable, moreover, that Shakespeare's own discussion of 'degree' should be treated more as a reflection of the resulting confusions than a straightforward restatement of the old commonplaces. Certainly there is something suspiciously fulsome about Ulysses's famous speech, and there is more than a touch of irony in the fact that it is declaimed by such a notoriously manipulative character. If we wish to investigate the real

[1] See *Troilus and Cressida*, I, iii, 75–137.

heyday of these assumptions, we must revert to the earlier part of the century: there we find the defence of 'order' and its association with 'degree' being presented not merely with complete conviction, but also with considerable aggression and force.

The aggression was supplied by those who wanted to protect the existing hierarchies against ambitious upstarts who were trying to improve their 'degrees' by rising through the ranks of society. The most famous polemic of this kind is Skelton's assault on Wolsey as 'a wretched poor man' of 'greasy genealogy' who had been raised by the king 'out from a low degree' to a position of undeserved power and inordinate wealth (pp. 353, 355). But an even more savage attack on such plebeian *arrivistes* was mounted by Humphrey in the opening Book of his treatise on nobility. He views with intense loathing those 'wretched upstarts' who attempt 'suddenly with their brightness' to 'dim the ancient families' (sig. G, 7b). And he commands them to remember 'the dung hill whence by God they were raised' to their positions of unmerited eminence (sig. B, 9a).

The positive commitment underlying such fulminations is always the same: good 'order' presupposes the maintenance of 'degree'. We find this cardinal assumption being defended even by some of the most radical of the Commonwealth writers. Starkey, for example, insists that 'the true common weal' is only achieved when all 'the parts as members of one body be knit together in perfect love and unity, everyone doing his office and duty after such manner that whatsoever state, office or degree any man be of, the duty thereto pertaining with all diligence he busily fulfil, and without envy or malice to other accomplish the same' (p. 62). The same outlook tends to be expressed even more forcefully in advice-books intended for kings and princes. As Budé insists, 'to confuse the degrees of authority and pre-eminence' is fatal to the stability of any monarchical government (p. 125). And finally, the same assumptions are presented most fully by the writers of advice books for the gentry and nobility. The clearest instance is Elyot's *Book Named the Governor*, the opening page of which defines 'a public weal' as 'a body living, compact or made of sundry estates and degrees of men' (p. 1). This is followed by a very strong expression of the belief that no commonwealth may be said to be well-ordered 'except it do contain in it degrees, high and base, according to the merit or estimation of the thing that is ordered' (p. 4). For as Elyot warns – in a passage later strikingly echoed by Shakespeare – if we 'take away order from all things', the result 'needs must be perpetual conflict'.[1] From this it follows, he concludes, that a true 'public weal' is bound to maintain

---

[1] See Elyot, *Governor*, p. 2. For a full account of the many parallels between Elyot and Shakespeare on the subject of 'order' and 'degree' see Starnes, 1927, esp. pp. 121–8.

'appointed degrees and places' both to 'impress a reverence and due obedience to the vulgar people or commonalty', and to assure the preservation of good order, harmony and peace (p. 5).

THE ROLE OF EDUCATION

If the practice of virtue by our rulers is the key to good government, this clearly raises a question of great practical importance: how are we to ensure that they duly acquire the necessary virtues? The answer characteristically proposed by the northern humanists – drawing directly at this point on the work of their *quattrocento* predecessors – was that the surest way of inculcating the virtues must be to furnish the leaders of society with an education in the *studia humanitatis*.

This commitment is most systematically defended in their specialised contributions to the philosophy of education. Sadoleto, for example, begins his discussion of *The Right Education of Boys* with a bold statement of the two key assumptions: good actions are the product of the virtues, while the virtues are the product of good training. He accordingly devotes his main attention to describing in considerable detail the type of education which he thinks will serve most effectively to encourage 'the pursuit of virtue' – a typically humanist course of study beginning with grammar and rhetoric and culminating in philosophy, 'the source and fountain-head of all the virtues' (pp. 67–8). Vives outlines precisely the same course of instruction in his treatise *On Education*, as well as suggesting a list of books which deserve to be read with the closest attention. In addition to the classic texts of ancient rhetoric and moral philosophy, he warmly recommends a number of modern writers who had already emphasised the closeness of the links between the study of the humanities and the practice of good government. On moral philosophy he particularly singles out Erasmus and Budé, while on the more detailed questions of political theory he cites Erasmus again, together with Patrizi and Sir Thomas More, all of whom he thinks are 'already great, or will soon be considered so' (pp. 157, 260).

Given this belief in the close connections between sound instruction and sound government, it is not surprising that many of the mirror-for-princes writers are almost as much concerned with pedagogic as with political advice. As Erasmus insists in *The Christian Prince*, 'the instruction of the prince in accordance with established principles and ideas must take precedence over all else' (p. 156). The implications of this assumption can be seen at their clearest in the organisation of a work such as Budé's *Education of the Prince*. He begins by declaring, in his first four chapters, that his main interest lies in promoting wisdom, prudence and 'science' in government. He immediately assumes, however, that if we ask how these values are to be attained, we are asking in effect how our rulers ought to be educated. So he assigns the next thirty chapters to considering what form of education may be expected to produce the most virtuous governors – taking it for granted that this in turn will produce the most virtuous government.

This sense of the paramount importance of education also serves to explain why so many of the humanists, ostensibly writing treatises of moral and political philosophy, include such extravagantly detailed instructions to the tutors of future princes and magistrates. Agreeing with Erasmus that 'men are not born but made', they clearly assume that even the smallest errors in training may be capable of having a deleterious effect on a child's subsequent performance in a position of authority (cf. Woodward, 1906, p. 116). One remarkable instance of the lengths to which they carried this belief can be seen in the second Book of Guevara's *Dial of Princes*, which considers 'how princes and great lords' should 'nourish and bring up their children' (fo. 80b). Guevara devotes no less than six chapters to the importance of breast feeding, considering everything from the 'seven properties which a good nurse should have' to the absurdity of various heathen superstitions on the subject (fos. 112b, 119a). The same extraordinary attention to detail can be found in Book I of Elyot's *Governor*, in which the merits of breast feeding are again canvassed, and a great deal of space is given over to a peculiarly English discussion about the forms of exercise most suitable for young gentlemen. Dancing ('signifying matrimony') is particularly recommended, on the grounds that it serves as 'an introduction unto the first moral virtue, called prudence'; but tennis is only allowed if it is 'seldom used', while football is strongly criticised for its 'beastly fury and extreme violence' (pp. 78, 92).

The outcome of this intense concern with the ideal curriculum was that, as the humanists became increasingly influential as advisers to princes, this in turn helped to bring about a revolution in educational theory and practice. It was the humanists who first introduced into northern Europe the immensely influential belief that a training in the *litterae humaniores* represents an indispensable requirement for public life. And it was they who first succeeded in consequence in breaking down the age-old distinctions – already abolished in Italy – between the education of the ruling classes and the education of 'clerks'. As late as the end of the fifteenth century we still find the old assumptions being voiced in such treatises as the anonymous *Book of Noblesse*. 'But now of late days', we are told, 'the greater pity is' that many young men 'descended of noble blood and born to arms' are setting themselves 'to singular practice' and 'strange faculties', such as learning 'the practice of law' and other 'civil matters', with the result that they 'waste greatly their time in such needless business' (p. 77). The humanists were keenly aware of such prejudices, and as late as the 1560s we still find Humphrey complaining that the nobility 'rarely delight' in 'learned wit and wisdom sealed with knowledge' (sig. X, 2a). Faced with such illiteracy, however, they devoted themselves above all to furthering the Platonic conception that, as Erasmus roundly expresses it at the start of *The Christian Prince*, 'you cannot be a prince if you are not a philosopher; you will be a tyrant' (p. 150). Again and again they cite the fact that Alexander the Great was taught by Aristotle – the best proof, as Budé insists, of 'the honour and great glory which arise out of the study of good letters' (p. 112). And at the same time they encourage kings, princes and gentry alike to recognise that, as Elyot puts it in *The Governor*, 'learning commends, not dispraises, nobility' (p. 42).

Humphrey grandly summarises the call that went out to the ruling classes of the age: 'Cease nobles therefore to hate learning'; recognise that those who 'glitter in bravery' ought also 'to glitter in mind' (sig. X, 2a, 4a). The point of major historical importance is that the call was widely heeded. The humanists succeeded in persuading the aristocracy that the time had come to recognise that the force of arms had largely given way in their society to the force of argument. The bleak alternative, as Edmund Dudley pointed out as early as 1509 in his *Tree of Commonwealth*, was to watch their traditional supremacy being eroded by 'the children of poor men and mean folk' who had mastered the new learning and were beginning to receive 'the promotion and authority that the children of noble blood should have if they were mete therefore' (p. 45). The lesson was quickly taken to heart: the sons of the nobility began to fill the universities of northern Europe in the latter part of the sixteenth century; their increasing literacy made it correspondingly plausible to claim that virtue and *vera nobilitas* were indeed to be found in their highest form in the traditional aristocracy; and this in turn helped to ensure that the threat posed by the revival of learning to the established class-structure was largely neutralised.

9

The humanist critique of humanism

So far we have examined the ways in which the northern humanists endorsed and developed the moral and political outlook characteristic of the Italian Renaissance. This has enabled us to underline a thesis which has sometimes been doubted, but which seems inescapable: that it is in fact appropriate to regard the political theory of the northern Renaissance essentially as an extension and consolidation of a range of arguments originally discussed in *quattrocento* Italy. It is no less important, however, to stress that these arguments were never simply reiterated in an uncritical or mechanical style. As we have already observed, a number of issues central to Italian political debate were scarcely accorded any attention in northern Europe. To complete our survey, we finally need to add that some of the theories evolved by the northern humanists must be understood not so much as continuations but rather as criticisms of earlier humanist themes.

HUMANISM AND THE JUSTIFICATION OF WAR

One important point at which a number of northern humanists tended to criticise rather than to follow their Italian precursors was in their analysis of the role of warfare in political life. As we have seen, the Aristotelian ideal of the armed citizen had played a major part in many *quattrocento* theories of statecraft. A willingness to fight for one's liberty had come to be seen as part of one's ordinary civic duties, while the business of warfare had correspondingly been viewed as little more than a continuation of politics by other means. By contrast, many northern humanists laid great emphasis on the stoic conception that, since all men are brothers, all warfare must in effect be fratricide. The most eloquent statement of this commitment was given by Erasmus in his oration of 1517 entitled *The Complaint of Peace*.[1] Peace speaks in her own person of 'the insults and

[1] The *Complaint* was Erasmus's definitive pronouncement on the horrors of war in Christian society, and was one of his most popular works, with thirty-two dated editions appearing in

repulses' she continually suffers at the hands of 'man's injustice' (p. 1). She begins by insisting that war is utterly opposed to the ideals of Christian fellowship. It is 'so unhallowed that it becomes the deadliest bane of piety and religion' wherever it breaks out (p. 2). Later she adds that war is no less an enemy of virtuous government, since 'the voice of law' is 'never heard amid the clang of arms', while 'the worst of men' always attain 'the greatest share of power' when peace is spurned (p. 81). She then declares that since the highest aim in any commonwealth is known to be the furthering of Christian fellowship and virtuous government, it follows that 'war must of necessity be held in the greatest conceivable abhorrence' (p. 82). It overturns all our best hopes, leaving us in 'the foul sink of sin as well as misery' (p. 82). So the oration concludes with a stirring call 'to all who call themselves Christians' to 'unite with one heart and one soul in the abolition of war, and the establishment of perpetual and universal peace' (p. 98).

It would of course be an oversimplification to suggest that this attack on the ideals of martial glory should be understood simply as a repudiation of earlier humanist attitudes. Several northern humanists were also in revolt against the venerable doctrine of the just war, which they tended to see as an even more dangerous source and justification for the prevailing violence of their age. The most influential exponent of this doctrine had been St Augustine. Although he had frequently called for the abolition of warfare in *The City of God*, he had also allowed two very important exceptions, both of which had subsequently been accepted by the Church and incorporated by Aquinas in his classic defence of the just war (cf. Adams, 1962, pp. 6–12). St Augustine had first of all laid it down in Book IV that 'since it would be worse for wrongdoers to rule over the just' than for the just to submit to wrongdoers, it follows that a war of the just against wrongdoers may not merely be 'a necessary evil' but may also be 'properly termed a fortunate event' (II, 59). And in Book XIX he had added that although 'the wise man' will always 'deplore his being compelled to engage in just wars', there may nevertheless be occasions on which 'the injustice of the opposing side' forces him to recognise 'the necessity of waging just wars' (VI, p. 151).

It is evident that when the so-called Christian humanists – particularly Colet and Erasmus – mounted their unqualified attacks on the horrors of

the course of the sixteenth century; cf. Bainton, 1951, p. 32. There are many other places, however, in which Erasmus describes his hatred of warfare in similar terms. The most important is his discussion of the adage '*Dulce Bellum Inexpertis*', 'war is sweet to those who do not know it'. For the major essay which Erasmus added under this heading to the 1515 edition of his *Adages*, see Phillips, 1964, pp. 308–53. For a full discussion of this essay, and of the *Complaint*, see Adams, 1962, pp. 86–109.

war, it was mainly this dangerous orthodoxy they were seeking to overturn. As Colet explains in his *Exposition* of St Paul's Epistle to the Romans, to defend the idea of a just war is to assume that it is possible 'to crush evil with evil'. But St Paul teaches that 'there is nothing that conquers evil but good', and that if we 'endeavour to crush evil with evil', we merely 'descend to evil' without achieving any good (p. 86). This means that the 'infliction of punishment, and undertaking of war, and all the other ways in which men labour to do away with evil, aim in vain at that object' (p. 86). For 'it is not by war that war is conquered, but by peace, and forbearance and reliance on God' (p. 97). A similar and even more explicit attack is mounted by Erasmus in *The Complaint of Peace* (cf. Fernandez, 1973, p. 225). Christians often claim, he says, to be fighting 'a just and necessary war' even when they turn their weapons against 'another people holding exactly the same creed and professing the same Christianity' (p. 51). But it is not necessity and justice that make them go to war; it is 'anger, ambition and folly' that supply 'the compulsory force' (p. 53). If they were truly Christian, they would instead perceive that 'there is scarcely any peace so unjust that it is not preferable, upon the whole, to the justest war' (p. 54). For peace is 'the most excellent of all things', and if we wish to 'prove ourselves to be sincere followers of Christ' we must embrace peace at all times (pp. 19, 91).

It is clear, however, that several of the northern humanists were less concerned with this traditional problem than with the more insouciant treatment of the art of war developed by a number of *quattrocento* humanists. They were particularly scandalised by the fact that force and violence were coming to be regarded as ordinary adjuncts of statecraft. The most complete repudiation of this outlook is contained in More's *Utopia*. Whereas the 'civic' humanists had characteristically argued that a good citizen ought to think of military service as part of his regular public duties, More informs us that the wise Utopians do everything they can to avoid 'sending their own citizens' into battle. They 'regard one another of such value' that 'they would not care to exchange any one of their own people' even in return for capturing 'the king of the opposite party' (pp. 205–7). Similarly, while the 'civic' humanists had invariably viewed the practice of hiring mercenaries with the gravest alarm and disapproval, More repeatedly tells us that the Utopians 'pay foreign mercenaries' on every possible occasion to fight on their behalf, and 'take care not to be obliged to fight in person as long as they can finish the war by the assistance of hired substitutes' (pp. 149, 211).

As well as rejecting the concept of the armed citizen, many of these theorists also attack the increasingly fashionable claim that the profession of arms should be regarded as the only worthy and honourable occupation for a gentleman. This was of course a traditional chivalric belief, but two factors had helped to give it a renewed prominence at the start of the sixteenth century. One was the widespread and self-conscious attempt to revive the ideals of the knightly code – a movement of social nostalgia which found expression in such writings as *The Book of Noblesse* and such spectacles as the Field of the Cloth of Gold (cf. Ferguson, 1960, pp. 23–6, 143–53). The other and connected factor was the interest shown by a number of Italian humanists in the project of civilising Europe's warriors – the aim being to imbue them with the appropriate notions of honour, glory and fame, and to reassure them that (in Castiglione's phrase) the pursuit of letters need not be detrimental to arms. The emphasis Castiglione and his numerous imitators placed on this scale of values helped to ensure that in many humanist circles the business of fighting attained an unparalleled glamour in the course of the sixteenth century. Othello's insistence[1] that 'big wars' serve to 'make ambition virtue' is clearly a humanist rather than a knightly commentary on his calling, while Sir Philip Sidney's noble death on the field of Zutphen may be said to represent the apotheosis of a Renaissance courtier as much as of a chivalric knight.

The sternest denunciation of these renewed preoccupations with the splendours of war, whether in their chivalric or humanist dress, can again be found in More's *Utopia*. We are told that the wise Utopians 'count nothing so inglorious as glory sought in war', and always prefer to gain peace by deceiving their enemies or buying them off with gold rather than by an indulgence in the expenditure of lives (pp. 201, 205). The same urge to deflate what Othello calls the 'pride, pomp and circumstance of glorious war' is no less marked in a number of other northern humanists.[2] It is true that by no means all of them would have agreed with More's contention that 'the honourable activities of peace' must always be preferred to 'the pursuits of war' (p. 57; cf. also p. 65). Budé, for example, continues to urge all 'true noblemen' to seek 'death with honour' in battle as a means of 'ennobling the reputation of their name and exalting their arms' (p. 33). But if we turn to the other mirror-for-princes writers, we generally find them agreeing that, as Guevara puts it in *The Dial of Princes*, 'if princes take upon them war for no other cause than to win honour', they will be sure to find this 'an unprofitable conquest' (fo. 174a). Erasmus carries over his hatred of warfare into his advice-book for princes, boldly criticising St Augustine at the end of *The Christian Prince* for conceding that wars can sometimes be just, and pleading with all rulers to recognise

[1] *Othello*, III, iii, 350–1. [2] *Othello*, III, iii, 355.

'how honourable and wholesome peace is', and 'how disastrous and criminal' it is to engage in wars (pp. 249, 251). Similarly, Guevara devotes a special chapter of his *Dial of Princes* to exhorting all 'princes and noblemen' to 'embrace peace and eschew the occasions of war', and includes a letter allegedly written by the Emperor Marcus Aurelius to his fellow-Romans in which he had despairingly asked them to consider 'what fame, what honour, what glory, what victory or what riches' won in warfare can possibly hope to justify the fact that 'so many good, virtuous and wise men' are always lost (fos. 172b, 175a).

HUMANISM AND 'REASON OF STATE'

A number of northern humanists also accused their Italian precursors of having shown an undue readiness to endorse the morally ambivalent notion of 'reason of state'. Some of them, it was suggested, had been too willing to concede that it might on occasion be legitimate for a ruler to discount the virtues, and to engage in a morally reprehensible course of action, if this could be shown either to be in his own best interests, or else to be a means of attaining a greater profit for the community as a whole.

Such a defence of *ragione di stato* had not of course been advanced by any of the more orthodox humanists of *quattrocento* Italy. As we have seen, however, the suggestion that good ends may be used to justify evil means had been a central feature of Machiavelli's political theory, and his principles had to some extent been endorsed by Guicciardini, who was one of the first political writers actually to use the phrase 'reason of state' (Church, 1972, p. 46). Furthermore, the desirability of adopting this less idealised view of princely conduct later became the central theme of an entire *genre* of political writing in sixteenth-century Italy, the most notable contribution to which was Giovanni Botero's treatise of 1589 entitled *The Reason of State*.[1] Botero is careful to distance himself from Machiavelli's increasingly sinister reputation, but the range of topics on which he offers advice is often strikingly similar: there are successive chapters on the treatment of subjects, the means of avoiding insurrections, the importance of defence, the raising of revenues and the maintenance of

[1] For Botero (1540–1617), and for the date of his treatise, see Waley, 1956, p. xv. Ferrari gives a list of similar works which appeared throughout Italy in the following generation, all with the same title, *Reason of State*. One was published by Girolamo Frachetta at Venice in 1592; another by Scipio Chiaramonti at Florence in 1615; another by Federigo Bonaventura at Urbino in 1623; another by Ludovico Zuccolo at Venice in 1626; another by Ludovico Settala at Milan in 1627; and so on through a long list of works which have been characterised by Meinecke as 'catacombs of forgotten literature by mediocrities'; cf. Meinecke, 1957, pp. 67 and n. Church, 1972, has recently rescued Frachetta from oblivion (pp. 64–6), but does not discuss any of the others.

military discipline. There is no doubt, moreover, that Botero is recognisably an inhabitant of Machiavelli's moral universe. His basic concern, he announces at the start of *The Reason of State*, is to consider those actions which a ruler might be said to have a sufficient reason for performing, even though they 'cannot be considered in the light of ordinary reason' (p. 3). Although he begins by discussing the importance of being guided by the principles of justice, he rapidly moves on to the more equivocal notion of political prudence, arguing in Book II that prudence and valour are 'the twin pillars upon which all government must be founded' (p. 34). And the first and basic maxim of prudence which he then proceeds to enunciate is this: that 'it should be taken for certain that in the decisions made by princes, interest will always override every other argument; and therefore he who treats with princes should put no trust in friendship, kinship, treaty nor any other tie which has no basis in interest' (p. 41).

Even before they became aware of this Machiavellian tradition of political argument, the northern humanists had characteristically set themselves to extirpate any temptation to argue that it might be legitimate to ignore the dictates of justice in the hope of attaining some greater benefit. Men often assume, as More admits in *Utopia*, that 'justice is only a low and plebeian virtue', and that 'everything is permissible' to kings (p. 199). This in turn means, as Elyot somewhat wearily agrees in *The Governor*, that the sort of injury 'which is done with fraud and deceit' is 'so commonly practised that if it be but a little it is called policy, and if it be much and with a visage of gravity, it is then named and accounted for wisdom' (p. 168). But this merely serves to show, he immediately adds, that kings and princes have no true conception of their duties. For any appeal to the guile of the fox, or to the 'violence or force of the lion', is not merely 'horrible and detestable' in 'the opinion of man', but is no less so 'in the sight and judgment of God' (p. 168). Elyot is thus completely convinced that even if a mastery of such politic arts could be shown to give rise to 'something that were good', the fact that such practices are 'repugnant to justice', combined with the fact that justice is the mainstay of good government, means that they must be avoided and condemned under all possible circumstances (pp. 169–70).

Erasmus reiterates the same conclusion in *The Christian Prince* – asking the crucial question already raised by Machiavelli in *The Prince*, and arriving at precisely the opposite answer. What is to be done, Erasmus enquires, if you find that 'you cannot defend your realm without violating justice, without wanton loss of human life' and 'without great loss to religion?' (p. 155). Machiavelli had replied that you must be prepared to do anything, however unsavoury, in order to 'maintain your state'. But

Erasmus answers that you must never do anything, even from the best of motives, which may injure the cause of justice. You must instead be prepared to 'give up and yield to the importunities of the age' (p. 155). Between Erasmus and Machiavelli – writing at the same moment from within the same intellectual tradition – lies the greatest of ethical divides. Erasmus assumes, very much in the spirit of Plato's *Republic*, that the fundamental question for the political theorist to consider must be how the rules of justice are to be preserved within the commonwealth. So he stands by the reckless grandeur of the maxim *fiat iustitia, ruat coelum*. But Machiavelli assumes, more in the spirit of a modern utilitarian, that the fundamental question to ask must be how to preserve the commonwealth itself. So he invariably takes his stand on the need for a prudent calculation of likely consequences.

Machiavelli's *Prince* was first printed in 1532, and thereafter the Machiavellian defenders of *ragione di stato* showed an increasing disposition to argue that, if the main aim of the political theorist is to offer genuinely useful advice on how to 'maintain one's state', then the less edifying aspects of prevailing political practice ought to be acknowledged and even recommended rather than merely outlawed. Confronted with this manifest betrayal of what they took to be the proper task of political philosophy, this in turn meant that the next generation of northern humanists became increasingly vociferous in their condemnations of 'reason of state', training their polemics in particular on the infamous figure of Machiavelli, the inventor of the doctrine and the leading 'politic atheist' of the age.[1]

One of the first to denounce Machiavelli by name was Reginald Pole, the hero of Starkey's *Dialogue*, whose *Apology to Charles V*, written in 1539, includes an attack on Machiavelli's political theory as destructive of all the virtues (cf. Raab, 1964, pp. 29–31). Within a few years we find another leading English humanist, Roger Ascham, commenting with similar revulsion in his *Report and Discourse* on 'Machiavelli's doctrine' that one may 'think, say and do whatever may serve best for profit and pleasure' (p. 160). But it was in France that the most systematic of these early attacks appeared, the *Anti-Machiavel* of Innocent Gentillet (1535–88), which was first published at Geneva in 1576 (Rathé, 1968, p. 4). Amongst the maxims Gentillet claims to derive from Machiavelli's writings on government is the suggestion that 'the prudent prince ought not to observe good faith when the observance of it is damaging to his

---

[1] This became the customary term of abuse in discussions about those writers who were said to be 'well practised in Machiavel'. See for example, James Hull, *The Unmasking of the Politic Atheist* (London, 1602), sig. A, 4a; sig. D, 4a; sig. E, 3b. Cf. Raab, 1964, p. 59.

interests' (p. 445). All Machiavelli's maxims, he declares, are 'vicious and detestable in the highest degree', but 'this one wins the prize over all the others concerning our duty towards other men' (p. 445). Gentillet begins his analysis of the proposition in typically humanist style by arguing that the acceptance of such a morality would bring about the destruction of 'all contracts, commerce, distributive justice and politics itself' (p. 446). And he concludes by adding, in the more thundering tones of the Calvinist preacher, that 'perfidy is so detestable to God and to the whole world, that God never allows the perfidious and the breakers of their word to go unpunished' (p. 477).

The same unequivocal rejection of Machiavelli's godlessness can still be found in the next generation in a number of Jesuit as well as humanist writings in Spain. The most extensive condemnation is contained in Ribadeneyra's treatise on *Religion and the Virtues of the Christian Prince*. Ribadeneyra clearly perceives that 'the principal buttress and most firm foundation' of the 'false political thinking' of 'Machiavelli and the politicians' is that the prince must practise 'feigned virtues' while at the same time following the crafty and violent methods of the lion and the fox (pp. 274, 279). It is indeed crucial, Ribadeneyra concedes, to raise the question of 'whether it is possible to tolerate any subterfuge in the prince' (p. 279). And it is right to insist that the main aim of our rulers must always be 'to act with prudence for the good of the commonwealth' (p. 282). But it is still a grave mistake to suppose that this justifies them in accepting 'the pestiferous doctrine of Machiavelli' (p. 282). Their prime duty, Ribadeneyra unswervingly concludes, is to work with 'the law of Christianity' at all times, never stooping to 'break the law of God and his religion' under any circumstances (pp. 282–3).

As the violence of sixteenth-century politics increased, however, and as the exponents of force and fraud increasingly trampled on the defenders of virtue, even the humanists found it difficult to sustain their lofty commitment to the ideal of justice as the only possible basis of political life. Some of them began to slip into allowing that, in cases where the pursuit of justice may actually prove to be incompatible with the preservation of the commonwealth, it may be justifiable to do what is useful rather than what is strictly right.

The first signs of this slide can be detected in the emphasis which a number of humanists began to place on the idea that all rulers have a duty to follow the dictates not merely of equity but also of prudence. An early instance of this implicitly less stringent view of political morality can be found in Budé's *Education of the Prince*. He begins, after describing the different types of rule, by asking how the 'science' of government can be acquired (p. 16). He admits, of course, that this is partly a matter of understanding the rules of justice, and devotes his third chapter to explaining that 'the virtue of justice' is one which 'princes ought to hold in the highest regard' (p. 20). Before turning to this conventional argument, however, he insists in his second chapter that the chief foundation of good government lies in appreciating the value of 'civil prudence' (p. 16). He concedes, moreover, that this somewhat equivocal notion needs to be defined in terms of 'politics' rather than 'moral philosophy', and he adds that is it 'more nearly related to, and has a closer affinity with, the rigour of law than the idea of charitable equity' (pp. 16, 19).

It proved to be a relatively short step from promoting prudence above virtue to endorsing the unequivocally Machiavellian contention that it may sometimes be appropriate, while feigning the virtues, to engage in 'profitable deceit' in order to protect the interests of the commonwealth. The first humanist writer in northern Europe to offer an unashamed defence of this viewpoint was Stephen Gardiner (c. 1483–1555), who developed the argument in the course of an advice-book addressed to Philip II of Spain in the early 1550s.[1] Gardiner's treatise, written while he was Lord Chancellor, takes the form of a history of early Britain, focusing on the reign of Vortigerius, the first king of the Britons, and subsequently on the coming of the Normans in 1066. As in so many humanist histories, however, the narrative is selected and deployed entirely to point up a series of practical lessons for existing rulers, Gardiner's main concern being to offer instructions to Philip – at the time when Mary Tudor had announced her intention of marrying him – on the question of what policies might most profitably be followed in governing the people of England. The result is in part a series of conventional humanist warnings about the need to avoid flatterers, to learn the lessons of history, and to encourage 'men of virtue and good will' (pp. 105, 108, 129). But Gardiner also exhibits an unblinking sense of the limitations of such advice, and proceeds to supplement his argument with an elaborate exposition of a purely Machiavellian conception of reason of state. He first of all agrees with Machiavelli – and quotes him as saying – that while it is vital that the prince should appear to be virtuous, it is not essential that he should actually possess all the virtues. For 'it suffices if the prince is prudent enough to know how to escape the infamy of the contrary vices, when he has to use them, and to avoid those vices which will lose

[1] Gardiner's treatise, entitled *A Discourse on the Coming of the English and Normans to Britain* was written between November 1553 and November 1555, and was evidently presented to Philip II, although it was never published. For these and other details about the manuscript see the Introduction to the excellent edition which has now been produced (Donaldson, 1975, esp. pp. vii, 2, 4).

him his state' (p. 149). Gardiner also agrees with – and quotes – Machiavelli's most characteristic dictum to the effect that a prince 'cannot observe all the things by which we are held good', since 'it is often necessary, to maintain his state, to act contrary to mercy, religion and faith' (p. 149). It is of course useful to appear 'merciful, generous and observant of faith', but 'the conditions of kingship' are such that any ruler who actually feels bound by these requirements will find that they 'bring him more harm than good'. Gardiner's final counsel is thus that while the prince must always keep up an appearance of 'faith, mercy and charity' – since 'these semblances gain him great reputation with the multitude' – he must ensure at the same time 'that he can change what he does like the wind according to the variety of fortune' (p. 149). Not merely the sentiments but the words are entirely taken – though without acknowledgement – from Machiavelli's *Prince* (cf. Donaldson, 1975, p. 16 and n.).

It was in France and the Low Countries, however, that the pure Machiavellian doctrine of *ragione di stato* gained its firmest foothold in the course of the sixteenth century. As the political fabric of both these countries collapsed under the impact of the religious wars, it came to seem less and less realistic to insist that the maintenance of justice must always be given precedence over the preservation of the commonwealth. Writing in Paris during the siege of 1590, Guillaume Du Vair felt compelled to admit that in desperate times it may instead be necessary to treat self-preservation as the first law of nature (pp. 117–62). Similarly, Montaigne in his essay 'Of the useful and the honourable' – written at almost the same time – agreed that the only possible response to what he called the 'divisions and subdivisions that tear our nation apart today' was to admit the place of 'prudence' as well as 'goodness' in government (pp. 600, 603). He himself, he tells us, prefers to keep out of politics and diplomacy, since he has a tender regard for his honour, and dislikes the idea of finding himself betrayed into deviousness and lies. He is quite certain, however, that we ought to acknowledge the indispensable role played by 'lawful vice' in the business of government (p. 604). He recognises, of course, that 'it is certainly unfortunate' when a 'sudden and unexpected accident of state necessity' forces a ruler to 'deviate from his word and his faith' (p. 607). But he sees no alternative to accepting that there are vices which not only 'find their place' in any government, but are useful 'for sewing our society together, as are poisons for the preservation of our health' (p. 600). Nor does he really think it reasonable to regard reason of state as a vice: 'vice it is not', for the prince has merely 'abandoned his own reason to a more universal and powerful reason' which shows him that an apparently evil action 'had to be done' (p. 607).

An even stronger and less apologetic commitment to the same conclusion can be found in the *Six Books of Politics* written by the great classical scholar Justus Lipsius (1547–1606). Lipsius published his *Politics* at Leyden in 1589, having moved there from Antwerp in the hope of avoiding the worst furies of the continuing revolt against Spanish rule (Saunders, 1955, pp. 27–30). His treatise is largely devoted to outlining a series of maxims of prudence, and in Book IV he boldly raises the question of 'whether mixed prudence, to wit, when there is deceit, ought to take place with a prince?' (p. 112). He notes that many moralists 'only approve the path which by virtue leads to honour', but he complains that 'they seem not to know this age', and are little better than children lost in the 'tempestuous sea of the affairs of the world' (pp. 112, 114). The truth is, he briskly asserts, that 'some kinds of persons rage too much against Machiavelli', not seeing that in times of violence and enmity it is obvious that any prince who wishes to survive must learn 'to intermingle that which is profitable with that which is honest' (pp. 113, 114). So Lipsius ends by aligning himself quite explicitly with Machiavelli's doctrine of reason of state. A prince who has 'to deal with a fox', he concludes, is certainly justified in learning to 'play the fox' himself, 'especially if the good and public profit' requires it (p. 113).

Having begun by counselling princes to uphold the dictates of justice at all costs, a number of leading humanists thus found themselves obliged to temper their advice with an increasing admixture of what Lipsius liked to call 'profitable deceit' (p. 197). They excused themselves by claiming that, in admitting the doctrine of reason of state, they were merely recognising the compulsive force of dire necessity. Sometimes they then attempted to tell themselves that this was not really a case of the virtues being discounted, since necessity itself might hopefully be counted as one of the virtues. This is the somewhat cynically optimistic outlook Shakespeare ascribes to John of Gaunt at the start of *Richard II*[1]. Seeking to commiserate with Bolingbroke on his sentence of exile, John's advice is to

'Teach thy necessity to reason thus;
There is no virtue like necessity.'

More commonly, however, the humanists comforted themselves by recalling the proverbial remark made by Publilius Syrius at the time of the final collapse of the Roman Republic: *necessitas non habet legem*, necessity has no law. Foreshadowing the easier political morality of the coming age, they agreed that if necessity cannot be made conformable to the law, the law will have to be made conformable to necessity.

[1] *Richard II*, I, iii, 277–8.

'UTOPIA' AND THE CRITIQUE OF HUMANISM

So far we have concentrated on the extent to which More's *Utopia* can be treated as a relatively typical contribution to the mainstream of northern humanist political thought. It seems essential to begin by adopting this perspective. First of all, this enables us to suggest a corrective to one of the most influential but misleading approaches to the interpretation of *Utopia* – the approach based on claiming that we cannot hope to understand More's argument unless we consider it in the context of a medieval rather than a Renaissance view of political life. R. W. Chambers, for example, insists that *Utopia* must be seen as a 'reaction' against the 'progressive' political ideas of its age, and that More is 'looking back' to 'corporate life in the Middle Ages' in an attempt to revive the dying ideal of 'medieval collectivism' (Chambers, 1935, pp. 132, 258). And Duhamel has gone so far as to add that *Utopia* must be considered 'perhaps the most medieval of More's works', since it is 'thoroughly scholastic in its method of construction' as well as being 'largely medieval in its style and content' (Duhamel, 1977, pp. 234, 246, 249). We have already seen, however, that the range of questions More considers as a political theorist, as well as the range of concepts and arguments he employs, serve to align him very closely with the other northern humanists we have discussed. He accepts, albeit ironically, that the proper stance for a political theorist to adopt must be that of acting as an adviser to princes. He shares the widespread humanist sense of the difficulties involved in offering any genuinely useful as well as praiseworthy political advice. He strongly endorses the general humanist belief in the centrality of the virtues in political life, as well as the more specific assumption that the upholding of justice must be treated as the fundamental aim in any virtuous commonwealth. And he reiterates the well-established humanist commonplace that the key to maintaining a well-ordered political society must lie in furnishing its citizens with the right kind of education in the *studia humanitatis*.[1]

A further reason for beginning with this emphasis on More's place in the mainstream of humanist thought is that – as in the case of Machiavelli's *Prince* – this provides us with a benchmark against which we can now hope to measure More's originality as a political theorist. Admittedly it has sometimes been implied that this further task hardly needs to be performed. Some scholars have treated *Utopia* simply as a contribution

---

[1] For the best discussion of More's essentially humanist allegiances, see Hexter, 1965, pp. lxiv–cv. For a valuable account of More's view of the Christian humanists as the natural teachers of Europe, see Fleisher, 1973, esp. pp. 128–36.

to a more general 'programme' of humanist reform, a programme which More is said to have worked out in close agreement with Erasmus, Vives, Elyot and their various followers.[1] There is no doubt that this interpretation helps to capture much of the spirit of More's book. But it also prevents us from grasping what is arguably one of the most important keys to understanding its meaning: the fact that, while *Utopia* is unquestionably the greatest contribution to the political theory of the northern Renaissance, it also embodies by far the most radical critique of humanism written by a humanist.

To offer this as a key to More's meaning is not of course to suggest that we may now hope to unlock all the doors into his mind. *Utopia* remains an exceptionally puzzling work, with a depth of irony which is sometimes hard to gauge, and a tone which is often disconcertingly variable. Sometimes More manages to strike an apparently effortless note of sweetness and light, as in his attack on the barbarities of hunting, his concern for the equality of the sexes, or his insistence on the value of religious toleration (pp. 129, 171, 219, 227). But sometimes he appears to be commending a remarkably unimaginative way of life in a strangely solemn style. We are told, for example, that the Utopians all wear identical clothes and live in identical houses in identical towns; they all get up at four o'clock in the morning to listen to academic lectures; they are summoned by trumpets to eat in communal halls while improving literature is read aloud to them; and they all go uncomplainingly to bed at eight o'clock in the evening (pp. 113, 121, 127, 129, 133, 141, 145).

More's tone will undoubtedly continue to affect each different reader in almost as many different ways. It is arguable, however, that if we now go on to examine the ways in which he is evidently concerned to criticise rather than endorse the accepted tenets of humanist political thought, this may at least enable us to suggest an answer to one of the major questions that arises out of the description of Utopia given in Book II. When Hythlodaeus comes to the end of his story, the figure of More in the dialogue first of all points out that 'the principal foundation' of the system Hythlodaeus has commended is a 'common life and subsistence – without any exchange of money' (p. 245). He then tells us that while he admires 'many features in the Utopian commonwealth', he 'cannot agree' with all that Hythlodaeus has said, since he thinks in particular that the Utopian system of communism is 'very absurdly established' (pp. 245–7). The question this raises is whether we are intended to sympathise with the figure of More when he finds fault with Hythlodaeus, or with Hythlodaeus when

[1] For this assumption see esp. Hogrefe, 1959, pp. 1 and *passim*. See also Caspari, 1968, esp. p. 127 and Southgate, 1955, esp. p. 254.

he unreservedly commends the Utopian way of life, or whether we are intended to think of their argument as having no clear resolution at all. This is the problem which has provoked the most intense and protracted controversy in modern scholarly discussions of More's work.[1] And this is the problem which it seems possible to reassess if we begin by considering *Utopia* as a humanist critique of humanism.

More's critique may be said to begin with the statement of a humanist commonplace: that virtue constitutes the only true nobility. He observes with exceptional bitterness that nowadays 'the only nobility' is taken to reside in lineage and wealth (p. 169). This means that people 'imagine themselves to be noble and plume themselves on it' simply because they happen to have had the good fortune 'to be born of certain ancestors' who in course of time became 'rich in landed estates' (p. 169). The outcome of this 'strange and sweet madness' is that these supposed nobles are then treated with 'almost divine honours' – are greeted with 'bared head and bent knee' – simply because of their inherited position and their wealth (pp. 157, 169).

This is not to say that More is opposed to the very idea of one man showing another a fitting honour, reverence or respect. He accepts the

---

[1] Two traditions of interpretation converge in accepting that More must have intended us to take Hythlodaeus's commendation of the Utopian system with complete seriousness. One arises out of seeing More as the tragic figure of a socialist born out of his time. This appears to have been Marx's view, and it was introduced into the literature on More by Kautsky, 1927. The same thesis has been revived and developed by Ames, 1949, esp. pp. 5–7, 27. For a discussion of this interpretation, see Avineri, 1962, esp. pp. 268–70. The same conclusion is endorsed by those who think of *Utopia* as an oblique yet serious statement of the ideals of Christian humanism. This is the thesis advanced by Hexter, 1965, esp. pp. lvii–cv. For a discussion of this interpretation see Skinner, 1967, esp. pp. 157–60. It is suggestive, as Allen points out in his study of the prefatory letters in *Utopia*, that all More's humanist contemporaries, and particularly Budé, seem to have assumed that he intended *Utopia* with complete seriousness as an ideal commonwealth. See Allen, 1963, esp. p. 106. The main traditions of interpretation, however, have been founded on assuming that More did not intend us to accept Hythlodaeus's wholehearted commendation of the Utopian way of life. The most usual argument in favour of this conclusion was originally proposed by Chambers: More intended, he argues, to portray the limits of rationalism, with the implication that the Christian commonwealths of Europe would be able to do much better if only they tried as hard. 'The virtues of heathen Utopia show up by contrast the vices of Christian Europe' (Chambers, 1935, p. 127). This contention has been broadly endorsed by a considerable number of scholars: see for example Campbell, 1930, esp. pp. 96–101; Donner, 1945, esp. pp. 68–75; Duhamel, 1977, esp. p. 237; and Fenlon, 1975, esp. pp. 117, 124. For discussions of this interpretation see Surtz, 1957b, esp. pp. 12–15 and Hexter, 1961, esp. pp. 22–6. More recently, a different reason has been suggested for accepting the same conclusion. More is said to be impartially presenting two rival points of view without unequivocally endorsing either of them. This thesis, which makes much of *Utopia*'s formal properties as a dialogue, was first presented by Surtz, 1957a, esp. pp. 182–4, and later developed in Surtz, 1965, esp. pp. cxxxiv–cxlvii. It has also been adopted by Bevington 1961, esp. p. 497. For a discussion of this interpretation, see Skinner, 1967, esp. pp. 155–6. Finally, a further reason which is sometimes given for supposing that More may not have wished us to take Hythlodaeus seriously is that he may not have wished us to take anything in the book seriously. This has been argued by Allen, 1957, esp. p. 156 and by Lewis, 1954, esp. pp. 167–9.

familiar humanist assumption that we ought to seek honour and even glory as the goals of our actions, and stresses that the wise Utopians always 'offer honours to invite men to virtue' (p. 193). His objection is merely to those who 'think themselves better men, the better coat they wear', who 'hold their heads high and think some extra worth attaches to them' because of their wealth, and become indignant if they are not paid the honour which they think to be due to their rank (pp. 167, 169). He invariably speaks of these 'so-called gentlefolk', who are 'commonly termed gentlemen and noblemen', in his heaviest tones of sarcasm (pp. 131, 241). And he always opposes their outlook with the claim that the only true nobility – the only valid title to be honoured or respected – lies in the possession of virtue. We are told that when the Utopians set up statues in commemoration of their 'great men', the reason for awarding them this honour is always that they have shown exemplary virtue and 'done great service to their country' (p. 193). Similarly, we are told that when the Utopians show 'more honour' to their priests than to anyone else, this is because they know that 'nothing but virtue' can help a man to aspire to the priesthood (p. 229).

It has sometimes been argued that, in mounting this attack on the hereditary aristocracy of his day, More's intention was to indicate his support for the eventual inheritors of their power, the protean 'new middle class'. Ames declares, for example, that *Utopia* must be seen as 'a product of capitalism's attack on feudalism, a part of middle-class and humanist criticism of a decaying social order' (Ames, 1949, p. 6). More, it is claimed, was striving to make the world safe for his own shrewd and career-ist kind. But this interpretation appears in the first place to be based on a *non sequitur*. It hardly follows from the fact that More saw himself as an enemy of the aristocracy that he must have seen himself as a friend of the merchants, lawyers and other members of the 'progressive class' described in Ames's account (pp. 5, 37). Furthermore, there is a good deal of textual evidence to suggest that More felt no less alienated from the usual aspirations of these typical members of the bourgeoisie. We are told that the Utopians 'absolutely banish' all lawyers from their commonwealth, on the grounds that they 'cleverly manipulate cases' and 'argue legal points' instead of concerning themselves with the truth (p. 195). And there is of course no place for merchants in the Utopian scheme of things, since the entire economy is run without the use of money, and all credit transactions are handled by the municipal government, with no private citizen ever being trusted to engage in any commercial enterprises (pp. 139, 149).

More's main concern in attacking the hereditary aristocracy seems rather to have been to question the unduly comfortable social philosophy of his fellow humanists. As we have seen, most of them had argued that virtue must be regarded as the only true nobility, but had then neutralised the radicalism of this contention by adding that the virtues are, as it happens, most fully displayed by the established members of the ruling classes. They had thus tended to conclude that the achievement of a virtuous commonwealth is not merely compatible with, but actually presupposes, the upholding of 'degree, priority and place'. By contrast, More insists that if we are genuinely concerned to establish a virtuous commonwealth, we must abandon the pretence that our present-day nobles are men of any real nobility, and abolish the entire structure of 'degree' in the name of ensuring that only men of true virtue are treated with due honour and reverence.[1]

He immediately admits, in a passage of almost desperate irony, that this solution will be dismissed as utterly absurd by everyone, and especially by 'the common people', who have all been brought up to believe that 'nobility, magnificence, splendour and majesty' represent 'the true glories of the commonwealth' (p. 245; cf. Stevens, 1974, pp. 17–18). Nevertheless, he remains adamant. He lays it down at the start of his description of Utopia that 'the one and only road to the general welfare' lies in the abolition of 'degree' in all its forms and 'the maintenance of equality in all respects' (p. 105). He declares that, by putting this principle into practice, the Utopians have been able to institute such a virtuous form of government that 'there is nowhere in the world a more excellent people nor a happier commonwealth' (p. 179). And he concludes by affirming that the structure of their society, based on the abolition of all social hierarchies, is 'not merely the best but the only one which can rightly claim the name of a commonwealth' (p. 237).

He gives two main reasons for insisting that the maintenance of 'degree' can never be compatible with the establishment of a virtuous commonwealth. The first is that, in any hierarchical form of society, it is inevitable that the worst type of people will always gain control. There is a remarkable difference at this point between More's reactions to the nobility and gentry of his age and the reactions of even his closest friends and followers. Erasmus, Vives and Elyot all tended to adopt a thoroughly genial attitude towards the ruling classes. As we have seen, they were anxious to prevent the status of the aristocracy from being eroded by social change, and they offered themselves as therapists to help them adjust to the unfamiliar world of the Renaissance. More, by contrast, never addresses himself to

[1] For More's attack on 'degree', see Hexter, 1964, esp. pp. 960–2, a most suggestive discussion to which I am much indebted.

the 'great lords' and 'governors' of his age except to insult them. He is unyielding in his claim that the sort of qualities which make for success in a hierarchical society will always be detestable. The rich and powerful can be relied on to be 'greedy, unscrupulous and useless', while the poor are generally 'well-behaved, simple' people whose industry is essential to the community, but whose habits of virtue and deference serve to ensure that they are always cheated of their just deserts (p. 105). The inevitable outcome is that 'so called gentlefolk', who 'are either idle or mere parasites and purveyors of empty pleasures' run the commonwealth in their own vile interests, while 'farmers, colliers, common labourers, carters and carpenters without whom there would be no commonwealth at all' are first of all 'misused' by their contemptible masters and are then abandoned to 'a most miserable death' (p. 241).

The other reason More gives for demanding the abolition of 'degree' brings us to the climax of his attack on the social inequalities of his age. No hierarchical society, he claims, could ever in principle be virtuous: for in maintaining 'degree' we encourage the sin of pride; and in encouraging the sin of pride we produce a society founded not on the virtues but on the most hideous vice of all. It is pride, he insists, which lies at the heart of every existing commonwealth. For it is obvious that 'the whole world' would 'long ago' have adopted 'the laws of the Utopian commonwealth, had not a single monster, the chief and progenitor of all plagues, striven against it – I mean Pride' (p. 243). The result is that no existing commonwealth can ever hope to achieve a genuine sense of justice or equity. For pride, that 'serpent from hell' inevitably 'entwines itself around the hearts of men' in any inegalitarian society, and effectively prevents them 'from entering on a better way of life' (pp. 243–5).

Having insisted that the good society must be founded on the eradication of all social distinctions, More turns to the practical question which concerns him most of all: how are the existing structures of 'degree' to be dismantled, so that the triumph of virtue can at last be attained? It is in raising and answering this question that he parts company most radically with his humanist contemporaries.

He begins by asking what it is that serves to uphold existing 'degrees', and serves in consequence to enthrone the sin of pride as the ruling passion of social life. The answer is obvious: it is the unequal distribution of money and private property which enables a few people to lord it over everyone else, thereby feeding their own pride and ensuring that deference is paid not to virtue but merely to rank and wealth. As Hythlodaeus declares at the beginning of his account of Utopia, 'it appears to me that where you have private property and all men measure all things by cash values, there it is scarcely possible for a commonwealth to have justice or prosperity – unless you think justice exists where all the best things flow into the hands of the worst citizens or prosperity prevails where all is divided among very few' (p. 103). More's diagnosis may thus be said to be based on taking with complete seriousness one of the most familiar maxims from St Paul's Epistles: the love of money, he agrees, is indeed the root of all evil.

If this is the sickness, then the cure, he claims, is no less obvious: money and private property must be altogether given up. Having stated the problem, Hythlodaeus is made to state the solution with no less force: 'I am fully persuaded', he goes on, 'that no just and even distribution of goods can be made and that no happiness can be found in human affairs unless private property is utterly abolished. While it lasts, there will always remain a heavy and inescapable burden of poverty and misfortunes for by far the greatest and by far the best part of mankind' (p. 105). Here again, and most dramatically, More is in effect accusing his humanist contemporaries of failing to recognise the implications of their own arguments. As we have seen, it was becoming a commonplace to point to the abuse of private property as the root cause of the prevailing social and economic problems of the age. Erasmus in his *Adages* even anticipated the essence of More's argument by speaking with revulsion of 'riches and their daughter Pride' (p. 328). But More alone follows out the train of thought to its full Platonic conclusion, even citing Plato himself with complete approval for 'his refusal to make laws for those who rejected that legislation which gave to all an equal share in all goods' (p. 105).

The solution More proposes to the problems of Europe is of course the one the wise Utopians have already adopted. They have abolished the use of money, and treat gold with contempt, using it only to fashion 'chamberpots and all the humblest vessels' (p. 153). They have thereby succeeded in abolishing 'degree', and in founding a system in which 'affairs are ordered so aptly that virtue has its reward, and yet, with equality of distribution, all men have abundance of all things' (p. 103). This in turn means they have managed to pluck out the sin of pride from their social life, and to extirpate 'the roots of ambition and factionalism along with all the other vices' (p. 245). They have succeeded, in short, in establishing a virtuous and harmonious commonwealth by following what More sees as the only possible pathway to that highest goal.

It will by now be evident that the starting-point of More's enquiry is one that he shares with many other humanists. He believes that one of the most urgent tasks of social theory is to discover the root causes of injustice and poverty. And he believes, like Erasmus and the later Commonwealth-men, that these evils are mainly caused by the misuse of private property – by 'riches and their daughter Pride'. What is unique about More's *Utopia* is simply that he follows out the implications of this discovery with a rigour unmatched by any of his contemporaries. If private property is the source of our present discontents, and if our basic ambition is to establish a good society, then it seems undeniable to More that private property will have to be abolished. This means that, when he presents his description of Utopian communism in Book II, he must be taken to be offering a solution – the only possible solution – to the social evils he has already outlined in Book I. And this in turn suggests that, in giving *Utopia* the title of 'the best state of a commonwealth', he must have meant exactly what he said.

Further Reading

(1) *Erasmus*. The most informative biography is still the one by Smith, 1923. Phillips, 1949, sketches the general context of Erasmus's thought. Born, 1965, analyses the intellectual background of his *Education of a Christian Prince*. There is a good general survey of Erasmus's political ideas in Mesnard, 1936, Chapter 2. For Erasmus's views on war and peace, see Adams, 1962 and Fernandez, 1973. For a special study of his biblical humanism, see Rabil, 1972.

(2) *More*. For the background of Tudor humanism, see Morris, 1953 (on political theory), Charlton, 1965 (on educational theory) and Caspari, 1968 (a general survey), all excellent accounts. The standard biography of More is by Chambers, 1935. The critical literature on *Utopia* is surveyed in Surtz, 1957a, Chapter 1, Avineri, 1962 and Skinner, 1967. Hexter, 1965, contains one of the most convincing discussions of the meaning of *Utopia*. See also Hexter, 1952 (on the composition of the book) and Hexter, 1961 and 1964 (two valuable interpretive essays). For contrasting interpretations see Ames, 1949 on *Utopia* as a 'middle class' manifesto; Duhamel, 1977, on its 'medievalism'; and Surtz, 1957a and 1965 on the allegedly inconclusive character of More's argument.

Bibliography of primary sources

Adalbert of Samaria, *The Precepts of Letter Writing* [*Praecepta Dictaminum*] ed
Franz-Josef Schmale (Weimar, 1961).

Agrippa, Heinrich Cornelius, *Of the Vanity and Uncertainty of Arts and Sciences*,
ed. Catherine M. Dunn (California, 1974).

Alberti, Leon Battista, *The Family*, trans. Guido A. Guarino, in *The Albertis of
Florence* (Lewisburg, 1971), pp. 27–326.

Three Dialogues, in *Renaissance Philosophy, Vol. I: The Italian Philosophers*,
trans. and ed. Arturo B. Fallico and Herman Shapiro (New York, 1967), pp.
28–40.

Alciato, Andrea, *Brief Annotations on the Last Three Books of Justinian's Code*
[*In Tres Posteriores Codicis Justiniani Libros Annotatiunculae*], in *Opera
Omnia*, 4 vols (Basle, 1557), vol. II, pp. 91–138.

The Extra Ornament of the Law [*Parergon Iuris*], in *Opera Omnia*, vol. II,
pp. 173–494.

On Magistrates and Civil and Military Offices [*De Magistratibus, civilibusque et
militaribusque officiis*], in *Opera Omnia*, vol. II, pp. 495–519.

The Paradoxes of the Civil Law [*Paradoxorum Iuris Civilis*] in *Opera Omnia*,
vol. III, pp. 6–177.

Anonymous, *The Book of Noblesse* (1475), ed. John G. Nichols (London,
1860).

Anonymous, *The Pastoral Eye* [*Oculus Pastoralis*] in *Antiquitates Italicae*, ed.
Lodovico Muratori, 6 vols (Milan, 1738–42), vol. 4, pp. 93–132.

Anonymous of Bologna, *The Principles of Letter-Writing* in *Three Medieval
Rhetorical Arts*, ed. J. J. Murphy (Berkeley, 1971), pp. 1–25.

Aristotle, *The Nicomachean Ethics*, trans. H. Rackham (London, 1926).

The Politics, trans. H. Rackham (London, 1932).

Ascham, Roger, *A Report and Discourse of the affairs and state of Germany* in
Roger Ascham: English Works, ed. William Aldis Wright (Cambridge,
1904), pp. 121–69.

The Schoolmaster, in *Roger Ascham: English Works*, ed. William Aldis
Wright (Cambridge, 1904), pp. 171–302.

Augustine, St, *The City of God against the Pagans*, trans. George E. McCracken,
William M. Green et al., 7 vols (London, 1957–72).

Bartolus of Saxoferrato, *Commentaries on the First Part of the Old Digest* [*In
Primam Digesti Veteris Partem Commentaria*], in *Opera Omnia*, 12 vols
(Basle, 1588), vol. I.

Commentaries on the Second Part of the Old Digest [*In Secundam Digesti Veteris Partem Commentaria*], *Opera Omnia*, vol. II.

Commentaries on the First Part of the New Digest [*In I Partem Digesti Novi Commentaria*], *Opera Omnia*, vol. V.

Commentaries on the Second Part of the New Digest [*In II Partem Digesti Novi Commentaria*], *Opera Omnia*, vol. VI.

Commentaries on the First Part of the Code [*In I Partem Codicis Commentaria*], *Opera Omnia*, vol. VII.

Commentaries on the Second and Third Parts of the Code [*In II and III Partem Codicis Commentaria*], *Opera Omnia*, vol. VIII.

Commentaries on the Last Three Books of the Code [*Super Postremis Tribus Libris Codicis Commentaria*], *Opera Omnia*, vol. IX.

A Tract on City Government [*Tractatus de Regimine Civitatis*], in *Opera Omnia*, vol. XI, pp. 417–21.

A Tract on the Guelfs and Ghibellines [*Tractatus de Guelphis et Gebellinis*], in *Opera Omnia*, vol. XI, pp. 414–17.

A Tract on Tyranny [*Tractatus de Tyrannia*], in *Opera Omnia*, vol. XI, pp. 321–7.

Becon, Thomas, *The Catechism* in *The Catechism . . . with Other Pieces*, ed. John Ayre (Cambridge, 1844), pp. 1–410.

The Jewel of Joy in *The Catechism . . . with other Pieces*, ed. Ayre, pp. 411–76.

Boccalini, Trajano, *I Ragguagli di Parnasso: or Advertisements from Parnassus*, trans. Henry, Earl of Monmouth (London, 1657).

Bodin, Jean, *The Six Books of a Commonweal*, ed. Kenneth D. McRae (Cambridge, Mass., 1962).

Boncompagno da Signa, *The Newest Rhetoric of All* [*Rhetorica Novissima*], in *Bibliotheca Juridica Medii Aevi*, ed. Augustus Gaudentius, 3 vols (Bologna, 1888–1901), vol. 2, pp. 249–97.

The Palm [*Palma*], in Carl Sutter, *Aus Leben und Schriften des Magisters Boncompagno* (Freiburg/Leipzig, 1894), pp. 105–27.

The Siege of Ancona [*Liber de Obsidione Ancone*], ed. Giulio C. Zimolo (Bologna, 1937).

Boniface VIII, *Clericis Laicos* [Bull of 1296], in *Quellen zur Geschichte des Papsttums und des Römischen Katholizismus*, vol. I, ed. Carl Mirbt and Kurt Aland (Tübingen, 1967), pp. 457–8.

Unam Sanctam [Bull of 1302] in *Quellen*, vol. I, ed. Mirbt and Aland, pp. 458–60.

Bonvesin della Riva, *The Glories of the City of Milan* [*De Magnalibus Urbis Mediolani*], ed. F. Novati, in *Bullettino dell' Istituto Storico Italiano* 20 (1898), pp. 5–188.

Botero, Giovanni, *The Reason of State*, trans. P. J. and D. P. Waley (London, 1965).

Brinklow, Henry, *The Complaint of Roderick Mors*, ed. J. M. Cowper (London, 1874).

Bruni, Leonardo, *A Dialogue* [*Dialogus*] in *Prosatori Latini del quattrocento*, ed. Eugenio Garin (Milan, n.d.), pp. 44–99.

A Eulogy of the City of Florence [*Laudatio Florentinae Urbis*] in Hans Baron, *From Petrarch to Leonardo Bruni* (Chicago, 1968), pp. 217–63.

A History of the Florentine People [*Historiarum Florentini Populi*], ed. Emilio Santini, in *Rerum Italicarum Scriptores*, vol. 19 (Bologna, 1926).

The Life of Dante, in *The Earliest Lives of Dante*, trans. and ed. James R. Smith (New York, 1901), pp. 79–95.

On Military Service [*De Militia*], in C. C. Bayley, *War and Society in Renaissance Florence* (Toronto, 1961), pp. 360–97.

An Oration at the Funeral of Nanni Strozzi [*Oratio in Funere Nannis Strozae*] in Stephan Baluze, *Miscellanea*, ed. J. D. Mansi, 4 vols (Lucca, 1761–4), vol. IV, pp. 2–7.

Budé, Guillaume, *Annotations on the Pandects* [*Annotationes in Pandectas*], in *Opera Omnia*, 4 vols (Basle, 1557, republished Farnborough, England, 1966), vol. III, pp. 1–399.

The Education of the Prince [*De l'institution du prince*] (Paris, 1547, reprinted Farnborough, 1966).

Buonaccorso da Montemagna, *A Declamation of Nobleness*, trans. John Tiptoft, in Rosamund J. Mitchell, *John Tiptoft (1427–1470)*, (London, 1938), Appendix I, pp. 213–41.

Carafa, Diomede, *On Rulers and on the Duties of a Good Prince* [*De Regentis et boni principis officiis*], in Johann A. Fabricius, *Bibliotheca Latina*, 6 vols (Florence, 1858), vol. 6, pp. 645–64.

The Perfect Courtier [*Dello Optimo cortesano*] ed. G. Paparelli (Salerno, 1971).

Castiglione, Baldesar, *The Book of the Courtier*, trans. Charles S. Singleton (New York, 1959).

Cicero, Marcus Tullius, *On Invention*, trans. H. M. Hubbell (London, 1949).

On Moral Obligation, trans. John Higginbotham (Los Angeles, 1967).

The Making of an Orator, trans. E. W. Sutton and H. Rackham, 2 vols. (London, 1942).

To Gaius Herennius: On the Theory of Public Speaking, trans. Harry Caplan (London, 1954).

Tusculan Disputations, trans. J. E. King (London, 1927).

Clichtove, Josse, *A Brief Work on the Office of the King* [*De Regis Officio Opusculum*] (1519), in *Opuscula* (Paris, 1526).

A Brief Work on True Nobility [*De Vera Nobilitate Opusculum*] (Paris, 1512).

Colet, John, *An Exposition of St Paul's First Epistle to the Corinthians*, trans. and ed. J. H. Lupton (London, 1874).

An Exposition of St Paul's Epistle to the Romans, trans. and ed. J. H. Lupton (London, 1873).

Compagni, Dino, *The Chronicle*, trans. Else C. M. Benecke and A. G. Ferrers Howell (London, 1906).

Contarini, Gasparo, *The Commonwealth and Government of Venice* (1543), trans. Lewes Lewkenor (London, 1599), in *The English Experience*, No. 101 (Amsterdam, 1969).

Crowley, Robert, *The Voice of the Last Trumpet*, in *The Select Works of Robert Crowley*, ed. J. M. Cowper (London, 1872), pp. 53–104.

The Way to Wealth in *Select Works*, ed. Cowper, pp. 129–50.

Dante Alighieri, *The Banquet*, trans. and ed. Philip H. Wicksteed (London, 1903).

Inferno in *The Divine Comedy*, trans. Charles S. Singleton, 3 vols (Princeton, 1970–5), vol. I (Princeton, 1970).

Monarchy, trans. Donald Nicholl (London, 1954).

Purgatorio in *The Divine Comedy*, ed. Singleton, vol. II (Princeton, 1973).

Diet of Roncaglia : Decrees [Curia Roncagliae] in Monumenta Germaniae Historica : Constitutiones et Acta Publica Imperatorum et Regum, vol. I, ed. Ludwig Weiland (Hanover, 1893), pp. 244–9.

Dudley, Edmund, *The Tree of Commonwealth*, ed. D. M. Brodie (Cambridge, 1948).

Egidio Colonna, *The Rule of Princes [De Regimine Principum]* (Rome, 1607, reprinted Darmstadt, 1967).

Elyot, Sir Thomas, *The Book Named The Governor*, ed. S. E. Lehmberg (London, 1962).

Erasmus, Desiderius, *The Adages*, in Margaret Mann Phillips, *The 'Adages' of Erasmus: A Study with Translations* (Cambridge, 1964).

The Complaint of Peace, trans. and ed. Alexander Grieve (London, 1917).

The Correspondence of Erasmus : Letters 1 to 141 ; 142 to 297, trans. R. A. B. Mynors and D. F. S. Thomson (Toronto, 1974, 1975).

The Education of a Christian Prince, trans. and ed. Lester K. Born (New York, 1965).

On the Philosophy of Christ [The *Paraclesis*], in *Renaissance Philosophy*, vol. II, *The Transalpine Thinkers*, trans. and ed. Herman Shapiro and Arturo B. Fallico (New York, 1969), pp. 149–62.

The Praise of Folly, trans. and ed. Hoyt H. Hudson (Princeton, 1941).

Preface to Laurentius Valla's Annotations to the New Testament, trans. Paul L. Nyhus in Heiko A. Oberman, *Forerunners of the Reformation* (New York, 1966), pp. 308–14.

Ferreti, Ferreto de, *The Rise of the Della Scala [De Scaligerorum Origine]*, in *Le Opere*, ed. Carlo Cipolla, 3 vols (Rome, 1908–20), vol. 3, pp. 1–100.

Fichet, Guillaume, *A Letter to Robert Gaguin [Épitre adressée à Robert Gaguin]*, ed. L.D. (Paris, 1889).

Ficino, Marsilio, 'Introduction to the Commentaries on Plato' in *Opera Omnia*, ed. M. Sancipriano, 2 vols (Turin, 1959), vol. II, pp. 116–18.

Fonte, Bartolommeo della, *An Oration in Praise of Oratory (Oratio in Laudem oratoriae facultatis]* [extracts], in Charles Trinkaus, 'A Humanist's Image of Humanism: The Inaugural Orations of Bartolommeo della Fonte', *Studies in the Renaissance* 7 (1960), pp. 90–147.

Frulovisi, Tito Livio, *The Life of Henry V [Vita Henrici Quinti]*, ed. Thomas Hearne (Oxford, 1716).

Gardiner, Stephen, *A Discourse on the Coming of the English and Normans to Britain*, ed. and trans. as *A Machiavellian Treatise by Stephen Gardiner*, by Peter Samuel Donaldson (Cambridge, 1975).

Gentillet, Innocent, *Anti-Machiavel*, ed. C. Edward Rathé (Geneva, 1968).

Giannotti, Donato, *The Florentine Republic [Della repubblica fiorentina]* in *Opere*, 3 vols (Pisa, 1819), vol. II, pp. 1–279.

The Republic of the Venetians [Libro della repubblica de Viniziani] in *Opere*, vol. I, pp. 1–243.

Guevara, Antonio de, *The Dial of Princes*, trans. Thomas North (London, 1557) in *The English Experience*, No. 50 (Amsterdam, 1968).

Guicciardini, Francesco, *Considerations on the 'Discourses' of Machiavelli on the first Decade of T. Livy* in *Selected Writings*, trans. and ed. C. and M. Grayson (London, 1965), pp. 57–124.

A Dialogue on Florentine Government [*Dialogo del reggimento di Firenze*] in *Dialogo e discorsi del reggimento di Firenze*, ed. Roberto Palmarocchi (Bari, 1932), pp. 1–172.

The Discourse of Logrogno [*Del modo di ordinare il governo popolare*], in *Dialogo e discorsi*, ed. Palmarocchi, pp. 218–59.

The History of Italy, trans. Sidney Alexander (New York, 1969).

Maxims and Reflections, trans. Mario Domandi (New York, 1965).

Heywood, John, *Gentleness and Nobility*, ed. Kenneth W. Cameron (Raleigh, North Carolina, 1941).

Hull, James, *The Unmasking of the Politic Atheist* (London, 1602).

Humphrey, Lawrence, *The Nobles, or Of Nobility* (London, 1563) in *The English Experience*, No. 534 (Amsterdam, 1973).

Innocent III, *On the Misery of Man* in *Two Views of Man*, ed. and trans. Bernard Murchland (New York, 1966), pp. 1–60.

John of Viterbo, *The Government of Cities* [*Liber de Regimine civitatum*], ed. C. Salvemini, in *Bibliotheca Juridica Medii Aevi*, ed. Augustus Gaudentius, 3 vols (Bologna, 1888–1901), vol 3, pp. 215–80.

Landucci, Luca, *A Florentine Diary from 1450 to 1516*, ed. Iodoco del Badia and trans. Alice de Rosen Jervis (London, 1927).

Latimer, Hugh, *Sermons*, ed. J. E. Corrie (Cambridge, 1844).

Latini, Brunetto, *The Books of Treasure* [*Li Livres dou Tresor*], ed. Francis J. Carmody (California, 1948).

Lever, Thomas, *Sermons*, ed. Edward Arber (London, 1870).

Lipsius, Justus, *Six Books of Politics or civil doctrine*, trans. William Jones (London, 1594), in *The English Experience*, No. 287 (Amsterdam, 1970).

Machiavelli, Niccolo, *The Art of War* in *Machiavelli: The Chief Works and Others*, trans. and ed. Allan Gilbert, 3 vols (Durham, North Carolina, 1965), vol. II, pp. 566–726.

The Discourses, trans. Leslie J. Walker, S. J. and ed. Bernard Crick (Harmondsworth, 1970).

The History of Florence in *Machiavelli: The Chief Works and Others*, trans. and ed. Allan Gilbert, vol. III, pp. 1029–435.

The Letters of Machiavelli: A Selection of his Letters, trans. and ed. Allan Gilbert (New York, 1961).

Opere, ed. Sergio Bertelli et al., in *Bibliotheca di classici italiani*, 8 vols (Milan, 1960–5).

The Prince, trans. George Bull (Harmondsworth, 1961).

Manetti, Giannozzo, *On the Dignity of Man*, in *Two Views of Man*, trans. and ed. Bernard Murchland (New York, 1966), pp. 61–103.

Marsiglio of Padua, *The Defender of Peace*, trans. Alan Gewirth (New York, 1956).

Montaigne, Michel de, *Essays* in *The Complete Works of Montaigne*, trans. Donald M. Frame (London, 1957), pp. 1–857.

More, St Thomas, *Utopia*, in *The Complete Works of St Thomas More*, vol. 4, ed. Edward Surtz, S. J., and J. H. Hexter (New Haven, Conn., 1965).

Mussato, Alberto, *Ecerinis* [*Ecerinide*], ed. Luigi Padrin (Bologna, 1900).

A History of the Achievements of the Italians after the Death of Henry VII [*De Gestis Italicorum post Mortem Henrici VII Caesaris Historia*] in *Rerum Italicarum Scriptores*, ed. Lodovico Muratori, 25 vols (Milan, 1723–51), vol. 10, cols. 569–768.

Nenna, Giovanni Battista, *Nennio, or A Treatise of Nobility*, trans. William Jones (London, 1595).

[Nevile, Henry], *The Works of the Famous Nicolas Machiavel* (London, 1675).

Osorio, Hieronymus, *A Discourse of Civil and Christian Nobility*, trans. William Blandie (London, 1576).

The Education and Training of a King [*De Regis Institutione, et Disciplina*] in *Opera Omnia*, 4 vols. (Rome, 1592), vol. I, pp. 253–562.

Otto of Freising, *The Deeds of Frederick Barbarossa*, trans. and ed. Charles C. Mierow and Richard Emery (New York, 1953).

Palmieri, Matteo, *On Civic Life* [*Della Vita Civile*], ed. Felice Battaglia in *Scrittori Politici Italiani*, 14 (Bologna, 1944), pp. 1–176.

Paruta, Paolo, *Political Discourses* [*Discorsi Politiche*], in *Opere Politiche*, ed. C. Monzani, 2 vols (Florence, 1852), vol. 2, pp. 1–371.

Patrizi, Francesco, *The Founding of a Republic* [*De Institutione Reipublicae*] (Paris, 1585).

The Kingdom and the Education of the King [*De Regno et Regis Institutione*] (Prato, 1531).

Petrarch, Francesco, *Il Canzoniere*, ed. Michele Scherillo (Milan, 1908).

The Life of Solitude [*De Vita Solitaria*], trans. and ed. Jacob Zeitlin (Illinois, 1924).

On Familiar Matters [*Familiarium Rerum Libri*], ed. Vittorio Rossi, 4 vols (Florence, 1968).

On Famous Men [*De Viris Illustribus*], ed. Guido Martellotti (Florence, 1964).

On his Own Ignorance and that of Many others, trans. Hans Nachod, in *The Renaissance Philosophy of Man*, ed. E. Cassirer et. al (Chicago, 1948), pp. 47–133.

On Memorable Matters [*Rerum Memorandum Libri*], ed. Giuseppe Billanovich (Florence, 1945).

Pico della Mirandola, Giovanni, *Oration on the Dignity of Man*, trans. Elizabeth Forbes in *The Renaissance Philosophy of Man*, ed. Ernst Cassirer et al. (Chicago, 1948), pp. 223–54.

Piccolomini, Aeneas Sylvius, *The Education of Children* [*De Liberorum Educatione*] in *Opera Omnia* (Frankfurt, 1967), pp. 965–92.

Plato, *Laws*, trans. R. G. Bury, 2 vols (London, 1952).

Poggio Bracciolini, 'Letter to Duke Filippo Maria of Milan' ['Poggius . . . Philippo Mariae . . . Duci Mediolani'] in *Opera Omnia*, ed. Riccardo Fubini, 4 vols (Turin, 1964), vol. III, pt. ii, pp. 179–87.

On Avarice and Luxury [*De Avaritia et Luxuria*], in *Opera Omnia*, ed. Fubini, vol. I, pp. 2–31.

On Nobility [*De Nobilitate*], in *Opera Omnia*, ed. Fubini, vol. I, pp. 64–83.

On the Misery of the Human Condition [*De Miseria Conditionis Humanae*], in *Opera Omnia*, ed. Fubini, vol. I, pp. 88–131.

Pontano, Giovanni, *On Fortune* [*De Fortuna*], in *Opera Omnia*, 3 vols (Basle, 1538), vol. I, pp. 497–584.

270 BIBLIOGRAPHY OF PRIMARY SOURCES

On Liberality [*De Liberalitate*] in *I trattati delle virtù sociali*, ed. Francesco Tateo (Rome, 1965), pp. 1–63.

On Magnificence [*De Magnificentia*], in *I trattati*, ed. Tateo, pp. 83–121.

The Prince [*De Principe*] in *Prosatori Latini del quattrocento*, ed. Eugenio Garin (Milan, n.d.), pp. 1023–63.

Ptolemy of Lucca, *Ecclesiastical History* [*Historia Ecclesiastica*] in *Rerum Italicarum Scriptores*, ed. Lodovico Muratori, 25 vols (Milan, 1723–51), vol. XI, cols 741–1242.

The Rule of Princes [*De Regimine Principum*], in St Thomas Aquinas, *Opuscula Omnia*, ed. Jean Perrier, vol. I (Paris, 1949), Appendix I, pp. 269–426.

Rabelais, François, *Epistle of Dedication to the Medical Letters of Manardus*, in *The Five Books and Minor Writings*, trans. and ed. W. F. Smith, 2 vols (London, 1893), vol. II, pp. 499–501.

The Histories of Gargantua and Pantagruel, trans. J. M. Cohen (Harmondsworth, 1955).

Remigio de' Girolami, *The Common Good* [*De Bono Communi*], extracts trans. in L. Minio-Paluello 'Remigio Girolami's *De Bono Communi*: Florence at the time of Dante's Banishment and the Philosopher's answer to the Crisis', *Italian Studies* II (1956), pp. 56–71.

The Good of Peace [*De Bono Pacis*], ed. Charles T. Davis, in *Studi Danteschi* 36 (1959), pp. 123–36.

Ribadeneyra, Pedro, *Religion and the Virtues of the Christian Prince against Machiavelli*, trans. and ed. George Albert Moore (Maryland, 1949).

Rinuccini, Alamanni, *A Dialogue on Liberty* [*Dialogus de Libertate*], ed. Francesco Adorno in *Atti e Memorie dell' accademia Toscana di scienze e lettere 'La Colombaria'*, vol. 22 (1957), pp. 265–303.

Rolandino of Padua, *A Chronicle of Padua* [*Patavini Chronica*], ed. Philipp Jaffé, in *Monumenta Germaniae Historica: Scriptores*, vol. 19, ed. G. H. Pertz (Hanover, 1866), pp. 32–147.

Romoaldo of Salerno, *Annals* [893 to 1178] [*Annales*], ed. W. Arndt in *Monumenta Germaniae Historica: Scriptores*, vol. 19, ed. G. H. Pertz (Hanover, 1866), pp. 398–461.

Sadoleto, Jacopo, *The Right Education of Boys* [*De Pueris Recte Instituendis*], in *Sadoleto on Education*, trans. and ed. E. T. Campagnac and K. Forbes (Oxford, 1916).

Salamonio, Mario, *The Sovereignty of the Roman Patriciate* [*Patritii Romani de Principatu*] (Rome, 1544).

Salutati, Coluccio, *Epistolae*, ed. Giuseppe Rigacci, 2 vols (Florence, 1741–2).

Epistolario, ed. Francesco Novati in *Fonti per la storia d'Italia*, 5 vols (Rome, 1891–1911).

'Letter to Giuliano Zonarini', trans. in Ephraim Emerton, *Humanism and Tyranny* (Cambridge, Mass., 1925), pp. 300–8.

'Letter to John Dominici', trans. in Emerton, *Humanism and Tyranny*, pp. 346–77.

'Reply' [to Giangaleazzo Visconti] ['Responsio'], in *Rerum Italicarum Scriptores*, ed. Lodovico Muratori, 25 vols (Milan, 1723–51), vol. 16, cols 815–17.

A Treatise on Tyrants, trans. Emerton, in *Humanism and Tyranny*, pp. 70–116.

Savonarola, Girolamo, 'On Political and Kingly Government' ['De Politia et Regno'] in *Compendium Totius Philosophiae* (Venice, 1542), pp. 576–99.

   A Tract on the Constitution and Government of Florence [*Trattato circa il reggimento e governo della citta di Firenze*] in *Prediche sopra Aggeo*, ed. Luigi Firpo (Rome, 1965), pp. 433–87.

Skelton, John, *The Complete Poems*, ed. Philip Henderson (London, 1931).

Smith, Sir Thomas, *The Commonwealth of England* [*De Republica Anglorum*], ed. L. Alston (Cambridge, 1906).

   A Discourse of the Common Weal of this Realm of England, ed. Elizabeth Lamond (Cambridge, 1893).

Starkey, Thomas, *A Dialogue between Reginald Pole and Thomas Lupset*, ed. Kathleen M. Burton (London, 1948).

Sturm, Johann, *The Education of Princes* [*De Educatione Principum*] (Strasbourg, 1551).

Thomas Aquinas, St, *The Rule of Princes* [*De Regno sive De Regimine Principum*] in *Opuscula Omnia*, ed. Jean Perrier, vol. 1 (Paris, 1949), pp. 221–67.

Torre, Felipe de la, *The Education of a Christian King, mainly taken from the Scriptures* [*Institucion de un Rey Christiano, Colegida principalmente de la Santa Escritura*] (Antwerp, 1556).

Valla, Lorenzo, *Annotations on the New Testament* [*In Novum Testamentum . . . Annotationes*], in *Opera Omnia*, ed. Eugenio Garin, 2 vols (Turin, 1962), vol. 1, pp. 801–95.

   A Declamation on the False Donation of Constantine [*De Falso . . . Constantini Donatione Declamatio*], ed. Walther Schwahn (Leipzig, 1928).

   A Letter to Candido Decembrio [*Epistola . . . Candido Decembri*] in *Opera Omnia*, ed. Garin, vol. 1, pp. 633–43.

   In Praise of Saint Thomas Aquinas, trans. M. Esther Hanley, in *Renaissance Philosophy*, ed. Leonard A. Kennedy (The Hague, 1973), pp. 17–27.

   Six Books on the Elegancies of the Latin Language [*Elegantiarum latinae linguae libri sex*], in *Opera Omnia*, ed. Garin, vol. 1, pp. 1–235.

Vegio, Maffeo, *The Education of Children* [*De Educatione Liberorum*], ed. Maria W. Fanning, 2 vols (Washington, D.C., 1933–6).

Vergerio, Pier Paolo, *On Good Manners* [*De Ingenuis Moribus*], trans. in W. H. Woodward, *Vittorino da Feltre and other Humanist Educators* (New York, 1963), pp. 96–118.

   'Letter in the Name of Cicero to Petrarch' ['P. P. Vergerio in nome di Cicerone a Francesco Petrarca'], in *Epistolario di Pier Paulo Vergerio*, ed. Leonardo Smith (Rome, 1934), pp. 436–45.

   On Monarchy or the best form of Rule [*De Monarchia sive de optime principatu*], in *Epistolario*, ed. Smith, pp. 447–50.

Vespasiano da Bisticci, *The Lives of Illustrious Men of the Fifteenth Century*, trans. as *Renaissance Princes, Popes and Prelates* by William George and Emily Waters, Introd. by Myron P. Gilmore (New York, 1963).

Villani, Giovanni, *Chronicle*, in *Cronice di Giovanni, Matteo e Filippo Villani*, ed. D. A. Racheli, 2 vols (Trieste, 1857–8).

Vives, Juan Luis, *On Education*, trans. and ed. Foster Watson (Cambridge, 1913).

Wimpfeling, Jacob, *Agatharchia, that is, Good Government. Or, the Epitome of a*

Good Prince [*Agatharchia, id est, Bonus Principatus: Vel Epitoma boni principis*], in *De Instruendo principe* . . . *Imago*, ed. M. A. Pitsillio (Strasbourg, 1606), pp. 181–206.

Zasius, Ulrich, *A Commentary on Cicero's Rhetoric to Herennius* [*In M. T. Ciceronis Rhetoricen ad Herennium Commentaria*], in *Opera Omnia*, 7 vols (Darmstadt, 1964–6), vol. v, cols 378–490.

An Epitome of the Custom of Fiefs [*Usus Feudorum Epitome*], in *Opera Omnia*, vol. iv, cols 243–342.

Judgments, or Legal Opinions [*Consilia, sive Iuris Responsa*], in *Opera Omnia*, vol. vi, cols 9–576.

Bibliography of secondary sources

Adams, Robert M. (1962), *The Better Part of Valor: More, Erasmus, Colet, and Vives, on Humanism, War, and Peace, 1496–1535* (Seattle, 1962).

D'Addio, Mario (1954), *L'Idea del contratto sociale dai sofisti alla riforma e il De Principatu di Mario Salamonio* (Milan, 1954).

Allen, A. M. (1910), *A History of Verona* (London, 1910).

Allen, J. W. (1957), *A History of Political Thought in the Sixteenth Century* (London, revd. ed., 1957).

Allen, Peter R. (1963), '*Utopia* and European Humanism: the Function of the Prefatory Letters and Verses', *Studies in the Renaissance* 10 (1963), pp. 91–107.

Ames, Russell (1949), *Citizen Thomas More and his Utopia* (Princeton, N.J., 1949).

Anderson, Perry (1974), *Lineages of the Absolutist State* (London, 1974).

Anglo, Sydney (1969), *Machiavelli: a dissection* (London, 1969).

Armstrong, Edward (1932), 'Italy in the time of Dante' in *The Cambridge Medieval History*, ed. J. R. Tanner et al., 8 vols (Cambridge, 1911–36), vol. 7, pp. 1–48.

(1936), 'The Papacy and Naples in the Fifteenth Century' in *The Cambridge Medieval History*, ed. J. R. Tanner et al., 8 vols (1911–36), vol. 8, pp. 158–201.

Avineri, Schlomo (1962), 'War and Slavery in More's *Utopia*', *International Review of Social History* 7 (1962), pp. 260–90.

Bailey, D. S. (1952), *Thomas Becon and the Reformation of the Church in England* (Edinburgh, 1952).

Bainton, Roland H. (1951), 'The *Querela Pacis* of Erasmus, Classical and Christian Sources', *Archiv für Reformationsgeschichte* 42 (1951), pp. 32–48.

Balzani, Ugo (1926), 'Frederick Barbarossa and the Lombard League' in *The Cambridge Medieval History*, ed. J. R. Tanner et al., 8 vols (Cambridge 1911–36), vol. 5, pp. 413–53.

Banker, James R. (1974), 'The *Ars Dictaminis* and Rhetorical Textbooks at the Bolognese University in the Fourteenth Century', *Medievalia et Humanistica*, New Series, 5 (1974), pp. 153–68.

Baron, Hans (1938a), 'Cicero and the Roman Civic Spirit in the Middle Ages and Early Renaissance', *Bulletin of the John Rylands Library* 22 (1938), pp. 72–97.

(1938b), 'Franciscan Poverty and Civic Wealth as Factors in the Rise of Humanistic Thought', *Speculum* 13 (1938), pp. 1–37.

(1955), *Humanistic and Political Literature in Florence and Venice* (Cambridge, Mass., 1955).

(1958), 'Moot Problems of Renaissance Interpretation: an Answer to Wallace K. Ferguson', *The Journal of the History of Ideas* 19 (1958), pp. 26–34.

(1961), 'Machiavelli: the Republican Citizen and the Author of "The Prince"', *The English Historical Review* 76 (1961), pp. 217–53.

(1966), *The Crisis of the Early Italian Renaissance*, 2nd edn. (Princeton, N.J., 1966).

(1967), 'Leonardo Bruni: "Professional Rhetorician" or "Civic Humanist"?', *Past and Present* 36 (1967), pp. 21–37.

(1968), *From Petrarch to Leonardo Bruni* (Chicago, 1968).

Bataillon, Marcel (1937), *Érasme et l'Espagne : Recherches sur l'histoire spirituelle du XVIe siècle* (Paris, 1937).

Bayley, C. C. (1961), *War and Society in Renaissance Florence* (Toronto, 1961).

Bec, Christian (1967), *Les Marchands écrivains : affaires et humanisme à Florence, 1375–1434* (Paris, 1967).

Becker, Marvin B. (1960) 'Some Aspects of Oligarchical, Dictatorial and Popular Signorie in Florence, 1282–1382', *Comparative Studies in Society and History* 2 (1960), pp. 421–39.

(1962), 'Florentine "Libertas": political Independents and 'Novi Cives", 1372–1378', *Traditio*, 18 (1962), pp. 393–407.

(1966), 'Dante and his Literary Contemporaries as Political Men', *Speculum* 41 (1966), pp. 665–80.

(1968), 'The Florentine Territorial State and Civic Humanism in the Early Renaissance', in *Florentine Studies*, ed. Nicolai Rubinstein (London, 1968), pp. 109–39.

Berlin, Isaiah (1972), 'The Originality of Machiavelli', in *Studies on Machiavelli*, ed. Myron P. Gilmore (Florence, 1972), pp. 147–206.

Bertelli, S. (1960), 'Nota Introduttiva' to Niccolo Machiavelli, *Il Principe e Discorsi* (Milan, 1960).

Bevington, David M. (1961), 'The Dialogue in *Utopia*: two sides to the Question', *Studies in Philology* 58 (1961), pp. 496–509.

Boase, T. S. R. (1933), *Boniface VIII* (London, 1933).

Bonadeo, Alfredo (1973), *Corruption, Conflict, and Power in the Works and Times of Niccolo Machiavelli* (Berkeley, Calif., 1973).

Born, Lester K. (1965), 'Introduction' to Desiderius Erasmus, *The Education of a Christian Prince*, ed. Lester K. Born (New York, 1936, reprinted 1965), pp. 3–130.

Bouwsma, William J. (1968), *Venice and the Defence of Republican Liberty* (Berkeley, Calif., 1968).

Bowsky, William M. (1960), *Henry VII in Italy: The Conflict of Empire and City-State, 1310–1313* (Lincoln, Nebraska, 1960).

(1962), 'The *Buon Governo* of Siena (1287–1355): a Mediaeval Italian Oligarchy', *Speculum* 37 (1962), pp. 368–81.

(1967), 'The Medieval Commune and Internal Violence: police power and public safety in Siena, 1287–1355', *The American Historical Review* 73 (1967), pp. 1–17.

Brinton, Selwyn (1927), *The Gonzaga – Lords of Mantua* (London, 1927).

Brucker, Gene A. (1962), *Florentine Politics and Society 1343–1378* (Princeton, N.J., 1962).

Bryson, Frederick Robertson (1935), *The Point of Honor in Sixteenth-Century Italy: an Aspect of the Life of the Gentleman* (New York, 1935).

Bueno de Mesquita, D. M. (1941), *Giangaleazzo Visconti, Duke of Milan (1351–1402)*, (Cambridge, 1941).

(1965), 'The Place of Despotism in Italian Politics' in *Europe in the Later Middle Ages*, ed. J. R. Hale et al. (London, 1965), pp. 301–31.

Burckhardt, Jacob (1960), *The Civilisation of the Renaissance in Italy*, trans. S. G. C. Middlemore: Phaidon Edn (London, 1960).

Bush, Douglas (1939), *The Renaissance and English Humanism* (Toronto, 1939).

Butterfield, H. (1940), *The Statecraft of Machiavelli* (London, 1940).

Cameron, Kenneth W. (1941), *Authorship and Sources of 'Gentleness and Nobility'* (Raleigh, North Carolina, 1941).

Campana, Augusto (1946), 'The Origin of the Word "Humanist"', *The Journal of the Warburg and Courtauld Institutes* 9 (1946), pp. 60–73.

Campbell, W. E. (1930), *More's Utopia and his Social Teaching* (London, 1930).

Cantimori, Delio (1937), 'Rhetoric and Politics in Italian Humanism', *The Journal of the Warburg and Courtauld Institutes* 1 (1937–8), pp. 83–102.

Carmody, Francis J. (1948), 'Introduction' to Brunetto Latini, *The Books of Treasure [Li Livres dou Tresor]* (California, 1948).

Cartwright, Julia (1908), *Baldesare Castiglione, the Perfect Courtier: his Life and Letters 1478–1529*, 2 vols (London, 1908).

Caspari, Fritz (1968), *Humanism and the Social Order in Tudor England* (Chicago, 1954; reissued New York, 1968).

Cassirer, Ernst (1946), *The Myth of the State* (New Haven, Conn., 1946).

Chabod, Federico (1958), *Machiavelli and the Renaissance*, trans. David Moore (London, 1958).

Chambers, R. W. (1935), *Thomas More* (London, 1935).

Charlton, Kenneth (1965), *Education in Renaissance England* (London, 1965).

Church, William F. (1972), *Richelieu and Reason of State* (Princeton, N.J., 1972).

Clark, A. C. (1899), 'The Literary Discoveries of Poggio', *The Classical Review* 13 (1899), pp. 119–30.

Cochrane, Eric W. (1961), 'Machiavelli: 1940–1960', *The Journal of Modern History* 33 (1961), pp. 113–36.

(1965), 'The End of the Renaissance in Florence', *Bibliothèque d'humanisme et renaissance* 27 (1965), pp. 7–29.

Collingwood, R. G. (1946), *The Idea of History* (Oxford, 1946).

Collinson, Patrick (1967), *The Elizabethan Puritan Movement* (London, 1967).

Cosenza, Mario Emilio (1962), *A Biographical and Bibliographical Dictionary of the Italian Humanists and of the World of Classical Scholarship in Italy, 1300–1800*: vol. 5, Synopsis and Bibliography (Boston, Mass., 1962).

Cowper, J. M. (1872), 'Introduction' to *The Select Works of Robert Crowley*, ed. J. M. Cowper (London, 1872), pp. ix–xxiii.

(1874), 'Introduction' to Henry Brinklow, *The Complaint of Roderick Mors*, ed. J. M. Cowper (London, 1874), pp. v–xxii.

Craig, Hardin (1950), *The Enchanted Glass: The Elizabethan Mind in Literature* (1935; reprinted Oxford 1950).

Croce, Benedetto (1945), *Politics and Morals*, trans. Salvatore J. Castiglione (New York, 1945).

Croft, H. H. S. (1880), 'Life of Elyot' in Sir Thomas Elyot, *The Book Named the Governor*, ed. H. H. S. Croft, 2 vols (London, 1880), pp. xix–clxxxix.

Davis, Charles T. (1957), *Dante and the Idea of Rome* (Oxford, 1957).

    (1959), 'Remigio de' Girolami and Dante: a comparison of their conceptions of peace', *Studi Danteschi* 36 (1959), pp. 105–36.

    (1960), 'An Early Florentine Political Theorist: Fra Remigio De' Girolami', *Proceedings of the American Philosophical Society* 104 (1960), pp. 662–76.

    (1965), 'Education in Dante's Florence', *Speculum* 40 (1965), pp. 415–35.

    (1967), 'Brunetto Latini and Dante', in *Studi Medievali* 8 (1967), pp. 421–50.

D'Entrèves, A. P. (1939), *The Medieval Contribution to Political Thought* (Oxford, 1939).

    (1952), *Dante as a Political Thinker* (Oxford, 1952).

Dewar, Mary (1964), *Sir Thomas Smith: A Tudor Intellectual in Office* (London, 1964).

    (1966), 'The Authorship of the "Discourse of the Commonweal"', *The Economic History Review* 19 (1966), pp. 388–400.

Dickens, A. G. (1959), *Lollards and Protestants in the Diocese of York, 1509–1558* (London, 1959).

    (1965), 'The Reformation in England' in *The Reformation Crisis*, ed. Joel Hurstfield (London, 1965), pp. 44–57.

Domandi, Mario (1965), 'Translator's Preface' in Francesco Guicciardini, *Maxims and Reflections of a Renaissance Statesman*, trans. Mario Domandi (New York, 1965), pp. 33–8.

Donaldson, P. S. (1975), 'Introduction' to *A Machiavellian Treatise* (Cambridge, 1975).

Donner, H. W. (1945), *Introduction to Utopia* (London, 1945).

Donovan, Richard B. (1967), 'Salutati's Opinion of Non-Italian Latin Writers of the Middle Ages', *Studies in the Renaissance* 14 (1967), pp. 185–201.

Douglas, Richard M. (1959), *Jacopo Sadoleto, 1477–1547, Humanist and Reformer* (Cambridge, Mass., 1959).

Duhamel, P. Albert (1953), 'The Oxford Lectures of John Colet', *The Journal of the History of Ideas* 14 (1953), pp. 493–510.

    (1977), 'Medievalism of More's *Utopia*', in *Essential Articles for the Study of Thomas More*, ed. R. S. Sylvester and G. P. Marc'hadour (Hamden, Conn., 1977), pp. 234–50.

Dunn, John (1972), 'The Identity of the History of Ideas', in *Philosophy, Politics and Society*, Series IV, ed. Peter Laslett, W. G. Runciman and Quentin Skinner (Oxford, 1972), pp. 158–73.

East, James R. (1968), 'Brunetto Latini's Rhetoric of Letter Writing', *The Quarterly Journal of Speech* 54 (1968), pp. 241–6.

Edelman, Nathan (1938), 'The Early Uses of Medium Aevum, Moyen Age, Middle Ages', *The Romanic Review* 29 (1938), pp. 3–25.

Egenter, Richard (1934), 'Die soziale Leitidee im "Tractatus de bono communi" des Fr. Remigius von Florenz', *Scholastik* 9 (1934), pp. 79–92.

Elton, G. R. (1968), 'Reform by Statute: Thomas Starkey's *Dialogue* and Thomas Cromwell's Policy', *Proceedings of the British Academy* 54 (1968), pp. 165–88.

(1972), 'Thomas More, Councillor (1517–1529)', in *St Thomas More: Action and Contemplation*, ed. Richard S. Sylvester (London, 1972), pp. 85–122.

Emerton, Ephraim (1925), *Humanism and Tyranny* (Cambridge, Mass., 1925).

Febvre, Lucien (1947), *Le problème de l'incroyance au XVIᵉ siècle: la religion de Rabelais*, revd edn (Paris, 1947).

Fenlon, D. B. (1975), 'England and Europe: *Utopia* and its Aftermath', *Transactions of the Royal Historical Society* 25 (1975), pp. 115–35.

Ferguson, Arthur B. (1960), *The Indian Summer of English Chivalry* (Durham, N.C., 1960).

(1963), 'The Tudor Commonweal and the Sense of Change', *The Journal of British Studies* 3 (1963), pp. 11–35.

(1965), *The Articulate Citizen and the English Renaissance* (Durham, N.C., 1965).

Ferguson, Wallace K. (1948), *The Renaissance in Historical Thought* (New York, 1948).

(1958), 'The Interpretation of Italian Humanism: The Contribution of Hans Baron', *The Journal of the History of Ideas* 19 (1958), pp. 14–25.

Fernández, José A. (1973), 'Erasmus on the Just War', *The Journal of the History of Ideas* 34 (1973), pp. 209–26.

Ferrari, Giuseppe (1860), *Histoire de la raison d'état* (Paris, 1860).

Fife, Robert H. (1957), *The Revolt of Martin Luther* (New York, 1957).

Figgis, J. N. (1960), *Political Thought from Gerson to Grotius, 1414–1625* (Torchbook edn New York, 1960).

Fisher, Craig B. (1966), 'The Pisan Clergy and an Awakening of Historical Interest in a Medieval Commune', *Studies in Medieval and Renaissance History* 3 (1966), pp. 143–219.

Flanagan, Thomas (1972), 'The Concept of *Fortuna* in Machiavelli' in *The Political Calculus*, ed. Anthony Parel (Toronto, 1972), pp. 127–56.

Fleisher, Martin (1973), *Radical Reform and Political Persuasion in the Life and Writings of Thomas More* (Geneva, 1972).

Franklin, Julian H. (1963), *Jean Bodin and the sixteenth-century Revolution in the Methodology of Law and History* (New York, 1963).

Garin, Eugenio (1965), *Italian Humanism; Philosophy and Civic Life in the Renaissance*, trans. Peter Munz (Oxford, 1965).

Geerken, John H. (1976), 'Machiavelli Studies since 1969', *The Journal of the History of Ideas* 37 (1976), pp. 351–68.

Germino, Dante (1972), *Modern Western Political Thought: Machiavelli to Marx* (Chicago, 1972).

Gewirth, Alan (1948), 'John of Jandum and the *Defensor Pacis*', *Speculum* 23 (1948), pp. 267–72.

(1951), *Marsilius of Padua: The Defender of Peace* Volume 1: *Marsilius of Padua and Medieval Political Philosophy* (New York, 1951).

Gierke, Otto von (1934), *Natural Law and the Theory of Society, 1500 to 1800*, trans. Ernest Barker, 2 vols (Cambridge, 1934).

Gilbert, Allan H. (1938), *Machiavelli's Prince and its Forerunners* (Durham, N. Carolina, 1938).

Gilbert, Felix (1939), 'The Humanist Concept of the Prince and *The Prince* of Machiavelli', *The Journal of Modern History* 11 (1939), pp. 449–83.

(1949), 'Bernardo Rucellai and the Orti Oricellari: a Study on the Origin of Modern Political Thought', *The Journal of the Warburg and Courtauld Institutes* 12 (1949), pp. 101–31.

(1953), 'The Composition and Structure of Machiavelli's *Discorsi*', *The Journal of the History of Ideas* 14 (1953), pp. 136–56.

(1957), 'Florentine Political Assumptions in the Period of Savonarola and Soderini', *The Journal of the Warburg and Courtauld Institutes* 20 (1957), pp. 187–214.

(1965), *Machiavelli and Guicciardini : Politics and History in Sixteenth Century Florence* (Princeton, N.J., 1965).

(1967), 'The Date of the Composition of Contarini's and Giannotti's Books on Venice', *Studies in the Renaissance* 14 (1967), pp. 172–84.

(1968), 'The Venetian Constitution in Florentine Political Thought', in *Florentine Studies*, ed. Nicolai Rubinstein (London, 1968), pp. 463–500.

(1969), 'Religion and Politics in the Thought of Gasparo Contarini', in *Action and Conviction in Early Modern Europe*, ed. Theodore K. Rabb and Jerrold E. Seigel (Princeton, N.J., 1969), pp. 90–116.

(1972), 'Machiavelli's "Istorie Fiorentine"', in *Studies on Machiavelli*, ed. Myron P. Gilmore (Florence, 1972), pp. 75–99.

(1973), 'Venice in the Crisis of the League of Cambrai', in *Renaissance Venice*, ed. J. R. Hale (London, 1973), pp. 274–92.

Gilbert, Neal W. (1960), *Renaissance Concepts of Method* (New York, 1960).

Gilmore, Myron P. (1952), *The World of Humanism, 1453–1517* (New York, 1952).

(1956), 'Freedom and Determinism in Renaissance Historians', *Studies in the Renaissance* 3 (1956), pp. 49–60.

(1973), 'Myth and Reality in Venetian Political Theory', in *Renaissance Venice*, ed. J. R. Hale (London, 1973), pp. 431–44.

Gilson, Étienne (1924), *The Philosophy of St. Thomas Aquinas*, trans. Edward Bullough (Cambridge, 1924).

(1948), *Dante the Philosopher*, trans. David Moore (London, 1948).

(1955), *History of Christian Philosophy in the Middle Ages* (New York, 1955).

Gray, Hanna H. (1963), 'Renaissance Humanism: the pursuit of Eloquence', *The Journal of the History of Ideas* 24 (1963), pp. 497–514.

(1965), 'Valla's *Encomium of St Thomas Aquinas* and the Humanist Conception of Christian Antiquity', in *Essays in History and Literature Presented by Fellows of the Newberry Library to Stanley Pargellis*, ed. Heinz Bluhm (Chicago, 1965), pp. 37–51.

Grayson, Cecil (1957), 'The Humanism of Alberti', *Italian Studies* 12 (1957), pp. 37–56.

Green, Louis (1972), *Chronicle into History. An Essay on the Interpretation of History in Florentine Fourteenth-Century Chronicles* (Cambridge, 1972).

Green, V. H. H. (1964), *Renaissance and Reformation*, 2nd edn (London, 1964).

Greenleaf, W. H. (1964), *Order, Empiricism and Politics: Two Traditions of English Political Thought, 1500–1700* (London, 1964).

Gregorovius, Ferdinand (1967), *A History of the City of Rome in the Middle Ages*, trans. Annie Hamilton, 8 vols (London, 1909–12, reprinted New York, 1967).

Grendler, Paul F. (1966), 'The Rejection of Learning in Mid-*Cinquecento* Italy', *Studies in the Renaissance* 13 (1966), pp. 230–49.

Grey, Ernest (1973), *Guevara, a Forgotten Renaissance Author* (The Hague, 1973).

Gundersheimer, Werner L. (1966), *The Life and Works of Louis Le Roy* (Geneva, 1966).

—— (1973), *Ferrara: The Style of a Renaissance Despotism* (Princeton, N.J., 1973).

Hale, J. R. (1961), *Machiavelli and Renaissance Italy* (London, 1961).

Hannaford, I. (1972), 'Machiavelli's Concept of *Virtù* in *The Prince* and *The Discourses* Reconsidered', *Political Studies* 20 (1972), pp. 185–9.

Haskins, Charles Homer (1927), *The Renaissance of the Twelfth Century* (Cambridge, Mass., 1927).

—— (1929), 'The Early *Artes Dictandi* in Italy', in *Studies in Medieval Culture* (Oxford, 1929), pp. 170–92.

Hay, Denys (1959), 'Flavio Biondo and the Middle Ages', *Proceedings of the British Academy* 45 (1959), pp. 97–125.

—— (1961), *The Italian Renaissance in its Historical Background* (Cambridge, 1961).

—— (1965), 'The Early Renaissance in England', in *From the Renaissance to the Counter-Reformation*, ed. Charles H. Carter (New York, 1965), pp. 95–112.

Hazeltine, H. D. (1926), 'Roman and Canon Law in the Middle Ages', in *The Cambridge Medieval History*, ed. J. R. Tanner et al., 8 vols (1911–36), vol. 5, pp. 697–764.

Herlihy, David (1967), *Medieval and Renaissance Pistoia* (New Haven, Conn., 1967).

Hertter, Fritz (1910), *Die Podestàliteratur Italiens im 12. und 13. Jahrhundert* (Leipzig/Berlin, 1910).

Hexter, J. H. (1952), *More's Utopia: The Biography of an Idea* (Princeton, N.J., 1952).

—— (1956), 'Seyssel, Machiavelli and Polybius VI: the Mystery of the Missing Translation', *Studies in the Renaissance* 3 (1956), pp. 75–96.

—— (1961), 'Thomas More: on the Margins of Modernity', *The Journal of British Studies* 1 (1961), pp. 20–37.

—— (1964), 'The Loom of Language and the Fabric of Imperatives: The Case of *Il Principe* and *Utopia*', *The American Historical Review* 69 (1964), pp. 945–68.

—— (1965), 'Introduction' to Thomas More, *Utopia* in *The Complete Works of St. Thomas More*, vol. 4 (New Haven, Conn., 1965), pp. xv–cxxiv.

Hirsch, Rudolf (1971), 'Printing and the spread of humanism in Germany', in *Renaissance Men and Ideas*, ed. Robert Schwoebel (New York, 1971), pp. 23–37.

Hirschman, Albert O. (1977), *The Passions and the Interests* (Princeton, N.J., 1977).

Hogrefe, Pearl (1959), *The Sir Thomas More Circle* (Urbana, Ill., 1959).

Holborn, Hajo (1937), *Ulrich von Hutten and the German Reformation*, trans. Roland H. Bainton (New Haven, Conn., 1937).

Hollis, Martin (1977), *Models of Man* (Cambridge, 1977).

Holmes, George (1969), *The Florentine Enlightenment, 1400–1450* (London, 1969).

— (1973), 'The Emergence of an Urban Ideology at Florence', in *Transactions of the Royal Historical Society* 23 (1973), pp. 111–34.

Hornik, Henry (1960), 'Three Interpretations of the French Renaissance', *Studies in the Renaissance* 7 (1960), pp. 43–66.

Huizinga, J. (1952), *Erasmus of Rotterdam* (London, 1952).

Hyde, J. K. (1965), 'Medieval Descriptions of Cities', *Bulletin of the John Rylands Library* 48 (1965–6), pp. 308–40.

— (1966a), *Padua in the Age of Dante* (Manchester, 1966).

— (1966b), 'Italian Social Chronicles in the Middle Ages', *Bulletin of the John Rylands Library* 49 (1966–7), pp. 107–32.

— (1973), *Society and Politics in Medieval Italy: the Evolution of the Civil Life, 1000–1350* (London, 1973).

Hyma, Albert (1940), 'The Continental Origins of English Humanism', *The Huntington Library Quarterly* 4 (1940–1), pp. 1–25.

Janeau, Hubert (1953), 'La pensée politique de Rabelais', in *Travaux d'humanisme et renaissance* 7 (1953), pp. 15–35.

Jayne, Sears (1963), *John Colet and Marsilio Ficino* (Oxford, 1963).

Jones, P. J. (1965), 'Communes and Despots: The City State in Late Medieval Italy', *Transactions of the Royal Historical Society* 15 (1965), pp. 71–96.

— (1974), *The Malatesta of Rimini and the Papal State* (Cambridge, 1974).

Jones, Whitney R. D. (1970), *The Tudor Commonwealth, 1529–1559* (London, 1970).

Jordan, W. K. (1968), *Edward VI*, vol. I, *The Young King* (London, 1968).

— (1970), *Edward VI*, vol. II, *The Threshold of Power* (London, 1970).

Kantorowicz, Ernst H. (1941), 'An "Autobiography" of Guido Faba', *Medieval and Renaissance Studies* 1 (1941–3), pp. 253–80.

— (1943), 'Anonymi "Aurea Gemma"', *Medievalia et humanistica* 1 (1943), pp. 41–57.

— (1957), *The King's Two Bodies: A Study in Medieval Political Theology* (Princeton, N.J., 1957).

Kautsky, Karl (1927), *Thomas More and his Utopia*, trans. H. J. Stenning (London, 1927).

Keen, M. H. (1965), 'The Political Thought of the Fourteenth Century Civilians', in *Trends in Medieval Political Thought*, ed. Beryl Smalley (Oxford, 1965), pp. 105–26.

Kelley, Donald R. (1966), 'Legal Humanism and the Sense of History', *Studies in the Renaissance* 13 (1966), pp. 184–99.

— (1970), *Foundations of Modern Historical Scholarship* (New York, 1970).

Kisch, Guido (1961), 'Humanistic Jurisprudence', *Studies in the Renaissance* 8 (1961), pp. 71–87.

Knapke, Paul J. (1939), *Frederick Barbarossa's Conflict with the Papacy* (Washington, D.C., 1939).

Knowles, David (1962), *The Evolution of Medieval Thought* (London, 1962).

Kontos, Alkis (1972). 'Success and Knowledge in Machiavelli', in *The Political Calculus*, ed. Anthony Parel (Toronto, 1972), pp. 83–100.

Kristeller, Paul Oskar (1956), *Studies in Renaissance Thought and Letters* (Rome, 1956).

(1961), *Renaissance Thought* I: *The Classic, Scholastic and Humanistic Strains* (New York, 1961).

(1962a), 'Studies on Renaissance Humanism during the Last Twenty Years', *Studies in the Renaissance* 9 (1962), pp. 7–30.

(1962b), 'The European Diffusion of Italian Humanism', *Italica* 39 (1962), pp. 1–20.

(1965), *Renaissance Thought* II: *Papers on Humanism and the Arts* (New York, 1965).

La Brosse, O. de (1965), *Le Pape et le concile* (Paris, 1965).

Lagarde, Georges de (1948), *La Naissance de l'esprit laique au déclin du moyen age*: vol. II: *Marsile de Padoue*, 2nd edn (Paris, 1948).

Lamond, Elizabeth (1893), 'Introduction' to *A Discourse of the Common Weal of this Realm of England*, ed. Elizabeth Lamond (Cambridge, 1893), pp. ix–lxxii.

Larner, John (1965), *The Lords of Romagna* (London, 1965).

(1971), *Culture and Society in Italy, 1290–1420* (London, 1971).

Lecler, J. (1960), *Toleration and the Reformation*, trans. T. L. Westow, 2 vols (London, 1960).

Lehmberg, Stanford E. (1960), *Sir Thomas Elyot, Tudor Humanist* (Austin, Texas, 1960).

(1961), 'English Humanists, the Reformation and the Problem of Counsel', *Archiv für Reformationsgeschichte* 52 (1961), pp. 74–90.

(1962), 'Introduction' to Sir Thomas Elyot, *The Book Named the Governor*, ed. S. E. Lehmberg (London, 1962).

Lewis, C. S. (1954), *English Literature in the Sixteenth Century, excluding Drama* (Oxford, 1954).

Lida de Malkiel, Maria Rosa (1968), *L'Idée de la gloire dans la tradition occidentale*, trans. from the Spanish by Sylvia Roubaud (Paris, 1968).

Limentani, U. (1965), 'Dante's Political Thought', in *The Mind of Dante*, ed. U. Limentani (Cambridge, 1965), pp. 113–37.

Lyell, James P. R. (1917), *Cardinal Ximenes . . . with an account of the Complutensian Polyglot Bible* (London, 1917).

Macaulay, Thomas Babington (1907), 'Machiavelli', in *Critical and Historical Essays*, ed. A. J. Grieve, 2 vols (London, 1907), vol. II, pp. 1–37.

McConica, James Kelsey (1965), *English Humanists and Reformation Politics* (Oxford, 1965).

MacIntyre, Alasdair (1966), *A Short History of Ethics* (New York, 1966).

(1971), *Against The Self-Images of the Age* (London, 1971).

McKeon, Richard (1942), 'Rhetoric in the Middle Ages', *Speculum* 17 (1942), pp. 1–32.

McNeil, David O. (1975), *Guillaume Budé and Humanism in the reign of Francis I* (Geneva, 1975).

Major, John M. (1964), *Sir Thomas Elyot and Renaissance Humanism* (Lincoln, Nebraska, 1964).

Mallett, Michael (1974), *Mercenaries and their Masters* (London, 1974).

Marrou, H. I. (1956), *A History of Education in Antiquity*, trans. G. Lamb (London, 1956).

Martines, Lauro (1963), *The Social World of the Florentine Humanists, 1390–1460* (Princeton, N.J., 1963).

Mattingly, Garrett (1961), 'Some Revisions of the Political History of the Renaissance', in *The Renaissance*, ed. Tinsley Helton (Madison, Wisc., 1961).

Mazzeo, Joseph A. (1967), *Renaissance and Revolution: The Remaking of European Thought* (London, 1967).

Meinecke, Friedrich (1957), *Machiavellism*, trans. Douglas Scott (London, 1957).

Menut, Albert D. (1943), 'Castiglione and the Nicomachean Ethics', *Publications of the Modern Language Association* 58 (1943), pp. 308–21.

Mesnard, Pierre (1936), *L'Essor de la philosophie politique au XVIᵉ siècle* (Paris, 1936).

Minio-Paluello, L. (1956), 'Remigio Girolami's *De Bono Communi*: Florence at the time of Dante's Banishment and the Philosopher's Answer to the Crisis', *Italian Studies* 11 (1956), pp. 56–71.

Mitchell, Rosamund J. (1936), 'English Law Students at Bologna in the Fifteenth Century', *The English Historical Review* 51 (1936), pp. 270–87.

(1938), *John Tiptoft (1427–1470)* (London, 1938).

Mommsen, Theodor E. (1959a), 'Petrarch's Conception of the "Dark Ages"', in *Medieval and Renaissance Studies*, ed. Eugene F. Rice (Ithaca, 1959), pp. 106–29.

(1959b), 'Petrarch and the Story of the Choice of Hercules', *Medieval and Renaissance Studies*, ed. Rice, pp. 175–96.

(1959c), 'St. Augustine and the Christian Idea of Progress: the Background of the City of God', *Medieval and Renaissance Studies*, ed. Rice, pp. 265–98.

Monfasini, John (1976), *George of Trebizond* (Leiden, 1976).

Monzani, C. (1852), 'Della vita e delle opere di Paolo Paruta', in *Opere politiche di Paolo Paruta*, 2 vols (Florence, 1852), I, pp. v–c.

Morris, Christopher (1953), *Political Thought in England: Tyndale to Hooker* (London, 1953).

Munz, Peter (1969), *Frederick Barbarossa: A Study in Medieval Politics* (London, 1969).

Murphy, James J. (1971a), *Medieval Rhetoric: A Select Bibliography* (Toronto, 1971).

(1971b), *Three Medieval Rhetorical Arts* (Berkeley, Calif., 1971).

(1974), *Rhetoric in the Middle Ages* (Berkeley, Calif., 1974).

Nauert, Charles G. (1965), *Agrippa and the Crisis of Renaissance Thought*, in *Illinois Studies in the Social Sciences* 55 (Urbana, Ill., 1965).

Nolhac, Pierre de (1925), *Érasme et l'Italie* (Paris, 1925).

Nordström, Johan (1933), *Moyen Âge et Renaissance*, trans. T. Hammar (Paris, 1933).

Noreña, Carlos G. (1970), *Juan Luis Vives* (The Hague, 1970).

Offler, H. S. (1956), 'Empire and Papacy: the Last Struggle', *Transactions of the Royal Historical Society*, 5th Series, 6 (1956), pp. 21–47.

Pacaut, Marcel (1956), *Alexandre III: Étude sur la conception du pouvoir pontifical dans sa pensée et dans son œuvre* (Paris, 1956).

Paetow, Louis J. (1910), *The Arts Course at Medieval Universities* (Urbana-Champaign, Ill., 1910).

Panofsky, Erwin (1960), *Renaissance and Renascences in Western Art* (Stockholm, 1960).

Parks, George B. (1954), *The English Traveler to Italy: the Middle Ages (to 1525)* (Stanford, Calif., 1954).

Partner, Peter (1972), *The Lands of St Peter: the Papal State in the Middle Ages and the Early Renaissance* (London, 1972).

Patch, Howard R. (1922), *The Tradition of the Goddess Fortuna* (Northampton, Mass., 1922).

Phillips, Margaret Mann (1949), *Erasmus and the Northern Renaissance* (London, 1949).

(1964), *The 'Adages' of Erasmus: A Study with Translations* (Cambridge, 1964).

Phillips, Mark (1977), *Francesco Guicciardini: the Historian's Craft* (Toronto, 1977).

Plamenatz, J. P. (1963), *Man and Society*, 2 vols (London, 1963).

Pocock, J. G. A. (1957), *The Ancient Constitution and the Feudal Law* (Cambridge, 1957).

(1971), *Politics, Language and Time* (New York, 1971).

(1975), *The Machiavellian Moment* (Princeton, N.J., 1975).

Previté-Orton, C. W. (1929), 'Italy, 1250–1290', in *The Cambridge Medieval History*, ed. J. R. Tanner et al., 8 vols (Cambridge, 1911–36), vol. 6, pp. 166–204.

(1935), 'Marsilius of Padua', *Proceedings of the British Academy* 21 (1935), pp. 137–83.

Price, Russell (1973), 'The Senses of *Virtù* in Machiavelli', *The European Studies Review* 3 (1973), pp. 315–45.

Pullan, B. (1973), *A History of Early Renaissance Italy* (London, 1973).

Raab, Felix (1964), *The English Face of Machiavelli* (London, 1964).

Rabil, Albert (1972), *Erasmus and the New Testament: The Mind of a Christian Humanist* (San Antonio, 1972).

Rand, E. K. (1929), 'The Classics in the Thirteenth Century', *Speculum* 4 (1929), pp. 249–69.

Rathé, C. Edward (1968), 'Introduction', to Innocent Gentillet, *Anti-Machiavel* (Geneva, 1968).

Redondo, A. (1976), *Antonio de Guevara (1480?–1545) et l'Espagne de son temps* (Geneva, 1976).

Reeves, Marjorie (1965), 'Marsiglio of Padua and Dante Alighieri', in *Trends in Medieval Political Thought*, ed. Beryl Smalley (Oxford, 1965), pp. 86–104.

Renaudet, Augustin (1922), *Le Concile gallican de Pise-Milan. Documents Florentines (1510–1512)* (Paris, 1922),

(1953), *Préréforme et humanisme à Paris pendant les premières guerres d'Italie (1494–1517)* (2nd edn, Paris, 1953).

Reynolds, Beatrice R. (1955), 'Latin Historiography: a Survey 1400–1600', *Studies in the Renaissance* 2 (1955), pp. 7–66.

Rice, Eugene F. (1952), 'John Colet and the Annihilation of the Natural', *Harvard Theological Review* 45 (1952), pp. 141–63.

(1958), *The Renaissance Idea of Wisdom* (Cambridge, Mass., 1958).

Richardson, Brian (1971), 'Pontano's *De Prudentia* and Machiavelli's *Discorsi*', *Bibliothèque d'humanisme et renaissance* 33 (1971), pp. 353–7.

(1972), 'The Structure of Machiavelli's *Discorsi*', *Italica* 49 (1972), pp. 460–71.

Ridolfi, Roberto (1959), *The Life of Girolamo Savonarola*, trans. Cecil Grayson (London, 1959).

(1963), *The Life of Niccolo Machiavelli*, trans. Cecil Grayson (London, 1963).

(1967), *The Life of Francesco Guicciardini*, trans. Cecil Grayson (London, 1967).

Riesenberg, Peter (1956), *Inalienability of Sovereignty in Medieval Political Thought* (New York, 1956).

(1969), 'Civism and Roman Law in Fourteenth-Century Italian Society', in *Explorations in Economic History* 7 (1969), pp. 237–54.

Robathan, Dorothy M. (1970), 'Flavio Biondo's *Roma Instaurata*', *Medievalia et Humanistica*, New Series vol. 1 (1970), pp. 203–16.

Robey, David (1973), 'P. P. Vergerio the Elder: Republicanism and civic values in the work of an early humanist', *Past and Present* 58 (1973), pp. 3–37.

Rousseau, G. S. (1965), 'The *Discorsi* of Machiavelli: History and Theory', *Cahiers d'histoire mondiale* 9 (1965–6), pp. 143–61.

Rubinstein, Nicolai (1942), 'The Beginnings of Political Thought in Florence', *The Journal of the Warburg and Courtauld Institutes* 5 (1942), pp. 198–227.

(1952), 'Florence and the Despots: some Aspects of Florentine Diplomacy in the fourteenth century', *Transactions of the Royal Historical Society* (1952), pp. 21–45.

(1957), 'Some Ideas on Municipal Progress and Decline in the Italy of the Communes', in *Fritz Saxl, 1890–1948: A Volume of Memorial Essays*, ed. D. J. Gordon (London, 1957), pp. 165–83.

(1958), 'Political Ideas in Sienese Art. The Frescoes by Ambrogio Lorenzetti and Taddeo di Bartolo in the Palazzo Pubblico', *Journal of the Warburg and Courtauld Institutes* 21 (1958), pp. 179–207.

(1960), 'Politics and Constitution in Florence at the end of the Fifteenth Century', in *Italian Renaissance Studies*, ed. E. F. Jacob (London, 1960), pp. 148–83.

(1965a), 'Introduction' to Francesco Guicciardini, *Maxims and Reflections* (New York, 1965), pp. 7–32.

(1965b), 'Marsilius of Padua and Italian Political Thought of his Time', in *Europe in the Late Middle Ages*, ed. J. R. Hale, J. R. L. Highfield and B. Smalley (London, 1965), pp. 44–75.

(1966), *The Government of Florence under the Medici (1434 to 1494)* (Oxford, 1966).

(1968), 'Florentine Constitutionalism and Medici Ascendancy in the Fifteenth Century', in *Florentine Studies*, ed. Nicolai Rubinstein (London, 1968), pp. 442–62.

Ruggieri, Paul G. (1964), *Florence in the Age of Dante* (Norman, Oklahoma, 1964).

Runciman, Steven (1958), *The Sicilian Vespers: a History of the Mediterranean World in the Later Thirteenth Century* (Cambridge, 1958).

Ryan, Lawrence V. (1972), 'Book Four of Castiglione's *Courtier:* Climax or Afterthought', *Studies in the Renaissance* 19 (1972), pp. 156–79.

Saint-Laurent, J. de B. de (1970), *Les Idées monétaires et commerciales de Jean Bodin* (Paris, 1907; reprinted New York, 1970).

Salvemini, Gaetano (1903), 'Il "Liber de regimine civitatum" di Giovanni da Viterbo', in *Giornale Storico della Letteratura Italiana* 41 (1903), pp. 284–303.

Sandys, John Edwin (1964), *A History of Classical Scholarship*, 3 vols (Cambridge, 1903–8; reprinted New York, 1964).

Saunders, Jason L. (1955), *Justus Lipsius: the Philosophy of Renaissance Stoicism* (New York, 1955).

Schellhase, Kenneth C. (1976), *Tacitus in Renaissance Political Thought* (Chicago, 1976).

Schevill, Ferdinand (1936), *A History of Florence* (New York, 1936).

Schipa, Michelangelo (1929), 'Italy and Sicily under Frederick II', in *The Cambridge Medieval History*, ed. J. R. Tanner et al., 8 vols (Cambridge, 1911–36), vol. VI, pp. 131–65.

Schwarz, W. (1955), *Principles and Problems of Biblical Translation* (Cambridge, 1955).

Seigel, Jerrold E. (1966), '"Civic Humanism" or Ciceronian Rhetoric? The Culture of Petrarch and Bruni', *Past and Present* 34 (1966), pp. 3–48.

— (1968), *Rhetoric and Philosophy in Renaissance Humanism* (Princeton, N.J., 1968).

Shapiro, Marianne (1975), 'Mirror and Portrait: the structure of *Il libro del Cortegiano*', *The Journal of Medieval and Renaissance Studies* 5 (1975), pp. 37–61.

Sheedy, Anna T. (1942), *Bartolus on Social Conditions in the Fourteenth Century* (New York, 1942).

Shennan, J. H. (1974), *The Origins of the Modern European State, 1450–1725* (London, 1974).

Simon, Joan (1966), *Education and Society in Tudor England* (Cambridge, 1966).

Simone, Franco (1969), *The French Renaissance. Medieval Tradition and Italian Influence in Shaping the Renaissance in France*, trans. H. Gaston Hall (London, 1969).

Sismondi, J. C. L. S. de (1826), *Histoire des Républiques Italiennes du moyen âge*, 16 vols (Paris, 1826).

Skinner, Quentin (1965), 'History and Ideology in the English Revolution', *The Historical Journal* 8 (1965), pp. 151–78.

— (1966), 'The Limits of Historical Explanations', *Philosophy* 41 (1966), pp. 199–215.

— (1967), 'More's *Utopia*', *Past and Present* 38 (1967), pp. 153–68.

— (1969), 'Meaning and Understanding in the History of Ideas', *History and Theory* 8 (1969), pp. 3–53.

— (1970), 'Conventions and the Understanding of Speech Acts', *The Philosophical Quarterly* 20 (1970), pp. 118–38.

(1971), 'On Performing and Explaining Linguistic Actions', *The Philosophical Quarterly* 21 (1971), pp. 1–21.

(1972a), ' "Social Meaning" and the Explanation of Social Action', in *Philosophy, Politics and Society*, Series IV, ed. Peter Laslett, W. G. Runciman and Quentin Skinner (Oxford, 1972), pp. 136–57.

(1972b), 'Motives, Intentions and the Interpretation of Texts', *New Literary History* 3 (1972), pp. 393–408.

(1974a), 'The Principles and Practice of Opposition: The Case of Bolingbroke versus Walpole', in *Historical Perspectives*, ed. Neil McKendrick (London, 1974), pp. 93–128.

(1974b), 'Some Problems in the Analysis of Political Thought and Action', *Political Theory* 2 (1974), pp. 277–303.

(1975), 'Hermeneutics and the Role of History', *New Literary History* 7 (1975–6), 209–32.

Smith, Pauline M. (1966), *The Anti-Courtier Trend in Sixteenth Century French Literature* (Geneva, 1966).

Smith, Preserved (1923), *Erasmus: A Study of his Life, Ideals, and Place in History* (London, 1923).

Sorrentino, Andrea (1936), *Storia dell' Antimachiavellismo Europeo* (Naples, 1936).

Southgate, W. M. (1955), 'Erasmus: Christian Humanism and Political Theory', *History* 40 (1955), pp. 240–54.

Spitz, Lewis W. (1957), *Conrad Celtis, The German Arch-Humanist* (Cambridge, Mass., 1957).

(1963), *The Religious Renaissance of the German Humanists* (Cambridge, Mass., 1963).

Starn, Randolph (1968), *Donato Giannotti and his 'Epistolae'* (Geneva, 1968).

(1972), ' "Ante Machiavel": Machiavelli and Giannotti', in *Studies on Machiavelli*, ed. Myron P. Gilmore (Florence, 1972), pp. 285–93.

Starnes, D. T. (1927), 'Shakespeare and Elyot's *Governour*', *The University of Texas Bulletin: Studies in English* 7 (1927), pp. 112–32.

Stevens, Irma Ned (1974), 'Aesthetic Distance in the *Utopia*', *Moreana* 11 (1974), 13–24.

Strauss, Leo (1958), *Thoughts on Machiavelli* (Glencoe, Ill., 1958).

Struever, Nancy S. (1970), *The Language of History in the Renaissance* (Princeton, N.J., 1970).

Surtz, Edward (1957a), *The Praise of Pleasure* (Cambridge, Mass., 1957).

(1957b), *The Praise of Wisdom* (Chicago, 1957).

(1965), 'Introduction' to Thomas More, *Utopia*, in *The Complete Works of St. Thomas More*, vol. 4 (New Haven, Conn., 1965), pp. cxxv–cxciv.

Tenenti, A. (1974), 'Le *Momus* dans l'oeuvre de Leon Battista Alberti', in *Il Pensiero Politico* 7 (1974), pp. 321–33.

Tilley, Arthur (1918), *The Dawn of the French Renaissance* (Cambridge, 1918).

Trinkaus, Charles E. (1940), *Adversity's Noblemen: The Italian Humanists on Happiness* (New York, 1940).

(1960), 'A Humanist's Image of Humanism: the Inaugural Orations of Bartolommeo della Fonte', *Studies in the Renaissance* 7 (1960), pp. 90–147.

(1970), 'In Our Image and Likeness': Humanity and Divinity in Italian Humanist Thought, 2 vols (London, 1970).

Ullman, B. L. (1941), 'Some Aspects of the Origin of Italian humanism', Philological Quarterly 20 (1941), pp. 212–23.

(1946), 'Leonardo Bruni and Humanistic Historiography', Medievalia et Humanistica 4 (1946), pp. 45–61.

(1963), The Humanism of Coluccio Salutati (Padua, 1963).

Ullmann, Walter (1949), 'The development of the Medieval Idea of Sovereignty', The English Historical Review 64 (1949), pp. 1–33.

(1962), 'De Bartoli Sententia: Concilium repraesentat mentem populi', in Bartolo da Sassoferrato: Studi e Documenti, 2 vols (Milan, 1962), II, pp. 705–33.

(1965), A History of Political Thought: The Middle Ages (Harmondsworth, 1965).

(1972), A Short History of the Papacy in the Middle Ages (London, 1972).

Van Cleve, Thomas C. (1972), The Emperor Frederick II of Hohenstaufen (Oxford, 1972).

Viard, Paul Émile (1926), André Alciat (Paris, 1926).

Vinogradoff, Paul (1929), Roman Law in Medieval Europe (2nd edn, Oxford, 1929).

Waley, Daniel (1952), Medieval Orvieto: The Political History of an Italian City-State, 1157–1334 (Cambridge, 1952).

(1956), 'Introduction' to Giovanni Botero, The Reason of State, trans. P. J. and D. P. Waley (London, 1956), pp. vii–xi.

(1961), The Papal State in the Thirteenth Century (London, 1961).

(1969), The Italian City-Republics (London, 1969).

Walzer, Michael (1966), The Revolution of the Saints (London, 1966).

Watt, John A. (1965), The Theory of Papal Monarchy in the Thirteenth Century (London, 1965).

Weber, Max (1968), Economy and Society, ed. Guenther Roth and Claus Wittich, 3 vols (New York, 1968).

Weinstein, Donald (1970), Savonarola and Florence: Prophecy and patriotism in the Renaissance (Princeton, N.J., 1970).

Weisinger, Herbert (1943), 'The Self-Awareness of the Renaissance as a Criterion of the Renaissance', Papers of the Michigan Academy of Science, Arts and Letters 29 (1943), pp. 561–7.

(1944), 'Who Began the Revival of Learning? The Renaissance Point of View', Papers of the Michigan Academy of Science, Arts and Letters 30 (1944), pp. 625–38.

(1945a), 'The Renaissance Theory of the Reaction against the Middle Ages as a cause of the Renaissance', Speculum 20 (1945), pp. 461–7.

(1945b), 'Ideas of History during the Renaissance', The Journal of the History of Ideas 6 (1945), pp. 415–35.

Weiss, Roberto (1938), 'Cornelio Vitelli in France and England', The Journal of the Warburg Institute 2 (1938–9), pp. 219–26.

(1947), The Dawn of Humanism in Italy (London, 1947).

(1951), 'Lovato Lovati, 1241–1309', in Italian Studies 6 (1951), pp. 3–28.

(1957), *Humanism in England During the Fifteenth Century* (2nd edn, Oxford, 1957).

(1964), *The Spread of Italian Humanism* (London, 1964).

(1969), *The Renaissance Discovery of Classical Antiquity* (Oxford, 1969).

Whitfield, J. H. (1943), *Petrarch and the Renascence* (Oxford, 1943).

(1947), *Machiavelli* (Oxford, 1947).

Wieruszowski, Helene (1971a), 'A Twelfth-Century *Ars Dictaminis* in the Barberini Collection of the Vatican Library', in *Politics and Culture in Medieval Spain and Italy* (Rome, 1971), pp. 331–45.

(1971b), '*Ars Dictaminis* in the time of Dante', in *Politics and Culture in Medieval Spain and Italy*, pp. 359–77.

(1971c), 'Arezzo as a Center of Learning and Letters in the Thirteenth Century', in *Politics and Culture in Medieval Spain and Italy*, pp. 387–474.

(1971d), 'Rhetoric and the Classics in Italian Education of the Thirteenth Century', in *Politics and Culture in Medieval Spain and Italy*, pp. 589–627.

Wilcox, Donald J. (1969), *The Development of Florentine Humanist Historiography in the Fifteenth Century* (Cambridge, Mass., 1969).

Wilkins, Ernest H. (1943), 'The Coronation of Petrarch', *Speculum* 18 (1943), pp. 155–97.

(1959), *Petrarch's Later Years* (Cambridge, Mass., 1959).

(1961), *Life of Petrarch* (Chicago, 1961).

Wilks, Michael (1963), *The Problem of Sovereignty in the Later Middle Ages* (Cambridge, 1963).

Wilmart, André (1933), 'L'"Ars arengandi" de Jacques de Dinant', in *Analecta Reginensia* (Vatican City, 1933), pp. 113–51.

Witt, Ronald G. (1969), 'The *De Tyranno* and Coluccio Salutati's view of Politics and Roman History', *Nuova Rivista Storica* 53 (1969), pp. 434–74.

(1971), 'The Rebirth of the Concept of Republican Liberty in Italy', in *Renaissance Studies in Honor of Hans Baron*, ed. Anthony Molho and John A. Tedeschi (Florence, 1971), pp. 173–99.

(1976), 'Florentine Politics and the Ruling Class, 1382–1407', *The Journal of Medieval and Renaissance Studies* 6 (1976), pp. 243–67.

Wolin, Sheldon S. (1961), *Politics and Vision: Continuity and Innovation in Western Political Thought* (London, 1961).

Wood, Neal (1967), 'Machiavelli's Concept of *Virtù* Reconsidered', *Political Studies* 15 (1967), pp. 159–72.

Woodward, William H. (1906), *Studies in Education during the Age of the Renaissance, 1400–1600* (Cambridge, 1906).

(1963), *Vittorino da Feltre and other Humanist Educators* (New York, 1963).

Woolf, Cecil N. Sidney (1913), *Bartolus of Sassoferrato* (Cambridge, 1913).

Index

Pontano, Giovanni, I. 117, 120–1, 127–8; II. 261n.

Popkin, Richard H., II. 28on.

popular sovereignty, theory of, in Calvinist thought, II. 223–4, 234–5, 312–13, 317–18, 332–4, 337–45, 347–8; in scholastic thought, I. 61–5; II. 116–17, 119–23, 148, 151–2, 345–8

positive law, II. 119, 148–9, 152–7, 164, 166–72, 182–4, 287–9, 292, 294–5, 310–19

Possevino, Antonio, II. 137, 143 and n., 171–2

Post, Gaines, II. 353 and n.

Postel, Guillaume, II. 244–7

post-Glossators, the, I. 9, 105, 204

Prague, Articles of, II. 35–6

Prato, I. 174

predestination, II. 6, 24–5

Previté-Orton, C. W., I. 64

princely virtues, concept of, I. 127–8, 133–6, 230

Principles of Letter-Writing, The, I. 28

printing, and spread of humanism, I. 195–6

property rights, II. 69, 152–4, 293–7, 320 and n., 327–9

Protestantism, origin of term, II. 195. See also under Calvinism, Lutheranism

Protestation, A, II. 304

Provence, II. 242

providence, contrasted with fortune, I. 95–6, 145–6; II. 278; equated with fortune, I. 97; role of, in political life, II. 66–7, 70, 95, 139–40, 161, 195–6, 202–5, 225, 301, 323–4

Ptolemy of Lucca, I. 52, 54–5, 59 and n., 79, 82, 144–5 and n., 147

Pufendorf, Samuel, II. 184, 347

Puritanism, I. 219, 225; II. 85, 123

Pyhy, Conrad von, II. 87

Quintilian, I. 85

Rabelais, François, I. 193 and n., 223 and n.; II. 258

Radical Reformation, the, origins of, II. 74–6; and pacifism, II. 77–9; and revolution, 77–8, 80–1; spread of, II. 76–7, 80–1

Raleigh, Sir Walter, II. 357–8

Ramus, Pierre, I. 107; II. 291

Ravenna, I. 5; University of, I. 7

Raymond of Toledo, I. 50

reason, and law of nature, II. 149–54, 166–75; limitations of, II. 3–4, 6, 8, 24–5

reason of state, concept of, attacked, I. 249–51; II. 143, 171–3 and n.; defended, I. 248 and n., 249, 252–4

Rebuffi, Pierre, II. 260, 262, 266–7

Reformation, Calvinist, see under Calvinism; Lutheran, see under Lutheranism; and Radicalism, see under Anabaptists, Radical Reformation

Regnum Italicum, I. 4 and n., 5–6, 13–14, 16–18, 22, 24–6, 57, 94, 113, 146; II. 351

Reinhard, Martin, II. 83

Remigio de Girolami, I. 52, 55–9 and n., 82, 147, 176, 182

Renaissance, the, and humanism, I. 102–12; Kristeller on, I. 102–4; and scholastic background, I. 101–2, 103–9. See also under northern Renaissance

republicanism, as best form of government, I. 41–2, 53–4, 79, 109, 140, 158–9; defended (1) by humanists, I. 152–89; (2) by scholastics, I. 144–52; in Florence, I. 73–84, 142–8, 152–89; Rome, I. 142–3, 148–52; Venice, I. 139–42, 171–2

Resby, James, II. 35

resistance to lawful authority, defended (1) by Anabaptists, II. 77–81; (2) by Calvinists, II. 209–17, 219–24, 227–38, 254–5, 267–8, 310–18, 319–20, 335–45, 347–8; (3) by Catholics, II. 121–3, 126–9, 177–8, 320–3, 326, 332–3, 345–8; (4) by legal theorists, II. 125–6, 197–9, 200–4, 208, 211n., 217–24, 234–5, 239, 267–8, 310–18, 320–3, 325, 335–8; (5) by Lutherans, II. 17, 74, 195–208, 217–19, 225–7. See also under revolution, defence of

Reuchlin, Johannes, I. 210–11; II. 27, 31, 52–3

revolution, defence of, II. 235–8, 239–41, 254–5, 275–6, 303, 309–10, 319, 323, 335, 339–48; and Calvinism, I. xiv–xv; II. 320–3. See also under resistance to lawful authority.

rhetoric, and classical literature, I. 35–8; philosophy, I. 86–9, 106–7, 193–4; political theory, I. 29–35, 38–48; teaching of, I. 27–8

Ribadeneyra, Pedro, I. 214, 251; II. 137, 143 and n., 171–3

Rice, Eugene F., I. 209

Ridley, Jasper, II. 211n.

Ridley, Nicholas, II. 190

Riesenberg, Peter, I. 53n

right, concept of a, II. 117 and n., 121–2, 176–8, 239–40 and n., 320 and n., 327–9, 335–9, 341, 344

Rimini, I. 25

Rinuccini, Alamanno, I. 153, 156, 177–8

Robert the Bruce, II. 121–2

Roberts, Michael, II. 83

Robey, David, I. 103

Rochefoucauld, François de la, I. 101

Rogers, John, II. 99

Rokycana, John, II. 36

Rolandino of Padua, I. 32–3

Rolando da Piazzola, I. 38

Romagna, the, I. 14, 25

Roman law, and absolutism, II. 124, 263–4, 266–7; and constitutionalism, II. 126–34, 183, 269–75, 321–3; denounced in England, II. 54–5; and humanism, I. 105–6, 201–4,